Women and the Cuban Insurrection

Using gender analysis and focusing on previously unexamined testimonies of women rebels, political scientist Lorraine Bayard de Volo shatters the prevailing masculine narrative of the Cuban Revolution. Contrary to the Cuban War Story's mythology of an insurrection single-handedly won by bearded guerrillas, Bayard de Volo shows that revolutions are not won and lost only by bullets and battlefield heroics. Focusing on women's multiple forms of participation in the insurrection, especially those that occurred off the battlefield, such as smuggling messages, hiding weapons, and distributing propaganda, Bayard de Volo explores how both masculinity and femininity were deployed as tactics in the important though largely unexamined battle for the "hearts and minds" of the Cuban people. Drawing on extensive, rarely examined archives including interviews and oral histories, this author offers an entirely new interpretation of one of the Cold War's most significant events.

Lorraine Bayard de Volo is Chair and Associate Professor of Women and Gender Studies at the University of Colorado Boulder. Previously the director of the Latin American Studies Center at her university, her fieldwork in Cuba, Colombia, Mexico, Nicaragua, and the United States centers on gender and war, revolution, political and sexual violence, and social movements. She is author of *Mothers of Heroes and Martyrs: Gender Identity Politics in Nicaragua, 1979–1999* (2001).

Women and the Cuban Insurrection

How Gender Shaped Castro's Victory

LORRAINE BAYARD DE VOLO

University of Colorado Boulder

CAMBRIDGE
UNIVERSITY PRESS

CAMBRIDGE
UNIVERSITY PRESS

University Printing House, Cambridge CB2 8BS, United Kingdom

One Liberty Plaza, 20th Floor, New York, NY 10006, USA

477 Williamstown Road, Port Melbourne, VIC 3207, Australia

314–321, 3rd Floor, Plot 3, Splendor Forum, Jasola District Centre,
New Delhi – 110025, India

79 Anson Road, #06-04/06, Singapore 079906

Cambridge University Press is part of the University of Cambridge.

It furthers the University's mission by disseminating knowledge in the pursuit of
education, learning, and research at the highest international levels of excellence.

www.cambridge.org
Information on this title: www.cambridge.org/9781107178021
DOI: 10.1017/9781316823378

First published 2018

Printed in the United States of America by Sheridan Books, Inc.

A catalogue record for this publication is available from the British Library.

Library of Congress Cataloging-in-Publication Data

Names: Bayard de Volo, Lorraine, 1966- author.
Title: Women and the Cuban insurrection : how gender shaped Castro's victory /
    Lorraine Bayard de Volo.
Description: First Edition. | New York : Cambridge University Press, 2018. | Includes
    bibliographical references and index.
Identifiers: LCCN 2017042287 | ISBN 9781107178021 (hardback)
Subjects: LCSH: Women—Political activity—Cuba—History—20th century/ | Castro,
    Fidel, 1926-2016. | Cuba—History—Revolution, 1959. | BISAC: HISTORY / Latin
    America / General.
Classification: LCC HQ1236.5.C9 B39 2018 | DDC 305.4097291—dc23 LC record
    available at https://lccn.loc.gov/2017042287

ISBN 978-1-107-17802-1 Hardback
ISBN 978-1-316-63084-6 Paperback

To Cory Riddle and Pierre Bayard de Volo

Contents

Preface

Having lived in Nicaragua at the end of the Contra War and immediate postwar period, I am mindful of both the trauma that war inflicts and the fact that a full reckoning with the physical and psychological trauma of the Cuban insurrection, including the collateral damage inflicted by all sides, is missing from this book. The wounds of war were terribly fresh during my Nicaragua fieldwork in the late 1980s and early 1990s, and interviewing war victims, I was immersed in the details. One day, while we walked the steep path to her house, María told me how, as a teenager, she faced a terrible choice when the Somoza regime's National Guard attacked her village: which of her two children to grab as she fled. She left her newborn infant and fled with her two-year-old. To survive, she joined the guerrilla and carried her son on her back, along with a gun, through the mountains until he too died. Wars, even those waged by leftist rebels in the name of liberation, are reliably traumatic and brutal. Armed rebellion, by definition, entails killing. Suspected traitors are executed after summary judgments. "Collateral damage" is endemic, and people are killed in crossfire, sometimes by guerrilla bullets (errant or otherwise) or botched homemade bombs. The military murders villagers suspected of sharing food with guerrillas. Guerrillas fire on teenage military conscripts.

It is difficult to reconcile the gains to gender equality implied by women engaging in one of the most masculine of pursuits – war – with feminist anti-militarism's insistence that scholarship must "recognize the sheer corporeality of the terrain" upon which attacks and ambushes are laid by rebels and regime alike.[1] Without such recognition, research is complicit in the process of rendering invisible the suffering of war victims, leaving them as disembodied statistics if they are counted at all. The corporeality of war does not render irrelevant women rebels' achievements, but it prompts the "sturdy suspicion of war" called for by feminist anti-militarism.² In the literature on the Cuban insurrection, including that on women rebels, with few exceptions the bloody reality of war and its long-term psychological costs are remote if not invisible. I have struggled against the sanitizing effects of the triumphal war story by seeking out and inserting details on collateral damage, regime repression, psychological trauma, sexual assault, summary executions, and the like. While not a full accounting, I hope there is enough here to engender a sturdy suspicion of this and all wars.

My research on Cuba began as part of a comparative project on gender, war, and peace processes in Latin America, supported by funding from the National Science Foundation and United States Institute of Peace, as well as from the University of Kansas. I conducted fieldwork in Cuba, Colombia, Nicaragua, and Mexico (Chiapas), gathering interviews, conducting participant observation, and searching archives, among other methods and sources. Measured by the volume of fresh details, the fieldwork and archival work were successful, almost too successful, and as I turned to the Cuban materials, I became convinced that an in-depth case study of conflict and militarization in that country was necessary before I could develop an effective comparative analysis across cases. I put the comparative project on hold to focus on Cuban conflict and militarization 1950–2000. Soon, the chapter devoted to the 1950s insurrection stretched to 130 single-spaced pages, at which point I began this book in earnest.

I have many people to thank for help on this long and winding road that is now a book. First, I would like to thank my two kids Theo and Shayne for providing so much love and entertainment between my first book and this one. Could I have finished this book sooner if I had managed more effectively to guard my time on the weekends and evenings from their needs and their diversions? Certainly, but I wouldn't have had it any other way.

This book is dedicated to the two adult men in my life. To my father, Pierre Bayard de Volo, who asked me every time he saw me, "When are you going to finish that book?" – thank you for all the reminders and for the love that inspired them. To my husband, Cory Riddle, thank you so much for your eternal patience and encouragement.

Very importantly, I also thank the Cubans who generously shared their memories and perspectives regarding the insurrection. Given the conditions under which they agreed to be interviewed, I do not list their names but recognize my indebtedness to their contributions.

The following people have read and commented on previous versions of this manuscript, in part or in whole, or have otherwise contributed in vital ways to my understanding of Cuban politics, war, insurrection, and gender: Linda T. Åhäll, Hannah Britton, Rob Buffington, Lee Chambers, Michelle Chase, Ann Cudd, Emmanuel David, Michaele Ferguson, Elisabeth Friedman, Misty Gerner, Donna Goldstein, Victoria González, Lily Guerra, Kwame Holmes, Rachel Hynson, Janet Jacobs, Alison Jaggar, Julie Kaarbo, Karen Kampwirth, Susan Kent, Betsey Kuznesof, Amy Lind, Polly McLean, Deepti Misri, Celeste Montoya, Joane Nagel, Gary Reich, Tony Rosenthal, Phil Schrodt, Lynn Stoner, Gwynne Thomas, Beverly Weber, and Chris White. My terrific Latin American Studies Center Works-in-Progress group at the University of Colorado Boulder has earned my eternal gratitude: Kaifa Roland, Christina Sue, Jennifer Bair, Joe Bryan, and Fernando Riosmena. What an amazing group of scholars! I owe an enormous debt to Dan Levine, Professor Emeritus at University of Michigan, for his continued support and priceless advice. Thanks to Debbie Gershenowitz, Senior Editor at Cambridge University Press, for her faith in this project and her rich and nuanced appreciation of Latin American political history, conflict, and gender studies. Thank you to the anonymous reviewers, who went above and beyond with their insightful, detailed feedback.

Notes

1. Thobani (2001, 291).
2. Ruddick (1989, 138): "Peace requires a sturdy suspicion of violence, even in the best of causes."

CHAPTER 1

Revolution Retold

What a Gender Lens Tells Us about the Cuban Insurrection

A photo by Spanish photojournalist Enrique Meneses portrays Fidel Castro reclining in a guerrilla camp at night, reading by candlelight. With the caption "Fidel Castro in the Sierra Maestra," he is framed as the subject of this photo. But what caught my eye and my imagination is the woman to his right, who sits beside him, head bowed, holding the candle for Fidel to read by. Who is she? Meneses does not tell us. In all likelihood, she is a bit actor who played a minor role in the insurrection. But without her and many more like her, Fidel would never have succeeded.

This book is, in part, a people's history of the Cuban insurrection.[1] The focus is principally but not exclusively upon women, whose history of activism has been acknowledged but remains largely unexplored.[2] Given the spotlight trained upon Fidel Castro and Che Guevara, and to a lesser extent other rebel leaders, a focus that includes rank and file women forces one off the literature's center stage to inquire about those who held the candle for Fidel to read by, smuggled messages down the mountain, planted bombs in theaters, or hid rebels in their home.[3] These are decidedly not the bearded rebels romanticized (or vilified) in the literature. Indeed, some guerrilla combatants were women. Such women combatants inform the post-1958 Cuban official historical narrative, the Cuban War Story central to the construction of the New Woman in the new revolutionary society.[4] But the attention to armed combatants – men and women alike – obscures two essential elements of the insurrection. First, as this study makes clear, insurrections are not only won or lost through bullets and battlefield heroics but through the more mundane tasks that women and lower-status men perform. Second, the Cuban War Story featuring guerrilla warfare obscures the battle for hearts and minds. The Castro-led July

26 Movement (M-26-7) put considerable effort into this latter battle, and women were central as both strategists and gendered subjects. This foray into a women's history of the Cuban insurrection aims not only to right the past wrongs of women's exclusion, important as that is. Collecting and analyzing details on women rebels – leaders and rank and file alike – reveals new insights into how this insurrection was waged and won.

Along these lines, I consider gender to be a tactic of war, the effectiveness of which depends upon the successful exploitation of dominant notions of femininity and masculinity.[5] Femininity was deployed when women, less likely to arouse military suspicions, transported weapons under their skirts or in false pregnant bellies.[6] Gender was also deployed when rebels mobilized mothers of youths killed by the dictatorship to plead with the US ambassador. Castro likewise armed a women's platoon to signal rebel commitment to equality as well as women's contributions to the future revolutionary society. As gender is a key means through which power, and thus politics and conflict, is understood, gender furthermore structured hierarchies in Cuban politics. In this way, rebels used gender to represent President Fulgencio Batista as an abusive, predatory, and corrupt masculine figure, in sharp contrast to rebel idealized masculinity. Government soldiers, upon capture, suffered injuries to their masculine status, even if physically unharmed. Bearded rebels were such "real" men that their victory took on an air of inevitability.

Accordingly, this book is not only a *her* story of the Cuban insurrection. By focusing on previously unexamined narratives of women rebels and using gender as a category of analysis, I return to a well-researched war story and come away with new perspectives.[7] Following rebel histories, priorities, and tactics, I examine not only the war of bullets, but also the war of ideas. This gendered approach to the Cuban insurrection, then, attends to two interrelated theaters of war: the war of flesh and blood and the war for hearts and minds.[8] Wars are fought in a material sense on physical terrain – the war of "flesh and blood" – but also through symbols and ideas – the war for "hearts and minds." In the former, people fight and are wounded, kill and die, and militaries make tactical plans to maximize enemy losses. Wars are also fought on cultural terrain, and states and rebel armies often commit significant resources to win hearts and minds and construct consent.[9] In both theaters of war, gender differences are magnified, minimized, or otherwise reshaped to best address the perceived needs of militarization. Gender is thus part of war's arsenal, waged at the level of ideas in the struggle to attach meaning to actions, processes, and relations.[10]

Much of what we know about the Cuban insurrection has been gleaned from what I refer to as the Cuban War Story – the dominant state-constructed narrative of how the Cuban insurrection was waged and won. As Sjoberg and Gentry note, "The best war story not only wins the war, it *is* the war."[11] Even beyond Cuba, too often the Cuban War Story *is* the war, as this particular narrative has been adopted with little critical reflection on the politics underpinning the repetitions and silences. This book engages the Cuban War Story, viewing it as one story among many.[12] This critical inquiry not only reveals new facets of the insurrection, but also of the post-1958 Cuban revolutionary state. In many ways, Cuba *is* its war story, and we learn much about Cuba through scrutinizing its war stories told and untold.

My agenda, then, is twofold: empirical and analytical. First, I document *what* women did and *how* they were (and were not) integrated into insurrection and militarism. Second, I analyze how gender was deployed tactically as well as how it operated as an organizing principle of the cultural constructs of war. This second approach is crucial in making sense of empirical findings. But a major impediment in the Latin American cases has been the relative lack of comprehensive information on how women contributed to and experienced political violence in the region. Despite some key works, we still know relatively little about how women engaged in, resisted, and were affected by the wars of flesh and blood in Latin America.[13] We know even less about gender and the wars for hearts and minds in the region. This book, then, provides a detailed account of women's contributions to the Cuban insurrection, an examination of how these new details challenge or build upon previous theories and narratives of war and Cuban politics, and a gendered analysis of war.

The empirical details of women and insurrection in twentieth-century Cuba are still relatively unexplored, with women rebels at once both present and absent in the literature.[14] That women participated in the insurrection is well known. The Cuban state has consistently celebrated those women among the rebel elite closest to Fidel. Thus, the Cuban War Story has hailed the four Heroines of the Revolution – Celia Sánchez, Vilma Espín, Haydée Santamaría, and Melba Hernández – along with the Marianas women's platoon. The literature has generally followed this narrative focus. In contrast, this book explores the diversity of women's activism against Batista's regime. In addition to introducing new information on well-known rebel women, I examine women's organizations that developed independently of Fidel's efforts and some women rebels who later fell out with the Castro government and were subsequently erased from the official war story. I also incorporate rebel women who were left out of the established Cuban War Story in a more benign fashion. Archives, memoirs, and Cuban print media spanning half a century contain a wealth of interviews with rank and file rebels and civilian supporters. Yet these have trickled out incrementally such that they have not significantly affected the dominant narrative focused on the bearded rebels engaging the enemy in the *Sierra*.[15] I collected Cuban women's rebel narratives from five decades of Cuban media, US declassified documents, archived interviews, memoirs, primary documents, and other material obtained during fieldwork, which cumulatively indicated that a diverse array of women were much more central to the effort than previously understood, particularly in the underground movement in the *llano* (plains, especially urban areas – as distinct from the *Sierra* or mountains).[16]

FF
Myf<

This retelling builds upon an important corrective to Cuba's political history concerning the *llano* underground, which was far more significant in the insurrection than previously recognized on or off the island.[17] Most scholarly accounts follow the dominant war story of Cuba's revolutionary government, which attributes rebel success to guerrilla warfare in the Sierra.[18] Julia Sweig aptly summarizes the revolution's "founding fathers' myth" that Che Guevara helped construct: "a handful of bearded rebels with a rural peasant base single-handedly took on and defeated a standing army, thereby overthrowing the dictator and bringing the revolutionaries to power."[19] After 1958, Castro discouraged "publicity concerning the underground exploits," the speculation for this being that it would "diminish the exclusive role he wished to attribute to his guerrilla troops, and to their inspired leader."[20]

Yet as Sweig documents, until the last eight months of the insurrection, the guerrillas had been "a virtual appendage of the July 26 Movement," rather than its vanguard, and most M-26-7 decisions regarding tactics, strategy, resource allocation, and political relations were made by "lesser known individuals from the urban underground" and not the guerrilla leaders in the Sierra.[21] Without the work of the *llano*, the rebel victory "would simply not have been possible."[22]

Fidel and the Sierra guerrillas ultimately led the insurrection and post-insurrection government partially by default, as *llano* leaders and competitors were killed off by Batista forces.[23] Thus, although Castro is typically cast as the undisputed leader of the anti-Batista movement, he did not emerge as such until the last eight months of the insurrection.[24] This guerrilla-centric focus of the official war story has also eclipsed the role of women, who were more active and prominent in the *llano*.

A second corrective is also possible through the work of historians such as Lynn Stoner and Teresa Prados-Torreira, who establish that the 1950s insurrection and women's place in it relied upon experiences and popular narratives of Cuba's previous wars and rebellions.[25] In part, this occurred symbolically, as rebels used previous women's contributions, especially as memorialized by Independence leader, journalist, and poet José Martí, to legitimize women's activism and inspire Cubans to rebellion. But as I show, women also drew upon their own experiences from previous insurrectionary moments to build the 1950s movement. Thus, tactics developed earlier were applied to the 1950s insurrection, and some women active in Cuba's 1930s rebellion transferred their political expertise to the 1950s struggle, lending a sense of continuity as well as efficacy.

Another element of this book's retelling of the Cuban insurrection involves denaturalizing familiar war stories to reveal how accepted truths depend upon gender narratives going unnoticed.[26] This latter approach begins with the notion established particularly within the feminist international relations (IR) literature that war stories do political work. "Gendered ideologies (masculinization and feminization) that are naturalized," Spike Peterson explains, "camouflage interests, agendas, and politics" to legitimize and gain support for war and nation-building efforts.[27] This dynamic can be seen in the valorization of armed insurrection over political negotiations, and the sharp distinctions between the idealized masculinity attached to rebels and the femininity or debased masculinity attached to Batista armed forces. Gender analysis, then, reveals how interests and agendas are depoliticized "even as the identities and practices they mobilize profoundly affect politics."[28] I also chart how behaviors and characteristics considered masculine or feminine structure sociopolitical opportunities. Modern militaries are often "a focus for national bonding and patriotism, which cuts across differences."[29] In such cases, according to Nira Yuval-Davis, nations signify modernity by including women as equal members of the nation and incorporating "*all* members of the national collectivity ... at least symbolically, into the military."[30] This helps explain the rebel leadership's receptivity to women rebels, despite the strong 1950s gender norms that militated against them. Rebel leaders further legitimized and appealed to women through the retelling of popular narratives of Cuba's previous rebellions. But Mary Hawkesworth cautions that when such historical narratives "are institutionalized within founding myths, notions of the 'national family' reinscribe fathers' rule and mothers' obedience as natural, even as they create and legitimate new race and gender hierarchies," alerting us to the subtle processes through which male dominance was naturalized in post-1958

Cuba.[31] This book, then, includes a gendered analysis of the founding myths of Revolutionary Cuba – the Cuban War Story – with a historical focus that incorporates prior foundational narratives.

Compared to gender, the manner in which ideologies of race structured hierarchies of power and naturalized inequalities in Cuba is more difficult to trace. This difficulty derives largely from the lack of references in primary sources regarding the race of most rank and file rebels (whereas their gender is virtually always noted), the nuanced spectrum of race and color terms in Cuba that complicate simplistic distinctions between Black and white, and a general silence concerning race in both rebel and Batista state narratives.[32] The Cuban revolutionary state, committed to social justice and inspired by independence hero Martí's call for a race-less Cuban identity, eliminated institutional forms of racial discrimination upon taking power.[33] But it dealt with ideological forms of racism largely by imposing an "official silence on race."[34] Given the Cuban state's control over media and scholarship on the island, little information on race and the insurrection remains, including the racial identities of rank and file rebels.

Building upon the above correctives, three main arguments and approaches are woven throughout this book. First, excavating women's multiple forms of participation is an effective means of capturing the more prosaic aspects of insurrection, including smaller-scale but multiple acts of rebellion and support upon which insurrections rely. Second, Castro and the rebel leadership placed greater emphasis on the war of ideas than is suggested in the literature and by the *foco* theory of guerrilla warfare associated with Che Guevara. Indeed, I argue that rebel success cannot be understood without attention to this war of ideas. Third, the rebels included gender as part of their arsenal, tactically deployed in the war of bullets and war of ideas. The M-26-7 rebels relied upon certain gendered logics that organized the way armed insurrection was interpreted, creating an alternative privileged masculinity. Although the revolution was officially committed to the liberation of women, gender continued to mark hierarchy during and after the insurrection. In the following pages, I examine each of these arguments in greater detail.

WOMEN REBELS: WHO WERE THEY AND WHAT DID THEY DO?

Stathis Kalyvas points to two gaps in the study of war. Social science research tends to ignore warfare itself, privileging instead "the study of social and political factors that are thought to affect the onset or termination of civil wars and revolutions."[35] Yet when warfare is examined closely, it is often reduced "to the exhaustive treatment of their military details – their tactics, techniques and firepower, while their political and social content is ignored."[36] This narrow focus extends to studies of the Cuban insurrection.[37] Post-1958 Cuba has produced reams of play-by-play accounts of the conflict, oriented toward guerrilla battles in the last two years of the anti-Batista movement. I move beyond the battlefields to incorporate a more holistic understanding of the day-to-day construction of the insurrection. A micro-level analysis with a gender lens, I propose, is key to better understanding armed insurrection, as it draws our attention to the more traditionally feminized, largely ignored, but still essential support tasks performed.[38]

In analyzing women's diverse contributions, I make several arguments. First, from 1952 to 1958, women participated primarily in the clandestine forces concentrated in the cities or *llano*, yet their contributions were later overshadowed by the intense focus on women guerrillas in the Sierra. Second, despite the Cuban representation of rebels as youths, many women were middle-aged and older, and often drew from experiences and skills honed from their activism in the 1930s. Third, though most women rebels were not armed, their work was at least as important to the actual war effort as women combatants' accomplishments in battle, despite the greater attention to the latter in the literature. Finally, rebel work was dangerous regardless of whether or not one carried a gun – a point that was instrumental in the eventual arming of women guerrillas.[39]

Certain Cuban women rebels hold a prominent place in the official Cuban War Story as well as independent research. Of the six founding members of what became M-26-7, two were women: Melba Hernández and Haydée Santamaría.[40] Two additional women, Celia Sánchez and Vilma Espín, became celebrated *llano* leaders who transferred to the Sierra. There are other rebel women who are well known in Cuba but less so elsewhere – including Teté Puebla, Pastorita Núñez, María Antonia Figueroa, Gloria Cuadras, Lidia Doce, and Clodomira Acosta. Furthermore, *Las Marianas*, the women's platoon, is notable not only for women's inclusion in combat but also for the attention they received in rebel and post-1958 state propaganda. Yet women clustered in the *llano* and in support roles barely register in the literature, which reflects the Cuban revolutionary equation that women's participation with gun in hand earned them their place as New Women in the New Society.[41]

Although I examine women combatants, it is a mistake to let guerrilla combat take analytical precedence over other forms of insurrectionary action. Not only does this misrepresent the insurrection, but it also ignores important rebel activity in which women played key parts. Here, I follow Cuban scholar Gladys Marel García-Pérez, who shifts attention from "the heroic and highly visible guerrilla *comandantes* to the many men and women who participated, typically in anonymity."[42] As rebel success did not depend exclusively on guns and combat, the *llano* underground and the active appeal for mass support are crucial aspects of the insurrectionary effort. In terms of danger, by which courage and thus masculine status are often measured, in both the *llano* and Sierra much of the effort spent by and danger posed to rebels occurred when evading the armed forces versus engaging in combat. *Llano* rebels and civilians often bore the brunt of the repression, compared to the less accessible guerrillas. Examination of the gendered distribution of danger has the effect of destabilizing old war stories.

A closer look at these women rebels has a similar destabilizing effect. A University of Havana study found nearly 30 percent were over 30 years old in 1952, indicating that by the insurrection's final year a significant proportion of women rebels were middle-aged and older.[43] This contrasts with the dominant representation of Cuban rebels as youths.[44] My own findings confirm this assessment, and the following chapters document the many contributions of middle-aged and older women to the insurrection.

Turning to women in guerrilla camps, a consensus in the literature places the Cuban guerrilla in the Sierra at roughly 5 percent women, most of whom formed the rearguard.[45] These numbers are low compared to estimates of women guerrillas in later Latin American conflicts, which range from 25 to 50 percent.[46] Barriers to women in the guerrilla include, "the structural constraint of women's roles in reproductive activities and traditional ideological constraints ... that define women's roles."[47] Mady Segal's comparative study includes the threat level and the lack of alternatives to explain the proportion of women in combat – that is, greater threat to the general population and fewer options for civilians to escape violence are theorized to produce more women in combat.[48] Indeed, personal safety is an underappreciated factor in theorizing guerrilla growth, as the guerrilla can offer relative protection from government forces. In Cuba, many tried to join the guerrillas to escape persecution in cities and towns. Yet as Cuban rebel men were more likely to be suspected, harassed, and pursued by Batista's forces, evidence suggests they were more likely to escape to the Sierra. Unlike the later Nicaraguan and Salvadoran cases, women with young children did not flee to the guerrilla and featured rarely as Cuban rebels in the *llano*.[49] Most Cuban guerrilla women were single and childless or, less commonly, mothers of adult children.

Ideology is also a consideration in rebel men's openness to women's participation. Though not explicitly feminist, a basic normative commitment to women's equality complemented the M-26-7 effort to build a movement. Fidel Castro stressed social justice and inclusion of the formerly marginalized, and male leaders did not bar skilled and trustworthy women, though they routinely assigned women "safer" duties of lesser status and authority. Unusually, women were prominent in the inner circle of the Cuban insurgency, and Fidel placed considerable trust in certain women.[50]

Susan Eckstein argues that Castro's policies were ideologically consistent when they suited his pragmatic goals.[51] Indeed, there were pragmatic reasons to include women in the rebel underground and guerrilla.[52] First, repressive forces were less likely to suspect women, detain them for interrogation, or attack them with lethal force. Taking advantage of this gender dynamic, leaders valued women rebels for their ability to feign pregnancy, flirt with authorities, or distract guards in idle chitchat or maternal concerns.

Second, Cuban women rebels had better survival rates and received shorter prison sentences than men and so, alive and free, assumed greater responsibility and sometimes moved into positions vacated by men who were killed, imprisoned, or exiled. It was a significant advantage to M-26-7 to have skilled and trustworthy women ready to step in.[53] Women were excluded as armed combatants in the two most suicidal confrontations – the attack on the Moncada garrison and the Granma expedition. Women had volunteered and trained for these battles, but rebel gender discrimination benefitted M-26-7, in effect if not by design. Because the very high mortality rates of both actions took out male leaders and potential leaders, women rebels were key to the survival and regeneration of the movement. A similar impulse kept women out of many smaller-scale violent encounters with authorities. *Llano* recollections, for example, include instances in which rebel men, sensing impending violence, ordered rebel women to leave. More generally, women were less prone to confrontational behavior with authorities, preferring escape over heroic but deadly firefights.[54]

CUBAN HEARTS AND MINDS

From published accounts both on and off the island, we know much more about specific physical battles – ambush sites, mines laid, location of trenches, and other step-by-step details of how a battle unfolded – than we do about rebel efforts to appeal to and engage with the Cuban public. Walter Laqueur, historian of guerrilla warfare, glosses over all but the military phase of the Cuban insurrection, arguing there was no "incubation" period in which "the emphasis was on organization, propaganda and conspiracy," and that "not that much preparatory work [was] needed for launching an insurgency."[55] Hugh Thomas, in contrast, more accurately maintains that Castro saw Cuba's insurrection as "really a political campaign" and worked as hard at "seeking to influence opinion as he did as a guerrilla seeking territory."[56]

Recent military theories of counterinsurgency strategy have endeavored to redirect the single-minded focus on kill or capture techniques toward a focus on "the country's people and their belief in and support of their government," making the winning of hearts and minds the primary objective.[57] A similar analytical focus should extend to the study of insurgency. The rebels' success in winning popular support comprises a driving puzzle of the book. In addressing such gaps in the study and practice of rebellion and war, I attend closely to the battle of hearts and minds (also termed the war of ideas). I propose that gender analysis that is also alert to race, sexuality, class, and other means by which power is structured and given meaning confirms the importance of this aspect of successful revolutionary insurgency and provides key insights into how it is achieved. Such a focus is all the more important as revolutionary movements tend to concern themselves not only with military victory, but with cultural and ideological transformation as well.

Che Guevara's accounts of guerrilla warfare inspired thousands of future revolutionaries in Latin America and beyond.[58] But the *foco* theory developed from Che's approach downplayed symbolism, propaganda, and the long, arduous process of winning a war of ideas.[59] Instead, a small, dedicated band of guerrillas would challenge the state's legitimacy and monopoly on violence through its military exploits, generating its own publicity from which popular support would follow. Che famously described "the perennial example of the guerrilla, carrying out armed propaganda (... that is, the bullets of propaganda, of the battles won or lost – but fought – against the enemy). The great lesson of the invincibility of the guerrillas taking root in the dispossessed masses."[60] These battles, in theory, pressured the regime to increase repressive measures, radicalizing the masses and generating popular support for the guerrilla.[61]

Bolivian *campesinos*, however, did not welcome Che and his largely foreign army in 1967, as he "hurried to fight battles against the ruling oligarchy's army instead of patiently educating, wooing and organizing the peasantry."[62] After Che's death in Bolivia, postmortem accounts compared *foco* theory unfavorably to the "classic" Maoist approach, a slow and arduous process of agitation and propaganda toward a mobilized population.[63] Edward Friedman differentiated between Che's bullets of propaganda and a war of ideas: "The revolution continues and grows because more people run forward to replace the dead. Che never sufficiently answers the question of what will make people willing to fight and die."[64] Nor did Che adequately acknowledge the extensive and costly underground rebel work in Cuba that began before his late-1956 arrival.

Though downplayed in the post-1958 Cuban War Story, Castro did not singularly aim to defeat the military on the battlefield but rather to profoundly undermine the Batista government. The rebels' survival skills during the military's 1958 summer offensive were a powerful contributor to Batista's fall, which complements Che's notion of "armed propaganda."[65] Yet Castro's war of ideas was often distinct from military engagements, sometimes even at the expense of military effectiveness. For example, in mid-November 1956 Fidel announced from exile his return to Cuba by year's end, which earned a rebuke from his Mexican military advisor: "Don't you know … a cardinal military principle is to keep your intentions secret from your enemy?"[66] Castro reportedly replied, "I want everyone in Cuba to know I am coming. I want them to have faith in the 26th of July Movement … I know that militarily it might be harmful. It is psychological warfare."[67]

For Timothy Wickham-Crowley, Cuba stands out among guerrilla campaigns for Castro's attention to media and the war of ideas: "Castro was able to place himself firmly in the minds of the Cuban people as a romantic, heroic, nationalist, legitimate, and revolutionary alternative to the Batista regime."[68] M-26-7 contrasted Castro with Batista, the latter portrayed as "brutal, dictatorial, illegal, and immoral" – repugnant to good Cubans regardless of their politics.[69]

The literature sometimes contrasts Cuba with Nicaragua and El Salvador for the latter's rejection of a *foco* approach in favor of the prolonged people's war strategy.[70] The greater participation of women in these Central American conflicts helped "guarantee a consistent presence upon which the prolonged war strategy relies."[71] As Karen Kampwirth rightly argues, "Given the need … for as many supporters as possible, they could hardly afford to reject the potential participation of 50 percent of the population just because those people were women."[72] However, the Cuban case itself did not rely on a *foco* strategy.[73] The common characterization of the Cuban case as *foco* in effect discounts the role of the *llano* and political alliances between the guerrilla and urban leftist organizations as well as rebel propaganda.[74] These blind spots have gendered implications, as rebel women and the gendered nature of the insurrection are missed or discounted when the urban underground and battle of ideas are de-emphasized. We also miss core aspects of the rebels' designs for mass support and mobilization post-insurrection.

GENDERED TACTICS, LOGISTICS, AND LOGICS IN INSURRECTION

According to Che, "tactics are the practical methods of achieving the grand strategic objectives".[75] I use the term "gendered tactics" in this sense – gender provided a practical means of achieving the desired strategic objective of rebel victory.[76] The rebels' gender transgressions – such as women taking on traditionally masculine tasks – must often be considered in this way, as means to a separate military or ideological end.

The arming of the Marianas women's platoon, I argue, is a prime example of gendered tactics in the rebel war of ideas.[77] The Marianas platoon was not tactically vital to combat. I propose that Fidel, in spite of resistance among rebel men, armed and trained women primarily in order to have an impact at the level of ideas, a symbolic act no less important than a military one. Indeed, Castro announced the Marianas on *Radio Rebelde* (Rebel Radio) and extolled them in his Santiago victory speech. My argument is that Fidel viewed such performances of equality at least in part as a rebel tactic, a practical means in pursuit of the longer-range guerrilla objective of overthrowing Batista and consolidating the revolution. As Che explained, tactics "are much more variable, more flexible than the final objectives, and they should be adjusted continually during the struggle."[78] In this sense, women combatants and other rebel gestures to gender equality were revocable features – complementary to the larger strategy of the revolution but not part of the revolution's inviolable core.

I use the term "gendered logics" to connote the manner in which gender differences structure our understanding of ourselves and the world around us. Gender, "the social organization of sexual difference," is expressed in the binary opposition masculinity/femininity, with one term supplying the other with meaning.[79] What is a man? A man is *not* a woman. Masculinity, as the valued term, is affirmed through rejection of the feminine – rejecting passivity, sensitivity, and weakness by projecting aggressiveness, toughness, and strength. Gender often functions through notions of difference that are accepted as natural to the point of social invisibility – the way things are. So deeply ingrained was the notion of women's passivity and political innocence that Batista's forces regularly failed to recognize known rebel women and allowed them to by-pass checkpoints.

Gendered logics help make sense of criticisms about the Cuban revolution's exaggerated expressions of masculinity. Cuban men in exile have contributed some of the most astute and pointed observations of masculinity in Castro's revolution. For example, Carlos Alberto Montaner charged, "[t]he Cuban Revolution is the business of machos ... Machos drive jeeps, have big pistols, and make revolutions ... [E]ach leader, each time he zips up his olive green fly and checks the lock on his pistol, reinforces his male ego and congratulates himself for being such a macho."[80] For Montaner, this "shows how little significance women really have in the decision-making circles in Cuba."[81]

The exiled Cuban writer Reinaldo Arenas similarly observed:

The Cuban man is condemned ... by a terrible machista condition. Fidel Castro ... is the total macho. When Fidel Castro speaks in the Plaza de la Revolución, it is like he ejaculates, he is taking possession of the masses, which are feminine. For this reason I divide the men into *machos machos* and *machos hembras* [roughly, masculine men and feminine men]. The *macho macho* is he who exercises power and the *macho hembra* is he who allows himself to be seduced by that power. This is very typical within Cuban masculinity. It is a paradox that, in a country that is so machista, everyone [men] tries to worship not the woman but the macho.[82]

How can a revolution that produced and celebrates heroines of armed rebellion and even incorporated armed women into its forces of liberation retain such a pronounced masculine accent? I understand the answer to lie in two related features of the revolution. First, the priority given to gender equality is a revocable feature of the revolution, pragmatically pursued when it suits regime stability and continuity. Second, the gendered Cuban War Story has been constructed such that the *macho macho* of Fidel and the revolutionary state are supported and emulated by the feminized masses. The insurrection and later the revolutionary state did not challenge the gender binary, thus reproducing gendered oppositions that continued to mark hierarchy.[83] Although officially committed to the liberation of women, the devaluation and rejection of the feminine undergirds gender inequality.

As this suggests, gender ascribes meaning beyond sexed bodies. As an "analytical category within which humans think about and organize their social activity," gender is a principal means of signifying power relationships.[84] As such, gender informs even those processes that appear gender-free, including the state, insurrection, and guerrilla warfare. In the contrast between Sierra and *llano*, the former was the privileged battle-ground – vested with masculine status that confirmed the masculinity of the men who fought there. And as Arenas suggests, the gender contrasts are not only between masculinity and femininity but also hierarchical contrasts within them. As I will explore, M-26-7 constructed rebel masculinity to favorably contrast with its representation of the debased masculinity or feminization of Batista's forces.

Che's "New Man"

The new model of masculinity is particularly evident in Che's "New Man." The New Man is guided by love for the people but able to forgo the "small doses of daily affection" enjoyed by ordinary men, is capable of great tenderness but also ready to coldly judge and execute enemies, rejects individualism and desire, and desires only to give selflessly to the cause.[85] Che had embodied men in mind in his discussion of the New Man. Given that his work is a globally influential reflection on guerrilla warfare, gender studies often look to Che's words to document and explain the lack of women in combat and the sexism inherent in guerrilla armies.[86] For example, Che explained:

> [in the guerrilla] a woman can perform her habitual tasks of peacetime; it is very pleasing to a soldier subjected to the extremely hard conditions of life to be able to look forward to a seasoned meal … the woman as cook can greatly improve the diet and, furthermore, it is easier to keep her in these domestic tasks; [such duties] are scorned by those [men] who perform them; they are constantly trying to get out of those tasks in order to enter into forces that are actively in combat.[87]

Reflecting upon this passage, Francesca Miller notes, "revolutions, no less than other military actions, were masculine; the soldiers were men, '*tiene[n] los cojones* [they have balls],' they were macho."[88]

Digging deeper into Che's writings, we find evidence of both his highest regard for the guerrilla fighter and his equation of the guerrilla fighter not only with men and masculinity but with becoming a real man. As José Moreno put it, for Che, life in the guerrilla "gives the fighter both an opportunity to become a revolutionary (which is the highest rank of the human species), and to become a man. Those who are not able to reach either stage, are advised to give up."[89]

Given dominant gender roles and the long-held understanding of war as exclusively masculine, Che's writings complement an understanding of the relatively passive, nonessential role of women in armed conflict.[90] Select quotes from Che mirror traditional gender patterns and thus have not given scholars much reason to pause over the question of women in the Cuban insurrection. But even as a focus on Che's writings can downplay women's contributions, they also lend useful insight into the structuring and deployment of gender in guerrilla war.

In sum, this book applies a gendered approach in three ways. First, it brings women rebels more fully into focus, in the process detailing quotidian acts of insurrection and thus providing a fuller account of the many contributions, large and small, by ordinary and extraordinary Cubans alike, starting at Batista's seizure of power and thus years before Castro and Che set up a guerrilla camp. Second, it considers gender as a tactical weapon in the rebel arsenal. Rebels purposefully and artfully deployed versions of femininity and masculinity to mobilize popular support and demoralize or shame the enemy. However, gender was not simply a weapon to wield, and rebels were in many ways gendered subjects rather than masters. Hegemonic masculinity – Cuban yet globally familiar – helps explain why scores of rebel men engaged in suicidal rebel schemes such as the Moncada Attack (1953) and the Granma Expedition (1956). That a few, including Fidel Castro, survived is testimony to the role of chance and Cuban rebel men's willingness to roll the dice – a willingness, I propose, propelled by hegemonic masculinity.[91]

HISTORY AS HANDMAIDEN: RESEARCH CHALLENGES IN CUBA

Cuba presents unique challenges for research on post-1952 politics. Foremost among these is the challenge of using sources produced in post-1958 revolutionary Cuba while remaining alert to the ways that revolutionary Cuba has used history on behalf of the state. This is a concern relevant to those using state-generated documents and narratives in any country. But the reach of the Cuban state is extensive, as the media is state-run, the universities (including research projects) are under close state oversight, and to a degree, the research done by foreign academics within Cuba is constrained.[92]

The revolutionary state produces and defends a specific version of history, upon which many academics studying Cuba have remarked. For Louis Pérez Jr., history in post-1958 Cuba serves "as handmaiden to the revolution," illustrating the need to use Cuban sources with caution.[93] Nicola Miller tells us, "the [Cuban] government kept a watchful eye on precisely which morsels of pre-revolutionary history were to be consumed and digested by the population ... a key element in mobilizing support, raising revolutionary consciousness and enforcing the identification of the Cuban nation with the revolutionary state."[94]

Virtually all media accounts from the island since 1958 were written in the service of the revolutionary state, delegitimizing the old order as corrupt and oppressive under Batista and the USA. At the same time, the revolutionary historiography "immortalize[ed] the social struggles of the past and claim[ed] direct lineal descent from those struggles" to support the state's claim to represent the interests of Cuban workers, *campesinos*, and women in order to integrate the masses into the Revolution.[95] Pérez maintains that the mobilization of women into the revolutionary process required an overhaul of traditional sexism.[96] With this aim, "increasing historiographical stress fell on the participation and contribution of women in all past struggles. The historiographical rehabilitation of women ... moved women toward the center of Cuban history and into the front trenches of revolutionary struggle."[97]

The challenge is to mine this "historiographical rehabilitation" for its details while remaining, to the degree possible, independent of the Cuban revolutionary state's own political aims and priorities. Attendant to this is my concern to more accurately recognize women's contributions without overstating them. Use of archival Cuban sources from pre-1959 and the early revolutionary period (roughly 1959–1962) is key to this aim, as is the inclusion of anti-Castro Cubans' recollections and analyses and non-Cuban observations and memoirs relating to the Cuban insurrection, including foreign journalists, witnesses, and participants as well as US State Department and US Embassy communiqués and reports. The diversity of sources allows for a form of triangulation, in which observations and claims from different perspectives are crosschecked and compared.

Cuban state media incrementally published interviews and articles on women's *llano* activities, which over five decades comprise a substantial body of information.[98] In their accumulation, these yield new insights into the *llano* struggle, the more prosaic aspects of insurrection, the diverse means by which women contributed to Batista's downfall, and the multiple paths by which gender threads through insurrectionary war, signifying power and forecasting Batista's defeat.

Julie Shayne has observed, "Cuba is an exceptionally challenging place for fieldwork, especially as a US citizen."[99] Over my fieldwork trips to Cuba, in addition to productive research in archives, particularly that of the Cuban Women's Federation, I spoke with many Cubans who gave their accounts of the insurrection, either informally or in meetings arranged through state channels. These were typically familiar stories that did not vary significantly from the state-endorsed version. I followed up on recommendations by Cubans for people they knew who had participated. I had greatest success when I went through state institutions (including the University of Havana), as one trusted revolutionary, vetted to speak to foreign press and academics, would point me toward another trusted revolutionary, typically another state official. As I was interested in events that occurred five decades prior, many rebel women had passed away or were unavailable owing to advanced age. Many of those remaining had been teenagers or very young adults during the insurrection, and their perspective reflected this subset of rebels. As interesting and impressive as these individuals were, they veered little from the well-trodden path already laid out in the official historical record. For some, I had already read interviews they had given and the interview produced few new insights. Questions designed to elicit new information or perspectives that varied from the familiar narrative were not as productive as I had hoped, and I sometimes held back to avoid engendering suspicion or discomfort. For example, I initially broached the subject of sexual assault during the insurrection. Respondents reported that, though it occurred, they had no specific information about it. In general, this was not a comfortable area of discussion for my respondents, and though it is a question I am regularly asked in public presentations on the Cuba insurrection, I have not pursued this sensitive topic in interviews. I also had little luck with seemingly less sensitive topics, such as the subject of women in rebel movements other than the Castro-led July 26 Movement. Fortunately, the documentary evidence provided a much fuller range of insights, and I draw primarily from these.

A final consideration concerns research in the context of US–Cuba relations. I received clearance from my university Institutional Review Board; however, the formal means of establishing and documenting consent for interviews for this topic was awkward at best. Given the nearly six decades of US hostilities toward Cuba, the troubled dynamics of a Cuban citizen granting formal consent for an interview to a US citizen on the subject of an insurrection not only against Batista but also US neo-imperialism were evident. I am indebted to the time and care with which many Cubans explained and recalled the insurrection. Interviews informed my research questions and findings, and helped guide the archival research itself and my analysis of it, including the over 2,600 entries with explicit focus on the theme of women and the revolution culled from the Cuban media 1975–1992.[100] Additional archival research was done with Cuban media in the 1950s (*Bohemia* and *Diario de la marina*), Princeton Latin American Pamphlet Collection (broadcast transcripts of *Radio Rebelde* and *Movimiento 26 de Julio* correspondence), the Cuban

Women's Federation (FMC) archives, online Cuban media sources, documentaries, Lyn Smith oral histories (US Library of Congress sound recordings), published interviews, recently released US State Department communiqués and additional material obtained through FOIA requests, and US media reports in the 1950s.

Notes

1. García-Pérez (1998).
2. Díaz Vallina, et al. (1994, 24); Díaz Vallina (2001, 7). Chase (2015) is a recent exception.
3. Szulc (1986) notes "the galaxy of Cuban revolutionary women who made the ultimate victory possible" (330). Smith and Padula (1996) maintain that without women, "Castro never would have succeeded" (22).
4. See Guerra (2012), who "draw[s] heavily on the grand narrative, that is, the [Cuban] state's own press, to tell radically different stories" (34).
5. Shayne (2004, 5).
6. Díaz Vallina, et al. (1994, 29); Díaz Vallina (2001, 7).
7. Harding (1986, 17); Scott (1999). See Enloe (2014) for how research that asks "where are the women?" can yield new insight into international politics. Yaffe (2014, 20–44) presents a good overview of the very well-worn paths of Cuban research.
8. This binary is expressed in various ways, including violence/media (Zarkov 2007) and coercive violence/hearts and minds (Biddle 2008, 347). I use the terms "war of ideas" and "hearts and minds" interchangeably.
9. Rodríguez (1996, xvi): "revolutions are also questions of words and wordings"; see also Saldaña-Portillo (2003).
10. Enloe (2000); Bernal (2000); Goldstein (2001); Zarkov (2007); Sjoberg (2013).
11. Sjoberg and Gentry (2007, 28). This entails vanquishing the enemy's triumphal narrative.
12. For example, Stout (2013, 168) remarks on the Castro-led rebels, including guerrillas "about whom a whole industry of lore and aggrandizement came into existence," in marked contrast to the rebel underground *clandestinos*, about whom much less is known.
13. Among the exceptions, see Prados-Torreira (2005); Viterna (2013); Kampwirth (2002); Luciak (1998, 2001); Taylor (1997).
14. For key scholarly inquiries into Cuban women, see Stoner (1991, 2003); Prados-Torreira (2005); Smith and Padula (1996); Chase (2010, 2015). See also Kampwirth (2002) and Shayne (2004), who include Cuba as a case in comparative analyses of women and revolution.
15. See Sweig (2002).
16. To mobilize women and support its claim to represent their interests, the post-1958 revolutionary state highlighted women's contributions to the struggle, incrementally publishing interviews and articles. Over five decades, these comprise a substantial body of information. Fieldwork interviews

informed the research questions and findings and helped guide the archival work, including 2,608 entries on women and the revolution culled from over fifty years of the Cuban media. *Granma*, *Verde Olivo*, and *Mujeres* were searched for references to women, including those covering women's participation in the insurrection (photocopied, transcribed in summary form, then thematically coded). I also searched *Bohemia* magazine (1956–1963) and *Diario de la marina* (1957–1958), which yielded many new names among the rank and file rebels. I built upon this foundation using primary and secondary documents. Using names found from these sources, I conducted internet searches that yielded additional information from a more diverse array of Cuban media sources. I constructed 107 biographical entries on women rebels and also compiled information on rebel events and activities. These are bolstered by archival Cuban sources from pre-1959 and the first years of the revolution, anti-Castro Cubans' published recollections, and non-Cuban observations, all of which reveal more heterogeneous narratives regarding events and interpretations.

17. Sweig (2002).
18. Ibid., 2. See also Childs (1995, 3); Halperin (1993). Key exceptions include Pérez (1976); Domínguez (1978, 110–133); García-Pérez (1998).
19. Sweig (2002, 1–2). See also Vellinga (1976, 246).
20. Halperin (1993, 188).
21. Sweig (2002, 9). See also Bonachea and San Martín (1974); Childs (1995).
22. Sweig (2002, 9).
23. Farber (2006, 117); Sweig (2002, 8); Childs (1995, 4); Domínguez (1978, 127). In addition to the high rebel casualty rates in the attack on the Moncada garrison in 1953 and the Granma landing in 1956, the rebel group *Directorio Revolucionario* was crushed in March 1957, M-26-7 leader Frank País was killed in July 1957, and the military put down a navy rebellion in September 1957. The llano's failed April 1958 general strike sealed its subordination to the Sierra.
24. Sweig (2002). For Castro's recognition of the continued importance of the llano, see Childs (1995, 4). Studies often begin with the guerrilla war in late 1956 (e.g. Kling 1962). Castro's own narratives exhaustively detail battles in the Sierra. His preference over five decades for the guerrilla olive green uniform embeds an association between himself, the revolution, and guerrilla warfare, in effect eclipsing the llano struggle and his own pre-Sierra political work (when he habitually wore suit and tie). Furthermore, Che's highly influential writings reflect his own experience as a Sierra-based guerrilla in the final two years of insurrection.
25. Stoner (1991, 2003); Prados-Torreira (2005).
26. Hunt and Rygiel (2006, 5–6); Tickner (2001); Cooke (1996).
27. Peterson (2010, 21).
28. Ibid.
29. Yuval-Davis (2004, 172).
30. Yuval-Davis (ibid.) offers Turkey, Libya, Nicaragua, and Eritrea as examples.
31. Hawkesworth (2005, 149–150). See also Enloe (1990, 1993, 2000); Peterson and Runyan (1999); Bayard de Volo (2012).

32. De la Fuente (1998); Sawyer (2000); Roland (2006). For exceptions to racial silence in Cuba, see Bayard de Volo (2012).
33. Roland (2006); Sawyer (2000); De la Fuente (1998, 2001).
34. De la Fuente (1998, 61).
35. Kalyvas (2005, 89). See also Kampwirth (2002, 5).
36. Kalyvas (2005, 89). Modern militaries often exhibit a similar shortsightedness. The US military prioritizes efforts to kill or capture the enemy rather than positively engage the civilian population (see Kaplan 2013; Ricks 2006; Sepp 2005). In addition to the US wars in Vietnam and Iraq (among others), this shortsightedness can be seen in the US-sponsored Bay of Pigs invasion in Cuba (Schlesinger 1965, 246).
37. Despite the vast literature on the Cuban insurrection, scholars outside Cuba tend to focus upon the post-insurrection phase; the scholarship that does focus on the insurrectionary period typically concentrates on the leaders and the Sierra Maestra (Pérez 1998, ix).
38. See Viterna (2013) for an exception.
39. Segal (1995, 762) argues that women are more likely to be included as combatants if the risk posed to them in combat is similar to that experienced as civilians.
40. Taber (1961, 34).
41. For discussion, see Kampwirth (2002) and Wickham-Crowley (1992, 22). Exceptions to this focus include Stoner (2003); García-Pérez (1999, 2009); Chase (2010, 2015).
42. Pérez (1998, ix–x).
43. Díaz Vallina, et al. (1994, 25). The study used interviews and files on women rebels from the Cuban veterans' association.
44. Díaz Vallina, et al. (1994, 25–27). The study indicates rebel women were overwhelmingly white and primarily middle class, with most unmarried and working outside the home. Sixty-three percent were employed as teachers, technicians, artists, university professionals, librarians, and small business owners; another 12 percent did industrial work and 2 percent worked in agriculture. As noted, Cuban sources rarely reference the race of rebels or civilian supporters, and the grainy photos that often accompany interviews and news articles on women ex-rebels are an unreliable means of determining race, particularly in terms of 1950s Cuba's dominant racial constructions.
45. Chapelle (1962a); Wickham-Crowley (1992, 216–17); Kampwirth (2002, 3); Foran, Klouzal and Rivera (1997, 32–3).
46. Kampwirth (2002, 2–3); Luciak (2001); Cupples (2006, 85). The percentages are in dispute (Vilas 1986, 108). El Salvador has been estimated as high as 40 percent women (for discussion, see Mason 1992, 64–65).
47. Lobao Reif (1990, 183).
48. Segal (1995, 762).
49. See Viterna (2013).
50. Possibly Fidel also viewed women as unlikely to challenge his leadership. The surviving male leaders were similarly less disposed to challenge Fidel's leadership, namely Raúl Castro, Fidel's younger brother, and Che Guevara,

an Argentine less interested in governing Cuba than in spreading revolution elsewhere.

51. Eckstein (2003, 12–13).
52. Scholars note that dominant notions of femininity can give an advantage to women rebels and activists. See Byrd and Decker (2008); Shayne (2004, 9, 43–4); Bouvard (1994); Fisher (1989), Schirmer (1993). This was also a clear theme in the 1965 film *The Battle of Algiers* (see Decker 1991).
53. See Viterna (2013) regarding women's greater survival rates in El Salvador's guerrilla.
54. See, for example, Santamaría (2003b, 37) and Marta Fuego Rodriguez interview, Lyn Smith Cuba Collection, regarding Pancho González.
55. Laqueur (1998, 392).
56. Thomas (1998, 1038).
57. Sepp (2005, 9).
58. Domínguez (1989); Childs (1995).
59. Debray (1967).
60. Guevara (1961 [1985], 211).
61. Moreno (1970, 117). Notably, Fidel's band of rebels initially generated popular support not through their military victories but through military defeats – Moncada and the Granma landing.
62. Friedman (1970, 135).
63. Mack (1975, 164, 175); Moreno (1970, 116); Friedman (1970).
64. Friedman (1970, 139). Once the rebels shifted from direct engagements like Moncada, for which Batista's military was most adequately prepared, to guerrilla warfare, the military advantage shifted to the rebels (Pérez 1976, 139).
65. In 1957, "Castro had informed Robert Taber that the guerrillas did not expect to overthrow the government singlehandedly but rather planned to produce a 'climate of collapse'" (Pérez 1976, 161).
66. Dubois (1959, 138).
67. Ibid.
68. Wickham-Crowley (1992, 174); see also Hampsey (2002).
69. Kling (1962, 45).
70. Shayne (2004, 7–8); Kampwirth (2002); Lobao Reif (1986).
71. Shayne (2004, 8); Viterna (2013, 63).
72. Kampwirth (2002, 9); see also Viterna (2013, 63).
73. Childs (1995).
74. Sweig (2002).
75. Guevara (1961 [1985], 58).
76. See Sjoberg (2013).
77. See Guevara (2013), especially 1957 diary entries.
78. Guevara (1961 [1985], 58).
79. Scott (1999, 2).
80. Montaner (1981, 87).
81. Ibid., 196.
82. Machover Ajzenfich (2001, 265–6). See also Arenas (1986, 218).
83. See Bayard de Volo (2012).

84. Harding (1986, 17); Scott (1999, 42).
85. Guevara (1965 [1969], 167). See also Rodríguez (1996); Saldaña-Portillo (2003); Bayard de Volo (2012).
86. Lobao Reif (1986, 153); Miller (1991, 146–7); Mason (1992, 64); Kampwirth (2002, 128); Shayne (2004, 45); Luciak (2001, 2).
87. Guevara (1961 [1985], 133).
88. Miller (1991, 147).
89. Moreno (1970, 116); see also Saldaña-Portillo (2003, 67–78).
90. Mason (1992, 64); Miller (1991, 147).
91. Fidel's narrow escapes are often attributed by his critics not to combat skills or luck but more cynically to his tendency to duck out early or hang back in battle.
92. See, for example, Dore (2012) and Hamilton (2012).
93. Pérez (1980, 83); see also Guerra (2012, 34).
94. Miller (2003, 149–50). See also Saldaña-Portillo (2003, 74–5).
95. Pérez (1980, 84). See also Eckstein (2003, 4).
96. Pérez (1980, 84).
97. Ibid. See also Miller (2003, 157).
98. See Klouzal (2008, 327).
99. Shayne (2004, 15). Like Shayne and many others, I did not have Cuban state institutional support for my research.
100. This research was part of a comparative project on women, war, and peace processes in Latin America funded by the National Science Foundation (SES-0242269), the United States Institute of Peace, and the University of Kansas.

CHAPTER 2

"How Can Men Tire When Women Are Tireless?"

Women Rebels before Moncada

Women's activism and the gendered logics deployed in the insurrection are better understood in light of women's prior participation in Cuba's wars of independence and 1930s rebellion. This chapter pursues several points along these lines that will inform later chapters. First, the 1950s insurrection and women's place in it were not created from scratch but rather drew from experiences of Cuba's previous wars and rebellions. In part, this occurred symbolically, as rebels used narratives of women's contributions in prior conflicts to legitimize contemporary women's activism and inspire Cubans more generally to rebellion.[1] But as I show, women activists also drew from their own previous insurrectionary experiences. Thus, tactics developed in the wars of independence were applied to the 1950s insurrection, and some women active in Cuba's 1930s rebellion transferred their political experience to the 1950s, lending a sense of continuity as well as efficacy.

A second and related theme, first identified by Cuban historian Gladys Marel García-Pérez, is the multigenerational aspect of the anti-Batista women's activism.[2] Building upon this, I further note that although the Cuban War Story frames it as an insurrection of youth, rebels in general and women in particular were often older than the term "youth" implies. The multigenerational anti-Batista women, when organizing as women, transcended much of the infighting and rivalry – some of it between generations – that characterized other anti-Batista groups.

José Martí, "La recepción en Filadelfia," *Patria*, New York, August 20, 1892; transl. by Stoner (1991, 29).

23

Several scholars note the continuities between the 1950s rebellion and its historical antecedents.[3] As Sweig summarized, most individual and institutional actors "on the Cuban political stage in the late 1950s were consciously playing out a drama that in fact began during the Wars of Independence against Spain and the American intervention in 1898, and continued in the 1930s."[4] Louis Pérez Jr. finds, "Cubans all through the first half of the twentieth century lived with and within their history. The past was remembered – relentlessly."[5] Pérez also points to the later reorganization of Cuban history to suit the goals of the post-1958 revolution in power, which meant "portray[ing] the revolution less as a break with the past than as a fulfillment of the revered heroes' mission."[6]

This chapter, then, explores women's participation in Cuba's wars of independence and 1930s rebellion to better understand subsequent women's activism and the gendered logics deployed. Building upon the work of historians, I document how the 1950s insurrection and women's place in it drew from experiences of Cuba's previous rebellions both symbolically and in terms of gender tactics. This lent continuity to the movement and status for the middle-aged and older women rebels. It furthermore interrupts the official Cuban War Story's celebration of youth as the authors of change, as rebels in general and women in particular were often older than the term "youth" implies. Finally, the anti-Batista women were effective in transcending the political and intergenerational rivalry that often characterized anti-Batista groups.

WOMEN REBELS OF THE PRE-1950S

Las Mambisas: Women and the Wars of Independence

Cuban armed resistance to Spanish colonial rule came in three waves: the Ten Years' War (1868–78), the Little War (*Guerra Chiquita*, 1879–80), and the War of Independence (1895–98). "Mambí" referred to rebel territory as well as the men and women who fought there. Women rebels were called Las Mambisas, and over half a century later, they were an important influence on the 1950s rebels, referenced as both inspirations and examples of women's capacity to support armed rebellion.[7] A few participants of those wars contributed to the anti-Batista movement. For example, following the 1953 attack on the Moncada barracks, some rebels fled to the house of Leocadia "Chicha" García Garzón, an Afro-Cuban woman who had served as a guide for the Mambí forces in 1895.[8] To confirm her rebel background, she showed Fidel a document signed by independence hero Antonio Maceo certifying her service as a rebel guide nearly sixty years prior.

The legacy of José Martí, independence hero and poet, helped secure Cuban women a place in the 1950s rebel movement. One Martí quote is cited throughout the post-1958 revolutionary era: "The people's campaigns are weak only when women offer them merely fearful and restrained assistance; when the woman of timid and quiet nature becomes excited and applauds, when the cultured and virtuous woman anoints the work with the sweet honey of affection – the work is invincible."[9] Martí's writings inspired anti-Batista rebels, including Castro and his M-26-7 co-founders.

Aside from post-1958 Cuban state publications, historians K. Lynn Stoner and Teresa Prados-Torreira have been most thorough in documenting Cuban women's involvement in its nineteenth-century wars of liberation. Prados-Torreira's research charts the many ways women undermined traditional authority to engender a revolutionary climate, "solidifying the notion that stepping outside the legal system was not only acceptable but heroic."[10] Women rebels were used as examples, "their courage often invoked to inspire the fighters. For how could Cuban soldiers hesitate to give their lives for the insurgency when their mothers, their sisters, their daughters were willing to do so?"[11] Women's participation also helped confront racist challenges to the Mambí cause. As thousands of Afro-Cuban men joined the rebels, the Spanish and their Cuban supporters used race to undermine rebel legitimacy. In response, the rebel men stressed their high moral caliber, representing themselves "as respectable nineteenth-century gentlemen who had the support of their pious mothers, wives, and daughters."[12] Indeed, as Prados-Torreira put it, Cuban women's "commitment to rebel ideals demonstrated the holiness of the insurgents' struggle. For was she not, as a woman, a non-partisan supporter, an apolitical player who merely wanted what was best for her children?"[13]

Prados-Torreira also notes the differences in class and race for these women, which were often determinants for the horizon of choices and opportunities the women confronted as well as the motivations behind their support for the Mambí cause. Most notably, "For black women, free or slave, maintaining the colonial status quo meant the survival of an oppressive, unjust system that considered them disposable."[14] In slavery, women often suffered the same deprivations, hard labor, and abuse as men, which made motherhood particularly trying. Slaves resisted colonial rule by struggling to keep their families together, maintain customs

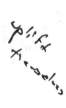

from their homeland, escape, and eventually, openly rebel against the Spanish colonial power.[15]

In the midst of war, once men joined the Mambí cause, their women relatives were guilty by association and had to flee their homes, often accompanying men into the *manigua* (rural, uncultivated regions).[16] These "family wars," as they were sometimes called, left little pretense that war was an exclusively men's affair.[17]

The following paragraphs introduce several Mambisas who inspired the 1950s rebels as symbols of heroism and sacrifice and who are regularly referenced in post-1958 Cuban sources.[18] These include Ana Betancourt, Mariana Grajales, Bernarda del Toro, Adela Azcuy, and Rosa "la Bayamesa" Castellanos.[19] Rebel leaders of the 1950s and later the Cuban War Story used their example to encourage women's participation as well as to legitimize women's place in the military.

Ana Betancourt, a white woman from a landholding family and supporter of the Mambí cause, called upon rebel leaders, as they sought to break the chains of race and class, to include women in their vision of a Free Cuba.[20] In the rebels' 1869 First Constitutional Assembly, Betancourt gave one of the first feminist speeches in Latin America: "Citizens: Everything was enslaved in Cuba: cradle, color, and sex. You want to destroy the enslavement of the cradle, fighting until death. You have destroyed the slavery of color by emancipating the slave. The time has come to free the women."[21] Betancourt's house was a center for conspiracy where she hid weapons and printed proclamations.[22] She continued even as the Spanish authorities monitored her, until she was forced to flee to the *manigua* with her husband for several years. She was then captured and imprisoned in 1871.[23]

Many stories featured women's and especially mothers' sacrifice in the wars.[24] Prados-Torreira argues that "the Mambisas' political potential was fully realized" through mothers: "Symbolizing pure, unselfish love, a mother's role as bearer of soldiers and her willingness to give up her children for *la patria* represented the ultimate testament to the worthiness of the rebel cause."[25] Of all the women rebels of the Wars of Independence, M-26-7 and later the revolutionary government most consistently referenced Mariana Grajales. Stoner places her among "Cuba's pantheon of war heroes."[26] Castro named the women's combat platoon after her, and Vilma Espín, head of the Federation of Cuban Women (FMC), described Grajales in 1982 as a "symbol of the brave and stoic Cuban woman, ready to offer herself to the cause of the country and also to offer that which is most precious to her, most beloved: her children."[27]

Grajales, a mixed-race woman from the Santiago area, lost her husband and nine of her eleven sons in the wars, including Antonio Maceo, one of the top military leaders of the Ten Years' War.[28] She is celebrated for having raised her children to oppose slavery and love Cuba, engaging them to swear on a crucifix their willingness to give their lives for their country.[29] She, along with her daughters and daughters-in-law, accompanied their menfolk into war. José Martí witnessed Mariana and her daughter-in-law María Cabrales venture on to the battlefield to rescue a wounded Antonio with only the covering fire of José Maceo to protect them, reflecting, "It is easy to be heroes with women such as these."[30] Martí's valorization of Mariana in another act of maternal heroism launched her as a powerful symbol. At news of the death of one son (and with three others wounded), she is said to have commanded her youngest: "And you, stand tall, it's time for you to go fight for your country."[31] As Stoner summarizes, "Mariana Grajales embodied all that was Cuba at that moment. She was a woman of color who symbolized that Cuba would be a nation of racial harmony. She was willing to sacrifice all that was most dear, the flesh of her flesh, for her nation. Cubans would never surrender."[32]

Bernarda del Toro, wife of rebel hero General Máximo Gómez, represented a feminine "Spartan selflessness" in rebel discourse.[33] She married Gómez in the *manigua* and lived there for ten years of war, giving birth in a rebel camp and, according to Martí, carrying her children "marching through battles in the cradle of her arms."[34] She lost infants to the harsh conditions and lost her oldest son in battle, was imprisoned, impoverished, and ultimately forced into exile.[35] Like Grajales, Bernarda stood as an ideal mambisa, a woman who sacrificed all for a free Cuba.[36]

Women's many contributions to Mambisa logistics were also later resurrected as worthy examples, inspiring and informing 1950s rebel techniques. Prados-Torreira found numerous accounts of women stealing, hiding, and transporting weapons. In 1897, women rebels in Las Villas stole weapons at night from the Spanish soldiers sleeping in the main square and hid them under their long, full skirts.[37] Rosario Morales and her two daughters were discovered with a storeroom in their house in which thousands of bullets were hidden in condensed milk cans.[38]

Women also served as couriers, running rebel messages, a dangerous act for which some were imprisoned. It was believed that women attracted less suspicion and thus could more safely carry rebel messages without being searched. They furthermore had the advantage of their many-layered clothing, in which messages, letters, and even medicine could be inconspicuously stored. Magdalena Peñarredonda or "General

Llellena," as she was known, was a trusted courier.[40] Rebel troops depended upon her to deliver crucial supplies as well as news of the war and even strategic military plans.[41] She crossed rebel lines almost daily for two years with messages, supplies, and money hidden in her petticoat or a briefcase with a false bottom until she was caught and imprisoned.

On a more quotidian level, *campesinas* opened their modest homes to Mambí troops, cooking for them, washing clothes, and sharing honey, candles, vegetables, and coffee.[42] Women also oversaw the production of gunpowder, clothes, horseshoes, and other war necessities in rebel *talleres* (workshops).[43] Established in the 1870s and staffed by women as well as injured men, these *talleres* proved vital to the rebellion.[44]

The most prominent war work for women was nursing, often under extremely dangerous conditions. Nursing took on both pragmatic and symbolic benefits for the rebels. The field hospitals, staffed largely by women scattered throughout the *manigua*, both reduced casualty rates and raised morale.[45] Adela Azcuy Labrador, a white Cuban woman from a middle-class family, served as both nurse and combatant. In 1896, Adela was in her mid-30s and with no children when she joined the Mambí army. She tried to enroll as a soldier but was only permitted to serve on the medical team. With medical and pharmaceutical expertise gained working in her first husband's pharmacy, she was well suited to the work.[46] She repeatedly went into battle to administer first aid and also to engage the enemy, once reportedly telling her commanding officer: "Commander, I came into the war to fight; if I have to die, I want to die like the brave, fighting."[47] Within months, she was promoted to second lieutenant. She wore a wide-rimmed hat with the Cuban tricolor and carried a machete and revolver into battle, along with her first-aid bag, participating in forty-nine battles, and ultimately earning the title of captain.[48]

Another woman nurse who also engaged in combat was Rosario Castellanos, known popularly as Rosa la Bayamesa. Rosa was an Afro-Cuban ex-slave who rose to Captain of Military Health, a rank granted her by General Máximo Gómez. In Oriente, in addition to working as cook, messenger, and most famously as a nurse, she also participated in the rebel machete charges that so terrified the Spanish soldiers.[49]

After the Ten Years' War, scores of women enrolled in the Mambí army, many serving as soldiers.[50] Others initially engaged in more traditional feminine rebel pursuits before taking up combat. Most were poor and Afro-Cuban women, who were more likely to live in rebel camps as they had fewer options than most white women to find safe refuge elsewhere.[51] Spanish troops tried to suppress the insurrection by burning crops and driving the rural population into concentration camps. Thousands died of starvation and disease, if not outright assault by Spanish troops. Facing death in this form, many women, along with men, preferred to join the rebels to fight colonial rule.[52] Isabel was one example, a young Afro-Cuban woman wounded in battle: "thanks to her youth, her feminine form not being so well pronounced, and her being dressed like a man, [she] had the look of a boy; thanks also to her seriousness and composure, she had achieved what no other woman had – she had served under General Maceo's command."[53] One male rebel reported that four women fought in his regiment.[54]

In sum, Las Mambisas were visible and indeed vital to the independence wars, creating a blueprint and legitimizing women's integration for later Cuban struggles. As later chapters will show, many of the gender tactics employed by women rebels of the 1950s were proven methods from over sixty years prior. Furthermore, as Prados-Torreira explains, "All nationalist projects include the creating of myths and symbols that help cement the bond among disparate elements of society. The Mambisas' involvement in the anticolonial cause became a defining aspect of Cuba's historical memory and lore."[55] The powerful symbolism attached to Las Mambisas, their suffering, sacrifice, and bravery for the rebel cause inspired later generations. As Martí wrote: "How can men tire when women are tireless?"[56]

Women and the 1930s "Revolutionary Generation"

The wars of independence were followed several decades later by the "revolutionary generation" of the late 1920s to mid-1930s, during which Cuban opposition to the government neared all-out war as President Gerardo Machado y Morales grew increasingly dictatorial.[57] Through revisions to the constitution, bribery, intimidation, and repression, Machado was reelected in 1928 to a six-year term. The Great Depression and a subsequent disastrous decline in sugar prices increased the opposition, including women from diverse sectors of society who organized as women's rights advocates as well as students, workers, and communists. By 1931, independence war veterans had joined forces with student organizations, labor, and sections of the middle class in calling for Machado's ouster. The resistance was widespread, extending even among traditional politicians and factions of the military and including shootouts in the streets, bombings, and assassinations. By 1933, the unrest prompted the United States to intervene in Cuban sovereignty, first by attempting to influence Machado, then by arranging his exit.

Provisional president Carlos Manuel de Céspedes was soon unseated by the "Revolt of the Sergeants," in which future dictator Fulgencio Batista figured prominently. Ramón Grau San Martín took office, and in the four months of his presidency, he instituted radical changes, including an eight-hour workday, university access for the poor, and women's right to vote. The United States refused to recognize Grau's administration, condemning it as communist. With little support other than the military, Grau stepped down in January 1934. As civil unrest continued, the presidency was held by four more men in succession – all of whom were directed by General Batista, who was officially elected to the presidency in 1940.

Grau and his followers – including many students – reconsolidated in the Partido Revolucionario Cubano-Auténtico, known as the *Auténticos*. Grau was elected to the presidency in 1944, promising social reform and an end to corruption, though his administration was soon itself accused of corruption. The disappointment and frustration that followed gave rise to a new political party in 1947 – the *Ortodoxos*.[58] Founded by Eduardo "Eddy" Chibás, the party included many future anti-Batista rebels.

Stoner maintains that women's active role in the wars of independence undermined arguments that women should remain at home during the 1930s rebellion.[59] Women indeed were prominent in the Machado-era resistance in feminist groups and other organizations. Relations between groups of activist women in the 1930s were strained, as they held significantly different visions of social justice and government. Cuban feminists were part of a broad-based antigovernment movement. Interestingly, they were "moderates among radicals, not radicals among moderates," and were thus acceptable to most factions of the resistance.[60] Despite disagreements, "Women presented themselves as the salvation of Cuban morality when men were discredited as public leaders."[61] The death of student Rafael Trejo in 1930, shot six times in the back by police, "made many women militants who otherwise would have stayed home."[62] Machado declared a state of siege, threatening violence against anyone other than family in the funeral procession for Trejo. In defiance, over one hundred women accompanied the body to the cemetery.[63] As Stoner writes, soldiers "were loathe to fire on women who were doing what women were supposed to do after outbreaks of violence – mourn the dead."[64] Among them was Teresa "Teté" Casuso Brau, later an important ally for Fidel in exile.[65] Despite initial hesitation, government forces were increasingly willing to repress women. Casuso had been badly beaten in the protests following Trejo's death. During hearings to review the police actions, Casuso shouted from the legislative gallery and bared her back and shoulders to

reveal her wounds, giving the lie to police claims that no one had been mistreated.[66] Several months later, after women shouted down Machado on
his balcony of the presidential palace, government forces targeted opposition women for repression. In February 1931, two women assaulted two
young women activists on the streets, scratching them and tearing off their
clothes, while four male collaborators held back the crowd.[67] The attack
indicated a coordinated effort to punish and silence women activists.

Women were also active in the Communist Party, including Leonarda
Vargas (described in the 1983 Cuban press as "a strong and very pretty
black woman") and the sisters Dulce María and Mercedes Estrada,
who worked in propaganda and agitation, handing out manifestos, fliers, and proclamations.[68] In the 1933 strike preceding the military coup,
Communist Party women marched carrying a document of women's
demands.[69] One young communist, sixteen-year-old América Labadí
Arce, was gunned down in Santiago by Machado's forces in 1933.[70] In
post-1958 revolutionary Cuba, she is featured among women martyrs.[71]

THE CUBAN UNDERGROUND POST-COUP, PRE-MONCADA

When polls revealed Batista to be running third in the 1952 presidential
elections, he overthrew President Carlos Prío Socarrás.[72] The March 10
coup initially encountered relatively little popular resistance, in part due
to widespread revulsion at corruption and crime under Prío.[73] As discontent grew, women began to organize across generations, and they did so
in diverse ways, including through their own women's organizations. In
the next section, I first examine several women of the 1930s generation
of activists – the "Revolutionary Generation" – who brought their experience and political acumen to the anti-Batista struggle. Then I turn to
anti-Batista women's organizations, tracing the largely unacknowledged
contributions of these groups to the insurrection.

Women of the 1930s Generation

Cuban historian García-Pérez uses the case of Eva Jiménez Ruiz to challenge a dominant representation of the insurrection as arising out of
nowhere under the leadership of a new generation.[74] Instead, she illus-
trates "the continuity and the rupture" of the 1950s insurrection and
those of previous generations, emphasizing gender. Toward this end, it is
important to bring into the historical record the participation of women
rebels beyond the few well-known heroines. García-Pérez points out

that neither the M-26-7 nor the student-led *Directorio Revolucionario* (Revolutionary Directorate or DR) had women's sections; furthermore, neither group included in their programs the interests of women, despite women's rights activism since the turn of the century.[75]

Eva Jiménez was born in 1907 into a family in which men and women alike struggled for Cuba's independence.[76] In the 1930s she joined the *Directorio Estudiantil Universitario* (DEU), protested against Machado, and with sister Graciela, hid rebels from the authorities. Eva continued her family legacy of activism into the early 1950s. For example, prior to Batista's coup, she accompanied Fidel and others to document corruption on President Prío's farm, where Prío was using military personnel to work on his private land. As a middle-aged woman, Eva helped the young men maintain their cover as tourists sightseeing in the countryside as they filmed at the farm.[77]

Eva, then, already had a history of political engagement when Batista took power in 1952. The day after the coup, Fidel took refuge at her house during the post-coup violence and mass arrests.[78] She stocked her kitchen and gave her maid the week off, as Castro spent two days writing an anti-Batista proclamation entitled, "Not a Revolution – A Bang!"[79] Eva and René Rodríguez then set about getting it published. As Eva described it, "My house came to be practically Fidel's office."[80]

Following disagreements with Fidel, she began to conspire with Professor Rafael García Bárcena and was a founding member of his National Revolutionary Movement (MNR) in May 1952. The group held meetings in her apartment to plan the first anti-Batista coup in April 1953. Hundreds of militants, including many university students, gathered for an organized assault on the Columbia military garrison in Havana. However, the police were tipped off, and a few hours before the planned attack, they rounded up some seventy activists.[81] García Bárcena was arrested in Eva's home, along with Eva and several others. Before they were transported to jail, García Bárcena passed her incriminating papers, which she burned under the pretense of making coffee.[82] Nonetheless, as the police searched her house, they found damaging evidence, including a sketch of the Columbia military grounds, guns, and bullets. Eva was sentenced to six months' imprisonment, a light sentence given the evidence against her.[83] Once released, she went into exile in Mexico, where Fidel and Raúl Castro arrived roughly nine months later. She returned to Cuba several years later and worked as an M-26-7 courier in Havana.[84]

Santiago M-26-7 leader Gloria "Cayita" Cuadras de la Cruz was another middle-aged woman who contributed to the continuity of activism across generations. Raised in a politically active family, in the 1930s Cayita was a founder of the *Directorio Estudiantil de Oriente* and was known as a brave and eloquent speaker.[85] At 19, she was wounded by police while leading a student protest.[86] She went on in 1947 to be a founding member of the *Ortodoxos*, collaborating with Castro as a fellow *Ortodoxo* delegate. As a vocal Batista opponent, in May 1953 she became a political commentator on radio station CMCR. In 1955–56, she also ran the newspaper *Cuba libre*, in which, like her radio broadcasts, she castigated the government, condemned political corruption, and supported Fidel's efforts.[87] Though she was in her mid-to-late 40s and with health problems – weakness, with trouble walking and breathing – she was imprisoned repeatedly and brutally assaulted several times.[88] Nonetheless, described as "one of the most combative *compañeras*," Cuadras often headed student protests and other mobilizations that confronted the Batista regime.[89] In the final years of the insurrection, she was in the M-26-7 General Command (*Estado Mayor*) and the Secretary of Propaganda in Oriente.

Aida Pelayo and Hilda Felipe are two prominent but lesser-known middle-aged rebels. Aida, a key figure in the 1950s underground resistance and co-founder of the *Frente Cívico de Mujeres Martianas*, became active as a teenager in the 1930s, participating in anti-Machado and Communist Youth activities, for which she was arrested several times before her twentieth birthday.[90] Aida was further politicized by the Spanish Civil War and participated in the solidarity movement with the Republicans of Spain as her husband, a Spaniard, returned to his country to fight.[91] A feminist, Aida advocated for women's right to vote, the right to public office, and access to well-paying jobs, also extending the struggle to underprivileged groups more generally.[92]

Hilda Felipe, a co-founder of the *Mujeres Oposicionistas Unidas* in 1956, recalled her early politicization: "I was forged in the union struggles."[93] Her mother was a communist, and Hilda became the secretary general of 470 textile workers by the age of eighteen. At first a member of the *Partido Socialista Popular*, she later joined the Communist Party.[94] An early supporter of the anti-Batista movement, Hilda, like Teté Casuso, ultimately cut her ties with the Castro government and went into exile.

Las Martianas: Martí Women's Civic Front

Shifting the lens from individual activists to women's anti-Batista organizations, among the most notable is the *Frente Cívico de Mujeres Martianas*

FCMM

(Martí Women's Civic Front, also known as FCMM or *Las Martianas*), which formed in 1952.[95] Aida recalled that Spanish Civil War veteran Pedro González came to her house after the coup and asked her what women were going to do, "because in Spain, women were very active."[96] The anti-fascist women of Spain inspired Aida, along with Carmen "Neneína" Castro Porta and Olga Román Sánchez, to create a women's organization.[97] The original group included middle-aged women who would become prominent in the insurrection: Pastorita Núñez, Martha Frayde Barraqué, Eva Jiménez, and Rosa Mier López.[98]

After months of meetings in Aida's house, forty women officially formed *Las Martianas* in November 1952.[99] Diverse in age, Las Martianas included the "30s Generation," who drew experience from the anti-Machado struggles and served as leaders of the organization, as well as the "Centenary Generation," younger women who became active in 1953, the centenary anniversary of José Martí's birth.[100] As their name indicates, *Las Martianas* drew inspiration from Martí, a unifying figure broadly supported by anti-Batista organizations. Similarly, they aimed to unite all women against the dictatorship without distinction of political positions, class, or religion.[101] Their founding principles included "elimination of individualism" and a rejection of personalism, as they hoped to "set an example of unity for other revolutionary groups that were splintered and divided."[102] Indeed, members responded to those insurrectionists in need, regardless of party affiliation or ideology. According to members, they operated in a cooperative, non-opportunistic fashion, an achievement that they believed set them apart from the fractiousness of mixed-gender, male-led anti-Batista groups.[103]

Ultimately, the organization included thousands of women, with an estimated six to seven hundred formally registered across branches in several provinces.[104] Members participated in various actions: medical assistance, street protests, production and distribution of leaflets, and the organization of an amnesty movement. They called meetings against Batista, collected money, and hid people from authorities. They marched in the streets with signs: "The blood of the good is not shed in vain."[105] But they also ventured into more dangerous and violent acts, including sabotage, weapons transport, prison escapes, and assassinations.[106]

In January 1953, Aida and at least eleven other members were arrested as they prepared leaflets.[107] As the police transported the women to jail, they sang and chanted "Down with Batista! Down with the assassin!"[108] Fidel and two other lawyers happened to hear the women's chants and followed the police vehicle to the station, where Fidel acted as their legal

representative.[109] Fresh out of jail January 27, 1953, the women participated in the midnight March of Torches, an anti-Batista protest com-
memorating the centenary of Martí's birth. Their large group marched
arm in arm, placed prominently with the politically influential Federation
of University Students (FEU).[110]

Las Martianas was a means of integrating women into such mass
protests, and the presence of women conveyed a broad opposition to
Batista.[111] The March of Torches as well as a student-led protest earlier in the month marked a turning point in the opposition, as protests
moved off campus and became more vulnerable to police repression.[112]
Las Martianas continued to work closely with the FEU, supporting and
participating in many of that group's initiatives. Fidel also met with members, strategizing future plans. Following his arrest after the Moncada
assault on July 26, 1953, Las Martianas mobilized to demand release of
the Moncada prisoners and to collect food and other items for them.[113]

Evidence points to Fidel's early interest in organizing women, and he
solicited the support of Las Martianas in a variety of ways. Upon Fidel's
release from prison in 1955, Fidel met again with Aida, Carmen, and
Pastorita Núñez, detailing the Moncada assault, analyzing the causes for
its failure, and claiming he now had sufficient experience and resources
to succeed.[114] As he prepared for exile, he tried unsuccessfully to transfer his weekly radio time slot on "Cadena Oriental de Radio" to Las
Martianas.[115] He visited them once more on the day he left, to bid them
farewell and solicit their opinions, then two *Martianas* accompanied him
to the airport.

In correspondence, Fidel encouraged the Martianas to become a wom-
en's section of the July 26 Movement.[116] Fidel was not the only opposition leader seeking such an alliance. The other main contenders to lead
the anti-Batista struggle also met with Las Martianas, including García
Bárcena (leader of MNR), Don Cosme de la Torriente (a hero of the
wars of independence pursuing a "Civil Dialogue" between the parties
and Batista), and ex-Presidents Prío Socarrás and Grau San Martín.[117]
Although individual Martianas joined M-26-7, the organization remained
formally unaligned. However, Las Martianas rejected collaboration with
Grau and the other political leaders, opting for Fidel's plans of armed
insurrection.

Founders Aida and Carmen were Las Martianas' most prominent members. Authorities accorded Aida with enough suspicion that they arrested
her in Havana following the July 1953 assault on the Moncada barracks.
Although not part of the attack, she was detained until the Moncada trial

ended in October. During the trial, Fidel asked rhetorically, "Why is Aida Pelayo here? Why is she always arrested every time a gunshot goes off in this country?"[118] Indeed, she was arrested at least fourteen times.[119]

In addition to clandestine work, Las Martianas followed Martí's emphasis on propaganda, which they considered essential.[120] They distributed their own propaganda and that of other groups, principally M-26-7 and the *Directorio Revolucionario*.[121] For several months, Las Martianas put out an underground bulletin called *Noticias y Comentarios* which other groups helped circulate.[122] When Radio Rebelde began its broadcasts from the Sierra Maestra in early 1958, Las Martianas printed and circulated the transcripts. Las Martianas also had a time slot – Saturdays from 9:00 to 9:30 p.m. – on *Radio Memória,* from which they issued declarations, gave news of the struggle, and denounced human rights violations. By such means, they distributed news and propaganda during media censorship, much of it aimed at developing a popular consciousness that armed struggle was necessary.[123]

Las Martianas also provided legal, moral, and material assistance to political prisoners and their families. For example, after discovering poorly buried corpses, Aida sought out family members of the victims to arrange a proper burial.[124] Martianas visited the morgue to identify bodies and attended to the grieving loved ones, protecting the families, and providing moral and material support.[125] They also collected funds for funeral services.

Las Martianas made many such small-scale contributions to human dignity. For example, upon hearing of the 1957 assassination attempt against Batista, after which many were killed, Naty Revuelta, Aida Pelayo, and Josefina "Fifi" Rodríguez hurried to the funeral home where the bodies of several rebel leaders had been taken.[126] They were arranging flowers for three rebels already prepared for burial when they found the body of leader José Antonio Echeverría, naked on the floor of a separate room. Naty covered his body with flower arrangements until his family could arrive with clothing. By the time Elvira Díaz Vallina, a university student and FEU member, arrived at the funeral home, a mass of people, mostly women, had already gathered outside, defying orders against mobilizing in the midst of the military crackdown.[127]

Las Mujeres Oposicionistas Unidas

Mujeres Oposicionistas Unidas (United Opposition Women or MOU) was formed in 1956 by women who were either members or sympathizers of the *Directorio Revolucionario*, M-26-7, *Resistencia Cívica*, the Popular Socialist Party (PSP), and other opposition organizations.[128] Founding MOU members included Martha Frayde, Natalia Bolívar, and Hilda Felipe, and membership totaled roughly forty women.[129] Hilda Felipe explained, "We went out into the streets to fight; it was the first time that Cuban women came together from all the tendencies that were against the dictatorship."[130] Indeed, like Las Martianas, the MOU aimed to transcend the political divisions impeding cooperation among anti-Batista groups and provide a means for women of these various groups, as well as unaffiliated "housewives," to collaborate.[131] The MOU was a coordination center for women from the various mixed-gender organizations that were often at odds with each other.[132] One member explained, "If those women from the Directorio needed to distribute a proclamation, the women from the PSP could print it on the mimeograph machine of their party. Meanwhile, the letters to the squads of Batista's army, urging them to take up our cause, were edited by M-26-7 women."[133] Members agreed not to prioritize one party over another in their MOU work: "[no] matter if a *muchacho* in danger was from the 13 de Marzo, the PSP or the M-26-7, no one asked what group they came from or what they had done."[134] The MOU supported political prisoners, gathering and delivering food, clothing and medicines, and securing legal defense. They negotiated with foreign embassies to obtain political asylum for rebels.[135] They also approached wealthy families sympathetic to the resistance to lend space in the family tomb to temporarily house the remains of rebels killed by Batista forces.[136]

The MOU, however, is rarely mentioned in the post-1959 Cuban state sources. No references were found in research through *Mujeres*, *Verde Olivo*, and *Granma* for the period 1975–92.[137] Founding member Natalia Bolívar referred to the MOU as "one of the forgotten chapters of history."[138] The MOU was relatively small at forty members, which partially accounts for its absence from the official Cuban War Story. But also telling is what MOU leaders did once the revolution took power. Two leaders, Hilda Felipe and Martha Frayde, grew critical of the post-1959 Castro-led government, and for this the state charged them with being traitors. According to Hilda, "Our crime was to think," but the state accused her, among other things, of working for the CIA.[139] Detained twice in the late 1960s, Hilda was imprisoned for nearly two years, followed by house arrest in the 1970s and exile in 1980.[140]

"Traitor" also follows Martha Frayde's name in post-1958 Cuban sources.[141] Frayde went into exile in 1957 but returned once Batista fled. The new revolutionary government put Frayde, a medical doctor, in charge of the National Hospital of Havana and later named her as the Cuban delegate to UNESCO. These postings ended in the mid-1960s, once she expressed reservations about Cuba's relationship with the USSR. Frayde was in her mid-50s when the government accused her of conspiring with the CIA and sentenced her to twenty-nine years in prison. An international effort rallied for her release, including such leftist intellectuals as Octavio Paz, Michel Foucault, Jean-Paul Sartre, Simone de Beauvoir, and Norman Mailer.[142] After three years, she was released in 1979 and went into exile.

The preceding profiles call into question the Cuban War Story's representation as an insurrection of youth and instead document intergenerational collaboration, which included middle-aged and older women, many of whom brought valuable experience from the 1930s rebellions. In the remainder of this chapter, I introduce the nascent rebel group led by Fidel Castro, with a focus on its two founding women.

FIDEL'S REBELS BEFORE MONCADA

The rebel movement that would become M-26-7 formed soon after Batista took power. Between the March 10, 1952 coup and early May, Fidel met with hundreds of activists and potential movement members.[143] Like Fidel, many early members were *Ortodoxos*. His group was informally referred to first as the Movement and later as the *Moncadistas* until the name July 26th Movement or M-26-7 was chosen, honoring the date of the assault on the Moncada barracks. The Havana apartment that Haydée Santamaría shared with brother Abel served as a center of operations.[144] The Santamaría siblings met Fidel at a memorial for a victim of the dictatorship.[145] Haydée, in her late 20s, had followed younger brother Abel from their small town to Havana. Ex-rebel Carlos Franqui later described Haydée as keeping house while Abel worked as an accountant for the Pontiac dealership.[146] Indeed, accountants (Jesús Montané and Abel), lawyers (Fidel and Melba Hernández), and a "housewife" (Haydée) formed the original nucleus of the revolutionary movement that would drive Batista from power.[147]

Attorney Melba Hernández joined Fidel's small group in May 1952. Elda Pérez Mujica introduced her to the Santamarías, and Melba returned a few days later to meet Fidel: "From then on, I went to their house morning, noon, and night."[148] Though five years his senior, she was struck by Fidel's extraordinary confidence: "At that time, many youth knew our duty to our country, but we weren't finding the right path. When Fidel spoke in that meeting, I had the immediate impression that he would know how to guide us."[149]

Jesús Montané Oropesa and Boris Luis Santa Coloma joined around the same time.[150] Jesús introduced Boris to Haydée in November 1952 and though twenty-three-year-old Boris was six years her junior, the two began to date. Although Jesús was married, he and Melba also became a couple. Notably, while M-26-7 was predominately male and white by the fall of Batista, its founding members were more diverse, particularly regarding the inclusion of women. According to Melba, both Fidel and Abel insisted on "the importance of the incorporation of the woman in revolutionary struggle," and the Cuban revolution indeed began with women comprising half the movement leadership under Fidel.[151] However, thereafter, new members were primarily men. During the March of Torches in January 1953, among the future Moncada assailants that "marched arm in arm," Melba and Haydée were the only women.[152] Notably, the two had not joined Las Martianas but instead had thrown their lot in completely with Fidel, and in this march, they were the only women within a tight formation of men exhibiting a military discipline, carrying torches spiked with nails.

Fidel demanded extraordinary discipline, including dramatic changes to members' social relationships.[153] The general staff was comprised of Fidel, Abel, Haydée, and Melba, who met weekly to discuss the activities and behavior of all the members.[154] As the movement grew, the general staff organized the movement into cells of ten to twenty-five people, and each cell took orders from the general staff – a "totally vertical structure" that differentiated it from other political groups at the time.[155]

The group prioritized propaganda, and Melba distributed the *Ortodoxo* bulletin produced by Raúl Gómez and Abel, first entitled *Son los mismos* (They're the Same) and then renamed *El Acusador* (The Accuser). On August 16, 1952, after the group put out 10,000 copies of the third (and last) edition of *El Acusador*, the Military Intelligence Service (SIM) discovered their clandestine print shop, destroyed the mimeograph machine, typewriter, and thousands of copies of the underground newspaper, and arrested six people, including Melba and Elda Pérez.[156] According to Melba, the officer in charge lectured the two women "that we were crazy, that we should stop doing this, that we weren't going to fix the country, that for two women this was very unseemly. Then he 'generously' set us free."[157] Lawyers Fidel (who had not been arrested) and Melba then gained the release of their male comrades.[158] The mo lenient treatment that the two women received from police, along with the patronizing attitude, was not unusual. Throughout the insurrection women often were considered less suspect and less dangerous as compared to male rebels, even when arrested alongside men carrying out the same activity.

In sum, the 1950s insurrection drew heavily upon Cuba's historical precedents – its wars of independence and the 1930s struggle. Not only did this help legitimize women's participation in the 1950s, but past women's gender tactics such as hiding weapons under skirts informed the anti-Batista rebels' methods. This anti-Batista mobilization was, furthermore, intergenerational and counted on the support of middle-aged women, many of whom brought important experience not formerly recognized. Finally, women were early key leaders and formed half of the movement that ultimately led the overthrow of Batista, a prominence that remained until the guerrilla ascendency in the final year of the insurrection.

Notes

1. Stoner (1991, 2003); Prados-Torreira (2005).
2. García-Pérez (2009, 54).
3. Sweig (2002); Stoner (1991, 2003); García-Pérez (1999); Pérez (1980).
4. Sweig (2002, 2).
5. Pérez (2013, 179).
6. Pérez (1980). See also Eckstein (2003, 4); Thomas (1998, 1491–92).
7. Stoner (1991); Prados-Torreira (2005).
8. Bonachea and San Martín (1974, 22).
9. Martí, *Obras completas*, 5:16–17, transl. by Prados-Torreira (2005, 94).
10. Prados-Torreira (2005, 4, 5).
11. Ibid., 5.
12. Ibid., 61.
13. Ibid.
14. Ibid., 37.
15. Ibid., 37–8.
16. Stoner (1991, 18); Prados-Torreira (2005).
17. Stoner (1991, 23); see also Prados-Torreira (2005, 50).
18. Stoner (1991, 27).
19. See, for example, Katia Valdes, "Cuba en la Mujer," *Verde Olivo* March 3, 1983, 6–9; Vilma Espín speech on April 10, 1982, transcribed in *Granma* April 13, 1982, 2.
20. See Stoner (1991); Prados-Torreira (2005).
21. Prados-Torreira (2005, 84).
22. Espín (1982, 2).
23. Prados-Torreira (2005, 84). After nearly dying of typhoid in prison, she went into exile and learned her husband had been killed. At the close of the

Ten Years' War, "Ana Betancourt was a broken woman in soul and body" (Prados-Torreira 2005, 86). See also Espín (1982, 2).

24. Stoner (1991, 27).
25. Prados-Torreira (2005, 62–3).
26. Stoner (1991, 20); Prados-Torreira (2005, 63).
27. Espín, (1982, 2); see also, for example, Margarita Hernández Perdomo and Marta Sánchez Llobregat, "La mujer Cubana en la lucha revolucionaria," *Verde Olivo* August 19, 1982, 24–7.
28. Prados-Torreira (2005, 63).
29. Ibid., 64.
30. Stoner (1991, 20).
31. Martí, *Obras Completas*, 5: 26–7, transl. by Prados-Torreira (2005, 65).
32. Stoner (2003, 74).
33. Prados-Torreira (2005, 62).
34. Espín (1982, 2); Prados-Torreira (2005, 62).
35. Prados-Torreira (2005).
36. Ibid.
37. Ibid., 105–6.
38. Ibid., 112.
39. Ibid.
40. Ibid., 115–17.
41. Ibid.
42. Ibid., 119.
43. Ibid.
44. Ibid., 54.
45. Stoner (1991, 20).
46. Prados-Torreira (2005, 128).
47. Rafael Azcuy González, "La oficial que mandó a la tropa," *Bohemia* February 20, 2007.
48. Prados-Torreira (2005, 128); Azcuy González (2007); Valdes (1983); Hernández and Sánchez (1982, 25).
49. Espín (1982, 2).
50. Stoner (1991, 28).
51. Prados-Torreira (2005, 129).
52. Stoner (1991, 30).
53. Prados-Torreira (2005, 129).
54. José Isabel "Mangoche" Herrera, in Prados-Torreira (2005, 129).
55. Prados-Torreira (2005, 151). See also Stoner (1991, 29).
56. Martí (1892), cited in Stoner (1991, 29).
57. Farber (1976, 49). Stoner (1991, 1997, 2003) offers an excellent analysis of women's organizing during this period, including ardent supporters of women's rights who "organized feminist, labor, and student demonstrations, and … professed variant forms of socialism" (Stoner 2003, 82).
58. Formally known as the *Partido del Pueblo Cubano* (Cuban People's Party).
59. Stoner (1991, 115).
60. Ibid., 111.
61. Ibid.

62. Ibid., 116.
63. Ibid., 117.
64. Ibid.
65. Ibid., 117, 119.
66. Ibid., 118–19.
67. Ibid., 120. The father of one victim, a powerful Havana chief justice, refused to allow the assault to go to trial as his daughter's sexual humiliation would reflect poorly on him.
68. Heidy González Cabrera, "Cincuenta años dejan su huella," *Mujeres* August 1983, 17.
69. Pérez (1990, 190); González Cabrera (1983, 17).
70. Hernández and Sánchez (1982, 24).
71. Valdes (1983).
72. García-Pérez (2009, 55) lists the following 1950s anti-Batista women's organizations: *Frente Cívico de Mujeres Martianas*; *Mujeres Oposicionistas Unidas*; *Frente de Mujeres Cubanas* (Oriente); in exile, there was a women's section of M-26-7 (New York) and a branch of *Frente Cívico de Mujeres Martianas* (Tampa, Florida).
73. Llovio-Menéndez (1988, 47).
74. García-Pérez (2009).
75. Ibid., 53, 55.
76. Ibid., 60, 64.
77. Jiménez in Castro Porta (1990, 132–9); Heidy Gonzáles Cabrera, "Eva Jiménez Ruiz constituye un hermoso símbolo de patriotismo y valentía," *Mujeres* October 1984, 14–17.
78. According to Jiménez (1990, 132), Fidel had accused Salas Cañizares of killing a student and thus felt endangered when the latter was named police chief.
79. Szulc (1986, 222).
80. Gonzáles Cabrera (1984, 14–17). Eva also joined *Las Martianas* and attended nightly meetings on the university campus.
81. Bonachea and San Martín (1974, 17). Batista authorities referred to the MNR assault dismissively as the "razor blade coup."
82. Jiménez in Castro Porta (1990, 133).
83. Eva stresses the continuity of her activism with that of her father's and grandparents'. She was held at the same prison where her rebel maternal grandmother was once imprisoned (ibid.).
84. In 1981, in her mid-70s, Eva was one of the first to join the newly formed Territorial Militia Troops (MTT).
85. Nereyda Barceló, "Gloria Cuadras: Estirpe de Mariana," *Mujeres* 160, November 28, 2003.
86. Carolina Aguilar Ayerra, "Reflexiones sobre la mujer en la Revolución," *Granma* August 27, 1987, 3.
87. Orlando Guevar Núñez, "Gloria Cuadras De La Cruz: mujer de flor y fusil" *Mujeres* 456, September 24, 2009.
88. Aguilar Ayerra (1987, 3).
89. Ibid.; Barceló (2003).

90. Maloof (1999, 55).
91. Ibid., 56.
92. Ibid.
93. Amador Morales (1991).
94. Ibid.
95. Cuban documents most commonly refer to the group as "Las Martianas." Members also referred to it as the "Frente" or "Mujeres Martianas."
96. Irene Izquierdo, "La 'maldita' Aida Pelayo," *Tribuna de la Habana* (n.d.), www.tribuna.co.cu/mujere/historia/maldita1.htm (accessed 6/16/09); see also Castro Porta (1990, 27–8).
97. See García-Pérez (1999).
98. Other original members included María Catalina Cortina Leyva, Rosa Roque González, Alicia de Armas Menéndez, Mercedes Rodríguez Rodríguez, María Teresa León Comensán, and María Iglesias Tauler.
99. Matilde Salas Servando, "Aida Pelayo: cubana símbolo de valor y dignidad," *Radio Metropolitana* March 6, 2008; Maloof (1999, 57). Castro Porta (1990, 29) lists the women present at FCMM's founding: Isabel Álvarez, Carmen Barredo, Amparo Canella, Carmen Castro Porta, María Catalina Cortina, Tomasa Crespo, Herminia Díaz, Maruja Iglesias, Eva Jiménez, Nieves López, Orfelina ("Nina") Martínez, Rosita Mier, Mercedes Núñez, Pastorita Núñez, Aida Pelayo, María Pérez, Petronila Portela, Mercedes Rodríguez, Olga Román, Rosa Roque, Mercedes Valdés, and Telma Vázquez.
100. Aida was General and Action Coordinator; Carmen Castro was Coordinator of Propaganda and Organization; Olga Román was Finance Coordinator; Concha Cheda was Support Coordinator; María Pazos was External Relations Coordinator; Guidelia García and Isabel Álvarez were Youth Coordinators (Lupiáñez Reinlein 1985, 99).
101. Maloof (1999, 45, 57); Salas Servando (2008).
102. Maloof (1999, 57).
103. See, for example, Castro Porta (1990, 29).
104. Maloof (1999, 57); Izquierdo (n.d.). Castro Porta (1990, 31) lists FCMM branches: Artemesia, Guanajay, Guane, Candelaria, Mariel, Cabañazas, San Cristóbal, Los Palacios, Consolación del Sur, Pinar del Río, Mantua, Bahía Honda, Havana, Güines, Madruga, Aguacate, Alquizar, San José, Nueva Paz, Catalina, Matanzas, Camagüey, Céspedes, Florida, Ciego de Ávila, Santiago de Cuba, San Luis, Guantánamo, Holguín, and Campechuela.
105. Rosa Rodríguez G., "Mujer pueblo, mujer nación" in *Tribuna* (n.d.). See also Elizabeth Bello Expósito, "Una marcha de luz," *Alma Mater* January 28, 2010, www.almamater.cu/sitio%20nuevo/paginas/universidad/2010/marcha%202.htm (accessed 2/2/10).
106. Lupiáñez Reinlein (1985, 100).
107. Also arrested were Nina Martínez, Tomasa Crespo, Nieves López, Pastorita Núñez, Josefa Denis, Olga Román, Rosita Mier, Eloisa Irigoyen, Mercedes Rodríguez, María Antonia Fariñas, and Eloisa Martínez (Pelayo in Castro Porta 1990, 55; Szulc 1986, 234).

108. Arianna Barreado, Paula Companioni, Rosario Alfonso, and Alejandro Ruiz, "La luz que desafío a la dictadura Batistiana" in *Juventud Rebelde* January 26, 2008; Rodríguez, (n.d.); see also Estefanía (2006).
109. Barreado et al. (2008); Izquierdo (n.d.).
110. Bello Expósito (2010). *Martianas* were again detained after the march (Castro Porta 1990, 51).
111. Barreado et al. (2008).
112. At a January 15 protest, student Rubén Batista was mortally wounded by police.
113. Carlos del Torro, "Nosotros sabemos cumplir con el deber que demanda la patria: 15 de Mayo, 1955–1985," *Granma* May 15, 1985, 5.
114. Castro Porta (1990, 33–4).
115. Ibid., 35.
116. See August 3, 1955 letter to Faustino Pérez and Armando Hart, in Franqui (1980, 93).
117. The feminine section of *Partido Revolucionario Cubana* (Cuban Revolutionary Party or PRC) arranged the meeting with Grau, as the women were beginning to question Grau's electoral route to change versus armed rebellion (Castro Porta 1990, 38–43).
118. Maloof (1999, 59). See also De la Cova (2007, 323n4).
119. Izquierdo (n.d.).
120. Ibid.; Castro Porta (1990, 31). Pelayo testimony in Maloof (1999, 58–9).
121. The FEU formed the clandestine DR in 1955 in order to carry out underground activities including sabotage and assassinations.
122. Naty Revuelta testimony, in Maloof (1999, 47).
123. Ibid.
124. Ibid., 58.
125. Castro Porta (1990, 3).
126. Revuelta testimony, in Maloof (1999, 47); Rodríguez Olmo's testimony in Teresa Valenzuela García, "Cuando se conquistó el cielo," *Pionero* March 3, 2010.
127. Teresa Valenzuela García, "Primera mujer elegida Presidenta de la FEU en Cuba," *Mujeres* 621, December 20, 2012. In the midst of this outpouring of compassion and grief, Castro criticized the FEU attack in *Bohemia* magazine (May 1957) as putschist, fascist, and irresponsible, arguing that FEU should have joined M-26-7 (see Guerra 2012, 15).
128. Castro Porta (1990, 1–4). Another organization, *Frente Democrático de Mujeres*, is mentioned in Díaz Vallina (2001).
129. Other members include Victoria Rodríguez, Vicenta Antuña, Nila Ortega, Esther Noriega, Zoila Lapique Becali, Clementina Serra, Anita Betancourt, Aurelina Restano, Celia Sánchez Agramonte, Marta Freyre, and Beba Sifontes. The revolutionary government labels Martha Frayde and Hilda Felipe as "traitors in exile" (Pedraza 2007, 117; Amador Morales 1991).
130. Amador Morales (1991).
131. Rosete (2002).
132. Ibid.
133. Ibid.

134. Ibid.
135. Ibid.
136. Ibid.
137. MOU is mentioned in Stoner and Serrano Pérez (2000) and Díaz Vallina (2001).
138. Rosete (2002).
139. Pedraza (2007, 117); Amador Morales (1991).
140. In the United States, she helped found the *Comité Pro Derechos Humanos de Cuba.*
141. For example, Izquierdo (n.d.).
142. Jean-Paul Sartre, "In a Cuban Prison" (Letter to the Editor), *New York Review of Books* December 7, 1978.
143. Szulc (1986, 224).
144. In addition to the Santamaría apartment, the homes of Fidel's sister Lidia and Melba's parents were also common meeting places.
145. Marta Rojas, "El que debe vivir," *Verde Olivo* August 6, 1978, 26. Haydée and Abel's parents, Spanish immigrants, are typically described as "humble workers" (see Maclean 2003).
146. Franqui (1980, 28).
147. Jesús Montané was an accountant for a car dealership; Fidel met him while financing his car (Franqui 1980, 49). Accountants Abel and Jesús knew each other from before the coup; both were Ortodoxos and met regularly. René ("Daniel") Ramos Latour (1932–58) was also an accountant and founding member of M-26-7 in Santiago.
148. Franqui (1980, 50).
149. Andux González et al. (1990, 15).
150. Melba would later marry Montané.
151. Szulc (1986, 227). Melba was the only person of color among the founders.
152. Melba Hernández testimony, *Verde Olivo* July 28, 1963, reprinted in Andux González et al. (1990, 38). Haydée's testimony, in Franqui (1980, 52).
153. Szulc (1986, 226).
154. Ibid.
155. Ibid., 227. Fidel appears to have been very engaged in the personal lives of his followers. Just before the Moncada assault, Fidel realized one of the men, engaged to his childhood sweetheart, might die at Moncada without having married her. Fidel quickly organized a wedding – from the legal requirements to the veil – and honeymoon. As it turned out, the man died at Moncada (Ibid., 251). Fidel insisted on a similar arrangement in Mexico prior to the *Granma* expedition.
156. Andux González et al. (1990, 35).
157. Ibid., 38.
158. Ibid.

CHAPTER 3

A Movement Is Born

Military Defeat and Political Victory at Moncada

On July 26, 1953, Fidel Castro and Abel Santamaría led 120 rebels in an assault on the Moncada garrison in Santiago de Cuba, the country's second largest city. As a diversion, forty more rebels attacked the Bayamo military garrison 70 miles away. The plan was to quickly take over Moncada, capture weapons, and broadcast news of the victory to rally the public. What followed instead was a disaster in which nearly 40 percent of the insurgents died and many others were captured. The scholarly literature on Moncada tends to focus on the rebel military strategy and shortcomings while noting the symbolic importance of Moncada.[1] The Cuban War Story – the dominant revolutionary state narrative – frames Moncada as a military defeat turned political victory. But thus far little analysis has been done to analyze how this symbolic power operated at the time so as to produce a political victory.[2] Taking a gender lens to this important episode, including the assault, courtroom trials, and post-assault support, I explore women's participation, the gendered division of rebel labor, and the struggle for hearts and minds in order to better understand how this crushing defeat became a rebel rallying-cry.

I first examine Moncada through a more comprehensive exploration of women's contributions and experiences than the literature has provided thus far. I then turn to the puzzle of how a potentially humiliating military defeat became a rebel victory, pointing to Castro's skillful use of gender as a discursive tool to reorder hierarchies, differentiate between good and bad, and evoke sympathy. Rebel courage, along with their underdog status and the military's brutality, caught the nation's attention, but Fidel still had to mold this attention into public support, and he did so through a language of masculine heroic martyrdom and feminine

46

vulnerability. In court, he effectively claimed popular support, mitigated the humiliation of military defeat, and framed the rebels as superior men. Indeed, a prominent effort within Castro's courtroom defense involved contrasting honorable rebel masculinity with the debased, assaultive masculinity of the regime – a successful discursive strategy that rebels continued to pursue throughout the insurrection. He further used women's testimonies to both enhance the emotionally evocative narrative and shield rebel men's masculinity from the feminizing attributes of victimization. Finally, I explore an argument developed more fully in the next chapter: the tactical benefits to women's participation. In this case, the male leadership's openness to women's participation (despite gender conventions), combined with the Batista forces' understanding of women as politically innocent and passive, gave the rebels a key advantage in the two years following Moncada, after most rebel men had been killed or imprisoned.

WOMEN AND THE REBEL ASSAULT ON THE MONCADA GARRISON

Fidel claimed of Moncada, "It was never our intention to engage the regiment soldiers in combat, but rather to seize the weapons and seize control by surprise, to call to the people and then meet with the soldiers and invite them to abandon the odious flag of the tyranny."[3] It was, in this version, to be a relatively bloodless seizure, a gesture of courage to rally people to the cause while simultaneously capturing weapons. By July 1953, the rebels functioned in a militarized and disciplined network of cells, and Castro and Abel Santamaría kept details of their Moncada plans secret until just hours before the assault.[4] Melba Hernández and Haydée Santamaría would be the only women participating.[5] Haydée, who had previously traveled to Santiago to help prepare the Siboney farmhouse, the base of operations, made the 500-mile trip again on July 22. Fidel sought out Melba the following day, reassuring her mother that Melba was preparing for a "safe mission."[6] The women transported suitcases packed with small-caliber guns, and Melba stashed extra guns in a long florist box. Like Las Mambisas of the wars of independence, rebel women transported weapons because they attracted less suspicion than their male counterparts. Indeed, a soldier rushed to help Haydée with her heavy suitcase when the train arrived in Santiago, dropping the luggage off at the feet of the surprised rebels there to meet her.[7] At Siboney, the women prepared for the arrival of the rest of the combatants, making chicken soup and ironing the crumpled, damp uniforms that were to serve as disguises the following day (many of which had been sewn by movement women).[8]

According to Melba, as rebels departed for the Moncada assault early the next morning, the women had no assigned roles: "They thought that Yeye [Haydée] and I would wait at the farm."[9] The women pressed Fidel to participate, and he agreed on condition that they go unarmed and assist Dr. Mario Muñoz in the civilian hospital.[10] Castro had already assigned rebel leader (and Haydée's brother) Abel to the hospital, along with some twenty rebels, to provide covering fire for the barracks assault. Both Abel and Fidel believed the hospital to be the safest place, and for that reason Abel reportedly resisted: "I'm not going to the hospital ... If there is a fight, I must be there."[11] As it turned out, Abel, along with at least seventeen other rebels captured at the hospital, were killed within hours.

Melba and Haydée's efforts to be included in the assault and Abel's dismay at his "safe" assignment speak to the status of combat over rear-guard, a theme reflected in this first battle and throughout the insurrection. Again and again in Cuban rebel narratives, many men and some women pursued combat assignments over purportedly safer roles. All roles were arguably vital to the insurrection, but to be held back from combat or protected from threats meant lesser status and, for men, a compromised masculinity.[12]

THE MILITARY DEFEAT

Of the 160 rebels assembled, sixty-one were killed, thirty-two were caught and convicted, and sixty-seven either escaped or were acquitted.[13] The post-1958 Cuban War Story stresses the Moncada rebels' youth – "The preparations and assault upon the Moncada Garrison were done by very young men and women" – following the revolutionary script in which youth are the authors of change.[14] In fact, the average age of those killed was twenty-six, as was Fidel himself.[15] The women were older than most of the men: Haydée was thirty and Melba was about to turn thirty-two. Though still relatively young, the rebels had advanced further into adulthood than commonly implied, with most at an age at which Cubans were expected to settle down. Indeed, a number of the men were married with children.

The women travelled to Moncada with Dr. Muñoz, who became lost in the unfamiliar city. Shots were already flying when they arrived, and they dashed through the crossfire to reach the hospital. The women attended to the wounded, but according to Melba, they also helped the rebel men defend the hospital, passing them bullets and loading rifles.[16]

The rebel military defeat was quickly evident, at which both Melba and Haydée's concern turned to protecting rebel survivors. Melba urged them to flee, but Haydée could not convince her brother. When Haydée pressed him to issue orders, Abel was fatalistic: "[W]e have to prepare ourselves to meet our death."[17] Nonetheless, the Moncada narrative often stresses that Abel did not include the women in this fate and urged them to save themselves: "You have a much better chance than anybody else of staying alive."[18] The women refused to flee without their comrades, and the men refused to leave at all, awaiting their fate. Eventually, Haydée convinced Abel to put on a hospital gown to pose as a patient, and the two women hid in the children's wing.

By 10:30 a.m., once the rebel men at the hospital had been captured and the female visitors allowed to leave, soldiers went in search of the women rebels.[19] Patients directed them to the infant ward, where Melba and Haydée were posing as new mothers. A nurse later explained that soldiers saw through the disguise "because mothers back then did not wear slacks."[20] Unlike the men stationed at the hospital, Haydée and Melba were not killed upon capture but rather were treated reasonably well until they arrived at the prison.[21]

In addition to losing her brother Abel, Haydée's fiancé Boris was also killed after capture.[22] Melba's boyfriend Jesús Montané was captured but survived. Some forty rebels managed to reach Siboney, where Fidel proposed continuing the struggle in the mountains. According to Fidel, about eighteen accompanied him, but the rest, "already disheartened," fled in other directions.[23] Most, including Fidel, surrendered within a week.[24]

Women and Rearguard Support

Shots continued to be heard inside Moncada a day after the attack. Many in Santiago saw the military's response as unnecessarily brutal and rallied in indignation, even though few knew who the rebels were. Vilma Espín recounted, "People were talking in the middle of the street, outraged; they didn't know who was inside, but they realized what was happening. [Soldiers] were murdering people there."[25] Vilma's sister Nilsa witnessed rebels shot in front of the hospital, but "we didn't know who they were, nothing, not even remotely."[26]

Anti-Batista women quickly mobilized. In Havana, Las Martianas member Naty Revuelta was the only person with advance knowledge of the assault. Naty and Fidel had begun their collaboration the previous year. Naty's husband, a wealthy physician, helped finance the anti-Batista resistance, and Fidel and his co-conspirators often met at their house.[27] Naty's assignment was to type Fidel's "Manifesto to the Nation" and deliver copies to political leaders and the press on the morning of the attack.[28] This was an important task, as Fidel anticipated that the regime would cut communication between Santiago and the rest of the country, impeding news about Moncada and his rebel movement.[29] She distributed the documents to about eight people but stopped for fear she was being followed.

Her fear was justified, as authorities quickly arrested suspects in Havana as well. Martianas leader Aida Pelayo was apprehended almost immediately, along with three other women gathered at her house.[30] Though her companions were released after three days, Aida was held for much longer, accused of possessing financial documents linked to the Moncadistas (as the Fidel rebels were now called). Eva Jiménez was serving time when Aida arrived in prison. Both women supported armed insurrection as the necessary path for political change, and inspired by Moncada, the two conspired with Rosita Mier, who lived near the prison.[31] Rosita sent the women meals containing hidden messages and set up a simple communication system with the prisoners by turning on and off the lights of her house.[32] Eva began collecting weapons to resupply the rebels through her contacts among male political prisoners (*Ortodoxos*), which Rosita stored in her house.[33]

Many other women rebel sympathizers, also inspired by Moncada but with little experience and few connections, concentrated on morale-boosting efforts and fundraising – support roles that fit traditional gender expectations. For example, Celia Sánchez and her sister Griselda spent the night after Moncada writing messages of support on small pieces of paper and inserting them into cigarettes to be delivered to the imprisoned rebels.[34] In Havana, Las Martianas collected funds for the rebels, which Maruja Iglesias and María Sifones traveled to Santiago to deliver.[35]

TURNING DEFEAT INTO VICTORY IN CUBAN HEARTS AND MINDS

The details of Moncada and Bayamo reveal the many mistakes arising from the poorly planned attacks by a militarily inexperienced leadership that recruited men ill-prepared for combat.[36] Would-be participants in at least two cars were lost on the way to Moncada. A flat tire decommissioned one car, forcing several men to stay behind. Essential supplies such

poor plus L[51]*/luk*

as wire-cutters were forgotten.[37] The rebel weapons were inadequate to the task of overtaking a military garrison equipped with machine guns. And few post-combat plans were conveyed to combatants.[38]

Such details could be seen to magnify the humiliation of the rebel military failure. Yet when asked in 1967 how she felt upon realizing the attack had failed, Haydée responded that she never believed it failed, a position echoed in the Cuban War Story.[39] Indeed, this militarily disastrous assault proved decisive in the battle for hearts and minds, though in a manner less by design than by skillful improvisation. The post-1958 Cuban narrative likens the Moncada assault to the "little motor that helps start the big motor."[40] That is, Moncada was not an end in itself but a means – a patriotic act of courage and rebel martyrdom to spark rebellion. As Louis Pérez put it, "the dimensions of the failure distinguished it from all others: the plan was as daring as its failure was spectacular."[41] Indeed, its success lay, in part, in its spectacular failure. The public's attention was captured by the rebels who stood up to tyranny in large part *because* they were understood to have been crushed by a cruel, dishonorable, even sub-human military.

The US embassy confidentially emphasized the regime's vicious response as the ultimate cause of its downfall, a position echoed in the literature. The US consulate officer in Santiago reported to the State Department that the local population perceived Moncada, "as something that only a fool would have attempted," and the "Castro legend started only through what is regarded by local residents as an act of brutality by the commanders and forces of the Barracks in slaughtering most of the survivors."[42] US Ambassador (1959–60) Philip Bonsal argued that Batista's war against Castro was lost as soon as it began owing to the government's ruthless response, which was out of proportion to the attack, followed by a massive yet flimsy government cover-up.[43]

Moncada unquestionably elevated Castro to the public stage.[44] The Cuban security forces previously had not registered Fidel as a rebel of much importance. A military report on Moncada inaccurately linked the attack to the Auténticos and former President Prío, only incidentally listing "someone named Fidel Castro" as a leader.[45] Recall Che Guevara's 1967 promotion of "the bullets of propaganda ... The great lesson of the invincibility of the guerrillas taking root in the dispossessed masses."[46] Moncada, as the first major rebel battle, arguably demonstrated not rebel invincibility but vulnerability, lack of skill, or lack of resolve. That Moncada ultimately became a rebel rallying cry – a means of mobilizing Cubans to arms – did not just happen by default owing to the Batista forces' brutal response but rather, I maintain, through a well-orchestrated and hard-fought war of words and ideas. Moncada stirred great debate, with many Cubans "either questioning or admiring [Castro's] manliness and courage."[47] Even among anti-Batista Cubans, there was doubt. For example, rebel Huber Matos recalled his reservations: "Fidel had led a daring assault, but he didn't go into Moncada, and he'd managed to save himself."[48] Though an undeniable rebel failure in a strictly military sense, assessments that focus on the military details – the rebels' mistakes and the military's brutal counterattack – miss the rebels' engagement in the war of words.

The interesting question in this light is, how did the rebels carve political victory out of military defeat? The rebel challenge was to enhance the opposition, organize it under Castro, and direct it toward a mindset of armed rebellion. Regardless of the original intent behind Moncada, once militarily defeated, rebels shifted to discursive battle.[49] As will be detailed, Fidel led the charge, launching a high-drama courtroom defense and actively pursuing public support from prison through his manifestos and communiqués, wresting it not only from Batista but also competing rebel cliques and political parties.[50] Haydée and Melba were central to Castro's martyrdom narrative as gendered witnesses and victims who evoked public sympathy. Furthermore, both women were Fidel loyalists who valued the importance of the war of ideas and, once released, worked diligently in waging it. Finally, as women, they were the only rebels at the hospital to survive and the first of the convicted rebels to be released. I propose here and explore more fully in the following chapter that the rebel leadership's openness to women in positions of responsibility lent the rebels a gendered advantage.

Gendered Witnesses

Government press censorship ensured that Batista's message reached the public. In a speech the following day, Batista observed that the attack looked to be the work of *locos* and mercenaries sent by men who did not even accompany them into battle. According to Batista, after ruthlessly attacking soldiers who were resting after a day of "ensuring the public's safety and families' happiness," the assailants went on to attack nearby families within their own homes.[51] Las Martianas attempted to publish a condemnation of the treatment of captured rebels in *Prensa Libre*, but only a headline appeared above a blank column with the words "not approved."[52] Despite government censorship, news seeped out. Journalist Marta Rojas returned to Havana, smuggling photos of bloody rebel bodies in Moncada hallways, which when released heightened public revulsion toward the regime.[53]

Unlike the fate of most of the men, including the unarmed Dr. Muñoz, Haydée and Melba were not killed upon capture. In fact, other than the cigar burn inflicted on Haydée several days later, they were physically unharmed. They were the first detained rebels observed by journalists and by July 28 had given statements to the press.[54] When oral historian Lyn Smith inquired several decades later if the women had been sexually abused, Melba replied, "No, listen Lyn, if they had touched us, me or Yeye [Haydée], they would have had to massacre all the *compañeros* that were [in prison] … They respected us."[55] In Melba's telling, Batista's forces understood the women as rebels beyond their reach.

For the two months before the rebels awaited trial, Fidel had Cubans' attention if not necessarily their admiration, and a discursive battle unfolded around the question of what kind of men these rebels were. Students demonstrated in support of the rebels while Moncada military chief Alberto del Río Chaviano vilified the rebels as "without scruples or respect for the customs or laws governing warfare, with instincts lacking of all compassion and respect."[56] As the trial began, Fidel aggressively challenged the regime's version of events, employing courtroom theatrics as well as a discursive strategy that relied upon gendered notions of innocence and victimization. On the first day, Fidel and the Attorney General quarreled so heatedly that the court ordered a postponement.[57] Further courtroom drama unfolded several days later, when prison officials notified the chief judge that Fidel was suffering a "nervous crisis."[58] Forewarned, Melba stood to declare "Fidel is not ill!" and removed a folded note from her headscarf warning of a plot to kill Fidel and noting "the two girls" to also be in danger as "unusual witnesses of the massacre of 26 of July."[59] In addition to justifying Fidel's absence, this dramatic moment enhanced the importance of the women's testimonies.

As survivors, the women had witnessed rebels killed after capture. Haydée challenged the court: "I left the civilian hospital with 25 *compañeros* and there are now two; we are missing 23. You, who are the justice system, tell us where they are."[60] Once transferred to the Officers' Club of Moncada, they witnessed additional torture.[61] Fidel positioned Haydée as the main witness to the torture and executions of captured rebels to powerful effect. A journalist noted courtroom commotion whenever the bailiff called the name "Haydée Santamaría Cuadrado."[62]

Whereas Haydée provided much of the trial's emotionally evocative content, Melba served as legal defense. In addition to Melba's legal training, several factors explain this division of labor. Haydée had lost both her brother and her boyfriend at Moncada, whereas Melba's boyfriend Jesús Montané not only survived but was married to someone else.[63] Furthermore, Haydée was a white woman who kept house for her brother, in contrast to Melba, who was mixed-race and a lawyer. Haydée's manifestation of white domesticity and legitimate loss arguably made her a more sympathetic figure, securing her victim status more firmly.[64]

"A military setback, but a political victory"[65]

The struggle to establish the Moncada rebels as brave warriors for a just cause or as incompetent bumblers is still being waged.[66] However, a focus on the military attack misses the political victory in the battle of ideas.[67] Key elements of Castro's legendary defense took on a gendered logic, particularly in establishing a contrast between the rebels as masculine protectors and the debased, assaultive masculinity of government forces. In this way, Castro both strengthened the case against the Batista regime and established the urgent need for an honorable man – personified by Castro himself and the rebels more generally – to confront it.[68] The following gendered discourse analysis draws from the court case and the published speech "History Will Absolve Me" to illustrate this logic. Some examples rely more clearly on gender than others, though these elements are interconnected. I begin with the most infamous episode debated in the courtroom: the tortures of Haydée's brother and fiancé. Then I examine other prominent narratives of Castro's defense.

Castro pitched the published version of his speech to the anti-Batista left – students, *Ortodoxo* militants, and others – which was "very confused and disoriented, given the failure and inactivity of the more traditional opposition politicians" following the coup.[69] With civil liberties suspended, the speech did not circulate widely at first. One account claims the document was little known until Batista fled, after which Castro "virtually disinterred" it.[70] However, other accounts maintain that throughout the insurrection the published speech "functioned as the manifesto of the revolution, the founding text of what it promised for Cuba's future."[71] For example, María López Larosa, a *campesina*, and Aleida March, a student during the insurrection, both recalled it as a powerful and well-known text that influenced their decision to join the rebels.[72] Vilma Espín similarly recalled the "tremendous impact" its publication had upon anti-Batista Santiago residents: "We were all fascinated, it spoke in a new language that laid out a program around which we could all unite in struggle."[73]

The most infamous episodes raised in trial concerned grisly physical tortures – gouged eyes and castrated testicles – and the use of these to psychologically torture other prisoners. Sergeant Eulalio González Amador (whom Castro referred to as *El Tigre*) reportedly visited the women prisoners holding a human eye, claiming it to be Abel's. The prosecutor drew out this story through his questioning of Haydée, who testified that a guard had also claimed her fiancé Boris was in the next room and that they had castrated him to make him talk.[74] Jesús Montané confirmed that an army officer held out to him a round mass of flesh in one bloody hand and a razor in the other and said, "You see this? If you don't talk, I'll do the same thing to you I did to Boris. I will castrate you."[75]

Fidel strategically worked such events into the trials. In his testimony, revised and published as "History Will Absolve Me," Castro told of the brutality inflicted on rebel men. The readers are enjoined to sympathize not only with physically brutalized men but also with emotionally traumatized women. That is, the reader experiences the physical torture of the men through the psychological torture of the women.

Frustrated by the valor of the men, [the guards] tried to break the spirit of our women. With a bleeding eye in their hands, a sergeant and several other men went to the cell where our comrades Melba Hernández and Haydée Santamaría were held. Addressing the latter, and showing her the eye, they said: "This eye belonged to your brother. If you will not tell us what he refused to say, we will tear out the other." She, who loved her valiant brother above all things, replied full of dignity: "If you tore out an eye and he did not speak, much less will I." Later ... they told the young Haydée Santamaría: "You no longer have a fiancé because we have killed him too." But still imperturbable, she answered: "He is not dead, because to die for one's country is to live forever." Never had the heroism and the dignity of Cuban womanhood reached such heights.[76]

Fidel's published speech contained detailed eyewitness accounts of regime brutality after the Moncada assault, a context in which most rebel witnesses were killed. Fidel almost certainly took license with the story. Historian Antonio de la Cova refers to it as "the Black Legend" and labors to prove it false.[77] Whether myth, fact, or somewhere in between, it is central to the Cuban War Story. In addition to eliciting support for the rebels and indignation against the regime, the passage valorizes a stoic patriotism in confronting rebel martyrdom.

Further unpacking the underlying logic reveals several additional factors intertwined and often gendered. First, gouging an eye and then displaying it to the victim's loved one constitute particularly repugnant acts of physical and psychological torture, reflecting poorly on the regime. A regime viewed as having attacked a man and his masculinity by crushing or cutting off his testicles also loses legitimacy. Additionally, given a common understanding of women as politically innocent, a woman as witness renders the testimony less politically motivated, with Castro simply conveying Haydée's described experience. Haydée's innocence is enhanced by references to her youth, and she is referred to as the "young Haydée." Finally, as a woman who lost both her brother and fiancé, Haydée's testimony evoked past and future innocent women grieving loved ones lost at the hands of the regime, a particularly emotion-laden theme.

A series of additional gendered factors ultimately played to rebel advantage. In the military bloodbath that followed Moncada, the women were spared while their male comrades were killed. Haydée in particular provided emotionally evocative eyewitness testimony. Among those convicted, the women's sentences were the lightest as the prosecution could not prove they had fired weapons.[78] Thus, the women's demands to participate in the assault, and Castro's last-minute acquiescence, meant the movement had surviving witnesses of military abuses who could give particularly powerful testimony at trial and receive light sentences. The fact that they participated also lent the women a legitimacy within the anti-Bastista community, including among armed insurgents, that women rarely enjoyed.[79]

The passage discussed above is the best-known example of Fidel's courtroom defense. But there are additional gendered logics threaded through his speech that inform later rebel discourse. In that sense, they too were influential in ways not recognized in the literature. In the remainder of this section, I identify and examine three key gendered themes running through Castro's courtroom defense: claiming popular support, mitigating the humiliation of defeat, and establishing the rebels as superior men. To begin, Castro claimed popular support for the rebel assault through what I term an "Even the Women" narrative. He declared that had Moncada fallen to the rebels, "even the women of Santiago de Cuba would have risen in arms. Many were the rifles loaded for our fighters by the nurses at the Civilian Hospital. They fought alongside us."[80] Setting the veracity of this claim aside, the discursive power rests upon the logic that the rebel cause was so just that even the women were inspired to rise above their naturally passive, peaceful, and apolitical nature to support the rebels.[81] This narrative powerfully echoes José Martí's idealized rebel women, Las Mambisas of the wars of independence, bravely fighting alongside the men:

The people's campaigns are weak only when women offer them merely fearful and restrained assistance; when the woman of timid and quiet nature become excited and applauds, when the cultured and virtuous woman anoints the work with the sweet honey of affection – the work is invincible.[82]

A second gendered theme concerned Castro's efforts to mitigate the humiliation of rebel military defeat and any corresponding blow to rebel masculinity, which he did by emphasizing the rebels' lack of military training and by acknowledging mistakes. As he underlined the lack of training, he also indirectly boasted of his own leadership: "The government itself said the attack was done with such precision and perfection that military strategists must have planned it. Nothing could have been farther from the truth! The plan was drawn up by a group of young men, none of whom had any military experience at all."[83] With this framing, the rebels come across as long on courage and commitment, if short on experience. Any attributions of military competency on the rebels' part thus appear all the more impressive. It also painted Batista into a corner, as the regime had an interest in exaggerating the military threat posed by the rebels at Moncada to justify the brutal force used to suppress it. But in insisting that such a militarily inexperienced rebel army was a true threat, the regime suggested itself to be vulnerable to poorly armed men with no military experience.

Castro also got ahead of the story by admitting to mistakes: "[F]or the sake of truth and even though it may detract from our merit, I am also going to reveal for the first time a fatal fact: due to unfortunate error, half our forces, and the better armed half at that, lost their way at the city's entrance and were not with us at the decisive moment."[84] Admitting such an error helped the rebels save face. A wrong turn in an unfamiliar city was mundane enough as to not reflect too poorly upon the rebels. It also invited the audience to consider what might have happened, had the rebels all arrived as planned.

It is a complicated maneuver to stake political victory on rebel military mistakes and weaknesses. Castro repeatedly asserted that Moncada was not a battle among equals, that the rebels were a small group of poorly armed and ill-prepared combatants. But it is difficult to play up regime brutality without putting the rebels in the feminized, and thus devalued, position as helpless victims. As suggested earlier, Castro mitigated this danger by using the Moncadista women, particularly "young" Haydée, to stand as victims and bear witness to the brutality. Castro then posed the Moncada men not as victims so much as heroes and martyrs: men who selflessly acted upon their ideals, which many Cubans shared, despite the odds.

Finally, Castro insisted that despite utter military defeat, the rebels proved themselves superior men. This he defended by emphasizing the particularly cruel and even animalistic nature of Batista's military: "When the shooting ended, the soldiers launched themselves like wild beasts on the city of Santiago de Cuba, and took out their fury against the defenseless population."[85] In the rebels' refusal to denounce the cause, divulge information, or even complain, they diminished the masculinity and humanity of their captors: "[Batista's forces] crushed their testicles and they tore out their eyes. But no one flinched. Nor did they lament or plead. Even when they had been deprived of their virile organs, our men were still a thousand times more men than all their executioners together."[86] As further evidence of the substandard, debased masculinity of Batista's forces, Castro highlighted their efforts "to break the spirit of our women."[87]

In a discursive maneuver that he deployed throughout the insurrection, Castro compared the rebels' and military's treatment of those they captured.[88] Noting that some sixty Moncadistas were captured during or shortly after the assault, he asked: "Where are our wounded? Only five of them have turned up; the rest were murdered. These figures are irrefutable. In contrast, twenty soldiers whom we held prisoner have been paraded in front of us here, and by their own words, they received not a single mistreatment from us."[89] Fidel added, "The honorable soldier does not kill the defenseless prisoner after combat, but rather, respects him. He does not finish off the wounded, but rather, helps them," declaring "Such cowardice has no justification."[90] Introducing a theme that he pursued over the next five years of insurrection, Castro denied the soldiers' honor while establishing that of the rebels. Yet he held out the possibility of redeemed masculinity for those soldiers who refuse to follow orders. Here, Castro implicitly makes a distinction among the soldiers between debased men and potentially true men, calling on soldiers to distinguish themselves from their brutal comrades and the dishonorable regime, thus sowing seeds of demoralization and dissension within Batista's ranks. In sum, Castro used the trial to indict the regime by contrasting it to idealized masculinity, defined primarily through bravery and honor.

BIRTHING PAINS: A MOVEMENT IS BORN

Many studies document the legacy of Moncada in Revolutionary Cuba.[91] Moncada was also a watershed moment for individual rebels. They gained experience and attention to their cause but lost trusted collaborators, friends, and loved ones. Curiously, the trauma and grief of this period is sparsely detailed in the Cuban War Story. Over a decade later, Haydée detoured from the dominant narrative, reflecting in very personal terms on the question, "Why was Moncada different from [other episodes of the insurrection]?"[92]

[The answer] came to me very clearly with the birth of my child. When my son Abel was born, that was a difficult time, a time just like any woman when she is having a child, very difficult. They were deep pains, they were pains that tore apart the insides, and yet there was strength to not cry, shout, or swear ... And why is there this strength ...? Because a child is about to arrive. In those moments it occurred to me that it was like Moncada.[93]

Comparing Moncada to the birth of a first child, Haydée explained: "[T]he first is different: we aren't prepared to receive it, we don't yet know if we can withstand the pain, if we will be a good mother, if we will know how to raise it. And this is different for us ... because [after the first] we know we can withstand [the pain]."[94] Although the rebel leaders were prepared to die at Moncada, they were not prepared for the brutality: "[O]ur faith in mankind always made us think that they were men [that is, humans]; ... we couldn't imagine that a society could convert men into monsters.[95] [Moncada] was a jolt, a pain, a joy that changed our life totally ... The transformation after Moncada was total."[96]

Haydée's framing of Moncada is remarkable for at least two reasons. First, war stories told from the perspective of a woman protagonist are rare – all the more notable in that she makes sense of the battle by likening it to childbirth. Second, Haydée's reflections provide unusual insight into the emotional trauma experienced by Cuban rebels. Yet the gendered imagery of childbirth and debased masculinity in which regime soldiers are monsters works to naturalize and thus legitimize the violence of armed insurrection, rendering it tolerable and necessary. Like a pregnant woman faces the inevitable pain of childbirth, the rebels must suffer the trauma of war. The pain for rebel survivors, then, is a requisite but transitory state, as a revolution is born. Notably, this birthing metaphor only allows for rebel pain, as it obscures the violence and pain inflicted by rebels.

FIDEL'S GENDER ADVANTAGE

As I have argued, a gendered analysis of Moncada lends new insight into the means by which this outright military defeat was a catalyst for insurrection. Castro wove an intricate narrative that staked political victory on rebel military mistakes and certain weaknesses. He heightened public sympathy for the rebels and revulsion at the regime by recounting not his own eyewitness testimony but that of Haydée, a grieving woman whom the regime cruelly taunted with the death of her loved ones. Castro further contrasted an honorable and courageous rebel masculinity with that of the military's debased and even subhuman masculinity.

Interestingly, though Castro is alternately admired and criticized for the exaggerated machismo on which he based his leadership, he diverged from traditional gender norms by including women in the rebel circle, entrusting them with decision-making and highly sensitive information, and in the end, assenting to their participation in Moncada.[97] He was willing to bend gender, but only to a point; women participated in the military assault but as unarmed assistants stationed at the civilian hospital. Though it is unclear how much his decision had to do with principles or pragmatics, I propose that this decision paid off.

Castro's willingness to challenge gender roles was in part successful given the regime's reluctance to view women as political, much less as rebels. The Batista military's differential treatment of men and women rebels was clear at Moncada – Haydée and Melba's survival appears miraculous unless we take gender into account. Batista soldiers were hesitant to kill women even as they could not be restrained from killing captured, unarmed men. Dr. Muñoz, an unarmed Moncada rebel, was struck by rifle butts then gunned down, still wearing his white physician's uniform. It appears that his gender rendered him killable in the eyes of the Moncada soldiers. Women, by contrast, had partial immunity from regime repression.

These two factors – Castro's acceptance of women rebels and the Batista regime's reluctance to imprison, torture, or kill women at the same rate as men – ensured that women rebels could carry on political work while the surviving rebel men remained in prison. I propose here, and pursue in the following chapter, that the combined effect of greater rebel roles for women plus their gendered semi-immunity proved essential to the movement's survival after key male leaders had been killed or imprisoned. It also gave Fidel's group an advantage over other anti-Batista groups. Melba and Haydée emerged from prison as skilled rebel leaders who had risked their lives and paid a high price for their convictions. Held in high esteem by fellow rebels and much of the general population, they were all the more effective at carrying the movement forward.

Notes

1. De la Cova (2007); Waters and Fernandes (2012); Bockman (1984).
2. Pérez (2015, 228); Eckstein (2003, 15). Daynes (1996) and Judson (1984) examine the meanings later attached to Moncada, though without a gendered account.
3. Castro (1976, 70).
4. Franqui (1980, 55); Edimirta Ortega Guzmán and Nelsy Babiel Gutiérrez, "La mujer cubana en el Moncada," *Mujeres* (Dossier Especial) 293, July 21, 2006.
5. Elda Pérez stayed behind to attend to her ill mother. De la Cova suggests Elda manufactured her excuse (De la Cova 2007, 57). Yet the original plan was for Elda – like Melba and Haydée – to help with preparations but not to actually participate in the attack. See also Shayne (2004, 118).
6. De la Cova (2007, 57–8).
7. Santamaría (2003a, 15).
8. Franqui (1980, 56); De la Cova (2007, 71).
9. Hernández interview, Lyn Smith Cuba Collection.
10. Ibid.; Franqui (1980, 57); Szulc (1986, 256). Abel had already left. Post-1958 Cuban accounts describe the women as demanding their right to participate (see Guzmán and Gutiérrez 2006). De la Cova, writing from an anti-Castro perspective, framed the event differently: "Fidel told the two women to wait in Villa Blanca until the rebels returned. The overprotective Haydée insisted on accompanying her younger brother Abel" (De la Cova 2007, 76); he later describes Haydée as "the domineering older sister" regarding her attempts to save Abel's life (De la Cova 2007, 114).
11. Szulc (1986, 255–6). Franqui (1980) reports that Abel also said derisively of the hospital, "that's where the women and the doctor are going" (58). Yet Melba recalls that Abel had already left for the hospital before Fidel agreed to allow Melba and Haydée to go to the hospital (Hernández interview, Lyn Smith Cuba Collection).
12. See Stiehm (1982); Goldstein (2001).
13. De la Cova (2007, xii). Eighteen of Batista's forces were killed.
14. Margarita Carmona López, "Oda a la alegría," *Mujeres* July 1988, 8–9.
15. De la Cova (2007, 261–6). My calculations are based on the ages compiled by De la Cova (2007).
16. Hernández interview, Lyn Smith Cuba Collection.
17. De la Cova (2007, 114). See also Santamaría (2003b, 37); Ortega Guzmán and Babiel Gutiérrez (2006).
18. Szulc (1986, 270); Franqui (1980, 60).

19. De la Cova (2007, 116).
20. Ibid.
21. Hernández interview, Lyn Smith Cuba Collection.
22. Santamaría (1967, 29); Franqui (1980, 60–1).
23. Bonachea and San Martín (1974, 22).
24. Ibid., 23.
25. Vilma Espín, interview in Franqui (1980, 62–3).
26. Espín, interview in *Santiago* 18–19, 1975.
27. Revuelta testimony, in Maloof (1999, 45).
28. Szulc (1986, 254). Fidel had planned for Melba and Haydée to return to Havana to help.
29. Naty Revuelta interview, Maloof (1999, 46).
30. Pelayo in Castro Porta (1990, 73).
31. Heidy Gonzáles Cabrera, "Eva Jiménez Ruiz constituye un hermoso símbolo de patriotismo y valentía," *Mujeres* October 1984, 14; Pelayo in Castro Porta (1990, 73).
32. Mier in Castro Porta (1990, 75).
33. Jiménez in Castro Porta (1990, 76).
34. Lilian Chirino, "Desde el Moncada hasta el Granma: dos de sus hermanas y compañeros de lucha aportan sus testimonios para darnos a conocer aspectos de la vida de Celia," *Verde Olivo* January 10, 1985, 41.
35. Maruja Iglesias testimony in Castro Porta (1990, 74–5). After an unsuccessful attempt to visit Haydée and Melba in prison, they gave their collected funds to Archbishop Enrique Pérez Serantes to buy supplies for the Moncada rebels in hiding.
36. Szulc (1986, 263) describes Fidel's plans as meticulously detailed.
37. De la Cova (2007, 126).
38. Falk (1988, 64). Prior to the assault, Castro voiced total confidence in victory and made no viable backup arrangements. Once the plans were announced to the assembled rebels, some argued the attack was suicidal and refused to participate – a reasonable assessment given that Moncada housed over 1,000 soldiers (Waters and Fernandes 2012, 138).
39. Santamaría (1967, 16).
40. See, for example, Pedro A. García, "El 'Moncada' fue el motor pequeño que echo a andar el motor grande," *Granma* July 25, 2000; Eckstein (2003, 15); Szulc (1986, 243).
41. Pérez (2015, 228).
42. Oscar Guerra, "Despatch from the Consulate at Santiago de Cuba to the Department of State," Foreign Relations of the United States, 1958–1960, February 21, 1958.
43. Bonsal (1971, 17).
44. Pérez (2015, 228).
45. Bonachea and San Martín (1974, 23). Report by Colonel Alberto del Río Chaviano, quoted in "Un resumen de los dolorosos sucesos de Oriente," *Bohemia* 9 de Agosto 1953.
46. Guevara (1961) 1985, 211.
47. Bonachea and San Martín (1974, 24).

48. Matos interview in Adriana Bosch, "Huber Matos: A Moderate in the Cuban Revolution," 2005, PBS *The American Experience*. Theories about Fidel's remarkable (or suspicious) ability to save his own life regularly appear in anti-Castro discourse.

49. Bonachea and San Martín suggest that Fidel's "refusal to profit monetarily from his increased popularity" after Moncada was also key in eliciting support, as honest leaders were scarcer than brave ones (Bonachea and San Martín 1974, 62).

50. For example, in a June 19, 1954 letter to Melba and Haydée, Fidel emphasized the war of ideas and asserted that the Moncadistas deserved the people's support because "our history [is] the most self-sacrificing" (Castro 2005, 184–5). According to Szulc (1986, 302), Fidel studied Carl von Clausewitz, who emphasized both the physical and moral factors of war, positing the latter as the "real weapon" (Clausewitz [1832] 1976, 184).

51. Batista speech to military audience at Camp Columbia, in *Diario de la Marina* July 28, 1953, 1.

52. Castro Porta (1990, 75, 258).

53. Szulc (1986, 274). The government sensor permitted *Bohemia* to publish the photos on condition that the accompanying text followed the state's version of events.

54. Ibid. Some men who denied taking part in the attack were also allowed to be interviewed by the press. See also Rojas (1988, xix); Alberto García Torres, "Declaran los detenidos," *Diario de la Marina* July 29, 1953, 1.

55. Hernández interview, Lyn Smith Cuba Collection.

56. No author, "Un resumen de los dolorosos sucesos de Oriente," *Bohemia* August 9, 1953.

57. Bonachea and San Martín (1974, 25–6).

58. Szulc (1986, 291).

59. Dubois (1959, 47); Szulc (1986, 291–2). Ultimately, Fidel's case proceeded separately, with Melba as his court representative.

60. Santamaría (1967, 21).

61. Ortega Guzmán and Babiel Gutiérrez (2006).

62. Rojas (1979, 258); Roberto Fernández Retamar, "De hecho, la vida de Haydee arranca de un pequeño lugar del centro de Cuba, y marcha hacia el centro de historia," *Mujeres* December 1991, 54–8.

63. De la Cova (2007, 34).

64. See De la Cova (2007) for race-based commentary.

65. Arnaldo Silva León, "Moncada: A Vision from Afar," *Cuba Socialista: Revista Teórica y Política*, November 2003. Another instance of this framing (military defeat and political victory) is Ortega Guzmán and Babiel Gutiérrez (2006).

66. In contrast to the Cuban post-1958 representation of Moncada, see De la Cova (2007).

67. Hampsey (2002, 95).

68. Young (2003).

69. Farber (1976, 187).

70. Ibid., 186.

71. Miller (2003, 147).
72. López Larosa interview, Lyn Smith Cuba Collection; *Aleida* March 2012, 18.
73. Espín, *Santiago* 18–19, 1975.
74. Szulc (1986, 289). For a critique of this testimony, see De la Cova (2007, 166).
75. Szulc (1986, 289); see also Dubois (1959, 50).
76. Castro also told the court of an incident on a bus from Boniato prison. Sergeant Eulalio González, recognizing the mother of Abel and Haydée Santamaría dressed in mourning for her son, loudly boasted that he had pulled out both of Abel's eyes (Dubois 1959, 78–9).
77. De la Cova (2007, 164–5); Szulc (1986, 289).
78. About nineteen other male participants in the attacks brought to trial were acquitted. The prosecution could not prove the women handled weapons in the attack; however, according to De la Cova (2007, 76), three rebel men who refused to participate in the attack at all upon hearing the plans received three-year sentences.
79. For example, Oltuski (2002): "Yeyé [Haydée] ... was our ideal revolutionary woman. She had been at Moncada, where her brother and fiancé were killed" (95).
80. Several years later, Frank País echoed Castro's "even the women" logic as well as Martí: "In Oriente even the women have gone out into the street ready for battle. The mothers, just as in the great demonstration of days past, marched in a challenge" ("La valerosa acción de Santiago de Cuba" in *Revolución* February 1957, reprinted in Hart 2004, 157).
81. Yuval-Davis (2004, 172).
82. Martí, *Obras completas*, 5: 16–17, transl. Prados-Torreira (2005, 94).
83. Castro (1976, 65–6).
84. Ibid., 66.
85. Ibid., 96.
86. Ibid., 98.
87. Ibid.
88. See De la Cova (2007, 156). See also Pérez (1976, 154) for compelling analysis of this comparison and its effectiveness later in the insurrection.
89. Castro (1976, 102).
90. Ibid., 104.
91. Waters and Fernandes (2012); Judson (1984); Daynes (1996).
92. Santamaría (1967, 6–8).
93. Ibid., 6–7.
94. Ibid.
95. Haydée used *los hombres* in this sentence. I retain the gender-specific "men" or "mankind" as I read her comments to reference a debased masculinity that approximated monsters, which would not hold the same meaning in English using gender-neutral terms.
96. Santamaría (1967, 7).
97. See, for example, Montaner (1981, 87).

CHAPTER 4

Abeyance and Resurgence

Sustaining Rebellion in Prison and Exile

Santamaría &
Hernández

After scores of rebel men died in the 1953 assault on the Moncada barracks and the remainder were imprisoned or exiled, the rebel movement fell into a three-year period of abeyance. Haydée Santamaría and Melba Hernández, released from prison after seven months and commanding new status in the resistance, were crucial to implementing Fidel Castro's orders, presenting the public face of the movement, and developing new alliances and broad-based support. Many other women followed Melba and Haydée's lead, mobilizing to support Fidel's cause.

Abeyance periods are not unusual in a movement's lifecycle. They are a holding pattern, a phase during which movements "scale down and retrench to adapt to changes in the political climate."[2] Research on movement abeyance is thus far based on cases of social movements in stable democracies, not armed insurrection. Cuba presents a very different setting, in which abeyance was imposed through military defeat, death, imprisonment, and exile. For its part, the scholarly literature on the Cuban insurrection has typically paralleled the Cuban War Story in passing over this phase to focus on the periods of armed conflict, which in effect has meant that this period in which women were primary protagonists has often been overlooked.[3]

In this chapter, we see that the early and unconventional inclusion of women gave the rebels a series of advantages that helped ensure the rebel resurgence in December 1956. With the capture, exile, and killing of so many rebel men in 1953, Castro relied heavily on women, a position complemented by a rebel commitment to equality. Though Castro was more progressive than the Batista regime in recognizing women as political agents, he nonetheless barred women from the riskiest assignments. The result, when combined with state forces' traditional gendered notions of women as apolitical, was that rebel women leaders survived and emerged from prison before rebel men with the skills and status to sustain the movement in abeyance, accompanied by newly mobilized women.[4]

As rebel tactics in this period revolved around building alliances and disseminating Castro's revolutionary vision, Haydée and Melba were the face of the movement, implementing the orders of their imprisoned and then exiled leader, developing activist networks, and cultivating a rebel collective identity.[5] Women also organized for release of imprisoned loved ones and for a general amnesty – a key determinant in the Moncada rebel men's early release in 1955.[6] Within the Cuban exile community in Mexico, predominantly middle-aged women participated through traditional gender roles, serving as hostesses facilitating men's plans, making social and political introductions, feeding and housing rebels, providing meeting space in their homes, storing weapons, accompanying men on errands as a security precaution, and pressuring Mexican authorities on behalf of imprisoned rebels. Finally, as the rebels returned from exile to take up guerrilla warfare in the Sierra Maestra, women helped plan and execute the Santiago uprising timed to coincide with the landing, arranged rural contacts for the guerrillas, and delivered supplies.

The traditionally feminine nature of much of the work has served to normalize and depoliticize it, rendering it invisible or unimportant to the dominant understanding of the insurrection. Yet as the abeyance literature makes clear, movements are not born of immaculate conception but rather cycle through ebbs and flows of mass activism, and the maintenance work during abeyance ensures that resurgence is possible.[7] Skilled and trustworthy rebel women were key to ensuring rebel resurgence in Cuba, and the movement was significantly advantaged by its openness to women's participation in two ways. First, women were less suspected, less repressed, and received lighter sentences and thus survived to maintain the movement in abeyance. Second, these trustworthy and skilled women deferred to men's leadership, which gave the Moncadistas (christened the July 26 Movement or M-26-7 by 1955) an advantage over the often counterproductive vying for power within rebel groups.[8] Notably, this gender advantage was both enabling and constraining to women rebels, securing them unprecedented status and authority in the rebel movement while placing combat and the top leadership positions off limits despite women's considerable skills and accomplishments.

MOBILIZING FOR THE MONCADISTAS

With the exception of Fidel's directives from behind bars, the published record of rebel activity is comparatively sparse during the 1953–56 period.[9] The focus here on women rebels reveals not only previously unappreciated rebel work in this period of latent rebellion but also yields insight into the human toll of the Batista regime, the loss of life, and the emotional turmoil that ripped through families – details relatively absent from the Cuban War Story's emphasis on armed combat. Through this focus, we also come across small acts in defense of human dignity and life, which chipped away at Batista's legitimacy while also helping to sustain a movement through a period of abeyance. These acts were typically initiated by anti-Batista women and arose out of gendered norms and expectations. They include women's mobilization to support the imprisoned Moncadistas, to properly bury victims of the regime, and to commemorate deaths so that they did not pass into obscurity.

Santiago women, for example, delivered food and medicine to the Moncadistas, washed their clothes, and delivered messages while the latter were imprisoned in Oriente.[10] Family members were key activists in this period. After her release, Melba organized prisoners' relatives, including the family of her imprisoned boyfriend, Montané. The Pro-Amnesty Committee for the Liberation of the Moncada Assailants, predominately women, collected food, clothing, and books for the prisoners, sometimes hiding messages in them.[11] They also mobilized an ultimately successful amnesty movement, distributing cards throughout Cuba that read "No more political prisoners or exiles in the land of Martí and General Antonio Maceo!"

Women worked in other ways as well. Those of the 30s Generation – with political skills developed over several decades – were important contributors. For example, after the military secretly buried thirty-two Moncada rebels in nine unmarked graves in a remote section of Santa Ifigenia cemetery in Santiago, Gloria Cuadras arranged with cemetery workers to mark the graves with wooden crosses.[12] The military destroyed the markers, yet she persisted and eventually all the graves had borders with crosses. Gloria, with Santiago leader Frank País and others, maintained the graves, and citizens of Santiago, particularly students, visited the gravesites regularly as the anti-Batista opposition grew.[13]

In another example, Las Martianas member Mercedes Valdés del Oro, upon learning that her son Hugo Camejo had participated in the

Moncada assault, traveled from Havana to Santiago to search for him.[14] She heard the military had dragged some Moncadistas by their necks behind a jeep, but local officials denied that her son had been among them. A woman approached Mercedes surreptitiously to confirm that her son was one of the dead. The military had abandoned the bodies, leaving it to a traumatized public to act on behalf of the families of these unknown men. Another Santiago woman had arranged their burial in her own family's plot, also lighting candles and laying flowers at the graves. Two years later, Mercedes returned to Santiago with the family of Pedro Véliz, the young man buried with Hugo, for permission to remove and transport the remains.[15] The judge denied the request. Facing a six-year prison term if caught, the families returned to the cemetery at night. They removed their loved ones' remains to the house of Mirtha de La Fuente, where they cleaned the bones, placed them in a suitcase, and rode the bus back to Havana for a proper burial.[16]

On other occasions, maternal resistance was more spontaneous and overtly oppositional. For example, on the first anniversary of the July 26 Moncada attack, Las Martianas helped organize a demonstration at the tomb of Rubén Batista Rubio, considered the first martyr of the Batista regime.[17] In attendance was Lala Rodríguez, mother of an imprisoned Moncadista.[18] Lala shouted down the police captain as the police interrupted the memorial and assaulted the attendees. Police fired guns in response, but Lala did not back off, inspiring the crowd. Such instances of women's resistance, with over half of the Moncadistas killed, imprisoned, or in exile, address a question that is rarely asked – how did the rebel movement survive and indeed grow in this post-Moncada period of rebel military defeat? Such instances of small-scale resistance by Moncadistas family members and Santiago women were cumulatively crucial in the nurturing of a rebel collective identity and oppositional consciousness among anti-Batista activists, supporting political prisoners, creating sites for memorials and crafting a historical narrative and symbolism around rebel sacrifice and regime brutality.[19] This was a gendered process, as women were socially designated as both nurturers and mourners and thus took primary responsibility for caring for prisoners, boosting prisoners' morale, calling for amnesty, preparing bodies, accompanying the dead to the cemetery, and attending to both the gravesites and the memories of the dead. In this way, gender informed this aspect of movement maintenance during rebel abeyance.

THE HEART OF THE STRUGGLE: WOMEN AND PROPAGANDA

Melba and Haydée left prison on February 20, 1954, after serving only seven months. With this "event of immense importance," Fidel now had two trustworthy and respected Moncada veterans in Cuba to resuscitate the movement.[20] In correspondence from prison, Fidel lauded the women's "full, exemplary loyalty" and confirmed both as "members of the top leadership and as leading representatives of the movement on the outside."[21] Both women dedicated themselves to implementing Fidel's orders, which first involved reorganizing the rebel movement that had dispersed with the post-Moncada mass arrests.[22] According to Haydée, many people were inspired by Moncada and approached them to join the movement.[23] But Fidel instructed the women to prioritize the war of ideas over building rebel ranks. In a lengthy April 17 letter to Melba, Fidel insisted, "Our propaganda must not let up for one minute because it is the heart of the struggle."[24] Toward these ends, he directed her on the publication of his courtroom defense speech. In a June 19, 1954 letter, he again emphasized propaganda, "Our immediate task ... is to mobilize public opinion in our favor, to spread our ideas and win the backing of the masses of people ... We have a right to the people's faith – without which, I repeat a thousand times, there can be no revolution."[25]

Ann Louise Bardach, in editing Fidel's prison letters, found the most salient feature to be Fidel's "ability to inspire others – over and over – to do his will. Indeed, Castro's correspondents appear to have centered their lives around him, attending to his needs and implementing his political strategies."[26] In this period, he particularly relied upon women – in addition to Haydée and Melba were his wife Mirta, sister Lidia, and Naty Revuelta.[27] Mirta smuggled letters out of prison for Fidel, many containing instructions for Melba and Haydée as well as much of his courtroom speech, composed in lime juice as an invisible ink, which the women ironed to reveal the hidden text. They produced a pamphlet of Fidel's speech in October 1954, titled "History Will Absolve Me," and mobilized hundreds of supporters to distribute copies as well as call for amnesty. Rebel leaders in Santiago such as Frank País, Vilma Espín, and María Antonia Figueroa began their collaboration with Fidel by distributing his speech. Haydée noted its propaganda value, which for people like País, Espín, and Figueroa – already committed anti-*Batistianos* – "was a revelation."[28]

Under Fidel's direction, Melba traveled to Mexico to meet with exiled Moncadistas, delivering funds and urging them to continue organizing.

In Havana as well, Melba and Haydée built alliances with other anti-Batista groups to push for amnesty.[29] They met with activists who would later prove vital, including Armando Hart (whom Haydée would marry in 1956) and Faustino Pérez. Melba and Haydée met Hart in 1954 at the home of Rafael García Bárcena, leader of the National Revolutionary Movement (MNR), when the women delivered propaganda and a message from Fidel.[30] Haydée and Melba continued to meet with Hart, explaining Fidel's program and "what Moncada represented."[31] In this sense, the Moncada assault was not presumed to speak for itself – Haydée and Melba were charged with helping Fidel craft and convey its meaning.

By early 1955, the pro-amnesty movement led by sisters Delia and Morelia Darias Pérez had collected twenty thousand signatures and presented them to the Cuban Congress.[32] In April, Congress passed and Batista signed an early release for Fidel and the remaining imprisoned Moncadistas "in honor of Mother's Day."[33] Women featured heavily in accounts of the May 15, 1955 event, tearfully celebrating Fidel's return to freedom. In Havana, a woman who lost a son at Moncada approached Fidel: "He hugged the lady tightly and both he and the bereaved mother cried."[34] Other mothers of fallen Moncadistas unfurled a flag and sang the national hymn.[35] US media reports described Haydée resting her head on Fidel's chest, as his freedom "for her signified 'to live again.'"[36]

Such traditional representations of women celebrating the male warriors' return suggests a movement frozen in time during Fidel's imprisonment and thus obscure women's low-key but vital organizing and propaganda work that sustained and grew the movement. That Melba and Haydée stepped into Fidel's shadow when he emerged from prison is not surprising given gendered understandings of politics and leadership at the time. Yet through women's work in this abeyance period, we can trace gender advantages to women's inclusion in rebel leadership: women survived Moncada and received short sentences, which meant that Fidel had trusted, skilled, and respected Moncada veterans who also deferred to his authority, stepping back upon his return as gendered norms dictated.[37] That is, the time-consuming and often counterproductive jockeying among men for leadership within the anti-Batista resistance points to an additional organizational advantage to entrusting women in the inner circle.[38]

Fidel met with many anti-Batista individuals and groups, confirming alliances and seeking resources. A few weeks before going into exile, he named the group the "July 26 Movement" (M-26-7) and identified its leadership: Haydée Santamaría, Melba Hernández, Armando Hart,

Jesús Montané, Faustino Pérez, José Suárez Blanco, Pedro Aguilera, Luis Bonito, Antonio "Ñico" López, and Pedro Miret.[39] Thus, now two out of the eleven M-26-7 leaders were women. He also appointed María Antonia Figueroa, a Santiago rebel in her mid-30s, as M-26-7 treasurer.[40] María Antonia, in turn, suggested Frank País as a like-minded leader in Santiago and set about recruiting him.[41]

EXILE IN MEXICO CITY

Castro went into exile in Mexico City in July 1955. Mexico had offered asylum to previous generations of leftists, providing a haven for Spanish Republicans as well as generations of Cubans. In the tight-knit community of Cuban exiles, women continued to play a prominent role during the abeyance and then resurgence periods. After two years of imprisonment, Fidel and other rebels constructed a domestic life in exile even as they prepared for an armed invasion of Cuba. Middle-aged Cuban women contributed in a manner that approximated a traditional maternal femininity, seeing to it that the male rebels were housed and fed and kept out of prison. Several allowed their homes to be used to store weapons. Sought by both Mexican authorities and Cuban agents sent by Batista, the Cuban rebels were not to venture out alone, and these rebel hostesses and benefactresses often accompanied Fidel and other men on errands.[42]

In addition to his brother Raúl, Jesús Montané, and his new friend, Argentine radical Ernesto "Che" Guevara, Fidel spent much of his time in exile with women – Melba (who arrived in October 1955), his sisters Lidia, Emma, and Angelita, Graciela and Eva Jiménez, María Antonia González, Teresa "Teté" Casuso, and his fiancée Isabel Custodio.[43] Fidel did not separate politics from other aspects of his life, and these women were involved in one way or another in the insurrection. Many Cuban exile men relied upon the women for housing and meals. But in reading women's recollections of the period, these women were very much a part of the rebel life, immersed in the political debates among the exiles and sought out by Fidel as sounding boards for his plans. Upon arriving in Mexico, Fidel went first to Eva Jiménez's house, where he explained to her his plans for an expedition to return to Cuba, and Eva helped him connect with other exiles.[44] With her sister Graciela, she housed several future Granma expeditionaries and "sponsored" them with weapons and supplies.[45] María Antonia González also opened her home as a meeting place for anti-Batista exiles, and it was there that Fidel met Che.[46] It was also a message and coordination center where newly arriving Cubans were processed. Fidel himself took many of his meals there.[47] In June 1956, Mexican authorities, tipped off about the Cubans' arms procurements and insurrectionary plans, detained several people in María Antonia's house, including María Antonia herself. Fidel and many others were rounded up elsewhere.[48] Eva, who was not arrested, went first to the press to denounce the arrests and then to the authorities to demand their release, where Mexican officials interrogated her and then advised that such activities were shameful for a woman.[49] Undaunted, she initiated a successful letter-writing campaign with María Antonia Figueroa and Las Martianas in Cuba to denounce the incarceration and possible deportation of the rebels.[50]

Teté Casuso, another prominent woman in this exile community, was well known among left-leaning Cubans as a student leader in the 1930s protests. Forced into exile several times because of her activism, she worked as a writer and actress in Mexico and, for several years before the Batista coup, served as commercial attaché in the Cuban embassy.[51] Teté became a key ally of Fidel in Mexico and arranged meetings with exiled members of the 30s Generation and former Cuban President Carlos Prío, who committed nearly a quarter of a million dollars to Fidel's movement.[52] The exiled rebels also stored a large cache of weapons at her house, for which she spent over twenty days in prison after Mexican police raided her house in November 1956.[53]

Love and Marriage in Exile

Exile marked a period of rebel domesticity, as couples formed and even married. Fidel was engaged to Isabel Custodio, a young, independent-minded, feminist activist and a far cry from ex-wife Mirta, whom he had divorced while in prison.[54] Isabel herself was part of the exile community in Mexico City, as her family had fled Franco's Spain. The family had moved to Cuba, only to be forced out for their communist affiliations, arriving in Mexico in 1943.

Isabel met Fidel when she accompanied Néstor Almendros, a young Spanish exile who had been sent by the leftist *Bohemia* magazine to cover the Cuban rebels imprisoned in Mexico.[55] Fidel caught sight of her, and once released from prison, he sought her out at Casuso's house. Despite their age difference (Isabel was eighteen, Fidel was thirty) and the fact that they had just met, Fidel proposed marriage. She recalls that they were rarely alone together and did not go on dates because, as he explained, he had dedicated himself to revolution and had no time for a traditional courtship.[56] Instead, Isabel shared the Cuban exiles' rebel life and attendant risks. She was abducted by Batista's secret police and held captive in a drugged state for three days until Fidel led an armed rescue.[57] Nonetheless, according to Custodio, the other rebels resented the time she spent alone with Fidel, and Che Guevara was particularly outspoken in his disapproval, lecturing that "a leader can't be distracted, a leader must dedicate all his time to the cause and can't spend time on romance."[58]

Isabel has been portrayed as a beauty, young and flighty. Yet she was an old hand at radical politics. As Spanish exiles in France, Cuba, and Mexico, her family was part of a tight-knit leftist community, and from a young age she was steeped in political debates.[59] In Mexico, her family worked and socialized with intellectuals such as Erich Fromm. As a university student, she was engrossed in leftist theory and action. Unbeknown to Fidel, she was part of a small underground anarchist-feminist-Marxist student group attempting to organize women factory workers.[60] Later, she was cofounder of *Movimiento Nacional de Mujeres* (National Women's Movement) in 1971, and in the 1980s and 1990s, she was a feminist newspaper columnist.[61]

Isabel clashed often with Che, whom she describes as situating himself as a "king," constantly quoting Marx and Lenin to the Cubans, who in that period were not well versed in communist theory. Isabel, in contrast, had grown up amid socialists and studied Marxism at the university. Intellectually armed, she frequently challenged Che, "and there were tremendous arguments. I have to say that he was very machista."[62]

Isabel and Fidel were to be married just prior to his return to Cuba, but hours before a judge was scheduled to perform the civil ceremony, Che pulled her aside and recited a long list of reasons why she should not marry Fidel. For the good of both Fidel and the revolution, he urged her, "Let him go."[63] It was a rare moment in which the two agreed. Five days before the Granma disembarked, she broke off the engagement.

For his part, Che married Hilda Gadea in Mexico and had a baby daughter during this period. Hilda was a Peruvian economist and *Alianza Popular Revolucionaria Americana* (APRA) member, exiled after Peru's 1948 coup. She was working in Guatemala for the progressive Árbenz administration when she met Che in 1954 and introduced him into leftist Guatemalan circles. The CIA-orchestrated coup against Árbenz forced Hilda to emigrate. She met up again with Che in Mexico, and they married in August 1955 when Hilda became pregnant. Che left on the Granma nine months after the birth of his daughter Hildita.[64]

A veteran militant and economist, Hilda had steady jobs in Guatemala and Mexico (including a job with the World Health Organization). In contrast, Che relied upon odd jobs (such as selling photos in the park) and poorly paid stints as a doctor.[65] In her autobiography, Hilda discusses her reluctance to marry: "I told him ... that I thought the most important issue at the time was the political struggle ... [F]irst I had to accomplish something for society, and to do that I had to be free."[66] Che responded that "it was wrong to think that political activists shouldn't marry ... He referred to Marx and Lenin, saying that marriage had not impeded them in their struggle. On the contrary, their wives supported them."[67] She still hesitated, perhaps because it was her own activism she thought might be compromised, not Che's. Her thoughts on women and activism were radical for the time: "I didn't feel that women reached fulfillment and self-realization through marriage. In my view, a woman should be contributing to social progress and therefore had to prepare for it and become financially independent."[68] Che respected her intellect and political commitments, expressing in poetry that "he did not desire beauty alone but, more than that, a comrade."[69] It was Hilda who introduced Che to the Cuban exiles.[70]

Notably, then, during this period of suspended rebellion in Mexico both Fidel and Che were in relationships with independent-minded, intellectually sophisticated, politically radical women. These women expressed ideals on women's rights that were particularly progressive for the 1950s, a period of feminist abeyance in much of the world.[71] There is no clear indication of how Fidel or Che's thoughts on gender were influenced by Isabel or Hilda, and both men moved on to women who more readily deferred their own interests to those of their men. It is remarkable nonetheless that in exile, both were attracted to women who understood themselves to be men's political and intellectual equals. However, these relationships, acceptable (if barely) to a rebel movement in abeyance, were less compatible with the rebel resurgence, and the rebel return to Cuba aboard the *Granma* marked the end of both couples.

THE *GRANMA* AND THE TRANSITION FROM ABEYANCE TO RESURGENCE

Melba and a Mexican woman, Marta Eugenia López, trained for the armed return to Cuba alongside the men, only for Fidel to decide just prior to departure that they, along with some fifty men, could not join the voyage owing to lack of space aboard the *Granma* – the yacht purchased for the journey.[72] Fidel told Melba that it would be "an inadmissible imprudence" to allow women since the yacht had no "facilities for a woman."[73] She recalled her disillusionment: "From the moment I arrived in Mexico, I had done whatever training any other *compañero* had done ... I was sure that I'd come along."[74] So Melba, M-26-7 leader and Moncada veteran, remained on shore as her husband Jesús Montané embarked with eighty-one men for Cuba in what was later described as a voyage of "unmitigated disaster."[75] An engine repeatedly failed, and at one point the yacht took on water so quickly that all desperately bailed with whatever was at hand. They fell behind schedule.

This caused problems for the Santiago rebels charged with producing an uprising to coordinate with the *Granma* landing. Santiago M-26-7 leader Frank País had conveyed to Castro that conditions were insufficient for a successful uprising.[76] But, increasingly harassed by Mexican authorities, Fidel insisted upon his earlier public promise to return to Cuba in 1956. Fidel also believed a mood of unrest prevailed in Santiago and elsewhere in Cuba, which he did not want to dissipate before his dramatic return. Their plans were widely known. In October, the press, Cuban government, and US embassy all anticipated the rebels' return in the next few weeks.[77]

Santiago M-26-7 hoped to delay the military from reaching the *Granma* landing site. This, however, would require the *Granma* to keep to schedule. When the Santiago rebels received the coded telegram that the *Granma* was to arrive November 30, preparations shifted to high gear, with women playing key roles in logistics and planning. Vilma Espín, Frank's assistant, delivered packages and transported people. María Antonia Figueroa and Nilda Ferrer oversaw the first aid kits, stocking and storing them at Nayibe Atala Medina's house. The night before the uprising, the women alerted sympathetic doctors to prepare for rebel and civilian casualties. Also, some twenty women took first aid classes, overseen by Vilma, who managed the nine first aid stations.[78] Nayibe was in charge of sewing 200 olive green uniforms as per Fidel's detailed instructions, which she did at home with the help of other movement women.[79]

The morning of November 29, Frank called together M-26-7 leaders, which included three women, Haydée, María Antonia, and Gloria Cuadras, along with Armando Hart, Léster Rodríguez, José Tey, Baudilio Castellanos, and Ramón Álvarez.[80] Frank, declaring the movement now militarized and under his command, revealed final details. Gloria, Ramón, Haydée, and Armando then recorded calls to action at Vilma's house, to be broadcast during the uprising.[81] On the eve of the planned uprising, Las Martianas of Santiago, in coordination with M-26-7, organized a combative women's protest demanding an end to government repression. They confronted a combined force of military and police under the command of the hated Colonel José María Salas Cañizares, which resulted in the arrest of twenty-six women, many of whom were beaten.[82]

With no communication link, the Santiago rebels were unaware that the *Granma* was running two days late. The uprising, meant to draw the military's attention away from the coast, occurred early November 30 with a surprise assault on police headquarters by M-26-7 combatants dressed in olive green. Rebel snipers aimed at Moncada to prevent soldiers from leaving the garrison. Several other public facilities were also attacked. Small battles occurred through much of the city. While sectors of the public showed support for the rebels, few joined the uprising.

At the command center, Frank, Haydée, Armando, Vilma, Gloria, Asela de los Santos, and Ramón Álvarez, among others, directed the actions, and received reports on the various engagements around Santiago.[83] They soon saw the uprising had failed, and there was no news of the *Granma*.[84] Some proposed escaping to the Sierra to meet up with Fidel's group, but Frank ordered them to remain at their posts. Haydée later recounted, "That day, I relived with tremendous vividness our experience during the assault on Moncada, when we were left waiting there while they surrounded us, and we couldn't get out. I had always thought that if we had left [Moncada] a bit earlier, many comrades would have survived, maybe even Abel."[85] They were not yet surrounded, so Haydée proposed they move into the street, firing on the enemy if necessary rather than waiting for them, certain that at least some could be saved.[86] But twenty-two-year-old Frank was in charge, and he had ordered the rebels to fight "until the end."[87]

Haydée once again found herself confronting a rebel leader's impulse to martyrdom. She appealed to him as a Moncada combatant "to make him listen to my point of view. And I told him, moreover, that he had a duty to live, that he had to stay alive because Fidel needed him."[88] Frank relented, instructing combatants to don civilian clothing and blend into the general population. Rebel snipers were deployed to hold Batista forces at bay while others hid weapons and filtered into the streets.[89] In the end, the rebels only lost three combatants, with at least four dead among Batista's forces.[90] But the uprising had failed. Batista placed the province in a state of "operations" and his forces on full alert – he had received word that a ship had departed from Mexico destined for Cuba.

Waiting for Fidel

The Cuban War Story for this period revolves around rebel leaders. Expanding the inquiry to include the work and insights of local leaders, rank and file members, and collaborators emphasizes the rebel movement's transition from abeyance to resurgence as bloody, traumatic, and militarily disorganized. Rather than waiting for a political opening, the rebels had attempted to forge their own. But this came at great cost, as only eighteen out of eighty-two *Granma* rebels managed to regroup as guerrillas in the Sierra Maestra. Survivors relied heavily on the rebel support network headed most notably by Frank País, Vilma Espín, and Celia Sánchez. Next to the impulsive and disorganized nature of the *Granma* expedition, those tasked with receiving, transporting, and supplying the *Granma* rebels appear systematic and orderly.

Like Melba, Celia had aspired to accompany Fidel on the *Granma*.[91] But Frank instructed her to remain in Cuba as the general coordinator of the insurrection in Manzanillo.[92] Celia proved to have excellent organizing skills. She oversaw preparations on the coast to receive the *Granma* and then establish communication between the urban underground and Fidel's rebels as the latter moved into the Sierra Maestra.[93] She collected money, reinforced the network of militants and collaborators in the zone, and organized the *campesino* community to aid the *Granma* rebels.[94] Celia also researched optimal landing sites, taking coastal charts from a maritime institute and a ship captain.[95] With word of the *Granma*'s pending arrival, Celia traveled with Micaela Riera to Campechuela to arrange transfer of the *Granma* men to the Sierra Maestra.[96] Alerting her rebel network, she stationed five trucks with supplies and several dozen men along the coast near the prearranged landing sites.[97]

Through Celia's efforts, scores of rebels and collaborators were mobilized to act. For example, Elena González Ricardo, from a family of rebel collaborators, joined M-26-7 in 1956, at the age of fifteen. When the *Granma* landed, her family prepared a bomb, which Elena and her two sisters planted on the Jobabito River bridge to impede the passing of troops.[98] Manzanillo M-26-7 women donned uniforms of black pants and a blouse, under which large zippered pockets held first aid supplies.[99] Eugenia "Gena" Verdecía Moreno proved a particularly valuable early contact.[100] She traveled to Santiago in search of dynamite for armed actions to coincide with the landing.[101] To convince Frank and Vilma that she could conceal and transport the explosives, she described a type of cartridge belt for dynamite sticks that she could hide under her clothing.[102]

Vilma had the belt sewn, and Gena returned to Manzanillo carrying some ten sticks of dynamite, caps, and fuses under her wide skirt.

After the *Granma* landing, M-26-7's first objective was to make contact with Fidel through Celia.[103] Yet contact was a long time in coming. News of the failed Santiago uprising, coupled with the *Granma*'s delay, led M-26-7 in the area to pull back. By the time that Griselda Sánchez, listening in on military radio communications, learned that a boat had landed and military were in the zone, Celia was traveling toward Santiago and could not be reached.[104]

When Celia and two M-26-7 men rode the bus to Santiago, she was recognized by agents of the Military Intelligence Service and detained while other agents searched for Celia's two companions.[105] Convinced she would be tortured and killed, Celia tried to escape.[106] She took advantage of their lax security upon capturing a woman and asked permission three times to go to a nearby shop under the pretext of buying first cigarettes, then matches, and then gum. The last time, she took off running up the busy street. "The surprise paralyzed them," then they ran after her.[107] She crawled into a marabú thicket (later requiring medical attention for thorns lodged in her head) and waited.[108] Eventually she spotted an acquaintance, and claiming car trouble, got a ride. Along the way, she convinced the driver to pick up her two male companions. This dramatic escape became well known in M-26-7, gaining her notoriety and respect in the movement.

During this time, Gena visited her family at the base of the Sierra Maestra in search of *Granma* survivors, and then, eight days after the *Granma*'s scheduled arrival, she accompanied Celia to Santiago to meet with rebel leaders. In addition to these dangerous episodes, Celia was juggling numerous other crises. For example, she had placed a young man as M-26-7 leader in Pilón, but his nerves failed, and days before the landing, his mother dumped all the weaponry he had been hiding onto Celia's patio. This endangered Celia and her family, given that their house had come under surveillance.[109] After several harrowing efforts, she eventually transported the arms to the guerrillas. Such examples speak to a relatively broad-based and disciplined resistance in which women played important roles as both leaders and rank and file.

The *Granma* Landing: Another Military Disaster
Turned Political Victory

The *Granma* left Mexico with eighty-two men under less than ideal circumstances. Their departure was rushed by pressure from Mexican authorities as well as Fidel's own determination to stick to his public pledge to return to Cuba by year's end. Celia had studied the coastal water depths and advocated landing spots that would place the rebels close to the Sierra. For various reasons, including navigational errors and dwindling fuel, the *Granma* landed instead in a swampy area filled with mangroves. In addition to the problems encountered at sea in their overburdened yacht with a failing engine, hours before landing a man fell overboard, and they searched for him for nearly an hour in the dark, wasting precious time and fuel. With dawn approaching and fuel running out, the navigator and captain could not precisely identify their location. Fidel ordered them to the nearest coast. The yacht grounded (described by one rebel as more of a "shipwreck") while still 100 yards from shore, about 16 miles past the planned landing site and that much further from the Sierra Maestra.[110] The rebels persevered, loading the lifeboat with their heavy weapons, which promptly sank. They had little choice but to carry the weapons they could salvage and wade ashore. Heavily weighted down and in danger of drowning, the men abandoned more weapons before reaching dry land. Beyond the shore, the nearly impenetrable mangrove swamp stretched out before them, and the Sierra Maestra lay some sixty miles away. Celia later lamented, "They couldn't have landed in a worse place than the swamp. If they had done it on the small beach, it would have been a breeze. They would have found trucks and jeeps with gas, and they could have stormed the garrison [in Pilón] with the guns they had."[111] Instead, after landing hungry and weak, the rebels waded through mud and dense mangrove thickets for hours.

Fidel summarized that then, "after three days without food, marching through strange country without a guide, we were surprised and routed by land forces far superior in number and by an aircraft squadron."[112] Yet Castro had not helped the fate of the mission by his earlier public declarations that he would invade Cuba before the year was out. Farber termed it "a nearly suicidal but politically effective slogan."[113] Tens of thousands of leaflets had been distributed throughout Cuba that read, "In 1956, We Will Return OR We Will Be Martyrs."[114] Batista's forces, thus forewarned and having suppressed the Santiago uprising two days prior, had ships and aircraft patrolling and the army and rural guard on high alert. Batista's military tracked the *Granma* rebels by following a trail of partially consumed sugar cane stalks as well as information supplied by *campesinos* whom the rebels had trusted. As Dosal summarized: "Castro selected a poor location to rest, failed to post sentries, and did not make arrangements for an orderly retreat. When the firing commenced, the rebels scattered in every direction," abandoning more weapons and supplies.[115] Many were quickly killed or captured.

Although Castro's public vow to return by year's end appears ill advised militarily, much of Castro's revolutionary plans played to a war of ideas.[116] His declaration, followed by the landing, was good propaganda. As with Moncada, the *Granma* expedition was a military disaster riddled with mistakes that became a propaganda victory, particularly once Castro's survival was confirmed.

Celia contacted Crescencio Pérez, described as "the old patriarch of the mountains," or, alternatively, a "local thief wanted by the rural police for numerous robberies and murder."[117] It was Crescencio's network, coordinated through Celia, that came to the rebels' rescue. On December 12, some *Granma* survivors arrived at a *campesino* house linked to the network. From there, the rebels were led to the home of Crescencio's brother Mongo, where many of the remaining expeditionaries regrouped, joined by eight *campesinos*.[118] At least forty-six of the original eighty-two men of the *Granma* landing had been killed or captured, and by the end of December, only eighteen guerrillas had rendezvoused in the Sierra Maestra.

Once the *Granma* survivors were in the Sierra, Celia served as the most immediate contact between the Sierra and the urban plains or *llano*, and she was the center of the organizational support, which was particularly crucial in the first couple of months.[119] Those charged with handling military logistics do not receive the same status or scholarly interest as combatants. However, the guerrillas' survival depended upon these supplies, the delivery of which was dangerous.

Around December 18 or 19, Manzanillo M-26-7 finally received word on the survivors and soon after had a list of requested supplies.[120] Gena Verdecía left for Santiago to deliver the message, then accompanied Rafael Sierra and Enrique "Quique" Escalona into the Sierra, reaching the rebels on December 23 with hundreds of bullets, some machine gun magazines, and nine sticks of dynamite, among other items.[121] Gena, the first M-26-7 woman to reach the guerrilla group, recalled the optimism at the camp once the supplies and weaponry arrived.[122] Carrying letters and a new supply list, Gena returned to Manzanillo with *Granma* survivor Faustino Pérez, posing as his fiancée to provide cover.[123] On to Santiago, Gena accompanied Vilma and Frank and picked up more weapons. Delayed by intensified searches and surveillance, Quique and Gena finally reached the Sierra guerrillas again on December 29, traveling first by car, then jeep, horseback, and finally on foot to deliver food, books, glasses for Fidel, and asthma inhalers for Che, in addition to more weapons.[124]

As she recounted: "[Fidel] was surprised to see me: '*Muchacha*, you are a Mariana Grajales!'"[125] Gena hoped to participate in an attack on a military post in Veguitas, but Celia prohibited the idea as too dangerous and instead sent Gena to accompany two M-26-7 men to search for a group of rebels who had followed a man falsely claiming to be under Fidel's orders.[126] When Fidel next saw Gena, he asked about women's support for armed insurrection. According to Gena, he had no immediate plans to station women in the guerrilla camps owing to lack of weapons, but "He already had in his mind the idea of women combatants. He had asked me the second time he saw me when I was going to take up arms."[127]

Like the Moncada assault, the *Granma* expedition was nearly suicidal but also had a rallying effect on public opinion. In a confidential report, a US consulate officer in Santiago wrote that Castro supporters insisted Castro would return in 1956: "As the year's end approached, it was obvious to all Santiagueros that Castro would have to make good his boast of returning or they would lose faith ... [T]here was waning interest in [Castro's] movement as December 1956 approached and Castro was now being regarded also as a braggart."[128] Once Castro and his troops did arrive and a fraction reached the Sierra Maestra, the same consulate officer reported, "Fidel Castro skyrocketed to fame ... His successful defiance of the Cuban Army became the source of great delight and satisfaction to less daring Santiagueros."[129]

Reflecting upon this period with a gendered lens, we find qualities that women brought to the movement benefitted it during its abeyance phase. However, as will become clearer in later chapters, during resurgence many of the same qualities limited women's status and power as leaders. I maintain that women's tendency to defer to male leadership was part of their appeal and an advantage women lent to Fidel's group. However, the rebel resurgence and rise of guerrilla warfare after the *Granma* landing shifted the gender dynamics such that although some individual women remained key actors and mobilized women figured prominently in rebel propaganda, a preferential option for men and armed combat was pronounced and pervasive.

Notes

1. Taylor (1989).
2. Ibid., 772.
3. Judson (1984) and Szulc (1986) are key exceptions, arguing that the rebels' time in prison was key for their maturation and ideological development. Szulc (1986) concludes regarding this period, "women have played a role that may well have been decisive" (310).

4. Viterna (2013, 144) notes advantages to guerrilla women's higher survival rates in El Salvador.

5. Taylor (1989, 770–1) stresses the cultivation during abeyance periods of activist networks (organizational ties especially among a committed core of activists), repertoires (movement goals and strategies), and collective identity (including a shared history and symbols).

6. Judson (1984).

7. Taylor (1989, 772).

8. See Judson (1984, 66).

9. Bardach and Conte Agüero (2007).

10. These women included María Teresa Taquechel Manduley, Alba Griñán Núñez, Rosa Chade, Nilsa Espín, Cuca Mont, and María Teresa Valentino.

11. Founders included the families of Jesús Montané, Juan Almeida, and Pedro Miret, Fidel's sister Lidia Castro, along with mothers María Esther Aguilera and Adriana González (Orlando Álvarez Gómez, "Su museo de la clandestinidad," *Verde Olivo* May 1990, 58–9; Suárez Ramos, "15 de mayo de 1955: la profecía de Fidel" in *Trabajadores* December 22, 2006.

12. Argentina Jiménez, "Rescate de los restos de los mártires del Moncada," *Tribuna de la Habana* July 21, 2007. The military tried to covertly transport the bodies to the cemetery on the afternoon of July 27, but Gloria's husband Amaro Iglesias followed them (Rojas 1988, 99–101). Gravediggers collaborated with the rebels in identifying where certain rebels were buried, including Abel Santamaría. Cuadras also founded *Frente de Mujeres Cubanas* in Santiago before joining M-26-7 as part of the General Command (*Estado Mayor*) and Secretary of Propaganda in Oriente (Barceló, *Mujeres* November 28, 2003).

13. Rojas (1988, 101). Two years later, René Guitart, father of a Moncadista, had the bodies removed to a separate tomb near José Martí's gravesite, topped by a thick slab to prevent the military from destroying it (Rojas 1988, 102–3); Jiménez (2007)).

14. Castro Porta (1990, 81–4). Camejo, along with Pedro Véliz, both "deserted" the rebel group hours before the attacks but were captured and killed by the military (de la Cova 2007).

15. Castro Porta (1990, 84).

16. Ibid.; EcuRed (n.d.), Síntesis biográfica, Pedro Véliz Hernández.

17. Rita Amat in Castro Porta (1990, 79–80).

18. Ibid. Melba, Haydée, Lidia Castro, and Rosita Mier were also there.

19. Taylor (1989) stresses collective identity and oppositional consciousness in abeyance, linked to a crafting of movement history and symbols.

20. Szulc (1986, 310). On the importance of trustworthiness and women rebels, see Viterna (2013).

21. Franqui (1980, 86) (letter is dated October 3, 1954; the recipient is not noted); June 19, 1954 letter to Melba and Haydée, Castro (2005, 182–4). Fidel's prison letters reveal his concern that a competing political party would gain momentum.

22. Guzmán and Babiel (2006).

23. Santamaría (2003b, 21).

24. Franqui (1980, 77).

25. Castro (2005, 184–5).
26. Bardach (2007, x).
27. Fidel's marriage suffered a fatal blow when his wife received a love letter that Fidel had written for Naty Revuelta (Bardach 2003, 45). On Revuelta, see also Szulc (1986); de la Cova (2007, 44, 45, and 49); Skierka (2004, 32). Prison personnel reviewed outgoing letters, and it appears they placed Fidel's letter to Naty in the envelope addressed to Mirta.
28. Santamaría (2003b, 22).
29. Hart (2004, 86).
30. Ibid., 84. García Bárcena, of the 1930s Generation, was arrested as he was about to launch an attack against the Columbia military barracks in April 1953.
31. Hart (2004, 86).
32. Holgado Fernández (2000, 266).
33. Smith and Padula (1996, 25). Batista was most concerned about ex-President Prío and his followers; in July 1955, the Cuban ambassador complained to the US State Department about this group's "revolutionary activities" against Batista while using the United States as its base (Henry A. Hoyt, "Memorandum of a Conversation," *Foreign Relations of the United States*, 1955–1957, July 1, 1955).
34. Dubois (1959, 95).
35. Ibid., 94; Del Torro, *Granma* May 15, 1985, 5. Soon after, Fidel and Naty rendezvoused, and a daughter was conceived. Around this time he also reportedly conceived a child with María Laborde (Coltman 2003, 100; Bardach 2009, 36).
36. Guzmán and Babiel (2006). See also Taber (1961, 50); Dubois (1959, 93).
37. The Federation of University Students (FEU) and its armed wing *Directorio Revolucionario* (DR) exhibited a similar dynamic: leaders barred women from the 1957 assassination attempt against Batista, assigning them to rebuild the movement should the action fail (Pedro Antonio García, "Presencia femenina en el Directorio Revolucionario," *Granma* March 13, 1991, 2). The DR lost nearly its entire leadership from the attack, as those not killed went into exile. In the subsequent reorganization, Mary Pumpido took a seat on the executive council and Elvira Díaz Vallina became the first woman FEU president. Elvira also joined M-26-7 and worked under Haydée to form an underground women's cell, mobilizing hundreds of Havana women on Moncada's fourth anniversary in July 1957 (Shayne 2004, 129–31). Marta Jiménez resumed her activism following the death of her husband, FEU leader Fructuoso Rodríguez, and birth of her child, representing the new DR women's section (Bonachea and San Martín 1974, 174; García 1991, 2). These women, in sum, follow the familiar rebel pattern. They were active and committed rebels held back from the riskiest actions; thus protected, they survived to fill in for the men killed or in exile.
38. Judson (1984, 66).
39. Hart (2004, 95).
40. Bonachea and San Martín (1974, 38); Hart (2004, 95). Also see Klouzal (2008), which relates María Antonia's story under the pseudonym "Petra."

Meetings were held at her house, and she oversaw communications during important actions.

41. Bonachea and San Martín (1974, 38).
42. Gonzáles Cabrera, *Mujeres* October 1984, 15. For example, Eva was with him when they met Tony Conde, the man who would sell Fidel a yacht and weapons for his return to Cuba.
43. Hart (2004, 99). Szulc (1986, 353). Several women note his comfort in working with women. Melba reflected, Fidel was "'stimulated' by the presence of women, that he always 'needs a woman' because 'he has a great trust in women,' but with him 'the intellect is above everything else'" (Szulc 1986, 352). Teté Casuso opined: "He is so masculine with women that he makes them feel beautiful and satisfied in his company, even just as a friend" (Matthews 1961, 146).
44. Gonzáles Cabrera (1984, 14). For a detailed analysis of Jiménez's rebel contributions, see García-Pérez (2009).
45. Gadea (2008, 150).
46. Jiménez in Castro Porta (1990, 135). See also Barrio and Jenkins (2003, 68).
47. Szulc (1986, 348); Coltman (2003, 102).
48. See Barrio and Jenkins (2003, 68).
49. Gonzáles Cabrera (1984, 17). Hilda Gadea was also held by police, along with her four-month-old baby, because a telegraph to Fidel but addressed to her was intercepted by Mexican authorities (Gadea 2008, 186).
50. García-Pérez (2009, 67–8). Most rebels were released after several weeks.
51. Casuso (1961, 87); Custodio (2005, 37). Casuso was the widow of Pablo de la Torriente Brau, a journalist and rebel of Cuba's 30s Generation. He survived serious injury protesting the Machado regime in 1930 but died six years later in the Spanish Civil War. After 1959, Casuso was a member of the Cuban delegation to the UN until her defection in 1960.
52. Szulc (1986, 353); Llerena (1978, 82–3); Bonachea and San Martín (1974, 66). This would be roughly US $2.25 million in 2017.
53. Dubois (1959, 135). The raid and loss of weapons was a major blow to the rebels, who were weeks away from returning to Cuba. According to Oltuski (2002, 101), the rebels caught the man who tipped off the Mexican police, and Melba, Oltuski, and a third rebel deliberated over whether and how to kill him.
54. Isabel's mother was a friend of Casuso, and Isabel (under the pseudonym "Lilia" in Casuso's memoir) often stayed at Casuso's house (Casuso 1961, 90; Custodio 2005, 34).
55. Custodio (2005, 37, 40); Casuso (1961, 92–3). Almendros went on to become an Academy Award-winning Hollywood cinematographer.
56. Custodio (2005, 83).
57. Ibid., 215–24. She remained unconscious for four more days.
58. Custodio interview in Mariusa Reyes, "Castro y el amor en México," *BBC Mundo* December 19, 2005; Custodio (2005) recalls overhearing Che lecturing Fidel that she was not a true revolutionary and would not sufficiently dedicate herself to the cause; furthermore, Fidel should not marry anyone – he should dedicate himself to his only true "girlfriend," the Revolution (109).

59. Custodio (2005, 21) Isabel's father Álvaro Custodio was a respected stage manager and writer.
60. Ibid., 59–61. Their collective, Las AZUCENAS, distributed feminist pamphlets disguised as recipes at factory entrances. According to Custodio, their activities were clandestine, and even their friends and families did not know; they disguised their political work by feigning frivolity, pretending to go to parties.
61. She wrote for the Mexico City newspaper *Excélsior* and the feminist magazine *Fem* and is also a novelist.
62. Daniel Archilla, "Isabel Custodio, la novia de Castro antes de la Revolución (interview)" *Ya era hora* December 19, 2008. According to Custodio (2005, 110, 141–2), Che referred to her, disapprovingly, as a little bourgeois doll (*burguesita amuñecada*) and lectured her that she was distracting Fidel from his projects and obligations.
63. Custodio (2005, 250).
64. Hilda returned to Peru with her daughter in December 1956, serving as National Secretary of Statistics for APRA and a member of the National Executive Committee (Gadea 2008, 6–7). She wrote to Che of her intent to reunite with him and participate in the guerrilla struggle in February 1958, but he indicated the time was not right (Gadea 2008, 7–8, 218). They divorced in early 1959, and Che married Aleida March, whom he had met in the last months of the insurrection.
65. Gadea (2008, 48, 183, 201).
66. Ibid., 66.
67. Ibid.
68. Ibid. Notably, her party APRA "explicitly recognized women as an essential element of the revolutionary struggle and developed a 'feminist platform'" (Jaquette 1973, 346).
69. Gadea (2008, 66).
70. Ibid., 46.
71. Taylor (1989).
72. García-Pérez (2009, 70).
73. Orfilio Peláez, "Yo me entrené para venir en el Granma," *Granma* August 25, 2006, www.granma.cubaweb.cu/2006/08/25/nacional/artico3.html (accessed 7/29/11); Álvarez (1980) (documentary film), Hernández interview at min. 84.
74. Peláez (2006).
75. McCormick et al. (2007, 341); Anderson (1997, 212).
76. Taber (1961). Enzo Infante, "Santiago Uprising: A Harbinger of Victory," *Verde Olivo* November 27, 1966, translated in *The Militant* 60(9), March 4, 1996. Fidel also called upon the Revolutionary Directorate (DR) to lead a Havana uprising to coincide with the *Granma* landing, but DR leader Echevarría refused, considering it a pointless waste of lives (Llovio-Menéndez 1988, 66).
77. Arthur Gardner, "Telegram from the Ambassador in Cuba (Gardner) to the Secretary of State," Foreign Relations of the United States, 1955–1957, October 16, 1956.

78. Álvarez (2009, 128).
79. Ibid.
80. William Gálvez, "Crónicas de la lucha revolucionaria preparando la guerra VIII a X partes," *Publicación Semanal* 3(156), December 29, 2006.
81. Álvarez (2009, 129).
82. Lupiáñez Reinlein (1985, 100–1).
83. Bonachea and San Martín (1974, 81). Infante (1996).
84. They expected the Moncada troops would soon be released; the commander had held them back, fearing another massacre (Bonachea and San Martín 1974, 81).
85. Santamaría (2003b, 36); see also Hart (2004, 140–1); Franqui (1980, 63).
86. Santamaría (2003b, 37).
87. Hart (2004, 140–1); Santamaría (2003b, 37).
88. Ibid.
89. Franqui (1980, 63).
90. *Diario de la Marina* reported three dead police and one dead soldier, two others gravely wounded and that rebels freed and armed some 200 prisoners from Puerto Boniato prison (García Torres, "Domina el Ejército la situación en la capital de Oriente," *Diario de la Marina* December 1, 1956, 1).
91. Heidy Rodríguez Rey, "Testigos de una victoria," *Mujeres* November 1976, 6.
92. Hart (2004, 162); Lilian Chirino, "Desde el Moncada hasta el Granma: Dos de sus hermanas y compañeros de lucha aportan sus testimonios para darnos a conocer aspectos de la vida de Celia," *Verde Olivo* January 10, 1985, 41.
93. Sweig (2002, 40); Tomás Diez Acosta, "Las comunicaciones en la guerrilla," *Verde Olivo* March 6, 1986, 36–9.
94. Katia Siberia García, "Celia y el Grupo de Apoyo," *Granma* December 28, 2006.
95. Siberia García (2006). The military found these charts aboard the *Granma*, traced them back to Celia, and confronted Celia's father with them, first wrapping them in a girdle, apparently as proof of her participation (Celia's testimony in Franqui 1980, 128).
96. Gálvez (2006).
97. Szulc (1986, 375).
98. Daisy Martin, "Vanguardias del MININT" *Mujeres* June 1978, 6; Elena later joined *Las Marianas*, the women guerrilla unit.
99. Magaly Sánchez Ochoa, "'Muchacha, tú eres una Mariana Grajales!' *Mujeres* October 1979, 7–9.
100. Coltman (2003, 117).
101. Sánchez Ochoa (1979, 7–9).
102. Ibid.
103. Hart (2004, 141–2).
104. Chirino (1985, 43).
105. Ibid.
106. Siberia García (2006).
107. Ibid.
108. Chirino (1985, 43); Siberia García (2006).
109. Chirino (1985, 42).

110. Franqui (1980, 124).
111. Ibid., 129.
112. Fidel's testimony in Franqui (1980, 129).
113. Farber (1976, 187).
114. Szulc (1986, 345).
115. Dosal (2004, 14).
116. Che wrote that a guerrilla campaign should be initiated by a handful of dedicated revolutionaries "without mass support or knowledge" – contrary to the *Granma*'s preannounced arrival (Dosal 2004, 14).
117. Bonachea and San Martín (1974, 88); Llovio-Menéndez (1988, 66).
118. Bonachea and San Martín (1974, 89).
119. Armando Hart, quoted in Diez Acosta (1986, 36); see also Manuel Díaz Hurtado, "La supervivencia en el ejercito rebelde: la alimentación durante la lucha," *Verde Olivo* February 27, 1986, 24–7.
120. Sánchez Ochoa (1979, 8).
121. Ibid.; Szulc (1986, 391). Che recorded Gena's arrival in his diary but incorrectly assumed one of the men with her was her husband (Guevara 2013, 35).
122. Sánchez Ochoa (1979, 8–9).
123. Ibid.; Szulc (1986, 392).
124. Sánchez Ochoa (1979, 8). They carried sixteen explosive charges, four submachine gun clips, three dynamite cartridges, and eight hand grenades (Ustariz Arze 2008, 110; Szulc 1986, 392–3).
125. Sánchez Ochoa (1979, 9). Several women reported similar greetings from Fidel upon arrival in camp, suggesting that he selected women rebels out for particular encouragement.
126. Ibid. Some of the group had evaded capture – among them a woman, Teté Puebla.
127. Ibid. After evacuating a wounded rebel to Havana, Gena sought asylum in the Peruvian embassy and went into exile, returning in time to join the guerrilla in its final months.
128. Guerra, "Despatch from the Consulate at Santiago de Cuba to the Department of State," February 21, 1958.
129. Ibid.

CHAPTER 5

Gendered Rebels

Barriers and Privileges

As the previous chapter demonstrates, women were key figures in the movement's abeyance period (1953–56) that spanned imprisonment and exile. Moreover, during the November 1956 Santiago uprising, women comprised nearly a quarter of the twenty-five M-26-7 leaders.[1] Yet there were no women aboard the *Granma,* and over the course of the insurrection's final two years, women were edged out numerically and in terms of leadership positions. This chapter begins by examining the paths that women took into the rebel forces and the barriers they confronted to address how a movement that began with relative gender equity ended as a male-dominated revolution. I approach this puzzle with an intersectional lens. Despite the rich body of intersectional research on contemporary Cuba, the Cuban insurrection has seen little research on gender, race, or sexuality, much less the intersection of these identities.[2]

Accordingly, I first explore the means by which femininity, same-sex sexuality, and Afro-Cuban identity were devalued and politicized in 1950s Cuba. Then, drawing from diverse primary documents, I build theory on barriers to rebel women's participation, focusing on family resistance, rejection by rebel men, and low-status assignments.[3] Turning to rebel men and masculinity, I find courage and honor to be a double-edged sword, a means of gaining masculine status, but a status that must perpetually be defended. Finally, I narrow the focus to women leaders to consider how, in the context of race, class, and age-based privilege, different expressions of femininity were valued or disparaged. Criticism lodged at Melba Hernández, a mixed-race woman, drew upon sexism and racism working in tandem. In contrast, comparing their relative (dis)advantages during the insurrection and in later representations, both Celia Sánchez and Vilma Espín benefitted from race and class privilege, yet they were differently advantaged in terms of the particular femininity they represented. While Celia was widely venerated, Vilma attracted more criticism, particularly as a power-hungry woman.

GENDER, RACE, AND SEXUALITY IN 1950S CUBA

The literature on gender relations in 1950s Cuba points to the division between *la calle* (the street and, more generally, public and political life) and *la casa* (the home) as men's and women's proper realm, respectively.[4] Women ideally belonged to the house and should not "run around in the streets" for fear of "gossip about the woman and perhaps the loss of virginity."[5] Margaret Randall describes women of that time "inhabit[ing] a narrow space ... so constrictive to women's opportunity and agency."[6] Lourdes Casal notes heavy pressure on women to marry, as a woman without a man was considered "incomplete and in a state of prolonged childhood and dependency."[7] Accordingly, unmarried, middle-aged women could still be called *muchachitas* (the diminutive for "girls"). Moreover, women were "not supposed to become involved in politics," which was "a male preserve."[8] Expectations varied across class lines. In their recollections of the insurrectionary period, poor and middle-class women from the countryside and provinces often describe very strict gendered expectations while some middle- and upper-class urban women enjoyed a greater range of movement beyond the home.[9] More generally, women were idealized as fragile, purer than men, easily frightened, weak, and in need of men's protection.[10] However, this varied in terms of race, as black and mixed-race women were often understood and portrayed in white-dominated discourse as hyper-sexualized seductresses.[11]

Reflecting these gender norms, in 1959 only 17 percent of women were in the paid labor force, largely in low-status, low-paying jobs.[12] One quarter of working women were domestic servants, and one out of six was a professional – overwhelmingly (84 percent) teachers.[13] Women had higher literacy rates and grade school attendance than men, but the number of women who had received some university education was less than half that for men.[14]

Cuban idealized masculinity functioned in binary contrast to femininity.[15] Masculinity and femininity did not overlap but rather defined one another: a man was not a woman, and vice versa. Ian Lumsden, like many others, notes the striking "exaltation of physical bravado so evident in Cuban machismo."[16] A "real man" was courageous, physically strong, confident, and virile.[17] He took risks and initiative while suppressing fear and strong emotions other than anger. "Real men" recoiled from engaging in any activity considered feminine and also strongly rejected male homosexuality. When Aida Pelayo recalled her interrogation by police chief Rafael Salas Cañizares, she disparagingly remarked on his "repellent androgynous figure."[18] Tellingly, the pejorative slang for a gay man, *maricón*, also indicated cowardice.[19] Casal adds, "To launch an accusation of homosexuality against a political enemy was one of the most terrible insults ... [It] was a way of calling him a woman, a direct attack on his masculinity, on his value as macho."[20] Guerrillas, for example, taunted government soldiers with, ¡*Ríndanse, maricones*! (Surrender, queers!)."[21] Not surprisingly, a real man "did not take orders from a woman; he refused to acknowledge or respect women in positions of power."[22] Finally, the ideal man provided for and protected his family, particularly women.[23] A man's own honor was at stake in his ability to protect women's honor, which entailed controlling women's behavior outside the home.[24]

Even more so than gender inequality, racial inequality and norms in 1950s Cuba have not been well documented. Early on, the revolutionary government declared the race problem solved, and thus, "it has become subversive to speak or write about it."[25] Minority Rights Group International, pointing to the "long-standing problem of information concerning race relations and minorities in the island," maintains that "assessment of the situation of Afro-Cubans remains problematic due to scant records and a paucity of systematic studies both pre- and post-revolution."[26]

Nonetheless, several detailed studies have emerged on race relations in this period, revealing the complexity of Afro-Cuban political leanings.[27] Though Alejandro de la Fuente maintains, "the participation of blacks and mulattoes in the [rebel] movement was far from negligible," there is consensus on the common perception at the time that Afro-Cubans were unsupportive of the anti-Batista insurrection.[28] Despite a significant Afro-Cuban population, disproportionately situated among the poorest ranks, the Cuban rebels were predominately white, including collaborators in the civic resistance. In her sample of women rebels, García-Pérez finds 85 percent were white.[29] Nearly all rebel leaders were white, and anti-Batista forces exhibited "almost complete silence" on race and racial discrimination.[30] In contrast, Batista's military, with a significant percentage of Afro-Cubans, "stressed that blacks and mulattoes should follow a mulatto like Batista, not a white middle-class radical like Castro or most other anti-Batista leaders."[31] Such factors reinforced "the notion that blacks were sympathetic to Batista or, at the very least, unsympathetic toward the revolutionaries."[32] An additional complication for rebels was the social prohibition against white women mixing with black men. As a white female former rebel explained, "A white woman with a black man was a problem for [middle- and upper-class whites]. It became the subject of gossip."[33]

Adding to the racial ambivalence, though President Batista was popularly understood to be mixed-race or *mulato*, he identified as white or attributed his brown skin to an Indian heritage.[34] Nonetheless, some sectors of the opposition were overtly racist in their critiques of Batista. Followers of ex-President Carlos Prío (whom Batista had ousted) depicted Batista and his military as vicious ape-like creatures and referred to Batista as *el mulato malo* (the bad mulatto) and the "black beast," setting up a dichotomy between "the white, educated middle class and an ignorant, bloody, predominately black army – a struggle between civilization and barbarism."[35] "Cuban mothers" wrote to the US Embassy describing Batista as a "beast" who belonged in "the African jungle."[36] Carlos Moore, who is Afro-Cuban, recalls in his memoir that whites "told corrosive *chistes* (jokes) portraying [Batista] as a dumb and incompetent Negro," critiquing Batista's Spanish, his table manners, and his "bad hair."[37] Anti-Batista lyrics were set to a tune in 1957, which when not sung out loud by whites was whistled provocatively:

> *Cascabel, Cascabel,*
> *Ya llego Fidel,*
> *pa' tumbar al negro mono*
> *que está en el poder!*

> Jingle bells, Jingle bells,
> Here comes Fidel,
> to topple the black monkey
> who's in power![38]

Some key Batista allies made overt appeals to Afro-Cubans. The infamous Senator Rolando Masferrer, who commanded his own feared paramilitary, "distributed fliers in Santiago claiming that Fidel Castro and his followers were antiblack."[39] Others warned that if M-26-7 triumphed, Afro-Cubans would be forced into slavery or massacred.[40]

Moore reports that some sectors of the Afro-Cuban community greeted Batista's coup "with undisguised satisfaction. They defended against racial mockery, which they took personally."[41] This senti

Soc:.l cLS; f#§-.. cc-ss

was amplified as top social clubs refused Batista membership because of his race.[42] Moore's observations of Afro-Cubans' reactions to the coup differ markedly from Cubans' reactions described by Louis Pérez, who wrote: "The March 10 coup changed everything, and what changed most was how Cubans saw themselves: with embarrassment and humiliation, with deepening doubt and diminished confidence."[43] Pérez links the sense of embarrassment and humiliation with the perception that Cuba was regressing from modernity and civilization, noting references to the "laws of the jungle" and "savage tribes."[44] Batista's race informed many white Cubans' fear of encroaching barbarism and provided a potent means of undermining his authority. A man of color was Cuba's strong man, and he faced racist tropes marking him as a savage beast and uncivilized monkey. But this embarrassment for some was a source of racial pride for others, and the discontent and unease described by Pérez did not cut equally across racial groups.

Race, gender, and sexuality thus inform the founding myths of the revolution. In what follows, I first explore gender, including specific forms that discrimination took and the gendered logics that supported them. I also examine hegemonic masculinity, considering the pressures it imposed on rebel men. Then, I turn to the cases of women leaders to explore intersectional dynamics through analysis of the ways in which they were celebrated and criticized. Though alert to race and sexuality throughout my research, I found that rebels are rarely identified in terms of race in Cuban or other sources, and homosexuality was only mentioned as an insult or to imply a scandal. Furthermore, identifying rebels by race through photos is an incomplete and unreliable method given that it does not capture the individual's own subjectivity nor even necessarily how the individual was "raced" by others. I include those instances I found in which race or sexuality is specified, recognizing that this is an initial and still incomplete analysis.

REBELS AND FEMININITY: GENDERED BARRIERS

Idealized femininity cut multiple ways for Cuban women rebels, enabling women to make certain contributions – such as smuggling weapons under skirts – while foreclosing others. But the gendered barriers are not well detailed in the literature. The Cuban War Story portrays rebel leaders such as Frank País and especially Fidel Castro as promoting women's participation.[45] Rebel narratives rarely detail gender discrimination and sometimes deny it. Indeed, when a Cuban journalist asked Vilma Espín in 1975 about the difficulties for women in rebel leadership, she replied categorically, "No one ever had this as a problem."⁴⁶ A 1994 University of Havana study reveals a different reality, as nearly half the former rebel women interviewed recalled the struggle as more difficult for women. Respondents reported three main difficulties: (1) their families did not support the idea of women rebels; (2) rebel men rejected them; and (3) they were assigned low-status work.⁴⁷ I explore how these three barriers were informed by the patriarchal ideology discussed previously,⁴⁸ drawing from narratives found in the Cuban archival evidence to flesh out the details and build theory on gender barriers and how these reinforced each other.

First, although some families had a positive influence on women's activism (discussed in Chapter 7), many resisted their daughters' participation out of fear for women's honor and safety as well as the belief that women should not engage in politics.⁴⁹ Aleida March had to lie to gain permission to leave the house: "My parents didn't understand and they certainly couldn't accept that a young woman would put herself and her reputation at risk" by working with the rebels.⁵⁰ Although Haydée Santamaría was a national leader, she too felt the weight of family disapproval: "My own mother was the kind of woman who thought that men were the only ones who had the right to make revolutions."⁵¹

Second, though the Cuban War Story emphasizes women's inclusion, there is ample archival evidence that men – rebels and collaborators – rejected or discriminated against them. I find this took several main forms: redirecting women from activism; undercutting their authority; or undermining their ability (often in the guise of protection).⁵² In one representative example, Maruja Iglesias traveled to Santiago with María Sifones as members of Las Martianas to deliver funds for the Moncada survivors. The Archbishop accepted the funds but urged the two young women to get married and form a family in place of politics. Then he sent them off with reading material about matrimony.⁵³ Such advice appears several times in rebel women's testimonies, suggesting the quotidian level on which gender boundaries were patrolled within the anti-Batista community. The strict gender division of labor marginalized women in political activism in part by posing marriage and activism as contradictory, a significant barrier given the pressure on women to marry.

Archived rebel correspondence also documents discrimination as men challenged women leaders' authority, a finding not surprising given the incompatibility between idealized masculinity and women's authority discussed earlier. For example, in a July 1957 letter to Fidel,

Frank País accused René "el Flaco" Rodríguez, *Granma* survivor and head of the Havana M-26-7 Action group, of undermining Haydée's authority in an attempt to wrest leadership of Havana M-26-7 from her.[54] Frank coordinated with her to reimpose discipline, and they even considered killing René but feared revenge from his followers.[55] Instead, Frank proposed that since René respected Fidel and Frank's authority, the two men should intervene to gradually wrest power away from René.[56]

Marta Fuego Rodríguez, a rank and file rebel, identified a masculine protectionism that undermined women's abilities:

Machismo was very rooted in our country ... [T]he man thought of himself as the boss, and he thought of women as something weak that he should protect ... And even they thought that women cannot think like a man or act with sureness, with the confidence and worth of a man ... [They would say,] "you will do the less difficult, less dangerous things" ... We men will do the more dangerous things, and we will protect you because you are very weak women ... You will help us, but you will not participate fully.[57]

Marta's reflections also point to the third barrier women were given minor, low-status assignments, a factor closely linked to rejection in the name of protection. Marta had been recruited into M-26-7 as a teenage *campesina* in Pinar del Río. She was highly dedicated and prepared to face risks, yet rebel men upheld gender inequality even as they welcomed her into the rebel fold: "Well, you're a woman, but you can help anyway. Of course, you won't be given the riskier tasks."[58] Those riskier tasks were a primary means of gaining status and authority. As such, barring women in the name of protection in effect meant barring women from leadership.

The above examples illustrate barriers to women's full participation and the gendered logic that supported them. Women's proper place was in the home, and their honor was questioned as they ventured beyond it. Moreover, women rebels were viewed as less capable than men and in need of men's protection, and thus best placed in presumably safer auxiliary roles. The literature also points to women's reproductive capacities as a structural barrier that intersects with class, as middle- and upper-class women often hired poor women to perform domestic tasks, freeing the former to participate.[59] I add that delayed marriage and childbirth were more feasible and likely for middle- and upper-class women, thus positioning them to engage more readily in rebel activities.[60] To varying degrees, then, marriage and motherhood also functioned as barriers to rebellion, detaching women from rebel life.

REBEL MASCULINITY: COURAGE AND HONOR

Though "rebel" was a masculinized identity, rebel men nonetheless faced their own gendered constraints, as the idealized traits of a rebel revolved narrowly around courage and honor. Though its specific performance varies, courage is a core expression of masculinity that cuts across cultures, has endured over time, and is especially pronounced in militarized contexts.[61] Masculine honor, in turn, is linked to control over, protection of, and provision for women.

Former rebel Marta Fuego suggests the link between rebel masculinity, courage, and protection of women in her story about a young man, Willy, whom she accompanied with bomb materials hidden in a cake box. When they spotted several policemen,

> Willy turned white. Without saying anything, I took the box from him, and I hurried off ... I saw he was very afraid. And afterwards I could tell he was very ashamed. I thought that with the fear he wasn't able to react. In those days we had very much the idea of the gentleman, and the man always tried to protect the woman. But in this case, it was I who protected him. And he was ashamed of that.[62]

Marta also related an admission by guerrilla Jesús Suárez Gayol, who recalled, upon finding himself surrounded, "'I was very afraid, I felt my heart was beating out of my chest, and my testicles were up to here,' in [my] throat."[63] This confession, Marta explained, made a lasting impression because it was the first time she had ever heard a man admit fear.[64]

Marta's reflections indicate the constraints masculinity posed to rebel men.[65] Indeed, evidence suggests the pressure to show courage sometimes pushed rebel men into counterproductively dangerous positions. Recall Haydée's account of two such defining moments, the first a disaster, the second a disaster narrowly averted. At Moncada, because her brother Abel and his men refused to flee the hospital once the 1953 attack had failed, most of the men were killed. Later, when the 1956 Santiago uprising failed, Frank also wanted to confront Batista's forces head on, and only Haydée's urging convinced him to abandon this suicidal plan.

Leaders' recollections are also revealing for their invocations of masculinity. Because courage structured hierarchies among men, certain forms of rebel activism were more attractive. This informed complex Sierra–*llano* power dynamics within the rebel forces, marking the Sierra guerrilla with more status. According to Vilma, even *llano* leader Frank had hoped to transfer to the Sierra because, for him, "going to the Sierra was to fight the enemy face to face, to not have to hide ... All that of going to the mountains, carrying a backpack, waging open warfare" was "the most that anyone could hope for."[66] Instead, Frank had to suffer the inflated egos of guerrilla men traveling to the *llano*. In a July 1957 letter, Frank complained to Fidel and Vilma about guerrillas visiting Santiago: "[They are] terribly rude, believing that everyone is their slave and obligated to serve them."[67] Though Santiago M-26-7 was already financially supporting "40 families of *compañeros* who are dead, imprisoned, or in the Sierra," it also supported these visiting guerrillas with shelter, food, and money.[68] Nonetheless, "Some tell us that we must give them more money, that we don't take care of them. Others ask for watches, money to go to the movies or to buy whatever ... Others have rejected the clothing that we have given them, telling us that they want it in such-and-such a size or ... that they don't like the color."[69] He asks Fidel to inform the guerrillas that they are not "kings" in the *llano* and will be treated the same as the rest, closing with: "The things that one must put up with here are terrible! René [Ramos Latour] is going crazy to leave [for the Sierra], he says, so that he can rest! And me too ...!"[70] Frank thus suggested not only that the guerrillas felt superior and entitled but also that the guerrillas actually had it comparatively easy. This correspondence, read through a gender lens, reveals Sierra–*llano* tensions that played out via notions of danger/safety and hardship/comfort, which reference and rely upon dominant and subordinate forms of masculinity. He who confronted the greater danger and hardships occupied the dominant masculine position. Frank, in actuality, faced extreme danger and was killed within weeks of writing this letter. Yet as a *llano* rebel he was denied the opportunity to confront the enemy head on in battle, the ultimate test of courage.

Similarly, Fidel's prison letters convey his anguish at not being able to confront his enemies, in this case to defend his masculine honor. In 1954, he became enraged upon discovering that his wife Mirta was on the Interior Ministry payroll. Mirta's brother, as Deputy Interior Minister, had surreptitiously arranged a salary for Mirta to supplement the allowance she received from Fidel's father during Fidel's imprisonment.[71] Once Interior Minister Ramón Hermida discovered this, he cut Mirta off. Fidel, upon hearing the news, was convinced the regime had manufactured it to insult him. In a letter to a friend, Fidel drew on crude homophobia to criticize Hermida while also worrying over the implications for his own masculinity:

Only a queer like Hermida, at the lowest degree of sexual degeneration, would resort to these methods, of such conceivable indecency and unmanliness ... Has a political prisoner no honor? ... Shouldn't a prisoner be allowed to challenge someone to a duel when he leaves prison? Must he graze on the bile of infamy in the impotence and despair of confinement? ... I am ready to challenge my own brother-in-law to a duel at any time. It is the reputation of my wife and my honor as a revolutionary that is at stake ... I would rather be killed a thousand times over than helplessly suffer such an insult![72]

Two weeks later and with "manly tears in [his] eyes," Fidel reported himself to be still suffering this "new pain, unknown and awful, one thousand times more distressing and despairing because of my cruel confinement behind bars."[73] A victim of this equation between masculinity and a man's ability to defend his honor, Fidel also wielded the charge of dishonor against Batista and his military. In sum, both men and women bore the weight of pronounced gendered expectations for their abilities and inclinations as rebels. While women had to struggle for recognition and responsibility, men were expected to maintain a front of fearlessness and honor.

WOMEN LEADERS: PRIVILEGE AND PREJUDICE

Thus far I have analyzed gendered constraints, a task facilitated by revolutionary Cuba's recognition of lingering gender inequalities, which encouraged some research and discussion of machismo even on the part of revolutionaries. However, research on racial barriers faces a greater challenge, as open discussion of race was suppressed with the logic that racism no longer existed and thus race was irrelevant. Age, too, is an underresearched factor. To access some intersectional insights, I turn to the women who have received the most attention in primary and secondary sources: Celia and Vilma, and to a lesser extent Melba and Haydée. Unfortunately, the record on Melba, the only woman of color in this group, dramatically recedes after the imprisonment of her husband Jesús Montané in the 1956 *Granma* landing.[74]

In what follows, in addition to exploring the tropes by which these leaders were celebrated, I also consider how they have been critiqued. This approach produces new insights into the gendered barriers confronting rebel women, suggesting as well how some women were sheltered through race and class privilege and certain versions of femininity, often informed by age.

Given the silence on race in the Cuban War Story, excavating the impact of racism on women rebels is a particular challenge. The reflections of anti-*Batistianos* who later opposed Castro are a unique source. Unencumbered by government censorship in exile, this community largely passes over Haydée and Celia to target Melba and Vilma. In the following, for example, critics draw on both sexism and racism in appraising Melba's participation in events leading up to Moncada:

[Jesús] Montané was mixing revolutionary activities with lust by pursuing an adulterous affair with Melba Hernández Rodríguez, a thirty-year-old mulatto customs attorney ... Ortodoxo leader Millo Ochoa regarded Melba as "having a racial inferiority complex because she always tried to pass off as white." Raúl Martínez indicated that she had a reputation after having various romances with other Ortodoxo Party youths. Ortodoxo activist Manuel Suardíaz Fernández bluntly described her as "trollop who liked younger men."[75]

Melba was only two years older than boyfriend Jesús, whereas Haydée was six years older than her boyfriend. Furthermore, as a lawyer, Melba had a college degree, whereas Haydée had a sixth-grade education.[76] Nonetheless, Suardíaz compares Haydée favorably: "Melba Hernández as a lawyer was worthless. She is a real slut [*putana*], she liked the young boys and was always [sexually] excited ... I sympathized with Haydée. She didn't have a great education but she was a pure idealist. She sacrificed."[77] Dismissing Melba's professional accomplishments, these narratives draw on the enduring myth of the hypersexual Afro-Cuban seductress, exploiter of men's weakness, to attack Melba.[78] In the gendered double standards of the time, rebel men were not criticized for extramarital affairs. Though such sources do not paint a full and accurate picture of the lived experience of rebel women of color, they offer a glimpse into the particular challenges these women faced.[79]

The post-1958 Cuban War Story portrays Melba as a rebel beyond reproach; however, at the time some rebels were critical of her, though without overt racial references. For example, in a July 1957 letter to Vilma, M-26-7 leader Frank lamented that Melba was "causing headaches again," by ignoring the chain of command: "Melba did not want any responsibility, nor did she want to work, which pleased me because personally I believed that she was a bit unhinged emotionally."[80] Frank's letter hints at the gendered tropes – women as irrational and overly emotional – by which women leaders could be undermined.

Age further complicates rebel gender dynamics. Unmarried women such as Vilma, Haydée, and Celia were often referred to as girls. Relatedly, collaborators and observers often misrecognized women leaders' status. For example, Vilma was *Paris-Match* photojournalist Enrique Meneses's initial contact in Cuba in 1957, and as a leader of the July 26 Movement in Santiago, Vilma arranged his passage to the Sierra Maestra.[81] Yet in March 1958 Meneses wrote, "Several other leaders had also arrived in the Sierra, as well as a number of girls, among them [Vilma Espín]."[82]

Examining age further, while the Cuban War Story is heavily invested in the notion that youth were the primary architects of the insurrection, the evidence suggests a significant proportion of women rebels were actually middle-aged. The University of Havana study of women rebels overrepresents women as youth by counting back from 1952 (the year of Batista's coup) to the birth year of the 675 women in their data set. Finding that 71 percent were under thirty years of age in 1952, it defines them as youths for the duration of the insurrection.[83] However, most women did not join the movement until the late 1950s, and a significant portion of that 71 percent would have turned thirty by 1959. In addition, nearly 30 percent of women rebels in the study were middle-aged even in 1952. Surprisingly, then, a significant percentage, perhaps the majority, of women rebels were thirty and above when rebel forces took power in 1959.

The intersection of gender and age is an underappreciated factor in understanding the limits to women leaders' authority. Cuba's four heroines were unmarried in the 1950s and were often referred to as youth and girls, yet in 1958 Celia was thirty-eight, Melba was thirty-seven, and Haydée was thirty-six.[84] Vilma was the youngest at twenty-eight, still a year older than future husband Raúl Castro. As noted, in 1950s Cuba, *muchacha* (girl) was a common way to refer to unmarried women even in middle age, a designation that worked against any official authority they had earned.[85] But although marriage might have socially advanced a woman from girl to adult, it did not necessarily clear a path to rebel status and authority, because marriage carried with it a strong social expectation that a woman would prioritize children, husband, and home, making rebel activism less feasible. That Vilma, Celia, Melba, and Haydée were unmarried women without children when they joined the movement is not incidental; indeed, few women rebels were married or had children.[86] However, being unmarried left a young woman vulnerable to insinuations about her virtue and sexual availability while calling a middle-aged woman's femininity and normative heterosexuality into question. Postinsurrection narratives attempt to get around this Catch-22, applauding these women for having dedicated themselves to the insurrection, delaying married life and the family they would otherwise presumably have desired.

Saint Celia and the Vilification of Vilma

In the remainder of this chapter, I explore Celia and Vilma's paths to leadership and compare the discourses through which they were lauded and criticized. Melba, as a woman of color, would have been an ideal case to consider here; however, little information about her post-Moncada rebel activism is available beyond what has already been discussed. Instead, in comparing these two white women from upper middle-class backgrounds, their relative race and class privileges are noted while working through the puzzle of Celia's saint-like status and the less favorable treatment Vilma has received.[87]

To begin, an intersectional lens applied to Celia's rebel work highlights the class and racial privileges she enjoyed. A white woman in her mid-30s, Celia lived near Manzanillo in the Oriente Province with her father, a widower, keeping house and working in his medical practice.[88] She was privileged economically and racially, not only as the daughter of a doctor but the granddaughter of one of Manzanillo's wealthiest Spanish merchants.[89] However, as Tiffany Thomas-Woodard argues, details of Celia's affluent background are largely excised from the public memory.[90]

An Orthodox Party activist, Celia at first opposed the 1952 coup through traditionally feminine support roles. To raise funds, she sold bonds and grew her hair to sell to a Havana salon for 25 pesos.[91] She had greater success once she turned to baking, with her upside-down cake especially popular. "Everyone bought them," recalled friend and collaborator Berta Llópiz, "from the workers at the sugar refinery to the people with money."[92] In mid-1955, Celia met Frank and joined the movement, at which point she took on riskier assignments.[93]

Celia is extolled in the Cuban War Story for several qualities: her disregard for class and social divisions; her hard work and organizing skills; her cunning and audacity; and her feminine and maternal tenderness. Celia's perceived disregard for the traditional class and social divisions, quite pronounced in small-town Oriente, proved an advantage in her recruiting efforts, particularly among the poorest sectors.[94] For example, she recruited Guillermo García, the first *campesino* to join the guerrilla. García maintained that even though "her economic situation was very good," for Celia "social distinctions didn't exist ... [S]he treated us all the same."[95]

As rebel leader Armando Hart eulogized, "In the Sierra, Celia was the heroine not only of the war, but also of work."[96] Cuban narratives credit her work as indispensable to guerrilla survival, particularly in their most vulnerable first months.[97] During her first visit to the Sierra guerrillas, on February 16, 1957, she helped put the temporary camp in order for journalist Herbert Matthews's upcoming visit, such that the ragtag group of men in torn clothing and shoes held together with wire appeared a more formidable army.[98]

She returned to Manzanillo charged with arranging passage for guerrilla volunteers.[99] Celia took over a building alongside the rice fields for this purpose, unbeknown to the absentee owner. She oversaw the camp, feeding and supplying the rebels as they awaited transfer.[100] The farm's owner arrived unexpectedly and demanded that Celia, by then a known rebel, leave. Implying dire consequences should the owner report her to authorities, Celia refused to budge.[101] Soon she had sent the fifty-three men to the Sierra, and by the end of March 1957, these reinforcements had replaced the men lost in the *Granma* landing almost four months prior.[102]

Stepping up her fundraising from bake sales, she directly targeted the wealthy, at times through veiled threats. A message to reluctant donors that Celia would visit them personally was reportedly enough to elicit a donation, as many feared association with this wanted woman.[103] For others, her threat was more direct: "Look, who are you with – Batista or us? ... I'm asking because our people might be confused and plant a bomb at your house, thinking you to be against us."[104] According to biographer Nancy Stout, in a letter to her father Celia reported, "I am encouraging us to begin to apply terrorism" to convince wealthy Cubans to give money to the rebel cause.[105]

As these examples suggest, the success of her hard work often depended on a thick skin, a cool head, and something of a hard heart – though this latter trait is passed over in official narratives.[106] In mid-April 1957, authorities conducted a house-to-house search on the block where Celia was hiding, awaiting the CBS journalists arriving to interview Fidel. She escaped with another rebel through a side window, returning once the coast was clear. But the shaken homeowners were desperate for the rebels to leave. Celia refused and simply went to bed.[107] The homeowners had dismantled the bed she was to sleep in, so she crawled into bed with their child. In the morning, she again ignored the distressed homeowners' pleas and insisted on having coffee, only leaving once she knew that the journalists had arrived. Marta Rojas recalled Celia as "profoundly kind" but notes that she could also be an "insurmountable concrete wall against which those disloyal to the Revolution and the enemies of Cuba dashed themselves to bits."[108] Indeed, Celia could be callous toward those in her way – not only avowed enemies but also rebel collaborators expressing ambivalence grounded in intense fear. However, the Cuban War Story uniformly lauds her "capacity for giving, personal selflessness, human sensitivity, and the great gentleness that only women are capable of."[109]

Many remember Celia as exceptionally well organized, with attention to the smallest details and a "tremendous capacity for paper-work."[110] Before Fidel coordinated work with Celia and other underground leaders, his two biggest actions – Moncada and the *Granma* expedition – shared a disordered bravado.[111] As one Fidel biographer put it: "Where Fidel was disorganized and chaotic, Celia was neatly efficient and calm. Where Fidel dealt expansively in grand schemes and dreams, Celia dealt with the details of life."[112] During his February 1957 visit to the Sierra, Frank became concerned about the guerrillas' lack of discipline.[113] Celia helped pen a letter to Fidel criticizing the poor quality and lack of discipline of his guerrillas. But once she transferred to the Sierra, Celia settled into the business end of the rebel army: "She ran things; it was she who tended to guerrilla 'headquarters,' to Fidel's voluminous correspondence, and to paying bills ... She became a kind of moving office, a floating bureaucracy."[114] One of Castro's principal political advisors, she was also prepared to take on menial tasks.[115]

Celia further concerned herself with human needs to a degree unmatched by male leaders: "whether a *campesina* was about to give birth, medical supplies, where the hospitals would have to be, the schools ... If a combatant had a sick relative in the *llano*, she made sure someone looked after them ... Celia was the soul of the Sierra Maestra."[116] When journalist Meneses traveled from the guerrilla camp to Havana to file a story, he carried letters from captured Batista soldiers: "In many of them Celia Sánchez had enclosed a hundred-peso note" for their families.[117] Thus, rather than grand gestures or military commands, Celia led through administering small but often meaningful acts that cumulatively contributed to the struggle for hearts and minds.

Many, such as M-26-7 leader Enzo Infante, respected Celia for her audacity and cunning. Enzo recalled upon meeting her in July 1957, he was already well versed in her brave exploits, including her escape from police custody: "Thus, the respect that one had for Celia was immense, because she had done what few men had dared to do."[118] She became well known for such exploits, her father proudly noting that Celia was no longer known as the daughter of doctor Sánchez, but rather he was known as the father of Celia Sánchez.[119]

She is celebrated in Revolutionary Cuba for her loyalty to Fidel: "[Celia] climbed the mountains of the Sierra Maestra along with Fidel – with short and hurried little steps so as not to be left behind and also to be able to alert him in time of any hazards along the way."[120] The specific nature of their relationship has long intrigued international observers, and she is often mentioned for this relationship more so than her own contributions.[121] Meneses, a photojournalist embedded with the guerrillas for several months, remarked upon Celia's "loyalty, her admiration for Fidel Castro, which I think disguised the fact that she was in love with him."[122] As Thomas-Woodard details, this is a sensitive topic within Cuba, "most often addressed at the level of rumor ... or not spoken of at all. A more common response, however, is an uncomfortable silence followed by the claim that Celia never married in order that she might fully devote herself to the needs of the Cuban people."[123] On the rare occasions she is publicly criticized outside of Cuba, this relationship is often raised: "[Celia was] 'the proverbial lion at [Fidel's] door' who also happened to be 'sharing his double bed.'"[124]

On October 17, 1957, Celia permanently transferred to the Sierra, serving as one of Fidel's main advisors while also attending to rebel needs like an ideal hostess or mother.[125] The Cuban War Story remembers her as a "mother – more than *compañera* – of each and every one of the combatants in the Sierra."[126] Guerrilla Teté Puebla explained: "She was loved by all. Those of us who were guerrilla fighters consider her the mother of the Rebel Army."[127] Enzo Infante recalled that when he arrived in the Sierra, Celia "worried whether I was cold, she provided me with more adequate clothing ... She received everyone who arrived for whatever reason, and she arranged it so that they were attended to with such kindness and their problems were resolved to the extent they could be."[128] The maternal role that she performed in the Sierra is suggested in a well-known April 1957 letter from Raúl Castro: "You have become our nearest shoulder to cry on, and for this all the weight falls on you."[129] Fidel wrote to Celia in 1957, "Even when a woman goes around the mountains with a rifle in hand, she always makes our men tidier, more decent, gentlemanly – and even braver."[130] Her femininity is often remarked upon. For example, she is often likened to or otherwise linked to flowers: "a violet in the grass" and "flower of the Sierra."[131]

Celia, then, largely escapes criticism. Her early death in 1980 partly accounts for this, but I propose that it also has to do with her social positioning and the specific version of femininity she performed. As a white, upper middle class, unmarried, middle-aged woman financially supported by a father who approved her activism, she had a rare combination of social privilege, financial means, and independence from familial demands that uniquely positioned her to commit fully to M-26-7. These attributes, along with her dual secretarial and maternal roles, also helped position her beyond moral reproach, particularly avoiding questions about feminine honor. Her organizational skills were applied in an unobtrusive, self-abnegating way, and she often took on relatively menial tasks, working in the shadows rather than threatening to steal the limelight. Her celebrated acts of courage involved nonaggressive efforts to avoid capture. As a guerrilla, she brought a femininity to the highly masculinized camps, with particular attention to attending to rebels' physical and emotional comfort in a maternal manner, which was by all accounts welcome.

Vilma, like Celia, is venerated in the Cuban War Story, yet she attracts more venomous commentary outside of official channels. A white woman in her 20s and the daughter of a lawyer for Bacardi rum, Vilma enjoyed a privileged background. As a university student, she joined Bárcena's MNR soon after Batista's coup.[132] One of the first women in Cuba to graduate with a degree in chemical engineering, in 1954 Vilma attended graduate school in the United States at the Massachusetts Institute of Technology. Returning to Cuba, she traveled through Mexico City to transport sensitive M-26-7 documents from Fidel to Frank.[133] She became Frank's assistant and driver, using her family car to transport rebel leaders.[134] Frank entrusted her with sensitive assignments, and she attended high-level meetings, which were often held at her family's house.[135]

On July 30, 1957, Batista forces gunned Frank down in the street. Half a century later, claims still circulate that Vilma was to blame.[136] Conspiracy theories have long held that Fidel double-crossed Frank to emerge as the undisputed leader, and these often point to Vilma as the underling who carried out Fidel's bidding.[137] Another theory is that, in love with Frank and embittered by his rejection, Vilma agreed to double-cross him. A critical Fidel biographer claimed Frank stopped informing Vilma of where he was hiding: "For months, Frank had been working closely not only with Celia, whom he liked, but also with Vilma Espín, whom he did not like. One of those delicately pretty but coldly self-righteous Communist 'girls,' Vilma had always taken a rigidly far-Left line within the movement, exactly the line that Frank most hated."[138] According to Frank's brother Agustín (in exile),

Vilma was a power grabber ... She had tried to become Frank's girlfriend or mistress, always with the thought of being a power behind the throne. Frank put her off, and in effect named others to be his eyes and ears. This bothered her very much. Vilma didn't know where Frank was the last week of his life. But she found out. The morning of his death she called him. Frank was angry that she had found out where he was. That afternoon he was killed.[139]

However, it is not clear how Agustín had access to details such as Vilma's intentions. Furthermore, any animosity that Frank felt toward Vilma is not reflected in the archived correspondence, including the period immediately preceding his death. For example, a July 10 letter from Frank to Vilma implies a familiar and trusting relationship: "All that you do is very well done, like always ... I am at your orders for whatever you need."[140] A few days before his death, Frank wrote to Fidel, "A big hug for one and all. Vilma sends a hug, too."[141] The formalities, at least, do not convey tension.

Bonachea and San Martín blame Vilma for lack of discipline and semi-neurotic meddling, arguing that she "indulged" in phoning Frank, possibly revealing his whereabouts to the police:[142]

It was common knowledge that an underground fighter did not make calls from private phones, or receive them except in an emergency. According to Vilma, she called Frank in order to find out "Why you have not called me? What is it that has happened?" Nothing could have been more trivial at this moment in País' life than to explain to Vilma the obvious reasons for his silence, particularly when the police ... had all private conversations wiretapped. Vilma, in her explanation of the events, says Frank called her twice, something which Frank's excellent conspiratorial habits leave open to debate.[143]

In Vilma's version of events, she was worried, not having seen Frank in ten days.[144] He moved often to avoid capture, and from his new safe house, according to Vilma, he called her several times.[145] About ten minutes after his last call, she heard gunfire. A telephone operator connected Vilma to police lines, and in this way, she learned of Frank's death.[146]

In the most detailed examination of Frank's death, Castro critic José Álvarez does not fault Vilma for carelessness. Since Frank used an untraceable phone and had his calls screened, he must have accepted Vilma's call or called Vilma himself.[147] Interestingly, Álvarez still portrays Vilma as an ambitious power-grabber based on her subsequent actions: "The power had passed to the Sierra, and it is there where Espín wanted to be. To be even more secure, she later marries the chief of the [Second] Front."[148]

Given the tenuous evidence, the sustained attention to Vilma's possible role in Frank's death is notable. The narratives draw from familiar gendered tropes: a woman scorned, a scheming woman as the power behind the throne, and feminine incompetence. By way of partial explanation, Celia and Vilma performed different versions of femininity. Celia symbolized a revolutionary and often maternal self-abnegation, having forgone marriage and family to serve as "mother of the Rebel Army" and later "sister and mother to all soldiers."[149] She died of cancer in 1980 at the age of fifty-nine, assuming a martyr-like status that placed her further beyond reproach. In contrast, Vilma was an urban, well-traveled woman with a university degree in a masculine field and graduate work in the United States, who spoke fluent English, and did not avoid the spotlight. Though admirable in a man, such traits are typically threatening in a woman and thus subvert her feminine status. After Batista fled, Vilma married Raúl Castro, took a high-profile post directing the Cuban Women's Federation, and in that role forcefully championed an increasingly communist party line. In sum, she did not perform Celia's self-abnegating, maternal version of revolutionary femininity so much as an apparatchik version, emerging as a cold, ambitious, ideological, and ultimately unsympathetic feminine figure to many.

To summarize, analysis of the dominant representations of women leaders provides insight into idealized femininity during the insurrection, which in turn informed post-1958 revolutionary Cuba. As Thomas-Woodard argues, saint-like Celia has been portrayed in a didactic manner – a lesson in idealized revolutionary femininity.[150] Haydée is often described in similar terms – modest and self-abnegating – and receives similar admiration at home and abroad. In contrast, Vilma and Melba were university-educated and more publicly assertive women who have received much less favorable treatment outside of official channels. The Cuban War Story becomes nearly silent about Melba, a woman of color, after Moncada. As a heroine of the revolution, she is venerated in the dominant discourse, yet commentary from the exile community hints at the heightened burden posed by the intersection of racism and sexism.

Notes

1. The twenty-five executive members were Haydée Santamaría, Vilma Espín, Melba Hernández, Celia Sánchez, Gloria Cuadras, María Antonia Figueroa, Fidel Castro, Frank País, Armando Hart, Faustino Pérez, Enrique Oltusky, Lester Rodríguez, Pedro Miret, Gustavo Arcos, Enrique Hart, Carlos Franqui, David Salvador, Jesús Montané, René de los Santos, José ("Pepe") Suárez, Luis Benito, Antonio ("Ñico") López, Gustavo ("Machaco") Ameijeiras, Mario Hidalgo, and Marcelo Fernández (Bonachea and San Martín 1974, 375 n13).

2. For excellent examples of intersectional approaches to revolutionary Cuba, see Roland (2006, 2011); Sawyer (2000, 2006); Guerra (2012); Fernandes (2006).
3. Díaz Vallina et al. (1994).
4. Fox (1973); Lobao Reif (1986); Pérez-Stable (1987); Casal (1987, 37). See also Rosendahl (1998, 58–9).
5. Rosendahl (1998, 59); Casal (1987, 37). See also Díaz Vallina (2001, 6); Fox (1973, 284).
6. Randall (2015, 16).
7. Casal (1987, 35–6).
8. Ibid., 36.
9. See, for example, Viñelas (1969, 9); Lumsden (1996, 32, 37–8); Casal (1987, 39).
10. Casal (1987, 38).
11. Randall (2015, 39); Cámara Betancourt (2000); Kutzinski (1993).
12. Bunck (1994, 91). See also Casal (1987, 34); Pérez-Stable (1987, 53).
13. Pérez-Stable (1987, 53–4).
14. Ibid., 53.
15. Casal (1987, 39); Scott (1988, 36).
16. Lumsden (1996, 53).
17. Casal (1987, 39); Bunck (1994, 91); Rosendahl (1998, 62).
18. Pelayo in Castro Porta (1990, 55).
19. Lumsden (1996, 29).
20. Casal (1987, 42). Rebel combatants nicknamed Raúl Castro "la China roja," translated as both Red (Communist) China and Chinese woman (Bardach 2009, 213). The nickname referenced Raúl's (vaguely) Asian features, long hair, and rumors that he was gay.
21. Macaulay (1970, 55).
22. Casal (1987, 42); see also Fox (1973).
23. Fox (1973, 283–4); Rosendahl (1998, 61).
24. Rosendahl (1998, 62); Lumsden (1996, 37).
25. Domínguez (1976, 280).
26. Minority Rights Group International (2015).
27. Moore (2008); De la Fuente (1998, 2001). See also Sawyer (2000, 2006); Roland (2006, 2011).
28. De la Fuente (2001, 251). A white rebel man told Macaulay (1970, 29) in 1958: "The Negroes here are pimps and *marijuaneros*. They flock to join Batista's army. *Los negros* are not revolutionaries ... They abandoned their wives and children; how could you expect them to be loyal to the Revolution?" However, Macaulay (1970, 35) notes of his own guerrilla unit: "among fewer than two dozen in this camp, three were black and two were mulatto."
29. García-Pérez (1999).
30. De la Fuente (2001, 252). Manifesto No. 1 to the People of Cuba, dated August 1955, called for an end to racial discrimination. See Moore (2008) for discussion of M-26-7's token use of Afro-Cuban guerrilla leader Juan Almeida in post-insurrection Cuba.

31. Domínguez (1976, 279); Moore (2008, 55).
32. De la Fuente (2001, 250–1).
33. Teté Puebla interview in Waters (2003, 30).
34. Moore (2008, 54, 60). De la Fuente (2001) describes Batista as "of dubious whiteness" (135), noting his race "was always a contested issue" (136). Many Afro-Cubans "expect[ed] a lot from Batista" owing to an assumed racial tie (De la Fuente 2001, 136). Moore (2008, 54) recalls his Afro-Cuban community referred to Batista as *El Mulatón* (the Big Mulatto).
35. De la Fuente (2001, 253).
36. Ibid.
37. Moore (2008, 55).
38. Ibid., 60. Translation mine.
39. De la Fuente (2001, 253).
40. Moore (2008, 64); De la Fuente (2001, 253).
41. Moore (2008, 54, 55).
42. Ibid., 57.
43. Pérez (2013, 185).
44. Ibid.
45. For País see, for example, Eugenia San Miguel interview, Gladys Castaño, "Lo que habia en él de grande y prometedor," *Mujeres* July 1982, 14–15; Espín (1975).
46. Espín (1975).
47. Díaz Vallina et al. (1994, 29–30). The study included eighty interviews with women rebels.
48. Lobao Reif (1986, 150); Shayne (2004, 131, 164).
49. Díaz Vallina et al. (1994); Chase (2010). Women's activism sometimes endangered male family members, as authorities turned on men either as the responsible party for women's suspected transgressions or at least convenient proxies. Security forces imprisoned teenage Fe Isabel Dovale in Bayamo in June 1958, and after two weeks of physical and psychological abuse, they released her but turned their aggression against her father and brother, imprisoning both (Magaly Sánchez, "Una mujer de su tiempo," *Mujeres* October 1979, 52–5). Similarly, police detained Hilda Benítez, a young rebel in Guantánamo, in July 1958 for over two months (Daisy Martín, "Enfermeras en el Segundo Frente," *Mujeres* November 1976, 48–50). Her family bribed police for her release, and she fled to the Sierra. Police responded by imprisoning her father and brother for three months. Family efforts to block daughters more so than sons from activism drew from the same gender ideology by which young men were seen by police as threats and thus targeted, often without provocation or evidence. In contrast, authorities often treated young women as minors, innocents led astray. They pursued, detained, and assaulted them, but not on a par with men. The dynamics discussed in this chapter suggest that women of color as well as poor and working-class white women would receive less protection from regime violence than white middle- and upper-class women.
50. March (2012, 24).
51. Randall (2015, 39).

52. Chapter 10 discusses discrimination against women in the guerrilla camps.
53. Maruja Iglesias in Castro Porta (1990, 74–5).
54. País to Castro, July 17, 1957, Princeton University Latin American Pamphlet Collection. Among other accusations, René Rodríguez spent $13,110.50 in two months (approximately US $113,000 in 2017, adjusted for inflation) on bombs, operating primarily on his own authority. René had also threatened to kill the M-26-7 treasurer if he did not release more money.
55. País to Castro, July 17, 1957, Princeton University Latin American Pamphlet Collection. René's challenge to Haydée's leadership is not well known. Franqui (1980, 207) includes the letter but excised this section. René became a high-ranking Cuban official, figuring prominently in the 1959 executions of Batistianos. In 1982, Rodríguez and Haydée's brother Aldo Santamaría were indicted *in absentia* by the United States for narco-trafficking.
56. País to Castro, July 17, 1957, Princeton University Latin American Pamphlet Collection.
57. Fuego Rodríguez interview, Lyn Smith Cuba Collection.
58. Ibid.
59. Lobao Reif (1986, 147–8).
60. Cuba's 1950–55 fertility rate was 4.15 children per woman aged 15–49 (United Nations Department of Economic and Social Affairs 2015). Cuban mothers' average age at childbirth in 1950–55 was 28.09. Cuban women's fertility rates were highest in their 20s, declining significantly in their 30s, with one of Latin America's lowest fertility rates for ages 15–19.
61. Goldstein (2001, 266–7). See also Bayard de Volo and Hall (2015): "masculine ideals [include] toughness, strength, bravery, controlled aggression, and mastery over emotions. Conversely, characteristics broadly identified as feminine [include] tenderness, weakness, fear, passivity, and emotionalism" (874).
62. Fuego Rodríguez interview, Lyn Smith Cuba Collection.
63. Ibid. Suárez Gayol died with Che in Bolivia.
64. Ibid.
65. See Goldstein (2001) for comparative analysis of gendered narratives and roles in war.
66. Espín (1975).
67. País to Castro, July 17, 1957, Princeton University Latin American Pamphlet Collection. See also Frank País to Vilma Espín, July 10, 1957, Princeton University Latin American Pamphlet Collection.
68. País to Castro, July 17, 1957, Princeton University Latin American Pamphlet Collection.
69. While rebel propaganda drew sharp contrasts between morally superior rebels and debased Batista forces, private rebel correspondence shows the contrast was sometimes difficult to sustain. In a July 1957 letter to Vilma, Frank wrote bitterly of *llano* rebel Julio Pérez, whom he had sent into the Sierra as a last option to avoid execution, with strict instructions that Pérez not return to the *llano*, even if ill: "He was involved in the 'loss' of some money... And now I have learned of his lack of morals in taking advantage (along with a few others) of the hospitality of some homes to seduce

the daughters or the women of the house. The things they have done are so unworthy of a revolutionary" (País to Espín, July 10, 1957, Princeton University Latin American Pamphlet Collection).

70. País to Castro, July 17, 1957, Princeton University Latin American Pamphlet Collection.

71. Coltman (2003, 97).

72. Castro to Luis Conte, July 17, 1954, Bardach and Conte Agüero (2007, 32–3).

73. Castro to Conte, July 31, 1954, in Bardach and Conte Agüero (2007, 35).

74. After the *Granma* left port without her, Melba returned to Cuba in 1957, and in 1958, she joined the Third Front Mario Muñoz in the Sierra.

75. De la Cova (2007, 34). Antonio de la Cova is a Cuban-American anti-Castro historian. Manuel Suardíaz was a Moncada rebel until the car transporting him to the attack had a flat tire. Suardíaz was imprisoned for nine years after he split with Castro, then went into exile.

76. Randall (2015, 11).

77. Manuel Suardíaz interview, Antonio de la Cova Latinamericanstudies. org Archive. See also Emilio Ochoa interview, Antonio de la Cova Latinamericanstudies.org Archive: "Melba is very racist. *In what sense?* Well, she doesn't recognize that she is half *mulata*."

78. See Roland (2011); Kutzinski (1993).

79. Roland (2011).

80. País to Espín, July 10, 1957, Princeton University Latin American Pamphlet Collection. Frank's letter possibly exhibits the strain of heightened persecution. His brother was killed a month earlier.

81. Meneses (1966, 15).

82. Ibid., 73. Celia and Vilma's authority was also diminished when they were described in relation to male leaders – as Fidel's secretary and Raúl's fiancée, respectively. See, for example, Dorschner and Fabricio (1980, 34, 302). Che, upon meeting Vilma in the Sierra, assumed her to be Frank's sister (Guevara 2013, 74).

83. Díaz Vallina et al. (1994, 25). The United Nations defines youth as fifteen to twenty-four years of age. In revolutionary Cuba, the definition of youth extends to the age of thirty and the Young Communists Union (UJC) is open to people between the ages of fifteen and thirty. See Luke (2012, 128).

84. Dubois (1959, 47); Szulc (1986, 291–2). Fidel Castro, recalling Moncada, described Haydée as "just a young thing," though he was four years her junior (Castro 2008, 122).

85. Casal (1987, 35–6).

86. Melba, for example, became less active after she married. However, Haydée's marriage to Armando Hart in 1956 did not seem to lessen her activism. Neither Melba nor Haydée had children during the insurrection. Vilma married Raúl Castro soon after Batista fled, and Celia never married.

87. Haydée was also white, with parents from Spain. Her family had a fairly good economic situation – a car and a relatively large home by local standards (Randall 2015, 36, 41).

88. With the exception of Huber Matos (born in 1918), Celia (born 1920) was older than leaders Juan Almeida (born 1927), Ché Guevara (born 1928), Armando Hart (born 1930), Camilo Cienfuegos (born 1932), and Frank País (born 1934).
89. Stout (2013, 128). The Sánchez family owned three farms ranging from roughly 400 to 2,000 acres each (Thomas-Woodard 2003, 175).
90. Thomas-Woodard (2003, 156, 161).
91. Interview originally published in *Granma* April 23, 1990; cited in Katia Siberia García, "Celia y el grupo de apoyo," *Granma* December 28, 2006, 1. See also Manuel Echevarría Díaz interview in Chirino, *Verde Olivo* January 10, 1985, 41; Ramón Sánchez, "Celia en el recuerdo: Una mujer excepcional," *Granma* January 11, 1990, 4.
92. Sánchez (1990, 4).
93. Chirino (1985, 41).
94. Hart (2004, 162); Geyer (1991, 165).
95. Lilian Chirino, "Celia me abrió el camino para incorporarme a la lucha," *Mujeres* May 1985, 7.
96. Thomas-Woodard (2003, 160). Armando Hart, "Transformemos el dolor que nos embargo en acicate y estímulo para cumplir nuestros deberes," *Verde Olivo* January 20, 1980, 8–13.
97. See, for example, Hart (2004, 164–5); Sweig (2002, 40); Acosta, *Verde Olivo* March 6, 1986, 36–9; Díaz Hurtado, *Verde Olivo* February 27, 1986, 24–7; Chirino (1985, 42).
98. DePalma (2006, 83); Hart (2004, 146).
99. Álvarez Tabío 1996 (1990); Szulc (1986, 405). See also Stout (2013, 156–63).
100. Álvarez Tabío 1996 (1990). See also Hart (2004, 162–3); Stout (2013, 157–61).
101. Álvarez Tabío 1996 (1990).
102. Ibid.; Stout (2013, 161).
103. Stout (2013, 131).
104. Chirino (1985, 41).
105. Stout (2013, 234).
106. Álvarez Tabío 1996 (1990).
107. Stout (2013, 174–5).
108. Thomas-Woodard (2003, 162).
109. Hart (2004, 163).
110. Meneses (1966, 54).
111. See Stout (2013, 62–72) for details on Celia and Frank's extensive preparations for the *Granma* landing.
112. Geyer (1991, 165); see also Stout (2013). For exceptions, see Sweig (2002, 40–1, 45–6); Stout (2013, 177).
113. Guevara (1971, 77); Espín (1975). See also Stout (2013, 150–1).
114. Geyer (1991, 165). Celia also oversaw the guerrilla camps at La Plata once Che left for Las Villas in late August 1958 ("Lilia Rielo" interview, *Bohemia* July 28, 1967, 14–17).

115. No author, "Celia, cabal imagen del pueblo" *Granma* January 11, 1982, 2; Hart (2004, 327); Dubois (1959, 353–4). Foreign journalists referred to both Vilma and Celia as secretaries. See Dubois (1959, 272); Meneses (1966, 55). Celia, indeed, often acted as Fidel's personal assistant. See, for example, Celia's letter to Teté Puebla requesting cigars for Fidel and Che; meanwhile, she mentions in passing that they have not eaten in two days (Castro 2011, 222, 466–7).

116. Puebla interview in Báez (1996, 415–16).

117. Meneses (1966, 55).

118. Enzo Infante, in Suárez Suárez and Puig Corral (2010, 90).

119. Siberia García (2006).

120. Eliseo Alberto, "La más hermosa y autoctona flor de la Revolución" *Verde Olivo* January 20, 1980, 4.

121. See Geyer (1991, 166). See also Castañeda (1997, 115) and Stout (2013, 236–41) for intriguing discussion of correspondence between Celia and Fidel.

122. Meneses (1966, 54); Geyer (1991, 167).

123. Thomas-Woodard (2003, 157).

124. Ibid., citing Anderson (1997, 235, 344).

125. Chirino (1985, 43); Stout (2013, 245).

126. No author (1982, 2).

127. Waters (2003, 34).

128. Enzo Infante, in Suárez Suárez and Puig Corral (2010, 90). See also Lester Rodríguez in Chirino (1985, 42).

129. No author (1982, 2); Thomas-Woodard (2003, 163, 175n10); Stout (2013, 190).

130. Stout (2013, 190).

131. El Indio Nabori poem "Pido permiso a la muerte," *Granma* January 12, 1980, 4; Ana Núñez Machín poem "De la patria y de Fidel," *Mujeres* March 1984, 50–1. CBS journalist Robert Taber emphasized the mariposa flowers that Celia wore, in his special report that aired May 18, 1957 (Stout 2013, 182–3).

132. Espín (1975); Szulc (1986, 229); Franqui (1980, 63–4).

133. Santamaría (2003b, 24).

134. Espín (1975); Santamaría (2003b, 24).

135. Hart (2004, 136–7); Espín (1975).

136. For example, see Phil Davison, "Vilma Espin Guillois: Hero of the Cuban revolution who became a powerful 'first lady' and advocate for women's rights," *The Independent* (UK), June 20, 2007: "After País was [killed]... there were rumours that Espín, one of only a few people who knew his hiding place, had sold him out. The theory, prevalent among anti-Castro exiles in Miami, was that Fidel Castro resented País's popularity and asked her to betray him. There was never any evidence to back such a theory."

137. See Álvarez (2009, 251); Sweig (2002, 42–6); Farber (2006, 67).

138. Geyer (1991, 174).

139. Ibid.

140. Letter from Frank País (David) to Vilma Espín (Norma), July 10, 1957, 3, 5, Princeton University Latin American Pamphlet Collection.
141. Franqui (1980, 213).
142. Bonachea and San Martín (1974, 146; 377n42). Jorge Domínguez (1975, 57) describes Bonachea and San Martín's effort to implicate Vilma as "questionable."
143. A former Santiago telephone operator told Bonachea and San Martín that after Vilma made this call, Colonel Cañizares gave the order to surround the entire block where Frank was hiding (Bonachea and San Martín 1974, 146, 377n42, 378n43).
144. Franqui (1980, 214); Hart (2004, 185–8).
145. Espín (1975).
146. Franqui (1980, 214); Hart (2004, 185–8).
147. Álvarez (2009, 241).
148. Ibid., 251.
149. Teté Puebla, quoted in Waters (2003, 34); Nancy Robinson Calvet, "Y aquí, en el corazon del pueblo," *Granma* January 13, 1980, 5.
150. Thomas-Woodard (2003).

CHAPTER 6

War Stories Celebrated and Silenced

Tactical Femininity, Bombing, and Sexual Assault in the Urban Underground

Marta Fuego Rodríguez, who had worked in the tobacco fields from a young age, became the sole wage earner for her family at the age of fourteen, when her father died and her mother retreated into mental illness. Several years later, in 1955, while still working, she gained admittance to a teaching college, and it was there that leaders of the university federation of teachers recruited her into M-26-7:

I transported weapons, bullets. At the time, the very wide skirts were worn, with a lot of starch. And they made bags out of thick cloth that we put on like a belt under the skirt, and inside we put weapons, bullets, documents, and also live phosphorous for the sabotage they did. [The phosphorous] we put inside a jar of facial cream, because it had to be within a liquid; if it was in the air and made contact with a spark, it would explode ... We took a tube of toothpaste and would wrap a document in nylon wrap and put it inside the tube and close the tube again. If the police searched us, we would just have creams and toothpaste.[1]

Motivated by the injustices and the inequality she observed around her, Marta was highly dedicated: "we were dying a little bit each day, and so it didn't matter to die [in the rebel underground]. And I told them I wanted to join the organization because my life was a struggle."[2] However, rebel men limited her contributions because she was a woman, assigning her less dangerous tasks:

I am sure they didn't see me as a comrade. They saw me as someone who could help. How could I help? Lending my house so they could sleep there, delivering a message, hiding a person in my house. They saw me in that way. But doing sabotage, transferring weapons, explosives, confronting a situation, or suffering and torture – they didn't see me that way. Confronting or murdering a *guardia* – no they didn't see me [doing that]. They saw me as a delicate and sweet woman.[3]

Though she did come to more dangerous missions such as sabotage and smuggling weapons, as her statement suggests, those contributions were at once more valued and less compatible with idealized femininity.

Marta's account encapsulates the various themes and goals of this chapter. Thematically, we find women's rank and file *llano* (urban) underground work to rely heavily on feminine norms, to be risky and require courage, to be important and yet discounted as "help." In examining such experiences and contributions, this chapter both engages with and looks beyond the post-1958 Cuban state's official historical narrative, the Cuban War Story. In addition to the important empirical details concerning women's experiences in the urban underground, this focus also enhances our understanding of how femininity operates in armed insurrection.[4] I argue that idealized femininity was a successful tactic deployed by women rebels in performing risky logistical work.[5] When rank and file women are acknowledged in the Cuban War Story, it is often through these contributions. Women's engagement in the hyper-masculine domain of warfare potentially challenged gender inequalities. Yet in emphasizing women rebels' deployment of idealized femininity to the exclusion of other contributions and experiences in the rebel underground, traditional gender relations were reinforced as much as challenged. The Cuban War Story left women's feminine default setting relatively undisturbed, signified by beauty products, full skirts, and especially pregnancy and motherhood, which in turn celebrated women as delicate, passive, innocent, and domestic.

Yet all rank and file women's contributions in the *llano* underground did not operate in this way. By working with documentary sources outside of or preexisting the construction of the Cuban War Story, I identify women's underground work and experiences that have been downplayed or omitted from the popular narrative: bombers and victims of sexual assault. Such cases disrupt traditional femininity by their association with particular forms of violence and sexuality. In planting bombs, women deployed traditional femininity to escape the notice of authorities; however, the direct hand they had in violence, including the danger posed to bystanders, belied gender stereotypes of women as peaceful, virtuous, and restrained.[6] Furthermore, though some *llano* rebel women spoke publicly about surviving sexual assault inflicted by Batista forces, the post-1958 revolutionary state's silence on this gendered form of torture in effect reinforced the sexualized shame attached to victims while also obscuring the risks rebel women faced in the underground.[7]

The writings of Cuban independence hero José Martí, often referenced in rebel narratives, help to situate this examination of femininity in the Cuban context. Martí declared popular insurrections to be weak when they do not enlist "the hearts of women," but when "cultured and virtuous" women, "timid and quiet in nature," lend active support, the struggle is invincible.[8] Thus, Teresa Prados-Torreira explains, "female virtue was the best proof of the cause's worthiness."[9] There is a certain gendered logic operating here, as (white, upper-class) women, otherwise insulated from the harsh realities of the real world, on occasion are able to perceive innocent truths.[10] Cuba was an heir to the Western tradition that links women to peace and men to war. But, as this gender logic goes, when a cause is so just and a regime so outrageously vile that the necessity for action penetrates even through "cultured and virtuous" women's socially sanctioned worldly innocence that they too rise up, this constitutes the ultimate legitimation for the taking up of arms.

This Martí quote is a familiar one in post-1958 state rhetoric, and the logic extends to the 1950s Cuban War Story: when "even the women" lent their support, the struggle was just and victory assured.[11] Yet such paradigmatic equations marginalized women rebels whose virtuous feminine nature was in question. In such cases, rebel history was modified to sustain rebel femininity as both courageous and virtuous by silencing instances of devalued femininity.

I will first detail censorship and repression in 1957–58 to set the context for women's clandestine work in the *llano*. As per the common understanding at the time, for rebels the *llano* was more dangerous than the guerrilla camps. I then turn to the privileged narratives and silences outlined above to explore why femininity was an effective war tactic, how it was deployed, and why some women using feminine tactics were acknowledged and celebrated while others were not. These selective celebrations and silences help explain how women's participation in the highly masculinized practice of war left gender inequalities intact.

BATISTA CENSORSHIP AND REPRESSION

Through censorship, financial control, and repression, the regime exerted powerful influence over the press, blocking the Cuban public's access to independent sources of information on the insurrection and government repression.[12] With such censorship, plus the post-1958 government narrative privileging the Sierra guerrilla struggle, details of repression against *llano* rank and file rebels and civilians are relatively scarce, clustered in published or archived interviews and secondary sources. Confidential US embassy reports and foreign media also offer some frank assessments of regime brutality. For example, the embassy reported in February 1958, "As a daily occurrence bodies of young men are found hanged or lying along the roadside with as many as 40 bullet holes."[13] A US State Department official confirmed the targeting of young men: "If an Army officer or soldier is killed, three, four or more youths are found shot to death the next morning."[14] Foreign journalists, listening to police radio, heard the National Police chief order that no prisoners were to be taken alive in a roundup of suspects.[15] Challenging the regime's façade of normalcy, rebel bombs routinely exploded in the cities, sending a message of popular dissent.

In this atmosphere of repression, *llano* rebels and collaborators concluded that rebels were safer in the Sierra.[16] The available evidence generally supports this.[17] Civilians in both the Sierra and *llano* often bore the brunt of retaliation by frustrated troops unable to locate rebels. For example, when guerrillas killed a Batista colonel, the military retaliated by executing eight young men from the nearby town.[18] In another reported instance, fourteen *campesinos* were dragged from their homes and hanged in retribution for a rebel highway ambush.[19] Batista forces also cleared out small towns near the Sierra, burning homes, confiscating land, and setting up roadblocks to test people for gunpowder residue, shooting those who tested positive.[20]   *retaliation*

In cities, the military and police staged the bodies of their victims: "Bodies of boys and men were found hanging from trees or lampposts or lying lifeless in automobiles with grenades on their persons, to convey the impression that they had been caught in terrorist acts."[21] In one alarming case, a doctor arranged a taxi to a medical clinic for a young man partially paralyzed after being shot in the back.[22] The military intercepted the taxi, and the young man, doctor, and taxi driver were all later found dead, having been beaten and shot.[23] In the military counterattack to the 1957 Cienfuegos Navy uprising, planes strafed and bombed city streets, "No one ever knew how many people were killed. The army, in mopping up operations, went into houses and took out any young man they could find and shot him."[24] It then used bulldozers to dig ditches into which the dead were dumped. A witness counted fifty-two bodies in one mass grave.[25] In sum, government repression in 1957–58 was generalized and civilians often bore the brunt as collateral damage.

repression

When the government targeted its violence, it aimed primarily at young men. Díaz Vallina notes, "the machismo of the forces of oppression, who considered women to be insignificant, weak and useless, [thus] concentrated on men in their search for revolutionaries."[26] The targeting of men, often asserted in media and rebel reports, is supported by a review of lists of the dead compiled by anti-Batista activists. For example, a group of "mothers, wives, daughters, and relatives of the victims" of the regime submitted a document to the Supreme Court listing people killed in the conflict between February 13, 1953 and June 19, 1957.[27] There were no women listed among the 226 names.[28]

A US Consulate official described the Santiago office as "accosted daily by frantic parents who want to get their youngsters to the United States because the local authorities are looking for them or else think that they are."[29] Once "burned" (*quemado* – their cover was blown), rebels typically sought safety through exile or the Sierra. The Sierra was "exile with dignity," where Fidel "had created a sanctuary for the urban cadres, a place where they could continue the struggle rather than perish in the cities."[30] Vilma Espín explained: "we were rewarded for our work [in the *llano*] with trips to the Sierra; when one of us was exhausted, he or she was given a few days' vacation up there."[31] She expanded on the psychological toll of the *llano* struggle: "[It] was a very high-pressure, very violent life. It destroyed people, made *los muchachos* very nervous; if someone suddenly arrived or brakes screeched, they jumped ... [I]n the Sierra, ... one thinks: 'Well, if they kill me, I will die in combat,' but [in the city] you feel like a hunted animal."[32] Veteran US war correspondent Dickey Chapelle described guerrillas as terror victims, who "believed they would be killed if they went back to their homes [in the *llano*]."[33] Indeed, some families sent their adolescent and adult children to the guerrilla camps to escape. Carmen Miera recalled, "I took the youngest one, 14 years old, up myself, and that day I could sleep peacefully because if they killed them, it would be with a bullet, in combat, but they no longer ran the risk of being tortured to death by Batista's thugs."[34]

M-26-7 rebel narratives include a hierarchy of better and worse deaths, with a preference to die fighting in the Sierra rather than be hunted down like prey in the city. For example, Fidel compared René Ramos's death favorably to those killed in the *llano*: "[René] did not fall defenseless to the assassin's bullet, he died with weapon in hand on the battlefield, and this is a consolation in the midst of the sorrow."[35]

As this suggests, there was also the allure of guerrilla life. A US embassy official reported M-26-7 in early 1958 Santiago to be "anything and everything to anyone and everyone," and described Fidel as a "Pied Piper" to youth.[36] Fidel's guerrillas particularly attracted young men, who also faced greater danger in the *llano*, given authorities' gendered notions of guilt and innocence.[37] There are many recorded instances in which authorities did not hold women rebels to the same level of scrutiny as they did men.[38] The clandestine nature of the work makes it impossible to determine the number of *llano* rebel women.[39] But women figured more prominently in the *llano* than the Sierra, with more responsibility and command.[40]

This gendered reading of the *llano* insurrection sheds new and critical light on the dominant Cuban War Story's elevation of the Sierra guerrilla struggle.[41] Many rebels sought transfer to the guerrillas as a refuge from the trauma and persecution in the *llano*, which afflicted men more so than women. Rebels also aspired to the guerrilla struggle for the opportunity to confront the enemy directly "with gun in hand" – a privilege generally reserved for men. In sum, because women were relatively less persecuted than men and because combat was gendered masculine, a higher proportion of women rebels were in the arguably more dangerous but less valorized *llano* struggle.

In what follows, I explore gender tactics and the rebel tasks that women, particularly the rank and file, performed in the *llano*. Recognizing the politicized nature of the Cuban War Story from which many of these revolutionary narratives are culled, I include narratives of the insurrection that were later disfavored.

GENDER TACTICS, MILITARY LOGISTICS, AND FEMINIZED LABOR

Though most women did not work outside the home, many urban rank and file women rebels and collaborators did. Two feminized jobs stand out: teachers and telephone operators. The list of teachers turned rebels includes Aida Pelayo, Leocadia Araújo, Clara Lull, Margot Machado, Esterlina Milanés, Asela de los Santos, and Aleida March. Indeed, a Cuban study of women combatants found teachers to be the third largest occupational category at 12.4 percent, behind students (24.4 percent), and "no occupation" (20.6 percent).[42] Considered a respectable job for women, teaching was one of the few that Cuban women held in large numbers.[43] Many women teachers report becoming radicalized as they were exposed to their teenage students' politics as well as the repression targeting young men. Some were also politicized through their membership in teachers' organizations.

Telephone operators, primarily women, also played important roles in the underground. Thanks to these operators, Santiago M-26-7 could make untraceable, unmonitored calls.[44] Rosita Casán, a Santiago telephone operator, explained: "We knew where the *compañeros* in hiding were, so whenever the military would monitor the phones, we had to warn them immediately."[45] They devised a system of passwords and countersigns. For example, a rebel would call and ask about Aunt Dora. If Aunt Dora was doing very well, that indicated the lines were free. But if she was doing poorly, the caller knew that the military was monitoring communications.

Operators also listened in on police and military calls and even arranged for rebels to eavesdrop. Aleida Fernández Chardiet, active in the student movement at the University of Havana, became an international operator when the university closed in 1957.[46] She routed a compromising conversation between Batista and US officials to a radio station, which then broadcast it.[47] Rebels sometimes asked operators to spy for specific information. In January 1958, rebels called Rosita for information on several captured rebels, and she later confirmed that Armando Hart and three others were being held. The following day, Rosita and Carlos Amat listened as one general ordered another to kill the captured rebels, "Get moving and do it fast! ... These degenerates mobilize quickly and they mustn't learn of this."[48] Using Rosita's secret phone line to the rebel headquarters, the rebels mobilized quickly to seize a radio station and broadcast news of the detention, urging the public to remain alert and prepare to protest.[49] The operators then heard the military leaders discuss this broadcast: "Imbecile! You've wasted a lot of time! Now there's nothing you can do."[50]

Most women were assigned to rebel logistics, work supporting the maintenance and transport of armed forces, including weapons transport, fundraising, nursing, supply acquisition, sabotage, uniform-making, and message delivery. Seemingly mundane and less consequential compared to combat, it receives less attention and status in both the Cuban War Story and scholarly analysis, though it is the primary way that women's contributions are celebrated. Many rebel women engaged in traditionally feminine work, such as sewing, which might seem peripheral to warfare. But in addition to aiding in camouflage capability and serving to distinguish rebels from others, the rebel *verde olivo* (olive green) uniforms and black armbands sewn by women impacted positively on combatants' morale. Che wrote of his early days in the Sierra, "It moved us greatly to receive clothes which had initials embroidered on to them by the girls of Manzanillo."[51] In early 1957, women sewed life-sized dummies, 200 of which appeared early one morning, hanging from electrical posts with a sign reading, "This is how informers die."[52] This type of work was relatively safe from the regime's reach and securely within gender norms.

M-26-7 treasurers were often women, and movement funds were entrusted to women. Micaela Riera Oquendo, M-26-7 treasurer in Manzanillo, excelled at collecting funds, often in collaboration with Celia. When Fidel and other M-26-7 members were detained in Mexico in 1956 and most of the weapons for the *Granma* expedition were confiscated, Melba Hernández and María Antonia Figueroa, M-26-7 treasurer for Oriente, were sent to collect Manzanillo funds for legal fees and more weapons.[53] In summer 1958, Pastorita Núñez was entrusted to collect war taxes from the sugar mills, which she transferred to Cuban bank accounts overseen by María Ruiz and to those Haydée Santamaría controlled in Miami.[54]

A combination of factors explains the association of women rebels and finance. Fundraising and bookkeeping fit more readily with women's gender roles as compared to more directly militarized roles. This would be especially true for educated, middle-aged women, as oversight of funds was a position of authority and trust likely viewed as more befitting these women rebels as compared to low-skill feminine jobs or armed conflict.

Urban women also ran rebel safe houses, and the movement habitually met in the middle-class homes of trusted women. Typically, women spent much more time at home than their male counterparts, and these trusted supporters performed feminized tasks as hostesses, which included following security protocol as well as housekeeping and ensuring the comfort of guests.[55] Additionally, women were better able to stay under the radar of the authorities and neighbors, and thus maintain a safe house less likely to be under surveillance or raided.

Melba Hernández's mother Elena stands out as an example. Melba's parents were rebels of the 1930s generation who supported Melba by opening their apartment to the rebels.[56] There, Elena oversaw torchmaking for the 1953 March of the Torches. Soon after, she supervised Delia Terry, Dolores Pérez, Elda Pérez, and Naty Revuelta in preparing supplies and uniforms for the Moncada attack, which they stored in the apartment.[57] On July 24, 1953, the apartment hosted the rebels' final Havana meeting before they left for the Moncada assault.[58] Other women, such as Rosita Mier, Rosaura Ararás, and Naty's mother also oversaw similar use of their homes.[59] This behind-the-scenes work is another vital contribution of women in insurrectionary contexts. In the Cuban case, it was a common way that women – often middle-aged and older women, and especially single women – contributed to the cause.

Women rebels sometimes reverted to gendered displays of hospitality or domesticity to throw authorities off-track. Haydée remembered hiding in a safe house with Vilma when police arrived. While Vilma escaped over the roof with sensitive documents, Haydée stayed behind to receive them: "'Would you like some coffee?' I gave them coffee. 'Would you like a drink?' I gave them drinks. Then they began the search, and I accompanied them through all the rooms."[60] The police never suspected they were in a rebel hideout.

Similarly, middle-aged and older women appealed to filial sympathies in younger soldiers as a gender tactic. In 1958, M-26-7 sent "Tía Angelita" Montes de Oca, in her mid-40s, to Miami to transport weapons back to Cuba. On her return, she saw airport authorities searching all passengers. She approached a soldier, "*Ay, mi hijo* [my son], let me sit down a bit, I'm feeling awful."[61] He accommodated her, and she tearfully explained that she was returning from Miami in a hurry to see a dying relative, and tragically, this search was delaying her. The sympathetic soldier escorted her out the door without a search and even helped her find transportation.

Women rebels often accompanied men because, according to Vilma, "a couple always awakens fewer suspicions than a group or a single person."[62] She drove *llano* leader Frank País under the theory that a woman driver would not alert attention because authorities scrutinized the person driving more so than the passengers.[63] There are many recorded instances of women driving men to action sites and meetings or rescuing them by car. This was a primary way that middle-aged women or younger married women of the middle and upper classes contributed to the cause. For example, *llano* rebel Pedro Romero sought refuge with Bohemia Coll after the Cienfuegos uprising.[64] Bohemia and her daughter disguised Pedro and then accompanied him and another militant to the Sierra to divert suspicion. Clara Lull was similarly valuable to young rebels. As her son told her, "we need respected people to accompany us on missions" for cover.[65] Using her identity as a middle-class, middle-aged woman to deflect police suspicion, Clara accompanied her son and other rebels on *llano* operations in her car, including one in which son Eduardito, M-26-7 leader René Ramos, and several others seized a radio station at gunpoint.[66]

The Deceivers: Skirts and Pregnant Bellies

The rebel division of labor did not automatically default to gender norms, as the *llano* rebels recognized by exploiting a tactical advantage to femininity as a cover for riskier tasks that might otherwise be assigned to men. Vilma later explained: "the young men out on the streets at night were in constant danger of being detained ... but this wasn't so true for the women, so we used *compañeras*" – to deliver messages, transport weapons and supplies, plant bombs, or to protest the arrest of *llano* rebels.[67]

A favored narrative of women's logistical work is that of women carrying documents and weapons under the wide, full skirts fashionable at the time. Rebel women sewed pockets or belted bags inside skirts, which they sometimes called "*engañadoras*" (deceivers).[68] "La Engañadora," a popular Cuban song recorded in 1951, tells of a voluptuous-looking woman who relied upon "falsies" (padding) for her curves. So these skirts hiding weapons, supplies, and documents were, in effect, rebel falsies. For example, M-26-7 assigned Iris Quindos a mission in Guantanamo: "I [wore] a tangerine colored skirt, very wide, with three layers. Underneath I wore petticoats with many pockets ... I carried so many bullets in my petticoats that it weighed a ton."[69]

Despite some close calls, the skirts were effective. Guards once stopped Fe Isabel Dovale while she was carrying sensitive documents under her *engañadora* skirt.[70] She claimed a stomach ache, and a soldier let her use the bathroom, where she flushed the evidence down the toilet. María López Larosa, in addition to stuffing her bra full of war bonds and hiding rebel documents under her skirt, took advantage of an enamored policeman by allowing him to accompany her when she served as a rebel courier:

I was afraid that he would touch me and feel things inside my skirt. So I got a suitcase and filled it with [clothes], and I asked him to accompany me ... He carried the suitcase and I walked on the other side, with the suitcase between us so he wouldn't accidentally touch me and feel the things I was delivering ... [P]eople would see me walking with this *guardia* and no one would suspect.[71]

The regime's suspicions grew, and authorities in Oriente prohibited women from wearing wide skirts or loose dresses, though they had a hard time enforcing it.[72]

As the United States increased efforts to intercept planes and boats smuggling weapons to Cuba, M-26-7 in Miami, headed by Haydée, turned to women such as Tía Angelita, discussed above.[73] According to Haydée: "[I]t was just the small arms that our *compañeras* could conceal in their skirts ... The need was great and there was no alternative."[74] Women also smuggled guns under their skirts to hijack planes to Cuba. In November 1958, three women with handguns taped to their legs accompanied three men to hijack a plane to Raúl Castro's zone of operation.[75]

Women rebels also feigned pregnancy to divert suspicion and bypass roadblocks, an effective ploy given that "no one would touch the belly of a pregnant woman."[76] As the rebels in Oriente searched for *Granma* survivors in December 1956, Celia Sánchez traveled by bus with Gena Verdecía to Santiago to meet with the Santiago leadership. Authorities were searching for Celia after she had escaped from detention days earlier, and to avoid detection, Celia had cut her hair and disguised herself as a pregnant *campesina*.[77] There were two other pregnant women on the bus, and when the bus was stopped and searched, one joked that the soldiers should also search their bellies.[78] Though the suggestion alarmed Celia, the fact that the suggestion was made in jest points to the absurdity of the idea and thus the efficacy of the tactic. Celia dressed in the same way on the return. Traveling under high military alert, they were the only passengers. This time, when the bus stopped at a military roadblock, instead of a search, the soldiers invited the driver and the two women into the station for coffee, then in consideration of her prominent pregnancy, a soldier helped Celia back into the bus.[79]

Haydée also used this ploy to transport detonators: "I did it so well that I not only looked like a pregnant woman, but if touched, I felt like one as well."[80] Once, when her car was stopped, she created "a real scene," telling the guards: "Look, I went to Bayamo to see the doctor because I was feeling bad, and I can't take any shocks ... If there's any problems let the soldiers come with us, please. I'm trusting in you to get us there."[81]

In another example, Ángela González del Valle was carrying weapons under her pregnant-looking belly, riding in a car with several M-26-7 men sought by authorities. When the authorities pulled them over, Ángela instructed the driver, "tell them that you are taking me to the hospital, that I'm in labor and am doing poorly. When they see this belly, they'll believe us."[82] Indeed, the soldiers allowed them to proceed without a search.

Even without pregnant-looking bellies, women sometimes claimed to be pregnant to divert suspicion. Haydée told of an instance in which she was hiding from police, crouched between two cars. She flagged down a man driving past: "[P]lease help me. I had to get down there [between the cars] because I'm pregnant, only two months, but I think I'm going to lose it."[83]

Pregnancy, then, provided an effective cover. I found no reports in which soldiers insisted upon checking women's bellies or detained cars carrying women feigning labor. Pregnancy, for most police and military, put women above suspicion, or at least posed a potentially embarrassing situation that soldiers and police preferred to avoid. Louis Pérez Jr.'s research documents both the national scorn against Batista's military and its impact on military morale, such that the army increasingly felt itself to be "an army of occupation."[84] In this atmosphere, soldiers perhaps welcomed the opportunity to come to the aid of a pregnant woman – the embodiment of innocence and vulnerability – and thus redeem themselves.[85]

GENDERED REBEL SILENCES: SEXUAL ASSAULT AND BOMBINGS

As I have argued, examining the Cuban War Story with a gender lens provides new insights into how the insurrection was won. Given that revolutionary Cuba tells war stories to construct a certain vision of nation and state, it also tells us about post-1958 Cuba. Stories of women rebels using dominant conceptions of femininity against the regime – tactical femininity – comprise much of the narrative space accorded to women.

But what lies at the other end of the spectrum? What are the disfavored narratives of the Cuban insurrection?[86] Which, if any, of women's war stories are left untold? I explore two gendered silences: women victims of sexual assault and women bombers.[87] Although during the insurrection both were important gendered narratives that served the anti-Batista cause, I propose that they unsettled the post-1958 revolutionary state's dominant version of femininity and accordingly were not featured in the official war story.[88]

Sexual assault comprises a weighty silence in the Cuban War Story. Authorities' lack of suspicion toward women did not fully immunize them from violence – indeed, once suspected as rebels, the violence against them sometimes took sexualized forms. Across cases of political violence and war, the femininity of a woman whom authorities understand as an enemy is viewed differently, and she is subjected to a different gendered standard than women seen as politically innocent. Her femininity is "read as 'tainted,' soiled, and by definition sexually aggressive and active – she becomes a whore."[89] Following this logic, as a whore, and thus devoid of feminine honor that honorable men are obligated to protect, she also becomes rapeable. Victims of sexual assault, in turn, are devalued in the virgin/whore dichotomy, and this devaluation in part operates through shame that suppresses their stories even among family, friends, and comrades.[90] Among Cuban rebel women who were sexually assaulted, we can assume that many internalized the shame and the blame, which silenced discussion about this form of regime brutality. In a few cases during the insurrection, however, women or their loved ones radically reversed this gendered logic and publicized the rapes in order to shame the dictatorship. I draw primarily from these examples but also note that in the post-1958 discourse these stories have disappeared. They were strategically mobilized against Batista, but once having served their purpose, they dropped out of public discourse.

It is difficult to assess the prevalence of sexual assault during the insurrection, though the accumulated evidence indicates that sexual assault and the threat of sexual assault were used to torture and punish as well as to spread fear.[91] A US journalist reported at the time that police commonly threatened women and girls they arrested with rape.[92] For example, three sisters, ages fourteen, sixteen, and seventeen, were taken by Santiago police as hostages to be detained until their father, a suspected rebel, surrendered himself. The infamous Colonel José María Salas Cañizares tormented the girls by threatening rape, remarking: "Are these the ones I have for tonight? Not bad, not bad."[93] There are also reports that women, when arrested, were routinely forced to undress in front of the police and then beaten.[94]

In October 1957, the *Directorio Revolucionario* (DR) rebels issued a statement to the international press alleging that on September 26, 1957, in addition to the eighteen dead bodies left by authorities in Oriente streets, two young women suspected of being DR members were sexually assaulted by the police, and then murdered, their naked bodies abandoned in a Havana suburb.[95] Teté Puebla, a member of the underground, explained that most members of her M-26-7 cell, which was comprised primarily of teenagers, had to go into the Sierra for safety: "The military would persecute the suspected rebels by imprisoning them and torturing them. If you were a woman, you were raped."[96] She explained that she overcame her reluctance to kill in combat because, "if we didn't kill them, they would kill us. When the military would come into our zone, they would kill peasants, burn their houses. They would tie the *campesinos* to wooden posts and in front of them burn down their houses and rape their daughters."[97]

The details that follow do not feature in the dominant post-1958 War Story; rather, they are testimony taken during the Batista era or soon after or reported through the foreign press. Moreover, this evidence of sexual assault often appeared unexpectedly in articles and interviews on various other topics. They concern several specific instances of sexual assault against rebel women, the details of which have been largely lost to revolutionary Cuba, perhaps out of an impulse to protect the victims' honor but also, I suggest, to protect a certain idealized representation of Revolutionary Cuba. To the extent that victims are themselves tainted by the assault committed against them (and even internalize a sense of shame), this association would impact sexual assault victims' ability to represent an idealized revolutionary femininity. This particular untold story was a missed opportunity to interrupt the shame attached to rape victims and instead buttressed the importance placed on women's sexual "purity."

Ángela González was a rare woman who came forward with her story. In her late 40s and a veteran of the 1930s protests, she was a member of an M-26-7 Action and Sabotage cell.[98] In the early morning of October 7, 1958, the police broke down her door and beat Ángela and two other women present. Ramón Calviño, an officer known for his cruelty, recognized Ángela: "he went insane, he tore my nightclothes, he hit me, he did everything."[99] The beating was severe, and Ángela suffered permanent injuries.[100] They stripped the women of their clothes: "When [Calviño] stripped me, I was handed over to [other officers], so they could rape and humiliate me."[101] She was imprisoned for several weeks and then went into exile.[102] Calviño fled when the rebels came to power but was captured in the 1961 Bay of Pigs invasion. In a public trial, televised and extensively covered in the Cuban print media, Ángela testified against Calviño, displaying her shredded, bloodstained bedclothes from the assault.[103]

Also captured in Ángela's home was seventeen-year-old Hidelisa Esperón Lozano, a member of M-26-7, the DR, and the *Las Martianas*.[104] According to Hidelisa, whose testimony was recorded fifty years after Angela's, her clothes were ripped off, and after being interrogated and beaten, she was dragged naked out of the house to the police station. There, she was raped several times and thrown, bloody and naked, in a room full of other tortured male prisoners. Still naked, she was taken to the cemetery in the early morning hours and ordered to run.[105] Hidelisa recalled that the third woman in the house was raped while still in the house.[106] While many rebels surely knew that these three women had been sexually assaulted, there are very few mentions of it in the literature.

The case of Esterlina Milanés, a fifty-year-old Catholic high school teacher, is another rare instance of documented sexual assault. Esterlina had been recruited by her students, and she drove them to deliver guns and plant dynamite, and often visited them in prison.[107] She also hid rebels after the March 13, 1957 failed assassination of Batista. By 1958, police had her under surveillance, and on February 24, five officers arrived at her home at dawn, firing shots as they pounded on her door and then beating her in front of her children. At the station, the officer identified her to the police captain: "This is *la vieja* [old lady] who visits the students [in prison]."[108] She recalled the tile walls and floor drains in the police chief's office, designed to facilitate cleanup after beatings.[109] There, she was punched in the face, pulled by the hair and ears, and pushed down stairs amid threats of death. Many of her teeth were knocked out during interrogations.[110] As she later testified, during the five days of detention, they sexually violated her with an iron rod, threatening "Talk, old woman, [or] we are going to perforate you."[111]

The young man with whom she had been driving when first spotted by police was also detained and tortured with electrical wires to his genitals.[112] He was the nephew of the Colombian ambassador to Cuba, and when the ambassador arrived to take him from policy custody, the young man insisted that Esterlina be released as well.[113] The ambassador took her home and sought medical attention for her. The attending physician "was so horrified and so disgusted with the abuses committed on his patient that he wrote a letter of denunciation which was published in the newspapers."[114] She fled to the United States disguised as a nun, with the Colombian ambassador and his wife escorting her to the airport in the embassy car and even walking her on to the airplane to ensure her safety. In the United States, walking with a cane, she toured on behalf of the rebels, publicizing regime atrocities and raising funds to send to Cuba. Her testimony appears in the Congressional Record, reprinted from a talk given before the US House of Representatives on May 12, 1958.[115] Esterlina also wrote open letters to the United Nations, the Organization of the American States, and the Inter American Press Association with her account of the abuse, producing a degree of international outcry.[116] In a letter to the press, she wrote:

> Other Cuban women before me have been in the same position but I don't want to hide anything notwithstanding the threats of death should I denounce these facts. These beasts did something more which I would not mention were it not for the firm conviction ripened while suffering, that the truth and only the truth should be said.[117]

Ángela and Esterlina both went public about their sexual assaults to condemn the Batista regime and later the counter revolutionary movement. These two middle-aged, politically engaged women took charge of their testimony, rejecting the self-censorship and shame that can be internalized by victims of sexual assault. But they are rare exceptions in a conflict in which rape by the armed forces was understood as a prominent form of aggression against women but also carried the power to silence its victims.

Two younger women, sisters Lourdes and Cristina Giralt, were also alleged victims of sexual assault.[118] They did not survive, and though they are among the most well-known female victims of the Batista regime, post-1958 Cuban sources do not mention the evidence of rape, in contrast to the versions reported by their family and in US publications at the time.[119] The sisters, in their early to mid-20s, were active in the *Resistencia Cívica* and *Las Martianas*, distributing rebel war bonds and propaganda, gathering supplies for the Sierra Maestra, and transporting weapons. Their Havana apartment was sometimes used as a meeting place for the *Resistencia*.[120] On Sunday, June 15, 1958, their brother dropped them off at home after a weekend with family in Cienfuegos. Unbeknown to them, the police had raided their building over the weekend seeking rebels suspected of an assassination attempt.[121] Police were waiting for them on Sunday, and as the Giralt sisters happened upon the scene, police opened fire. When they carried the sisters downstairs and loaded them into a police car in front of witnesses, it is not clear whether the women were alive or dead.[122]

Their employer José Ferrer, also active in the *Resistencia Cívica*, made inquiries when the sisters did not come to work Monday morning. Ferrer told a US journalist that he and the women's brother found them that afternoon, "half naked and badly bruised, in the morgue. The eyes of both were blackened and across their breasts were bullet holes. Their blouses had been torn from them ... The pedal pushers of one were torn near the vagina, which indicated an attempt at rape. Stains of semen were evident to substantiate that theory."[123] Police added to the suspicion of rape when they only permitted autopsies to those parts of the women's bodies struck by bullets (the upper torsos).[124]

The murder of the Giralt sisters appeared in US newspapers. Exiled former Prime Minister Manuel Antonio de Varona declared, in a letter published in *The New York Times*, that the sisters had been sexually assaulted before being killed, asking how US citizens, "even after learning of such hideous conduct on the part of Batista, still insist on helping the tyrant responsible for those crimes."[125] Before 1959, censorship prevented open acknowledgement in the press of sexual assault by Cuban authorities. After, revolutionary state media exalted the Giralt sisters as martyrs, tragic victims whose fate demonstrated "the criminal nature of the Batista tyranny, its devaluation of human life regardless of the sex or age of its victims."[126] However, the sexualized nature of the police assault is excised from the narrative.

An internalized shame dissuaded other victims from reporting. Several women who had been held by the infamous Colonel Esteban Ventura at Havana's Fifth Precinct considered documenting "how women are defamed and abused when they fall in[to] Ventura's claws."[127] They discussed producing a signed record of abuses they had suffered, "keeping them secret until the Dictatorship falls because otherwise they would be ashamed, and to deliver the document to the Tribunal which is going to judge that monster called Ventura" once Batista is overthrown.[128] Ultimately, they decided against it, "because the things to be told are such that they could not be told."[129]

There were other references to rape in the international media. Miami-based journalist René Viera, in early 1958, compared the sexual assault on Esterlina to assaults he had previously reported against several other anti-Batista women – Martha Frayde, Lilia Figueroa, and TV actress Alicia Agramonte.[130] Soon after Batista fled, Agramonte confronted her accused rapist Captain José Castaño Quevedo when he was tried in the revolutionary courts. Following the testimony of Agramonte and many others, Castaño was sentenced to death and executed (reportedly at Che Guevara's hand).[131]

References were sometimes indirect or implied. In late 1957, the bilingual newspaper *Las Americas* contained an appeal to "women of America": "Persecuted, wounded, with our bodies black and blue from blows received, our clothes turned down, placed in cells with men who abuse us, the women of Cuba will continue while it is necessary ... Let the others carry their shame. We, with our dignity intact above all insults, and you women of the Continent, by our side."[132] Rebel propaganda obliquely referenced sexual assault. On April 8, 1958, an M-26-7 Radio Rebelde broadcast called to Cuban women: "our sullied honor demands justice ... *Compañeras*, it is better to die fighting ... than to live when not even our sacred condition of womanhood is respected."[133] Later that year, Radio Rebelde referred to "the intimate tragedies that befall [women]."[134] These particular references to sexual violence notably call on women to mobilize and defend themselves, whereas traditionally it fell to men to defend women's honor. They also suggest a broad public fear, encouraged and amplified by rebel propaganda, of sexual assaults committed by Batista's forces. This argument will be further developed in Chapter 8, which details guerrilla leaders' efforts to prevent sexual assault in their ranks and in the areas they controlled.

Finally, these sexual assaults were racialized, sometimes overtly, with race informing understandings of guilt and innocence. Women whose assaults were publicized – Ángela, Esterlina, and the Giralt sisters – embodied white or light-skinned middle-class femininity. In this sense, the privilege of light skin at least partially shielded them from public second-guessing regarding whether or not the act was consensual. I furthermore found two instances in these cases in which the race of the perpetrators was specified, apparently to enhance the perception of guilt or the horrific nature of the crime. When oral historian Lyn Smith interviewed her in 1981, she asked Esterlina if she was sexually violated while detained by authorities. Esterlina (speaking in English) replied: "Yes, two times. Two [black men]."[135] Similarly, the Miami M-26-7 in 1958 published an account of the assault on the Giralt sisters: "They were met [at the police station] by two negro policemen who raped them. Proof of this sadistic act was found in their bodies."[136] So little is known about what happened to the sisters, who were white or light-skinned, particularly once they arrived at the police station, that reference to the race of the rapists must be understood as a fabrication designed to enhance the perception that the assault occurred and also heighten the revulsion of a white audience: "such a savage action can only come from sick and rotten brains, an act which surpasses the limits of political crime to be converted into an unbelievable act of ferocity."[137]

A second gendered silence of the insurrection concerns women bombers. Though bombing in civilian areas was prevalent during the insurrection, the post-1958 Cuban War Story, as a triumphal war narrative, downplays such acts.[138] While Cuban sources sometimes mention women's participation, any impact on the general population, including psychological and physical trauma, is not part of the official history. We gain a glimpse into women's participation in these common rebel acts through oral histories and through reports of rebels being injured or killed.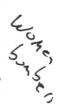

In rural areas, M-26-7 sabotage was often meant to threaten the profits of big landowners or foreign-held businesses: "Either Batista without the *zafra* [harvest] or the *zafra* without Batista."[139] María López Larosa engaged in rural sabotage alongside her husband and others, burning sugar cane fields and sawing down telephone and electrical poles at night.[140] Marta Fuego Rodríguez helped burn tobacco-drying houses.[141] Using a slingshot, they propelled ping pong balls inserted with slow-release capsules of spontaneously flammable material onto the thatched roofs. Such sabotage, which pressured the military to dilute its anti-guerrilla campaign in order to protect property, presented relatively little danger to civilians.[142]

Urban sabotage and bombings posed greater danger to civilians. Rebels targeted police and military officers, planted bombs, attacked and derailed trains, and fired on buses during strikes.[143] They aimed to create a climate of disorder, rebellion, and economic instability that put the regime on the defensive.[144] Sometimes they avoided crowded public places, bombing bridges and power lines, for example, to interrupt normal operations and weaken public confidence in the government.[145] However, bombs also exploded in plazas, theaters, and nightclubs, wounding and killing civilians.[146]

International media focused less on the rebel bombings than government repression, as US Ambassador Earl Smith later complained: "Little mention was given to the violence of the terrorists. In Cuban public squares, bombs were set off by the revolutionaries. Women and children were maimed. Bombs were placed by the Castro rebels in theaters, schools, stores wherever crowds gathered."[147] Similarly, in the post-1958 Cuban sources, when bombings are mentioned or an ex-rebel reflects upon having planted bombs, civilian casualties are not acknowledged. As such, little information is available regarding the civilian toll.

This omission covers men and women bombers alike, though as feminist IR scholars note, the narratives attached to violence and terrorism are deeply gendered such that women are particularly condemned for departure from their purported feminine nature.[148] Documents reveal that women manufactured and planted bombs in various cities.[149] In Bayamo, Fe Isabel Dovale Borjas made bombs using TNT extracted from the unexploded bombs dropped by military planes.[150] Members of Las Martianas, working on their own and in collaboration with M-26-7, engaged in arguably terrorist acts in Havana. Aida Pelayo, for example, worked with "dynamite, live phosphorous, the burning of shops, the bombs," and participated in three assassination attempts against Police Chief Esteban Ventura.[151] In 1955, Aida and Olga Román commissioned and planted their first bomb. Their ride fell through, so they carried the bomb on to a bus and rode around the city, waiting for the stores to close before planting it at a shop front door, where it soon exploded.[152]

Eighteen-year-old Urselia Díaz Báez died while planting a bomb.[153] With M-26-7's Havana Action and Sabotage group, Urselia had previously planted bombs at the Bacardí building, a bar, and the Ten Cent store.[154] On the evening of September 3, 1957, with the explosive device attached to her thigh, she accompanied Antonio Sánchez to Cine América. The bomb was to explode at 9 p.m. to coincide with two other theater bombs around the city – a time that, presumably, civilians would be attending the theater. But the bomb exploded prematurely as she planted it in the women's bathroom, killing her.[155] Though Urselia is sometimes celebrated in the Cuban War Story, information on civilian injuries resulting from such acts, which has the power to shift the narrative from heroine to terrorist, is omitted.[156]

The collateral damage of the armed insurrection itself was numerically (and ethically) significant. One of the best sources is a two-part volume published in June 1958 by M-26-7 in Miami, which lists names, dates, and details culled from Cuban and Miami-based Spanish-language news outlets and other sources regarding detentions, bombs, and casualties.[157] It includes many reports of bystanders hurt or killed by rebel bombs and shoot-outs, and many women's names appear alongside men's as collateral damage casualties.

FAVORED NARRATIVES AND SILENCES: GENDER AND THE CUBAN WAR STORY

I have suggested that the urban underground used traditional femininity – particularly notions of women as passive and politically and sexually innocent – as a tactic of war. The Cuban War Story celebrates the skirts and false pregnant bellies hiding weapons as documentation of rebel women's contributions and their ingenuity at duping the repressive regime. In contrast, it is relatively silent on the contributions and experiences of women rebels that more fundamentally unsettle the gender status quo: sexual assault victims and urban bombers.

What do these favored and silenced narratives tell us? In the former, women performed versions of idealized femininity even as they contributed to the highly masculinized domain of warfare. In testimonial accounts, the stories are typically told with a touch of glee: a woman outwitted the dictator's henchmen! But this gender tactic was used in the service of the larger strategy of insurrection. Women's contributions to armed insurrection potentially destabilize gender relations, yet the Cuban War Story left traditional gender relations largely intact by positioning them as exceptional and temporary. As Laura Sjoberg finds, women incorporated into militaries must be masculine enough (for example, exhibiting courage) without losing their femininity.[158] Celebrated deployments of femininity in the otherwise masculinized armed insurrection both documented the broad support for the insurrection (even the women mobilized!) and confirmed that women's participation in masculinized warfare did not masculinize women. In this sense, the Batista regime's sexism was a weakness that could be exploited by the rebels. But sexism itself was not targeted for overthrow.

I propose that the state's erasure of sexual assault also drew from and contributed to this logic, as sexual assault reflects back upon the victim. Some women victims and their surviving loved ones powerfully condemned the dictatorship for waging its war on women's bodies. But these testimonies do not complement the post-1958 Cuban War Story. The state silence is perhaps partly intended to protect women's privacy, but state silence even in cases in which victims broke their own silence reinforces an internalized shame for rape victims. Ultimately, these gaps in the Cuban War Story have the same effect as the favored stories in leaving the gender binary masculinity/femininity intact.[159] Tactical femininity thus operated in two theaters of war. In addition to the tactical deployment of femininity in logistical operations for the insurrection, this exploration also reveals the tactical femininity operating in the gendered war of hearts and minds.

Notes

1. Fuego Rodríguez interview, Lyn Smith Cuba Collection.
2. Ibid.
3. Ibid.
4. Sjoberg (2013, 217–18).
5. Lobao Reif (1986, 153–4); Shayne (2004).
6. Sjoberg and Gentry (2007, 50); Sjoberg (2013, 231). I propose that women bombers pose a deeper threat to the gender status quo than do women guerrillas, whose violence can be more readily represented as defensive and directed against an armed and dangerous threat.
7. See Theidon (2012); Campanaro (2000–2001).
8. Prados-Torreira's translation (2005, 94), from José Martí, *Obras completas*, Volume 5, Havana: Editorial Nacional de Cuba, 1963–66, 16–17. See also discussion in Chapter 2.
9. Prados-Torreira (2005, 94).
10. Elshtain (1987, 4, 140) terms such representations "Beautiful Souls." See also Hegel (1977); Sjoberg and Gentry (2007).
11. Yuval-Davis (2004, 172). See, for example, Frank País' account of the Santiago uprising (Hart 2004, 157). Twenty years later, *Verde Olivo* profiled a military woman: "the Revolution is indestructible, because even the women, who are the mothers and wives and workers, take up the AKA-47 to look after the present and the future" (Jorge Luis Blanco, "Para que no pase el enemigo," *Verde Olivo* June 6, 1976, 20–5).

12. Only six out of over sixty newspapers were financially independent of hand-outs from Batista or local officials (Guerra 2012, 40). See also Ambassador Earl T. Smith, "Despatch from the Ambassador in Cuba (Smith) to the Department of State," Foreign Relations of the United States, 1955–1957, September 16, 1957. International newspapers were also censored in Cuba. A *New York Times* journalist found his paper on Cuban newsstands with articles on Cuban unrest cut out (DePalma, 2006, 67–8). See also Phillips (1959, 328, 344); DuBois (1959, 258).

13. Guerra, "Despatch from the Consulate at Santiago de Cuba to the Department of State," February 21, 1958.

14. C. Allan Stewart, "Memorandum from the Deputy Director of the Office of Middle American Affairs (Stewart) to the Deputy Assistant Secretary of State for Inter-American Affairs (Snow)," Foreign Relations of the United States, 1958–1960, July 24, 1958.

15. Ibid.

16. See Draper (1962, 14); Halperin (1993, 188).

17. Castro estimated 1,000 Sierra rebel deaths by late 1958 and over 10,000 *llano* deaths in five years due to state repression (Chapelle 1962a, 329). These figures are difficult to confirm. Macaulay (1970, 14), a US citizen who joined the M-26-7 guerrillas, describes the guerrillas (in contrast to the urban underground) as "safe and sound in the sierras."

18. Phillips (1959, 333).

19. Macaulay (1970, 114). Macaulay notes that, in contrast to repression against peasants, upper-class opponents to Batista were tolerated or allowed to escape into exile. Peasants could not escape abroad and so their only refuge was with the guerrilla.

20. Phillips (1959, 345).

21. Dubois (1959, 182).

22. Ibid., 183–7; Phillips (1959, 331–2).

23. 26th of July Movement 1958, Part 1, no page numbers; Dubois (1959, 183). This murder enraged the Cuban medical community. Dubois also reported in Havana in 1958, "the bodies of 98 political prisoners were scattered through the streets, riddled with bullets ... in reprisal for a raid on a police station" (Dubois 1959, 334–5).

24. Phillips (1959, 329). See no author, "Calm Restored to Cuban Scene," *The New York Times* September 8, 1957, 11.

25. Dubois (1959, 177–8).

26. Díaz Vallina (2001, 7).

27. "Accusation Made to the Supreme Court by Relatives of Persons Violently Killed during the Last Years," in 26th of July Movement 1958, Part 1, no page numbers.

28. As this study documents, women were sometimes detained, tortured, and killed. The point remains that Batista forces overwhelmingly targeted men.

29. Guerra, "Despatch from the Consulate at Santiago de Cuba to the Department of State," February 21, 1958.

30. Jorge Eduardo Gutiérrez Bourricaudy, "Tortura y represión hacia la mujer durante el Batistato," *Caliban: Revista Cubana de Pensamiento e Historia*

October–December 2011; Bonachea and San Martín (1974, 173). See also Phillips (1959, 342).

31. Franqui (1980, 139).

32. Espín (1975) 2006.

33. Chapelle (1962a, 328).

34. Iraida Rodríguez Pérez, "Días de amor y de guerra," *Mujeres* 1990 (no. 5), 48. See also Carmen Cortés Pérez interview, Heidy González, "De la Savia de Mariana," *Mujeres* December 1981, 12–13.

35. Castro radio address, Radio Rebelde August 1, 1958, 2, Princeton University Latin American pamphlet collection. See also Castro (2011, 305–11).

36. Guerra, "Despatch from the Consulate at Santiago de Cuba to the Department of State," February 21, 1958.

37. Goldstein (2001).

38. For example, though sought by authorities, Haydée entered the same prison in which she had been incarcerated after Moncada to visit her boyfriend Armando. She posed successfully as his sister, raising no suspicions among prison guards despite her rebel fame (Hart 2004, 260–2); see also Meneses (1966, 81); Marta Rojas, "Quizás los momentos más difíciles," *Granma* May 5, 1988, 4. Women rebels were less likely to be captured or killed. During the April 1958 strike, for example, Ramona Barber Gutiérrez was with Marcelo Salado Lastra, Havana M-26-7 Action Chief, when surrounded by government forces (Zoila Martínez, "La huelga de abril 9," *Mujeres* April 1977, 4–5). Marcelo nudged Ramona aside, and a man working nearby pulled her into an office, where she hid until the soldiers left with Marcelo's body (which had thirty-three bullet holes in it). Though also an M-26-7 activist, the soldiers ignored her.

39. Shayne (2004, 122). One Cuban study found 25.5 percent of women *llano* rebels had been detained and 2.4 percent tortured (Díaz Vallina et al. 1994, 26).

40. Armando Hart's (2004) memoir demonstrates the centrality of women *llano* rebels, containing hundreds of references to women carrying out revolutionary activities – many of whom had not been mentioned in the literature previously.

41. Sweig (2002).

42. García-Pérez (1999, 131).

43. Women constituted 51 percent of university teachers, 90 percent of secondary teachers, and 84 percent of primary teachers (Pérez 2015, 240).

44. Espín (1975) 2006. See also Stout (2013, 130); Chirino, *Verde Olivo* January 10, 1985, 43.

45. Hart (2004, 269). Rosita Casán in *Santiago* June–September 1975; excerpts of the Casán interview were translated and reprinted in "How swift action saved life of Cuban revolutionary leader Armando Hart," *The Militant* 68:1, January 12, 2004.

46. Rebeca Díaz Acosta, "Aleida Fernández, la joven que desafió al tirano," Radio Güines 11 de Febrero de 2010.

47. Alina Carriera Martínez, "El precio de retar al tirano," in *Cuba Ahora*, noviembre 7, 2007. In February 1958, security forces shot Aleida at a checkpoint.

Though unclear whether her death was an accident, her funeral developed into a mass anti-Batista protest. See Díaz Acosta (2010). Aleida was from a prominent family; Batista lamented the "disgraceful accident," referring to Aleida as the daughter of an "old friend" (no author, "Piden se investigue la muerte de la Sra. Fernández Chardiet," *Diario de la Marina* February 13, 1958, p. 1, 18A). See also "Editorial: Por el serenamiento de las pasiones," *Diario de la Marina* February 14, 1958, 4A.

48. Casán (1975) 2004.
49. Amat (1975) 2004; Pedro Prada, "Los días mas felices de mi vida," *Verde Olivo* November 1988, 23.
50. Casán (1975) 2004.
51. Guevara (1971) (February 1, 1957), 68.
52. Olga Lara García interview, Magaly Sánchez Ochoa, "Junto a la Revolución," *Mujeres* May 1980, 7.
53. Magaly Sánchez Ochoa, "Una vida entregada a la Revolución," *Mujeres* June 1981, 15–17.
54. Pastorita Núñez, "Tengo la Revolución en la sangre" (interview), *La Jiribilla* VII, January 3–9, 2009. While stationed in the United States, Haydée bought weapons from the Mafia, and "sewed bullets into tiny individual pockets on the undersides of … skirts … that's how she got many of them back into Cuba" (Randall 2015, 17).
55. Middle- and upper-class women often had domestic workers to perform the cooking and housework, though many sent housekeepers out on errands or gave them time off during meetings.
56. Melba's father Manuel had been imprisoned for six months for participating in strikes. Ortega Guzmán and Babiel Gutiérrez, "La mujer cubana en el moncada," Oficina de Asuntos Históricos Consejo de Estado, *Mujeres* (Dossier Especial) 293, July 21, 2006. Hernández interview, Lyn Smith Cuba Collection.
57. Guzmán and Gutiérrez (2006).
58. Mirtha Rodríguez Calderón, "En tiempos de lo grande ellos supieron dar ejemplo," *Mujeres* July 1983, 5.
59. De la Cova (2007, 45). Rosaura was the mother de Raúl Martíriez Ararás, who participated in the Bayamo assault.
60. Santamaría (2003b, 26–7).
61. Heidy Rodríguez Rey, "La Tía Angelita," *Mujeres* April 1977, 17. Soon after, police captured Tía Angelita and her daughter as they transported weapons, and the two were imprisoned for one month.
62. Espín (1975) 2006.
63. Ibid.
64. Isolina Triay, "Dos luchadoras para un tiempo heroico," *Mujeres* January 1983, 6. María Josefa Corces told a similar story of how a young woman saved her husband, who had been detained in a hotel used as an impromptu jail: "a *muchacha* staying there with her parents … offered to help him. The rest were assassinated. The young woman lent him her father's clothing, dyed his hair, and by pretending he was her boyfriend, snuck him out of there" (ibid.).

65. Prada (1988, 22).
66. Ibid., 23.
67. Espín (1975) 2006. When Frank País was arrested, for example, Vilma immediately contacted "his mother and the girls, who went to create a scandal at the station so that they wouldn't kill him" (Espín [1975] 2006; Espín interview in Alfredo Reyes Trejo, "El Primer Refuerzo," *Verde Olivo* June 5, 1977, 32). See also Shayne (2004, 130).
68. Sánchez, *Mujeres* October 1979, 52–5; Waters (2003, 30).
69. Isolina Triay, "Triunfo la unidad," *Mujeres* September 1983, 16.
70. Sánchez (1979, 52–5).
71. López Larosa interview, Lyn Smith Cuba Collection.
72. Phillips (1959, 332); no author, "Cuban Army Style Note: No More Sack Dresses," *Chicago Daily Tribune* July 6, 1958, 3.
73. Santamaría (2003b, 51).
74. Ibid.
75. DuBois (1959, 326). Hijacking carried with it predictable civilian casualties. Another hijacked Cubana flight (the first international hijacking from the United States) on November 1, 1958 crashed into the ocean after attempting to land near Raúl Castro's guerrilla base. Out of the twenty on board, six survived.
76. Teté Puebla, in Waters (2003, 30). Teté noted the risk to a rebel woman's reputation when seen pregnant one day and not pregnant soon after.
77. Siberia García, *Granma* December 28, 2006.
78. Sánchez Ochoa, *Mujeres* October 1979, 7–9.
79. Ibid.
80. Santamaría (2003b, 47). See also Shayne (2004, 129–30).
81. Santamaría (2003b, 47–8).
82. Angela González del Valle, interviewed by Iraida Campo, "Siempre serás María Elena," *Mujeres* May 1976, 18.
83. Santamaría (2003b, 43).
84. Pérez (1976, 153).
85. Rebels operated from a similar gender script, and there are few accounts of rebel women who were actually pregnant or with young children. Marta Jiménez cut a poignant figure as the grieving pregnant widow of martyred rebel Fructuoso Rodríguez, yet this representation eclipsed her own contributions. At the time of Fructuoso's death, she had reduced her activism owing to her advanced pregnancy, in part because it was difficult to disguise herself. A photo of Marta in the funeral procession for her husband is striking for its juxtaposition of defiant militancy and embodied maternity (Pérez Cabrera Arístides 2006, 361–2; García, *Granma* March 13, 1991, 2). She leads the pallbearers, visibly pregnant, holding to her husband's coffin and shouting. Rosa Menocal, eight months pregnant, drove two rebel men wounded in the Presidential Palace attack to a safe house (Dubois 1959, 158). Armando Hart's sister picked him up in a car with her baby daughter after he escaped from prison (Hart 2004, 183). The urgency of these two situations explains the departure from the norm. In a few instances, women who were visibly pregnant used their condition as a diversion. Martha Oltuski insisted on

accompanying husband Enrique when he planted live phosphorous in a Havana store during Christmas season: "she was pregnant, so we would not arouse suspicion... [N]o one had noticed a thing, and we made it out into the street before the flash and explosion" (Oltuski 2002, 103–4). Pregnancy protected women only up to a point. After her husband Luis Felipe Almeida was killed in the 1957 Presidential Palace assault, María del Carmen Báez was imprisoned when she was eight months pregnant. She was not beaten but was subjected to psychological torture. Her baby was stillborn while she was in prison (Iraida Rodríguez Pérez, "Estrellas en las montañas," *Mujeres* January 1989, 54).

86. Of the facets of the insurrection not recorded in the official Cuban War Story, I highlight two additional ones here. The first concerns the psychological toll of war and Post-Traumatic Stress Disorder (PTSD). Evidence can be found tucked in Cuban memoirs. For example, Aleida March recalled a 1958 night she spent with Camilo Cienfuegos in a safe house: "I had to sleep in a bed that was close to his. I will never forget his nightmares; it seemed as though he was fighting the enemy in his sleep. I found it impossible to sleep that night" (March 2012, 33). Also, Haydée Santamaría exhibited signs of PTSD and committed suicide two days after the anniversary of Moncada in 1980 (Randall 2015, 28–9). A second silence concerns collateral damage caused by rebels. For example, Connie Wollam, wife of the US vice-consul, visited the pediatric ward of a Santiago hospital and met an adolescent girl who had lost her legs when traveling with her parents by jeep on the Central Highway – expecting an army convoy, rebels had detonated a mine (Dorschner and Fabricio 1980, 270).

87. Evidence suggests that sex workers working as rebel spies is another untold war story. Sex work is gender transgressive and overtly sexualized, operating within the feminine binary virgin/whore, in which sex work defines what the ideal woman is not. Havana in the 1950s had an estimated 2,000 brothels, most catering to tourists (Bonachea and San Martín 1974, 33). Brothels paid off the police, and police also acted as procurers and ran their own prostitution rings, sometimes supplying drugs (Bonachea and San Martín 1974, 33–4; see also Lewis et al. 1977, 237–56). Such corruption turned diverse sectors against Batista, including some sex workers such that, according to one source, *llano* rebels "gathered much of their intelligence information from sex workers and then relayed it to the rural areas through women sex workers. Their mission consisted of 'debriefing' as much as possible any important customer connected with the government agencies" (Bonachea and San Martín 1974, 34). Bonachea and San Martín maintain, "[Sex workers'] cooperation was very decisive, particularly during the last months of the regime. Some of them were assassinated by the police who traced information leakage to some [brothels]. Several revolutionaries ... owe their lives to prostitutes who helped them evade police persecution" (Bonachea and San Martín 1974, 354n13).

88. Sjoberg and Gentry (2007).
89. Schirmer (1993, 55).
90. Stephen (1995, 812); Schirmer (1993, 55).

91. Díaz Vallina et al. (1994, 27) note that the infliction of terror and torture predominately occurred during police detention rather than in the prisons, where judges had close oversight.

92. DuBois (1959, 267–8).

93. 26th of July Movement 1958, Part 2, no page number.

94. Ibid. For example, Pilar Menéndez was detained with another woman; their clothes were taken off and then they were beaten as many other policemen watched.

95. Bonachea and San Martín (1974, 73n50, 363); they cite Ramón Prendes, *Statements by the Federation of University Students to the Inter-American Press Association* (Havana: October 16, 1957, 2).

96. Puebla interview, Lyn Smith Cuba Collection.

97. Ibid.

98. Campo (1976, 18–19); González interviewed in Guillermo Bernal and Rafael Rodríguez, "El primer día de libertad," *Verde Olivo* December 29, 1983, 28; Angelita González, testimony in Martínez Triay (2006).

99. González in Bernal and Rodríguez (1983, 28).

100. Angela González, testimony in Martínez Triay (2006).

101. Ibid.

102. Campo (1976, 18–19); González in Bernal and Rodríguez (1983, 28). When Batista fled, Angelita's accused torturer Calviño escaped to the United States then returned in the 1961 Bay of Pigs invasion and was captured (Bernal and Rodríguez 1983, 28).

103. Ángela González's recorded testimony (Editora Girón 2010 [1961]). The trial was announced on September 8, 1961 and held the same day; Calviño was found guilty of crimes committed prior to the invasion and executed hours later (Richard Eder, "Cubans Execute 5 April Invaders," *The New York Times* September 9, 1961, 7). These televised trials did not have the formal legal protections of a rigorous defense for the accused. Ángela gave an emotionally evocative testimony, displaying bloody clothes that did not seem to have been tested or formally entered into evidence. That this trial was more spectacle than blind justice, however, does not in itself undermine the claim that sexual assault occurred. It is also corroborated by Hidelisa Esperón's 2011 testimony.

104. Gutiérrez Bourricaudy (2011). See also Rodríguez Calderón (1990, 66–7).

105. Ibid. 66.

106. Ibid.; Gutiérrez Bourricaudy (2011).

107. Milanés interview, Lyn Smith Cuba Collection.

108. Gladys Castaño, "Hasta el ultimo instante de mi vida," *Mujeres* February 1980, 51.

109. Chapelle (1962b, 256).

110. Rodríguez Calderón (1990, 63); Dubois (1959, 214).

111. Milanés letter to the Cuban Press and the Inter-American Press Association, Havana, March 7, 1958, in 26th of July Movement 1958, Part 2, no page number. See also Díaz Vallina (2001, 7); Chapelle (1962b, 256). The doctor who examined her testified that she suffered "multiple bruises and lacerations on the gluteal regions, as well as bruises throughout the body and

serious internal lacerations in the vagina, as well as deafness from break-
age of a tymphanum" (Rene Viera in RELOJ, translated and reprinted in
26th of July Movement 1958, Part 2, no page number). Viera was a Cuban
American political columnist based in Miami.

112. Milanés interview, Lyn Smith Cuba Collection. There are several refer-
ences to sexualized torture of men, targeting testicles. For example, Pedro
René Fraga died as a result of torture: "The savages destroyed his testicles.
Those men were envious of his manhood and of the manhood of the young
Cubans who are fighting" (26th of July Movement 1958, no page numbers). Cuban historians report no known cases of men rebels being raped
(Gutiérrez Bourricaudy 2011). Chase (2015) footnotes, "it is clear that some
imprisoned men were raped, but this [has] not been publicly spoken of"
(238n117).

113. Milanés interview, Lyn Smith Cuba Collection; Dubois (1959, 214).

114. Dubois (1959, 214).

115. Congressional Record – Appendix, 1958, A 4343.

116. Dubois (1959, 214).

117. Esterlina Milanés letter to the Cuban Press and the Inter-American Press
Association, Havana, March 7, 1958, in 26th of July Movement 1958,
Part 2, no page number.

118. Sometimes referred to as Giral or Girol.

119. Chase (2015) discusses the Giralt sisters "who were raped and killed by
security forces, but in tones of pathos and sexual victimization rather than
bravery or military glory," arguing that such references to women's martyrdom "make sense only when framed in terms of sexual exploitation"
(59; 226–7n72). However, the sexual victimization of the Giralt sisters was
largely if not completely absent in the post-1958 framing, including the
source Chase cited (Casals 1989, 165).

120. Naty Revuelta testimony, in Maloof (1999, 46).

121. Nidia Díaz, "Toda la patria está en la mujer: Si ella falla, morimos: si ella
nos es leal, somos," *Granma* June 15, 1983, 2.

122. Díaz (1983, 2); Manuel Antonio de Varona, "Crime in Cuba Described;
Continued Aid to Batista Queried in View of Sisters' Fate," *The New York
Times* July 10, 1958, 26.

123. DuBois (1959, 267).

124. Ibid., 268. An official police communiqué claimed the women were caught
in crossfire on Saturday night and died during transport to the hospital.
They also reportedly found communist literature and a large cache of arms
and ammunition in the women's apartment.

125. De Varona (1958, 26). De Varona fled Cuba again in 1960. In the plans for
the Bay of Pigs invasion, de Varona was to head a US-backed provisional
government.

126. Carlos Del Torro, "Las hermanas Giralt," *Granma* June 15, 1988, 3. For
martyrdom, see, for example, Daisy Martín, "Las hermanas Giralt," *Mujeres*
May 1978, 8–9; no author, *Granma* August 3, 1979, 3; Magaly Sánchez,
"Viven en la obra de la Revolución," *Mujeres* June 1980, 12–13; Daisy
Martín, "Hay que ayudar a que Fidel triunfe," *Mujeres* June 1983, 42–3;

Díaz (1983, 2). The sisters are represented as both agents and victims, who know the risks of activism and are prepared to give their lives.

127. 26th of July Movement 1958, Part 2, no page number.

128. Ibid.

129. Ibid.

130. René Viera, RELOJ article 1958, translated and reprinted in 26th of July Movement 1958, Part 2, no page number. Lilia Figueroa, in her 20s and not a rebel collaborator, was detained and tortured for eight days by Esteban Ventura.

131. See Guerra (2012, 78–9) for more on Castaño, who was accused of many crimes, including torture and murder. This March 4, 1959 trial is still debated and Agramonte's testimony called into question even though fifteen others testified against him. For example, Fontova (2008) draws from his interview with Castaño's son (also named José Castaño) to assert: "'What made the thing even more absurd was the woman they picked to claim the role of rape victim. Good grief. All Cuba was laughing over this one.' The woman who testified against the very handsome Jose Castaño was a failed actress, a failed radio personality, and a failed journalist named Alicia Agramonte. She was also – surprise! – a Cuban Communist Party member... The woman was hideous. Of course, an ugly woman can be raped. But Cubans knew that even more hideous than her face and body was Alicia's soul" (Fontova 2008, 129).

132. 26th of July Movement 1958, no page number.

133. Princeton University Library microfilm – no author, "Consigna definitiva para los grupos armados," Radio Rebelde abril 8, 1958.

134. Radio Rebelde transcript of 18 November 1958, reprinted in n.a., "'A la mujer Cubana!" *Granma* November 18, 1978, 2.

135. Milanés interview, Lyn Smith Cuba Collection. Audio partially indistinct – Milanés either uses the term "negroes" or a racial slur.

136. 26th of July Movement 1958, Part 2, no page number.

137. Ibid. Notably, in both instances, testimony was directed to audiences outside of Cuba (including largely Cubans in the United States, in the Giralt case).

138. Triumphal war narratives typically justify violence while minimizing victim-ization (Huston 1983, 273; Sjoberg and Gentry 2007, 28). Rebel sabotage, assassinations, and especially urban bombing are politically sensitive as they can be categorized as terrorist acts – to varying degrees and depending on context, they arguably carried an intent to instill terror and disregarded civilian safety. *Llano* rebels used threats of violence against civilians, bomb-ing theaters, restaurants, and department stores to discourage attendance and thus deprive businesses of profit in order to pressure the regime. Vilma recalled the Santiago rebels issuing "dead city" directives to citizens, "'Don't go to the movies, don't do this or that ...' We started to sabotage all the social activities ... [B]y April or May [1957] everything was dark ... and no one went anywhere" (Espín [1975] 2006). According to Llovio-Menéndez, the Federation of University Students in 1954 had a policy of setting bombs not in order to harm or kill anyone, "but only to amplify our presence by shock and noise, to keep the capital city on edge, and to remind people that

there was opposition to Batista's dictatorship. Empty theaters and deserted parks were favored targets for our bombs" (Llovio-Menéndez 1988, 62).

139. Pérez (1976, 158); Daniel M. Braddock, "Despatch from the Embassy in Cuba to the Department of State," *Foreign Relations of the United States, 1958–1960*, February 18, 1958.

140. López Larosa interview, Lyn Smith Cuba Collection. See also María Matilla Clares, in Magaly Sánchez Ochoa "María Matilla Clares, La Madre Heroica," *Mujeres* April 1980, 22–5.

141. Fuego Rodríguez interview, Lyn Smith Cuba Collection.

142. Pérez (1976, 158–9).

143. Cuban rebel groups M-26-7 and the DR had differing approaches to sabotage and bombings. Reportedly, in 1958 Fidel Castro ordered M-26-7 members in Havana to stop terrorism as it was ineffective (see Phillips 1959, 384–5). Braddock (1958).

144. Bonachea and San Martín (1974, 75).

145. Ibid., 227; DePalma (2006, 66).

146. Bonachea and San Martín (1974, 75, 227).

147. Smith (1962, 41).

148. Sjoberg and Gentry (2007, 41–50).

149. Martínez (1977, 4–5).

150. Sánchez (1979, 52–5).

151. Izquierdo, *Tribuna de la Habana* (n.d.); see also Maloof (1999, 58).

152. Pelayo in Castro Porta (1990, 86).

153. Valdes, *Verde Olivo* March 3, 1983, 6–9.

154. Sarabia (1980).

155. While Urselia is often mentioned in Cuba as a woman martyr, details of her activism are scarce, including her earlier bombing actions. Several other women martyrs not associated with terrorism (the Giralt sisters, for example) receive more media recognition. A case similar to Urselia's, though virtually absent in the Cuban War Story, is that of seventeen-year-old Magaly Martínez, who lost her arm when a homemade bomb exploded on New Year's Eve 1957 in the cabaret of the Tropicana Casino, the only serious injury from the blast (English 2007, 180–1); Jean Stein, "All Havana Broke Loose: An Oral History of Tropicana," *Vanity Fair* September 2011. Though she refuses to discuss it, she likely was attempting to plant the bomb.

156. Urselia's story appeared regularly in 1980s Cuban media during the massive national defense buildup. For example, "Youth like Urselia Díaz Báez did not hesitate to face death in carrying out dangerous assignments during the days of clandestinity" (Valdes 1983, 7).

157. 26th of July Movement 1958, Parts 1 and 2.

158. Sjoberg (2013, 235).

159. Bayard de Volo (2012); Lancaster (1992).

CHAPTER 7

"Stop the Murders of Our Children"

Mothers and the Battle for Hearts and Minds

In honor of Mother's Day 1957, thirty-seven Cuban mothers who had lost a rebel son or daughter claimed, on the basis of "tears and innocent blood shed," the right to speak and be heard, calling on Cuban women "to safeguard Cuba, to protect other mothers from suffering this agony":

> For a woman there is nothing that can be compared to the life of a son, a brother, a husband, and this is the time to prove it. Thus we appeal to our sisters to aid in the crusade for redemption which will detain the river of blood and tears which drown us ... It is essential that this Mother's Day should set the date on which the Cuban mothers join together to raise their voices as one and say to the government: ENOUGH.[1]

In an insurrection so closely associated with bearded young men in olive green fatigues, this maternal call to action is a dramatic counterpoint. Given that two decades later, the Nicaraguan and Salvadoran revolutionary movements would include robust maternal organizations, and the mothers of the disappeared in Chile and Argentina would help bring down dictatorships, it is not surprising to find middle-aged Cuban women mobilized in the insurrection, particularly as mothers.[2] However, apart from a few photos and anecdotes, revolutionary Cuba has not included maternal protest as a prominent part of its war story, nor have these protests or the middle-aged and older women marching in them received much attention in the literature.[3] A variety of factors converge to create this gap: the Cuban revolution idealized youth; guerrilla warfare in the Sierra was privileged over the *llano* and the war of ideas; and men's

---

Frank País, "La Valerosa Acción de Santiago de Cuba," *Revolución* February 1957, reprinted in Hart (2004, 157).

contributions were valued over women's. By exploring women rebels over the age of thirty-five – their backgrounds, their paths to activism, and their modes of participation – this chapter challenges these dominant narratives, revealing an insurrection that was generationally diverse, waged significantly through ideas, and with valuable contributions by women.[4]

Drawing from testimonials, memoirs, rebel propaganda, US State Department communiqués, and post-1958 Cuban media interviews, this chapter examines these women from three angles. I first explore specific cases of women rebels and collaborators, identifying several trends: previous political experience, familial rebel networks, and a form of collaboration marked by affectionate respect. The chapter then turns to this generation of women rebels' most powerful contribution, the anti-Batista protests led by mothers of the regime's victims, showing them to have far-reaching consequences in galvanizing domestic opposition, capturing international attention and support, and undermining the regime's legitimacy. Indeed, I argue that maternal protest was one of the most effective tactics against Batista in the war of ideas. Finally, I analyze rebel propaganda, tracking how it represented and appealed to women, especially mothers, through three prominent war narratives: Beautiful Souls lending virtue and purity to calls for an end to regime violence, Spartan Mothers stoically grieving the loss of sons while carrying on the struggle, and Combatant Mothers participating in the revolutionary movement alongside their children.[5] Together, these were powerful weapons in the rebel battle for hearts and minds.

GENERATIONS OF WOMEN REBELS

Cuban revolutionary discourse praised young people for their enthusiasm and purity.[6] As per Che, youth were "free of original sin," untainted by the vices of previous generations.[7] Furthermore, as proposed in previous chapters, rebels tactically referred to women rebels as "young" to connote innocence and vulnerability during the Batista era. However, García-Pérez, in stressing the continuity between the revolutionary generations of the 1890s, 1930s, and 1950s, challenges revolutionary Cuba's celebration of youth as its central driving force.[8] The idealization of youth as well as their numerical dominance within the insurgency have obscured the contributions of those who came of age in the 1930s or prior, and many episodes and forms of struggle as well as categories of rebels remain largely unexamined. I draw here from 107 biographies compiled from interviews and testimonies of women rebels and collaborators collected from three

Cuban newspapers – *Granma, Verde Olivo,* and *Mujeres* – as well as other sources, including oral history recordings and transcripts, autobiographies, and secondary sources.[9] I narrowed the pool to thirty-nine cases of women aged thirty-five and over by 1958. From these, several trends emerge in terms of the women's backgrounds and contributions as well as common discursive threads in the narratives, discussed later.

Though rebels under thirty-five were the majority, the struggle against Batista was more open to older generations of women than implied by Che's rhetoric and the internationally recognized representation of Cuban rebels as bearded young men. In addition to women leaders of M-26-7 and the anti-Batista women's organizations discussed in Chapter 2, many more middle-aged and older women were among the rebel rank and file and collaborators. In examining these women's activism, three themes emerge. The first is previous experience. Many came from politically engaged families who fought in the wars of independence or themselves had participated in the 1930s Cuban protests or the Spanish Civil War, bringing political insights and experience that younger rebels respected.[10] The second theme is familial and cross-generational rebel networks. These middle-aged and older women's rebel biographies reveal a pattern of intergenerational cooperation, as virtually all collaborated with young people, particularly their students and young adult children. Finally, this collaboration was markedly affectionate and familial in nature. In addition to the numerous instances in which women collaborated with their young adult children, the familial network was also signaled by pseudo-familial nicknames sometimes given to the women, such as *La Tía* (Aunt) or *La Abuela* (grandmother).[11] Rebel testimonials and memoirs contain many reverential references to this generation of women rebels.

Clara "Clarita" Lull's rebel history exhibits these features. Her parents were rebels in Cuba's struggles for independence, and Clarita grew up amid veterans recounting war stories and discussing politics, which influenced her own activism.[12] She began her rebel career as a high school student in the Machado era. Two decades later, Clarita and husband Eduardo ventured into Moncada to bear witness to the bloody aftermath of the 1953 assault. In 1956, she joined the *Resistencia Cívica* and formed a cell of nine women. Eventually, she and son Eduardito realized they were both underground rebels, and he recruited her to work directly in M-26-7. She helped organize mothers' protests in Santiago timed for the *Granma* landing, "dressed up as if for a party, with necklaces and everything," a dress code conveying middle-class respectability to the media that also provided some protection.[13]

Leocadia "Cayita" Araújo is a similar case. She had lost her father and six siblings in Cuba's wars of independence. As with many middle-aged and older women rebels, she was a teacher. In the 1930s, she organized teacher strikes against Machado, for which she was brought before tribunals nearly twenty times.[14] Two decades later, Cayita hid Moncada assailants and also helped organize the mother-led "Protest of Silence" on January 4, 1957, collaborating with her rebel daughter María Antonia Figueroa, an M-26-7 leader in Santiago. Rebel leaders Fidel, Haydée, Armando Hart and others later remembered her with great affection and respect, identifying her as a source of inspiration. Hart described her as "an inexhaustible source of optimism for us," a "teacher" of revolutionaries.[15] Fidel wrote her effusive letters from the Sierra: "I am anxious to see you again and to listen to you with great emotion."[16] Years later, when Cayita joined the Cuban Communist Party, Fidel personally signed her membership card – one of only two such cards.[17]

A woman called La Tía held a similar relationship with University of Havana student rebels. José Luis Llovio-Menéndez recalled the esteem his rebel group held for La Tía: "We students often visited her house, where she presided over our protracted discussions and impassioned debates on politics. Many of our actions were planned at La Tía's; she was always there to offer advice and help."[18] This contrasts with the hierarchical, patriarchal mode often expressed by men of the older generation during this period.[19]

Some Cuban women rebels such as Carmen Miera and Trinidad Carvajal were veterans of the Spanish Civil War. Carmen lived the triumphs and tragedies of the Spanish Republican forces, at one point being surrounded and under siege by fascists on a Spanish battlefield for fifteen days.[20] She fled with her husband following the Republican defeat, arriving in Cuba in 1940.[21] Fifteen years later, Carmen and her husband were M-26-7 collaborators with two guerrilla sons in the Sierra Maestra.[22] Another middle-aged rebel of the 1950s, Trinidad Carvajal, was born in Cuba in 1901 to Spanish immigrants.[23] Politically active at the University of Havana, she joined the Communist Party in 1927, working with Julio Antonio Mella until his assassination. Her family supported the Spanish Republican cause, and Trinidad traveled twice to Spain to deliver arms and funds. There she joined the *Guerrilla Gallega*, and as the only woman in a unit of eighty-two men, she served as an armed combatant.[24] When the guerrilla captain died in her arms, the men named her *Capitana*. Two decades later, as a middle-aged teacher in Cuba, she hid rebel students from authorities and drove them to the base of the mountains to join the guerrilla.[25] Trinidad herself was targeted, and she was imprisoned twice and tortured.

As can be seen in these examples, women aged thirty-five and over often came to the 1950s insurrection with extensive political experience, including armed insurrection, from prior activism and family history. Many were also politically mobilized through their children, inspired by them, stepping in to their rebel responsibilities when a son or daughter was killed or imprisoned, and maintaining a maternal vigilance to protect their children. Women whose children were members (or suspected members) of M-26-7 were furthermore pressured and mistreated by police. M-26-7 leader Armando Hart recalled that the police "went to my house ... and mistreated my mother. She told them she didn't know anything about me. They beat her. The bastards [*muy cabrones*] beat a defenseless old woman so that she would speak against her son, but they were wrong, my old lady was tough."[26]

Among the most prominent was Margot Machado Padrón, a leftist teacher in her late 40s who joined the rebels through her three children, all members of M-26-7.[27] The Pino Machado family was "an important center of conspiracy" for M-26-7, with contacts throughout the province of Villa Clara.[28] Margot's son Julio, Santa Clara Chief of Action for M-26-7, was killed with another rebel in May 1957 when a bomb they had manufactured exploded prematurely.[29] Her other son and daughter were also imprisoned. Margot stepped in to assume many of their M-26-7 responsibilities and soon became M-26-7 Coordinator in the province of Las Villas, an area that included the Escambray mountains, which became a key rebel stronghold.[30] She used her job as school inspector for the province as cover to travel throughout the region doing M-26-7 work.[31] Frank País noted the rebel movement in that region as functioning well under Margot's leadership.[32] García-Pérez suggests that with examples such as Margot Machado, the symbolism of the Cuban mother moves beyond that of Mariana Grajales: "no longer in their condition as mothers forging patriot families, but in a capacity of equality with their children in the participation and leadership of the struggle."[33]

Rebellion for María Matilla Clares of Guantanamo was also a family affair. Approaching her 50th birthday, María joined M-26-7 without realizing that her children were also members. At first, they hid rebel work from each other, but they soon found each other out, and the family collaborated. During a 1957 strike, María answered her door to find an army officer holding a gun to son Arnaldo Trutié's chest.[34] He was taken away, and she feared he would be killed unless she forced authorities to acknowledge that he was in custody.[35] Desperate, she visited the wife of the lieutenant who had detained him to make a maternal plea: "My son is not innocent, he is fighting for the country, but I speak to you mother to mother, and I want to know if he is still alive."[36] The woman intervened, and her husband passed María a message from her son. Badly tortured, he was eventually released, at which point her sons left for Havana.[37] Now with greater freedom to develop her own rebel activities, her house became a movement headquarters, with meetings, bomb-making, sewing, and storage of arms, medicines, and other supplies for the Second Front. María transported weapons and participated in sabotage. At one point, police pursued a young rebel to her house, where they found two M-26-7 leaders and two women sewing rebel armbands and uniforms along with a cache of weapons.[38] For this, María was imprisoned for forty-four days. After one son was again detained, her three children escaped into the Sierra, and by August 1958, at the age of fifty, María herself arrived at a guerrilla camp, reuniting with daughter Tisbe before moving to another camp to be closer to her sons, where she served as a nurse's aid in a rebel field hospital.[39]

These examples illustrate the common paths to rebellion for middle-aged and older women rebels. The women often described themselves as radicalized through family histories of activism in the wars of independence. Many were veterans of prior political struggles and thus were respected as patriots with valuable lessons to impart, inspiring and teaching the next generation. Another clear trend in the narratives is their entry into rebellion alongside or recruited by adult children. Finally, I note the familial and affectionate tone of the relationships many of these women maintained with younger rebels, which was inspirational to the latter and contributed to the social glue binding rebel networks.[40] In addition to such individual contributions, middle-aged and older women also mobilized collectively, motivated by the threats that the Batista regime posed to their children and other young people in their lives. I examine such instances below and then analyze gendered discourse representing and appealing to women in this age group.

MOTHERS' PROTESTS

On December 30, 1956, after some thirty rebel bombs exploded in Santiago, military patrols and Military Intelligence Service (SIM) units detained suspected rebels. Several days later, the tortured bodies of four young men, including fifteen-year-old William Soler, were found. Public outrage followed, and M-26-7 called for a women's Protest of Silence. Armando Hart later identified the importance of this protest for M-26-7, occurring as it did a month following the failed Santiago uprising and the *Granma* landing: "we all went to work organizing it. It was an event that showed the strength of the July 26 Movement already among the masses."[41] M-26-7 women were particularly involved, including Vilma Espín, Fela Tornés, Cayita Araújo, Amalia Ros, and Pilar Serrano.[42] Despite M-26-7's active hand in organizing this protest, participants represented it as an initiative of the women leading the march. With such a significant showing of women, the march signaled a broader, organized civic resistance to Batista.[43]

The January 4 Protest of Silence began at the Dolores Church.[44] Scores of women, many in black, emerged after attending mass. As they marched down a central Santiago street, groups of women joined them along the way.[45] Soler's mother headed the protest, with a large banner that demanded: "Stop the murders of our children!" As an estimated 500 to 1,000 women marched, sympathetic crowds gathered along the sidewalks.[46] It was an emotionally evocative event for many, as the women represented a profound maternal grief, directing the blame clearly on the regime. One US journalist reported, "Men watched from the doorways and many wept."[47] According to M-26-7 leader Hart, "Many of the men were moved to tears by their impressive march. Stores closed their doors, and I saw an officer of the US Army, eyes wide open, overcome with emotion. The store employees gradually joined the march at the initiative of the owners themselves. The soldiers sent to disperse that wave of women … were also moved."[48] Troops from the Moncada barracks and the police approached with rifles ready. The women negotiated for an hour and a half with authorities to continue their march, blocking traffic all the while. When authorities ultimately denied their right to proceed, the women sang the national anthem then broke into smaller groups, with some heading to newspaper offices and radio stations to publicize their cause.[49]

Frank País, deploying the "even the women" narrative inspired by Martí, wrote of the protest:

In Oriente even the women have gone out into the street ready for battle. The mothers, just as in the great demonstration of days past, marched in a challenge to [the regime]. The mothers of all Oriente shouted with all their might: "STOP THE MURDERS OF OUR CHILDREN! DOWN WITH THE MURDERERS!" And when the mothers raise their voices like that, it does not take long before they see their promises fulfilled.[50]

The power of maternal supplicants is also suggested in María Antonia Figueroa's recollection of the march.[51] When a soldier used his rifle to block their path, her mother Cayita Araújo responded: "Son, you think that you have power because you have a weapon, but you do not have power. The rich who sent you to do this have the power. You could be my son. Are you not going to let me get through so that I can protest the assassination of our sons?"[52] At that, he let her pass.

Both Frank and María Antonia's framing suggest the power of maternal protest, in which women such as Cayita make appeals through a frame that suggests a maternal relationship with an audience that might otherwise consider them a threat.[53] Indeed, the collective organizing of middle-aged and older women channeled a symbolic power, as their appeals as mothers proved difficult to ignore. In his radio address following another maternal protest, the Archbishop of Santiago, Monseñor Enrique Pérez Serantes, referenced "the hopes and pleas of many mothers who in their pain ask us to intervene in this fight that is so fraught, so complicated, and of such importance" to preface his decision to "break the silence" and call for peace between the warring parties.[54] The efficacy of maternal mobilizing is further indicated below, as US diplomats question whether women in these marches were "really" mothers, suggesting that mothers have an inherent right to protest regime atrocities in a way that others do not.

In addition to protests, women also figured prominently in funeral processions.[55] Indeed, by 1957 funeral processions and burials for rebels were an occasion in which women were particularly likely to be arrested, presumably because they represented a higher proportion of participants than in other protests.[56] Nonetheless, there are also reports of marches held by women from church after mass to protest police killings, during which only men were arrested.[57] For example, in June 1957 in Caibarién, women held a march after church, in which seven men were arrested, with no mention of women's arrests.[58] A month later, women in black protested after mass, during which two men were arrested, again with no mention of women's arrest (though women were reportedly mistreated).[59] These cases illustrate the relative gender immunity that made women's mobilizations viable and effective as a rebel tactic. They were both emotionally evocative to many Cubans while also less likely to bring extreme repression. Indeed, repression against protesting women – "mothers" – was counterproductive to the regime, placing it in a Catch-22 situation in which it had to either allow the protests to proceed or crush them. Either decision would produce a rebel victory

funeral
processions

tactical role of women

in the war of hearts and minds. Thus, it is little surprise that at least on occasion, police and soldiers attacked and arrested only men in or near the march.

However, as such mobilizations continued, Batista forces were sometimes more aggressive in confronting them. On May 28, 1957, the bodies of four young men, bearing signs of torture, were found hanging from trees in Oriente, further galvanizing rebellion.[60] Women organized a protest, but as they gathered at mass in the Santiago church beforehand, police entered armed with submachine guns, and as the women began their march, police roughly broke it up.[61] A month later, at the burial of Frank Pais's brother Josué, women turned on an undercover state intelligence agent, taking off their shoes and hammering him with their high heels.[62] Such protests and processions led by women-as-mothers were effective in attracting press coverage. Indeed, this particular protest made it into *The New York Times* and reflected very poorly on Batista. They are also often mentioned (if briefly) in memoirs, having touched an emotional chord for many rebels and observers.

March of Mothers following the Death of Frank País

The most significant march led by mothers occurred following the assassination of M-26-7 leader Frank País in Santiago on July 30, 1957. In this case, the powerful symbolism of mobilized mothers brought international attention to the Batista regime's repression and disregard for civil rights. It even sparked controversy between the United States and Cuba, and prompted op-ed pieces in US papers, a campaign to recall the US ambassador, and senate hearings.

René Ramos, in a letter to Celia the day after the protest, described the march and M-26-7's role:

> quickly we were able to mobilize the women, asking them to dry their tears and go to work; they rescued [Frank's] body that had by then been taken to the cemetery and they transported it to the place that we chose: the house of his girlfriend, which was in the center of the city, very far from the cemetery, in order to make the journey as long as possible.[63]

He elaborated: "There weren't conservatives and radicals, rich and poor, black and white. No! There was only one people determined to face down whatever risks."[64] Vilma also emphasized the popular response, claiming that she received countless phone calls from the *Resistencia Cívica* as well as shop owners and workers ready to go on strike.[65] In response, Batista suspended constitutional guarantees, including freedom from search and arrest without cause and the rights of habeas corpus, prompt trial, movement, speech, press, and assembly.

On July 31, the day of the funeral, in a previously scheduled visit, the new US Ambassador, Earl T. Smith, arrived in Santiago to receive keys to the city.[66] Nearly all businesses were closed in protest against the killing of this popular rebel leader, including the electric and telephone companies. Police forced some banks to open, but many of the workers refused to work.[67] The US embassy estimated that 60,000 people attended the funeral or lined the streets as the funeral procession went past.[68]

M-26-7 women such as Vilma and members of Las Marianas organized a demonstration of women in mourning to correspond with the ambassador's visit.[69] Conservative Cuban daily *Diario de la Marina* reported that women formed into groups along several streets and the park by early morning and estimated that 400–500 marched, wearing black and carrying signs.[70] When the US ambassador arrived at the *Palacio Municipal* (City Hall), the women gathered nearby in Céspedes Park, singing the national anthem, chanting *libertad* (freedom), and applauding the ambassador.[71] According to one foreign journalist, the women were "begging [the Ambassador] to intervene in order to prevent their sons being killed."[72] M-26-7 leader Hart later commented: "The ambassador's wife, who was 'unaccustomed' to watching such things so close up, was upset to see the police beating the women, who were shouting, 'Murderers!'"[73]

Police chief José María Salas Cañizares ordered the women to disperse, and when they refused, the police charged the demonstrators, beating the women dressed in black mourning clothes and attacking them with water hoses, injuring many. Gloria Cuadras fought back, famously biting the police chief's finger.[74] At least thirty women were arrested.[75] Olga Lara García recalled an elderly woman detained with her. Salas Cañizares said, "We're going to let this *viejita* (little old lady) go. How would she have been mixed up in this mess?"[76] Once she was at the door, however, she turned around and yelled, "'Cañizares, son of a bitch!' and then sprinted off like a deer, and they lost her. Cañizares went crazy with rage. He stopped in front of us with a machine gun and looked like a ferocious beast."[77] Gloria Cuadras, with pre-existing health problems, was beaten and threatened for several days and then released for health reasons.[78] Middle-aged M-26-7 member Amalia Ros was not so fortunate. After being tortured under detention for four days, her health rapidly declined, and she died the following year at the age of fifty.[79]

This protest speaks to the steady chipping away at the regime's legitimacy. As discussed more fully in the next chapter, the growing public contempt for Batista's forces, as demonstrated by the older woman after Salas Cañizares had shown her leniency, presented a severe morale problem contributing to the regime's undoing.[80] The police and military's role in beating and arresting women in mourning surely did not help their reputation or their own sense of themselves as men who are traditionally called upon to protect women.

Rebels remember the mothers' protest and Frank's funeral as "a situation of very great emotion and indignation. It was genuine."[81] The women's demonstration and the subsequent repression also made an impression on the US ambassador.[82] Yet Ambassador Smith took a cynical approach to the Batista government and the protestors alike. Upon hearing of the murders the night before his Santiago trip, Smith "wondered if the event was accidental, or might the shooting [of País] have been done for the purpose of getting me to call off the trip to Oriente."[83] He was suspicious of the protestors as well, noting that the announcement of his trip to Santiago six days prior had given the opposition time to prepare for a demonstration. He further wondered about the protestors' age and maternal identity: "Many were too young to have been mothers of grown sons. They were obviously recruited for the occasion."[84] Thus, he questioned whether the emotion and indignation he witnessed were staged or genuine on the basis of whether the protestors were predominately mothers of murdered rebels. He was nonetheless "appalled by the unnecessary roughness and brutality of the police."[85] In his words, "The women, in attempting to break through the police lines, brought down the wrath of the police and the Army Intelligence men upon them. Fire engines arrived and the firemen turned the hoses on the women. The police unnecessarily beat them back with their clubs."[86]

After witnessing the repression, Ambassador Smith gave reporters an initial response: "I think it unfortunate that some of the people of Santiago de Cuba took advantage of my presence here to demonstrate and protest to their own government."[87] Yet not wanting it inferred that he approved of the government's brutal response, he promised a press conference. One of the State Department's foremost concerns was for Smith to distance himself from his predecessor Ambassador Arthur Gardner, a close friend of Batista believed to have "intervene[ed] on behalf of the government of Cuba to perpetuate the Batista dictatorship."[88] At the press conference, Smith declared:

The American people are saddened and concerned over the political unrest which has led to bloodshed in Cuba. I have received a letter signed by the Mothers of Santiago de Cuba. This will receive my careful attention and consideration. Any form of excessive police action is abhorrent to me. I deeply regret that my presence in Santiago de Cuba may have been the cause of public demonstrations which brought on police retaliation. I sincerely trust that those held by the police as a result of their demonstrations have been released.[89]

As Smith noted in his memoirs, his statement "created a furor."[90] Batista's political allies campaigned to have Smith recalled and Cuban pro-Batista papers issued harsh attacks against him, which some US newspapers reprinted. According to an embassy report, Cuban government spokesmen "bitterly attacked the Ambassador in the press, charging stupidity, incompetence, prejudice and intervention."[91] Rolando Masferrer, Cuban senator, paramilitary leader, and close Batista ally, wrote an editorial in the paper he owned attacking Smith, who, he asserted:

[W]ith utter disregard for official courtesy, ... lands in Santiago de Cuba, as a degraded belligerent, to talk in favor of the rabble rousers and terrorists ... What was the Santiago police doing when the proud pro-Consul arrived? Using water hoses against a Communist Demonstration, a good show organized for the candor of the seven-foot blockhead they sent to us from Florida.[92]

Smith's statement also set off controversy in Washington – controversy that followed Smith for years. The political storm was such that US Secretary of State John Foster Dulles intervened in support of Smith's imperfect but "human" statements.[93] A *New York Times* editorial also weighed in, supporting Smith: "He did more to restore happy relations in one stroke than the most skillful traditional diplomacy could have done in many months. Does this mean that the State Department's attitude toward the dictatorial regime of President Batista has changed? Cubans evidently now believe so."[94] Indeed, for a short period, Ambassador Smith was popular in Cuba. He recounted that when he attended the horse races in Havana soon after, the largely Cuban audience gave him a standing ovation, which Smith interpreted as "an eager tribute to an American respect of humanity, so clearly expressed at Santiago."[95]

But the controversy in the United States surrounding Ambassador Smith's rather tepid disapproval of excessive police force against the women did not die down. Indeed, the US Senate Sub-Committee on Internal Security Hearings in 1960 focused on the incident in its inquiry into who bore responsibility for losing Cuba to the Soviets. Smith's predecessor, Ambassador Arthur Gardner, expressed surprise in the hearings that Smith even went to Santiago, "down near where Castro was" (and Cuba's second largest city), explaining "they put on a professional parade for him – the women all in black, supposedly the widows and so on of Castro people that had been killed or murdered, or whatever they talked about."⁹⁶ Then, "unfortunately, the police, in order to break up the meeting, used a hose on them. The result was that he, Smith, said that in his country nothing like that would ever happen, we never treat them that way ... And the Cuban Government became infuriated."⁹⁷ Ambassador Smith, questioned in the same hearings, claimed to be carrying out the main task assigned to him by the State Department: to correct the impression that the United States was "too close to the Batista government ... [and instead] to have the U.S. Embassy considered as being impartial."⁹⁸

Photos of such mothers' marches circulate in revolutionary Cuba, displayed at the Museum of the Revolution in Havana and appearing with newspaper articles looking back at the insurrection. Rebel memoirs and interviews also regularly make mention of the protest. But the diplomatic controversy it launched is less well known, and the significance of these women's protests is obscured by the attention given to the guerrilla war.

Largely lost in the literature is that this protest and the other mother-led protests were key gendered moments in the battle for hearts and minds domestically and internationally.⁹⁹ Observers' descriptions speak to their emotionally evocative nature, providing insight into the narratives that particularly motivated Cubans to move from bystander to collaborator or rebel. The protest functioned similarly to other forms of nonviolent resistance in Cuba. In this instance, the protestors' innocence was secured by their identity as respectable middle-aged and older mothers in mourning. The Batista regime found itself caught in the international spotlight beating unarmed women for calling for an end to the killing of their children. Moreover, the US ambassador, by his own account, was forced to condemn the actions of the United States's closest ally in the hemisphere.

MATERNAL TROPES/GENDERED APPEALS

Tracing the rebel histories of women in this age group and also examining the mothers' protests in Oriente, I find that these women's activism largely preceded and informed rebel propaganda that represented and appealed to women. That is, M-26-7 responded to women's successful examples of activism by developing propaganda appeals with particular frames that reached out to middle-aged and older women. In what follows, I chart three discursive trends of such women's rebellion: Beautiful Souls, Spartan Mothers, and Combatant Mothers. While the first two support a traditional association of masculinity and war, the latter legitimizes and calls forth women's active participation in insurrection.

Not long after Batista's coup, women's collective voice often followed the discursive tradition of Beautiful Souls, observing from a position of innocent transcendence, hovering above the evils of the world and reminding society of human virtue and morality.[100] For example, a "group of distinguished ladies" described as "faithful interpreters of the noble sentiments of our people," submitted a protest to the Cuban political magazine *Bohemia* in 1953 expressing "fear that the reaping of human lives may be converted into a system bringing mourning and blood to the whole nation."[101] The article proclaimed, "When the Cuban women exhort us to use good judgment and not to let violence reign our public lives, they ... [include] all Cubans regardless of their political way of thinking. To hear in reverent silence this fine, sensible, sympathetic and humane appeal, is a duty to everyone."[102]

After the *Granma* landing in late 1956, the families of the *Granma* rebels had grown increasingly distressed at the lack of news as to the fate of loved ones. As rumors circulated that Fidel and Raúl Castro had been killed, their mother Lina Ruz de Castro issued a statement: "I suffer as the mothers of soldiers and revolutionaries, but if Fidel and Raúl decide to die, I pray that they might die with dignity ... I weep for my sons, and I would embrace [in] the same way the mothers of the companions of my sons as the mothers of the soldiers who have died in this painful war."[103] In the discursive tradition of Beautiful Souls, Lina Castro expresses a maternal transcendence above politics, suffering for her sons while extending the hand of peace to the families of their enemies.

A second mobilizing identity by which rebel propaganda represented mothers was that of Cuban Spartan Motherhood – women following the example of Mariana Grajales, sending sons off to war and stoically grieving their death. At the death of Josué País, Cuban narratives describe his mother Rosario as suppressing her grief at the side of her son's body, saying with sadness and deep bitterness but dry-eyed: "What a shame ... ! They have cut short a life that began so full of hope."[104] Cuba's Spartan Mothers, then, mastered their emotions, feeling but not showing them. Fathers were sometimes similarly valorized. For example, in writing to the father of a rebel who died at Moncada, Fidel recognized both mother and father for their sacrifice: "Because [your son] offered himself and you offered him, your courage in the face of sorrow is as heroic and generous as his was in the face of death. He would be so proud of you ... As with you, also with your wife. I know she is a Spartan mother."[105]

Several of the women's narratives at the beginning of this chapter follow a third prominent rebel effort to represent and appeal to mothers: Combatant Mothers, in which women participated in the revolutionary movement alongside their children.[106] This example of revolutionary solidarity evoked a novel form of equality as well as suggested the rightness of the cause, when even the mothers join their rebel children in the struggle against Batista. In a theme repeated by other mothers, Ester Montes de Oca Domínguez recalled her son Luis, who responded to her fears for his rebel involvement by reminding her that it was she who had taught him to always put the love of country before even the love of one's mother.[107] Thus framed, rebel sons and daughters were following their mother's ideals. Both of Ester's sons, aged seventeen and eighteen, were killed in August 1957.

Cuban women exiled in Mexico wrote "To our sisters of America and Cuba" in November 1957, calling upon women to stand in "solidarity and support" alongside their men:

They, with us, are writing a page of history that cannot be more dramatic and instructive ... Cuban women today are above all fighters. The prisoner felt our presence, as has every woman in mourning [...] [Our presence] is in the Sierra Maestra, it was in Cienfuegos with the popular uprising on September 5, 1957, it is everywhere. Women in villages, peasants, housewives, women intellectuals, teachers, scientists, artists have risked their lives carrying out human and concrete tasks, oblivious to outdated romanticism.[108]

As seen in this passage, unlike the Beautiful Soul and Spartan Mother mobilizing identities, which sustained the idea of armed insurrection as exclusive to men, here women are called upon as combatants, risking their lives both in support of and alongside men.

For women aged thirty-five and over, this struggle was often expressed through a Combatant Motherhood identity. The influential 1957 maternal protests in Santiago demonstrated the propaganda potential of mothers. Direct rebel appeals to mothers as potential contributors to the cause increased, especially in the second half of 1958. Against a popular conception of women as apolitical, the alternative maternal discourse often reached back to the wars of independence to project a representation based upon Mariana Grajales and other mambisas – one that went beyond supporting their menfolk to legitimize women's direct participation in rebellion, particularly in the name of their children and Cuba.

Other historical examples were also used to normalize and valorize the idea of women rebels alongside men. For example, a November 1958 rebel radio broadcast traced women's history of struggle on the island, from independence – "in spite of the conventions of that epoch" – to the 1930s and into the 1950s.[109] With such a history,

Women can't shy away from their responsibility in the present day ... They were with the men of Moncada ... They are active in the clandestine work in the cities. The savage tortures never frightened them ... [T]here is still more: women go up into the Sierra and descend to the Llano to demonstrate with rifle in hand their love of freedom. Forward women, don't falter![110]

In *Radio Rebelde* broadcasts supporting the April 1958 general strike, another theme emerged: references to attacks on women's honor alongside maternal grief and Cuban women's history of struggle:

CUBAN WOMEN: You have seen the blood of your children run through our streets, ... you have seen your flesh destroyed by the blows of the cruel tyranny, join us as well in the struggle for the freedom of the country. Help in what you can, so that this oppressive and criminal regime disappears from our country. To the street – recover the dignity the despot has violated. To the street – defend our virtue and our sacred condition of womanhood. To the streets, Cuban women![111]

Through documenting and analyzing the multiple instances in which women responded to this call and went into the streets to face down the Batista regime, this chapter has maintained that middle-aged and older women were numerically and symbolically more prominent in the insurrection than the dominant war narrative conveys. Cumulatively, these stories challenge the Cuban War Story's focus on the leaders, the young, the Sierra guerrilla, the men, and the battle of bullets. The cases examined here, focused on an age group often ignored not only in Cuba but more generally in insurrection, speak to the importance of the rank and file, the older generations, the *llano*, the women, and the battle of ideas.

Notes

1.   Havana, May 1957, translated and reprinted in 26th of July Movement 1958, Part 2, no page number. The letter is signed by thirty-seven women – following each woman's name is the name of her son who died.

2.   See, for example, Bayard de Volo (2001); Stephen (1997); Noonan (1995); Schirmer (1993); Fisher (1989); Navarro (1989).

3.   See Chase (2015, 78–9). Examining maternal protest in the Cuban insurrection, Chase argues that women used maternal representations such as innocence and naivety strategically.

4.   García-Pérez (1999).

5.   Elshtain (1987); Bayard de Volo (2001).

6. Luke (2012, 132–4).
7. Guevara (1965 [1969], 166). Some rebels were indeed quite young, including cases of literal rebel girls. For example, thirteen-year-old María Esther de la Rosa Álvarez joined M-26-7 as a messenger and contact, her adolescence serving as a cover (Heidy Gonzáles Cabrera, "Cita con Fidel," *Mujeres* November 1985, 14–15). Rosa Berdeja, at fifteen, sold war bonds, distributed the underground newspaper, and helped rebels hide (Gladys Castaño, "El mismo pueblo, la misma decision," *Mujeres* January 1982, 4–6). M-26-7 assigned sixteen-year-old Piedad Ferrer important revolutionary tasks, such as debriefing rebels returning from the Sierra and aiding foreign journalists. Enrique Meneses of *Paris-Match* described Piedad as, "a pretty and courageous messenger, ... who smuggled my report out of the island between two starched petticoats" (Meneses 1966, 66). However, rarely did children under fifteen participate in direct hostilities, and I found no record of women bringing their children with them as they escaped into the guerrilla camps, in marked contrast to the Central American cases two decades later as well as Cuba's own Wars of Independence (Viterna 2013; Bayard de Volo 2001; Prados-Torreira 2005). In the few incidents of women rebels with young children who were forced into the Sierra for their own safety, they left their children with family or friends rather than bring them into camp.
8. García-Pérez (2009); Luke (2012).
9. I draw from three Cuban newspapers for the period 1960–91: *Granma, Verde Olivo,* and *Mujeres* as well as the Lyn Smith oral histories (audio recordings) housed at the US Library of Congress and the many Cuban media historical reports published or archived online.
10. See Pérez (2013, 173–6). "[T]he aspirations that informed the hopes of a generation contained within their telling deeply emotional content: a people learning history through the lives of loved ones. Vast numbers of young men and women of the republic sat in the presence of their history, privy to the past as a matter of first-person experiences and through which they developed emotional bonds to their history" (Pérez 2013, 174).
11. María Lara Fonseca, known as "La Abuela," was a rebel courier in her early 60s.
12. Prada, *Verde Olivo* November 1988, 20–4.
13. Ibid., 22.
14. EcuRed (n.d.). Síntesis biográfica, Leocadia Araujo Pérez.
15. Hart (2004, 135).
16. Klouzal (2008, 85).
17. María Antonia, in Klouzal (2008, 85); EcuRed (n.d.). Araujo Pérez.
18. Llovio-Menéndez (1988, 62).
19. Husbands were either co-collaborators who participated alongside their rebel wives or were absent, either literally or from the narrative. For example, María Fernández Aguilera and her husband Manuel Cespedes were referred to affectionately within the movement as "Los Tíos" (Magaly Sánchez, "Tíos, una palabra para el amor y la guerra," *Mujeres* January 1981, 10–12). They transported rebels, arms, and supplies. Their house was located in a busy part of Santiago that helped conceal the continual comings

and goings of rebels. Under this protection, the national and provincial leadership of M-26-7 held important meetings there. A clandestine rebel radio station operated from there, which transmitted instructions, slogans, and news. See also no author, "Datos biográficos de María Lara Fonseca 'La Abuela'" *Granma* August 3, 1979, 3; no author, "Fallecio María Lara Fonseca 'La Abuela,'"*Granma* July 24, 1981, 4.

20. Rodríguez Pérez, *Mujeres* 1990 (no. 5), 47–8.
21. Cuadriello (2009, 446).
22. Rodríguez Pérez (1990, 47–8). Julio manufactured a form of napalm for rebels in Santiago.
23. Graciela Navas Armas, "Una Cubana mas allá del tiempo," *Verde Olivo* June 1989, 48.
24. Ibid. (1989, 49); Rosa María Lecrere also participated as a teacher of Spanish war orphans.
25. Navas Armas (1989, 46–9).
26. Hart in Bernal and Rodríguez, *Verde Olivo* December 29, 1983, 29.
27. García-Pérez (1999, 122).
28. Hart (2004, 117).
29. Eliseo Alberto, "Justo reconocimiento," *Verde Olivo* September 9, 1979, 52; García-Pérez (1999, 122). García-Pérez was the only survivor of the bomb blast.
30. Hart (2004, 262).
31. García Pérez (1999). Margot went into exile in Venezuela in 1958; upon returning after Batista fled, she was named Vice Minister of Education.
32. June 27, 1957 letter from Frank País (David) to Fidel Castro (Alejandro), from Princeton University Library microfilm (Princeton University Latin American Pamphlet Collection): "Documents of the Movimiento 26 de Julio," May 1957–December 1958, Roll 2; García-Pérez (1999, 122); March (2012, 24).
33. García-Pérez (1999, 121).
34. Magaly Sánchez Ochoa, *Mujeres* April 1980, 22–5.
35. Ibid. Decades later, she recalled praying: "My God, if he has to die, let him die like a man and not like a traitor." Such remarks are not unusual in women's interviews published in the Cuban media.
36. Ibid.
37. Martín, *Mujeres* November 1976, 49.
38. Ibid.
39. Raúl Castro sent her a personal note on her 70th birthday in 1978. Sánchez Ochoa (1980, 22–5); Rodríguez Rey, *Mujeres* April 1977, 16–17.
40. See Shayne (2004).
41. Hart (2004, 142).
42. Sarabia (1983, 74).
43. Taber (1961, 87).
44. Hart estimates nearly 3,000 women marched (Hart 2004, 143); elsewhere, the estimation is 800 women (Herbert L. Matthews, "Rebel Strength Gaining in Cuba, but Batista Has the Upper Hand," *The New York Times* February 25, 1957, 1) and as low as 500 women (Thomas 1998, 912).

45. García Torres, "Manifestación de madres en Stgo. de Cuba," *Diario de la Marina* January 5, 1957, A1, B20.
46. Ibid., B20; Hart (2004, 142).
47. Taber (1961, 86).
48. Hart (2004, 143)
49. Sarabia (1983, 74–5). One Cuban paper reported that the police and military were "calm and persuasive" (Torres 1957, B20).
50. Frank País' account of the uprising in Santiago, November 30, 1956: "La Valerosa Acción de Santiago de Cuba," *Revolución* February 1957; reprinted in Hart 2004, 157.
51. See Bayard de Volo (2001).
52. Shayne (2004, 133).
53. Bayard de Volo (2001).
54. García Torres, "Aquellos que de verdad amen a Cuba deben sacrificarlo todo en aras de la paz," *Diario de la Marina* May 31, 1957, A1.
55. When Thelma Bornot's cousin was killed in Oriente in February 1958, the funeral procession was dominated by women. Members of Batista's rural guard lined the route and began shooting and beating mourners at the cemetery entrance ("Testimonio Thelma Bornot", *Mujeres* July 1978, 46).
56. For example, at the burial of the four rebels killed in the Humboldt Seven police attack, of the fourteen arrested, nine were women (26th of July Movement 1958, Part 2, no page number).
57. Women's protests were common in June and especially July 1957, occurring in many parts of Cuba, including Santa Clara and the small cities of Caibarién, Güines, and Campechuela (see 26th of July Movement 1958, Part 2, no page number). In Santa Clara in July 1957, Esther Jorge Méndez was badly beaten and hospitalized; at a July 1957 women's march in Campechuela, many women were detained.
58. 26th of July Movement 1958, Part 2, no page number.
59. Ibid.
60. Herbert L. Matthews, "Populace in Revolt in Santiago de Cuba," *The New York Times* June 10, 1957, 1,10.
61. Ibid. One report indicates that *Las Martianas* members were arrested by police after going to mass in Santiago for the young men (26th of July Movement 1958, Part 2, no page number).
62. Stout (2013, 193).
63. Princeton microfilm, August 1, 1957 letter, Ramos ("Daniel") to Celia ("Aly"), p. 4; see also Bonachea and San Martín (1974, 146). Frank's younger brother Josué had been killed the month before. "[Police Chief] Salas Cañizares is said to have come to the cemetery when Josué was being buried and told Señora País to advise her sons 'not to make any trouble'. Frank's mother, according to witnesses, replied that she still had two sons 'to give to Cuba'" (Meneses 1966, 51).
64. Princeton microfilm, August 1, 1957, roll 2, p. 2.
65. Vilma Espín, "Déborah" (entrevista). Revista *Santiago* 18–19 (junio–septiembre de 1975), 57–97. Oltuski (2002) describes the Civic Resistance as "mainly including professionals, women, and businessmen. Their main

activities were fundraising and passing out propaganda, but they also offered their homes for meetings and as places to hide" (109).

66. Smith (1962, 18).
67. García Torres, "Está triste y preocupado el pueblo de E.U. por el desasosiego existente en Cuba, dijo Mr. Smith," *Diario de la Marina* August 1, 1957, A1, B8. The influential *Diario de la Marina* was a Catholic, conservative Havana paper, and particularly in this climate of censorship and repression, it did not focus often on rebel activities. Thus, the report on the women's protest and the ambassador's visit was unusual for its topic and level of detail, suggesting that this mothers' protest combined with the ambassador's visit and resulting general strike captured the paper's attention in a way that other events considered major by M-26-7 itself did not.
68. Earl T. Smith, "Foreign Service Despatch, from the Embassay in Cuba to the Department of State," August 7, 1957.
69. Espín (1975, 57–97).
70. García Torres (1957, A1); Phillips (1959, 327). Phillips estimated roughly hundred women, though she did not witness the event.
71. García Torres (1957, A1).
72. Meneses (1966, 51).
73. Hart (2004, 187). The ambassador's wife is largely absent from the US versions, including Ambassador Smith's recounting.
74. Ibid.
75. García Torres (1957, A1, B8). Olga Lara García, one of those arrested, estimated sixty women were arrested (Sánchez Ochoa 1980, 7). A month later, women placing flowers where he had died were arrested.
76. Sánchez Ochoa (1980, 7).
77. Ibid.
78. Barceló (2003). She recovered and transferred to the Second Front, where she worked with Radio Rebelde.
79. Nidia Sarabia, "De nuestra historia: Amalia Ros (1908–1958)," *Mujeres* February 1983, 45; EcuRed (n.d.) Síntesis biográfica, Amalia Ros Reyes.
80. Pérez (1976, 153).
81. Hart (2004, 187).
82. Dubois (1959, 173).
83. Smith (1962, 18).
84. Ibid., 19.
85. Ibid.
86. Ibid.
87. Ibid., 20.
88. Ibid.
89. Ibid., 21.
90. Ibid., 22.
91. Smith (1957, 3) (Latin American Studies Archives).
92. *Tiempo* article, translated and reprinted in 26th of July Movement 1958, Part 2, no page numbers.
93. Smith (1962, 24).
94. *The New York Times* editorial, August 3, 1957, quoted in Smith (1962, 25).

95. Ibid., 26.

96. United States Senate, Sub-Committee on Internal Security Hearings, United States Senate, Eighty-Sixth Congress, Second Session, Part 9, August 27, 1960, Testimony of Arthur Gardner (Latin American Studies Archives).

97. Ibid.

98. Ibid. August 30, 1960, Testimony of Earl E. T. Smith (Latin American Studies Archives).

99. See Chase (2015).

100. Elshtain (1987, 4–6).

101. *Bohemia*, "The Death of Mario Fortuny" November 27, 1953; translated and reprinted in 26th of July Movement 1958, Part 1, no page numbers.

102. Ibid.

103. Szulc (1986, 382); Coltman (2003, 117).

104. Leonardo Padura Fuentes, "Recuerdan aniversario 50 del asesinato de Josué País, Floro Vistel y Salvador Pascual," *Diario de la juventud cubana* June 30, 2007.

105. Castro's Letter to René Guitart from prison on the Isle of Pines, July 17, 1954, in Bardach and Conte Agüero (2007, 54).

106. Bayard de Volo (2001).

107. Teresa Mederos, "Esther Montes de Oca: Maestra, educadora siempre," *Mujeres* December 1985, 14–15.

108. "A nuestras hermanas de América y de Cuba," México, 6 de noviembre de 1957, reprinted in García-Pérez (1999, 124). The letter was signed by Marta Frayde, Clara Martínez Luzco de Blanco, Ofelia L. Gronlier, Pura del Prado, Emma Castro Ruz, Lidia Castro, Esther Pérez de Pino, and Agustina Castro Ruz.

109. "¡A la mujer Cubana!" Radio Rebelde broadcast November 18, 1958, reprinted in *Granma* September 18, 1978, 2. In contrast, Lobao Reif found "no attempt to mobilize specifically women" (1986, 155).

110. "¡A la mujer Cubana!" *Granma* September 18, 1978, 2.

111. Princeton University Library microfilm, Radio Rebelde April 9, 1958.

CHAPTER 8

Masculinity and the Guerrilla War of Ideas

This chapter covers the rise of guerrilla warfare in 1957–58 and begins an inquiry into how guerrilla warfare was gendered. After an overview of the shift in command from the *llano* to the Sierra, it turns to how the guerrilla war was waged and won, arguing for the important role of the rebels' hearts and minds campaign. Despite the Cuban War Story's near-exclusive celebration of guerrilla military engagements, echoed in more muted tones in much of the literature, I show how the guerrillas relied upon a gendered war of ideas that both exploited military weaknesses and attracted popular support.

The rebels pursued several tactics in this struggle for hearts and minds. On the basis of sheer numbers, weapon power, supplies, and training, Batista soldiers appeared to comprise the superior military and express hegemonic masculinity. But rebel rhetoric challenged these soldiers' masculinity, representing instead the rebels – ragtag, poorly armed, and not formally trained – as the superior men. Rebels also divided the Batista military from within, distinguishing between most soldiers, who were men of honor, and *Batistianos* who were men without honor – indeed, corrupt rapists and assassins. M-26-7 dealt swiftly and harshly with accused rapists and positioned itself as the army that did not rape, which I argue was an important means of winning civilian support. As Fidel Castro's star rose, it too was tied to gender, and he performed *machismo* to increasing acclaim. Representations of Celia Sánchez served as the feminine rebel ideal against which Fidel's masculinity has been measured and celebrated.

Sánchez

165

M-26-7 GUERRILLAS AND THE APRIL STRIKE

Once the small group of *Granma* survivors reached the relative safety of the mountains in late 1956, they set about gaining support among the local population. Bonachea and San Martín note the power of Fidel's "mere presence in the Sierra Maestra," which contributed significantly to his popularity.[1] The Sierra had a considerable advantage over the *llano* in that the latter, operating clandestinely, had limited ability to rally support.[2] For example, *Chicago Tribune* reporter Jules Dubois, in the month before Frank País's death, had been unable to interview him "because he was changing hide-outs so frequently that it was dangerous both to him and to me to insist on it."[3] The guerrillas in the Sierra at this time were more accessible to journalists, and Fidel welcomed them.

Frank's death in July 1957 had a significant impact on the rebel division of labor.[4] M-26-7 immediately responded with violence, killing eleven suspected informers in one week in Santiago.[5] This was very effective, in Vilma's words, "because it terrorized them and after that betrayals were rare."[6] Rebel correspondence reveals Fidel to have been bitter and indignant over Frank's death, but it also allowed him to promote people who more readily deferred to his leadership. While René Ramos Latour ("Daniel") formally moved into Frank's position, Vilma assumed much of Frank's responsibilities in the Santiago underground, acting as chief of organization.[7] Fidel assigned Celia to fill Frank's responsibilities to the Sierra. Additional rebel authority was thus placed in women's hands yet under conditions that secured Fidel as the undisputed leader of M-26-7 and the Sierra as the center of conflict. Indeed, he instructed Celia in no uncertain terms, "The proper order should now be: 'All guns, all bullets, and all supplies to the Sierra!'"[8]

Many Cubans made their way up the Sierra to join the guerrillas. But leaders turned away most for lack of rifles, and Castro's guerrilla force remained relatively small until the insurrection's final months. They often avoided Batista troops, and the latter increasingly avoided the guerrilla. Rank and file Batista soldiers reportedly asked civilians in the Sierra not to reveal to their officers the location of the rebels, which fed the perception that many soldiers did not want to fight.[9] Engagements with Batista's forces were relatively rare and usually occurred on the guerrillas' terms. While the guerrillas were effective at evading Bastista's forces, civilians did not fare so well, and the repression against civilian populations turned more people against the authorities until "hatred against anything resembling a military uniform became almost universal."[10]

Though Castro enjoyed more public attention than any *llano* leader, the guerrillas were dependent upon the *llano* for supplies, and in early 1958 many orders still issued from the *llano*.[11] The *llano* leadership argued for a national strike, believing that popular support was sufficient to ensure success. National M-26-7 leaders met in the Sierra in early March, including Fidel, Haydée Santamaría, Vilma Espín, Marcelo Fernández, René Ramos Latour, David Salvador, Miguel Ángel Ruiz Maceiras, and Faustino Pérez. There, they agreed to the national strike.

Women rank and file rebels were assigned support roles in the strike. Pastorita Núñez's orders were to form a Havana *Comando Femenino* to provide medical attention. The twenty-two Comando women received first aid training and scoured Havana for secure locations to serve as safe houses and first aid stations.[12] Members prepared hundreds of Molotov cocktails, a substantial undertaking that involved acquiring, transporting, preparing, and storing "industrial quantities" of gas cans, fuses, and bottles.[13] Women also served as drivers. For example, M-26-7 assigned Piedad Ferrer to chauffeur a foreign journalist around Havana to observe the strike and interview rebel participants, while Emma Pérez drove M-26-7 leader Faustino Pérez (no relation) to machine-gun strike-breaking city buses.[14]

Despite high hopes and significant preparations, the strike went badly outside of Oriente. Government forces struck back aggressively, killing militia captains as well as lawyers who tried to come to their defense. A US journalist heard Havana's police chief tell officers over police radio that he wanted no reports of captured rebels, only deaths.[15] By dawn the next morning, Havana's morgue held ninety-two bullet-ridden bodies.[16] M-26-7 estimated two hundred killed in Havana alone.[17]

According to the US Consul in Santiago's confidential report, though the strike was a failure elsewhere, "Castro's war of nerves and propaganda effort was very effective" in Oriente.[18] There, many businesses closed and workers stayed at home as militias and guerrilla columns attacked Batista forces. Yet businesses began to open on word that the national strike had failed. By the second day, because striking Oriente workers were losing jobs for a strike failing everywhere else, Vilma directed Santiago workers to return to work and alerted Havana to call off the strike.[19]

THE SIERRA TAKES OVER FROM THE *LLANO*

Despite an organizational structure in which *llano* leaders held considerable decision-making power, many observers viewed M-26-7 as the "Castro movement" with rebel authority emanating from the Sierra. This

confusion is evident in a February 1958 US Embassy report after debriefing a US journalist who had spent two weeks with the guerrillas: "[Vilma
Espín and another *llano* leader] spoke of Castro as merely the military
commander for the movement, subject to the will of the Directorate. In
contrast, Castro spoke and acted as an absolute ruler, and appeared to
be obeyed as such."[20] The internal tensions over leadership and tactics
implied in such observations came to a head with the failed strike. Batista
claimed the rebel movement was waning, and observers such as US journalist Ruby Hart Phillips, based in Havana, agreed, "It did look like it.
The rebels faced setbacks on all fronts."[21]

   The failure opened up intense debate over tactics and leadership.
Vilma's decision to call off the strike in Santiago, where the strike had
been successful, set off a dispute with René Ramos, urban militia leader.[22]
Poststrike repression drove hundreds of urban militia, under René's command, into the hills, and René proposed that these militias conduct small-
scale attacks to wear down the regime and prevent the military from
concentrating on the Sierra.[23] Vilma refused to help René make his case,
for which he accused Vilma of insubordination.[24] By this time, Vilma had
been in the Sierra for over a month, and it was now too dangerous for
her to return to the *llano*.[25] Celia, too, was clearly oriented toward the
Sierra and in agreement with Fidel's plan to concentrate leadership and
the struggle there.[26]

   Fidel convened a May 3 national meeting at Los Altos de Mompié to
propose that all national leaders transfer to the Sierra. Many M-26-7
activists had been killed, captured, or transferred into the Sierra for their
own safety. The Sierra guerrilla camps were growing while the urban
groups, under siege following the strike, had been reduced or dispersed.[27]
The meeting, described as exhausting, tense, and even violent, included
Fidel, Che, Vilma, Haydée, Celia, and seven other men.[28] The three
women, identified by Castro biographer Tad Szulc as "Fidel's closest personal associates in the Directorate," provided, along with Che, a crucial
counterbalance to the *llano* men there to defend themselves.[29] Historian
Julia Sweig summarized the outcome: "Once the vanguard, the urban
underground had finally been relegated to the revolution's rearguard."[30]
The National Directorate was dissolved, Fidel assumed command, and
the struggle centralized in the Sierra.

   With this, the size of the national leadership was reduced and oriented
toward guerrilla warfare. This shift had implications for the women leaders, as they either transferred abroad or lost formal positions.[31] Haydée
was placed in charge of fundraising in exile and left for the United

States.[32] Celia and Vilma, based in the Sierra, were without formal titles or authority. Celia and, to a lesser extent, Vilma now relied on soft power – commanding respect and affection, and exercising authority on that basis as well as their relationships with the Castro brothers, as opposed to formal command backed by the authority to coerce and punish.[33] René, chief planner of the failed strike, came out ahead of the women in leadership assignments.[34] René, Faustino, and David transferred to the Sierra and remained in the national leadership under Fidel. Having handed over command of *llano* groups, they were in effect demoted; nonetheless, these men remained in the top echelon and endowed with formal authority.[35]

The reason for Celia and Vilma's disappearance from the formal ranks of leadership is unclear. Recognized as trusted Fidel loyalists, perhaps unlike the men of similar rank they did not push for formal leadership roles. Furthermore, in this comprehensive shift toward guerrilla warfare, there is nothing in the documentary record to indicate that women were viewed as potential military commanders capable of leading armed troops into battle. Finally, in the midst of this leadership shakeup, Celia and Vilma were developing personal relationships with Fidel and Raúl Castro, respectively, which also helps make sense of the informal authority that the women now exercised.[36]

With this restructuring, guerrilla and civic resistance increased, matched by government repression. The US consul in Santiago reported rebel activity and government repression to be increasing by June: "At the moment there is a large sugar warehouse on fire on the waterfront, with everybody immediately assuming it is sabotage. A local pastor had a funeral Monday, and says he counted 19 unidentified bodies at the cemetery ... Trains are being attacked again."[37] Much of the repression by government forces targeted those they could reach: *campesinos*, students, and other civilians. Increasingly, young men and some women sought out Castro's guerrillas. With the weapons shortage, unarmed rebels were more a burden than an asset, and many were turned away. Reinaldo Arenas wrote of his efforts to join the rebels, meeting a group of forty-five men and seven women whom the rebels had turned away because they were without rifles.[38] Arenas, too, was instructed to return to the city, kill a *guardia*, and take his rifle: "If you bring a rifle or shotgun, we'll [accept] you at once."[39] By March 1958, rebels had completed landing strips and began to fly arms into Cuba.[40] More weapons were captured from the military during its Summer Offensive in 1958.[41] Thus, summer 1958 marked the point at which the weapon shortage eased, though did not disappear.

M-26-7 was not the only rebel group dedicated to armed insurrection. About nine months after its failed assassination attempt against Batista on March 13, 1957, the *Directorio Revolucionario* (DR) and other armed groups established fronts in the Escambray Mountains in the central province of Las Villas, and within six months controlled much of the area.[42] An estimated 800 DR guerrillas were in the Escambray by September 1958, plus 150 new recruits in training and another fifty people serving as messengers.[43] They thus outnumbered M-26-7 guerrillas, which counted roughly 300 at the time. M-26-7 leaders were more particular about who they accepted as guerrilla combatants. Escambray was also more easily accessible, and rebels persecuted in Havana increasingly escaped there. The DR guerrillas inflicted hundreds of casualties against the military.[44] Their success was such that in October 1958 Castro sent Che to Escambray to centralize guerrilla command.[45]

ENGENDERING THE WAR OF IDEAS

How did this small band of guerrillas defeat Batista's military of tens of thousands? The question echoes the approach overwhelmingly adopted in the literature – a focus on what the guerrilla did right, often in triumphal military terms. An alternative explanation is that the rebels did not defeat Batista so much as succeed in "making Batista destroy himself."[46] Yet this explanation also focuses on rebel military tactics, to which Batista responded with generalized terror against the population, eliciting universal revulsion and the regime's collapse. A fuller understanding requires that we look into the war of ideas – the hearts and minds campaign through which the rebels exploited the Batista military's shortcomings. Louis Pérez's account of the Cuban armed forces details much of its self-destruction, and the analysis that follows builds upon these findings to explore the rebels' exploitation of military weaknesses through a war of ideas.[47] This extends the explanation for the rebel victory more broadly than the literature typically recognizes, beyond battlefield victories – which were relatively few and only partially account for the defeat of an army of tens of thousands – to consider military weaknesses as well as the gendered symbolic nature of the winning strategy.

Pérez identifies five problems in the armed forces contributing to its defeat. First, the military was trained and armed as a US ally in the Cold War and thus was unprepared for rural, low-intensity, guerrilla warfare. Batista declared, "From the military or national security point of view ... [Castro's rebels have] no significance at all," a perspective from which a series of inadequate and floundering responses flowed.[48] Second, by mid-1957 the military applied a "campaign of extermination," turning the Sierra Maestra into a free-fire zone.[49] It forcibly relocated thousands of *campesinos*, badly alienating the rural population, with many resisting relocation or joining the guerrilla.[50] Third, the military was fractured, divided between the professional academy officers and the political appointees. The division was exacerbated by the growing civilian contempt for the armed forces.[51] Pérez tells us: "Whatever self-view soldiers held – whatever perception they had of the cause for which they fought – suffered in the looking-glass image refracted by the civilian population."[52] As a commander who defected to the rebels tellingly remarked: "We felt as if we were an army of occupation."[53] Fourth, weapons captured by rebels or abandoned by soldiers in retreat, combined with the 1958 US arms embargo, further undermined the military's self-confidence in waging war and its faith in the government. Meanwhile, this benefitted the rebels, who used the military as their main source of weaponry.[54] Fifth, the government instituted obligatory military service, and thousands of young men were drafted, "[h]astily trained, inadequately armed, [and] hurled against the guerrilla veterans."[55] The collapse of these units in battle further demoralized the military.[56]

The literature rarely gives these factors their due in explaining rebel victory. Though very damaging, these were not necessarily fatal flaws, and a fuller understanding of the fall of Batista requires that we look to how the rebels seized upon these military weaknesses through its war of ideas.

Toward this end, the Sierra rebels created Radio Rebelde as well as the newspaper *El Cubano Libre*. With the established Cuban press under government censorship, rebel broadcasts and newspapers were a rare source of anti-Batista news and the rebels' means of mass communication.[57] Initiated in February 1958, Radio Rebelde grew quickly to include over thirty stations, and by July 1958, Havana residents could pick up the signal.[58] Its nightly schedule included news of guerrilla victories and rebel speeches, in addition to music and personal messages from rebels to their families. Che felt the radio lacked a woman announcer and appointed young Olga Guevara (who later moved in to armed combat with the Marianas).[59] After the April 1958 strike, Violeta Casals became the voice of women on rebel radio. A TV and radio actress in her early 40s, Casals was known for her catch-phrase, "Radio Rebelde here, from the free territory of Cuba ..."[60] The government was sufficiently threatened that it interfered with Radio Rebelde transmission, arrested people found listening to rebel radio, and even ordered radio dealers to report the names and addresses of those purchasing a radio.[61]

The heavy censorship led the international media also to rely on news generated and controlled by the guerrilla. Women rebel couriers were key liaisons and informants. As a US journalist detailed, "They placed soldiers in all commercial radio stations, at the telephone exchanges, and threatened any reporter who tried to get a story out. We began to have to depend on travelers and rebel sources. The rebels continued to send couriers back and forth, mostly girls."[62] These women messengers were crucial at this stage of the war in delivering the news the guerrillas wanted the world to hear.

Additionally, 1957–58 sources, including rebel leaders' own explanations as well as observers' remarks, indicate that a hearts and minds campaign was a significant part of the rebel war strategy and often targeted military morale.[63] In late 1958, Fidel explained to a reporter that "his secret weapon lay in his enemies' minds; they did not want to risk themselves for what they presumably were sworn to defend."[64] Compounding this, the rebels' carefully cultivated reputation for treating prisoners humanely led many soldiers to conclude that it was preferable to surrender than to risk their lives fighting back.[65] Fidel Castro stressed decades later the importance of the "living testimony" of soldiers, captured and then released, which circulated throughout the military, spreading news of both "the humanitarian treatment received and the power of the rebel forces, able to defeat a full battalion, destroy their reinforcements and capture in combat such a large number of prisoners."[66] As he summarized to a reporter during the insurrection, rebel victory depended "not so much on arms as it does on morale. Once we capture the heart of the soldier, he will find it hard to fight those who treated him so well. To kill a soldier or to imprison him would only serve to make defeated units resist. A free prisoner is the perfect answer to the tyranny's propaganda."[67]

Journalists' observations confirm and expand upon these tactics. As one reporter noted, with each initial hail of guerrilla bullets came the military's "moment of truth": engage the guerrilla or drop arms and flee.[68] "By all the military theory since Hannibal, Batista's men still held the advantage. If machinery won wars, they would have been victorious."[69] The rebels stood firm while the well-armed military increasingly fled, not only placing distance between themselves and the guerrilla, but also confirming the difference between substandard and real masculinity expressed by the two militaries. Military desertions and defections became commonplace.[70] Following its failed summer offensive, "the army virtually ceased to resist the drives of the rebel counteroffensive ... [T]he army no longer wished to fight."[71]

In its war of ideas, I propose that rebels waged a gendered offensive, redefining masculine hierarchies both between Batista's forces and the rebels and within Batista's forces. The rebels represented themselves as a brave and invincible force, undermining the traditional measures that cast Batista's as the superior army and inverting hierarchies within masculinity. Though bedraggled and rough in appearance, small in number, and poorly armed, the rebels were increasingly successful at posing themselves as real men, measured by honor, courage, and sacrifice.[72] Rebels furthermore exploited tensions within Batista's military by distinguishing between honorable and debased masculinity. The rebels positioned themselves as honorable men, hailing like-minded soldiers, pulling them toward the insurrection.

In the remainder of the chapter, I explore three facets of this gendered hearts and minds campaign in greater depth. First, I consider rape prevention as a means of invoking both feminine and masculine honor to rebel advantage. Second, I examine the guerrillas' casting of masculine honor as a means to undermine soldiers' morale and attract them to the rebel side. Finally, I analyze the rebels' particular brand of counter-hegemonic masculinity, which displaced traditional hegemonic masculinity in some ways while challenging *Batistianos'* claim to traditional masculinity in others.

Rape Prevention as Rebel Tactic

Rape has historically been understood as an inevitable companion to warfare. However, the literature on the Cuban insurrection provides very little reflection on the frequency and tactics of sexual violence. As I show in Chapter 6 and prior examples in this chapter, anti-Batista propaganda identified government forces as rapists, and in several instances women gave powerful public testimonies detailing their experience of sexual assault. Batista forces indeed committed acts of sexual violence – among them rape, threats of rape, forced nudity, and sexualized torture. Evidence points to its perpetration as acts permitted, encouraged, or committed by officers on a case-by-case basis as part of the repertoire of violence. The literature tells us that a military's reputation for rape can communicate its dominance and terrorize the civilian population, and in this way (and others), armed groups use sexual assault as a war tactic.[73] But what about a reputation of *not* raping?

Scholars have taken up this important question only recently.[74] As Elisabeth J. Wood details, perpetration of sexual violence can produce negative repercussions for a military in terms of supply of troops, intelligence, and other necessary inputs from civilians.[75] More broadly, it can weaken the "legitimacy of the war effort in the eyes of desired supporters."[76] Thus,

> [A]n armed group ... that sees itself as the embryo of a new, more just social order is likely to restrain its use of sexual violence because such violence violates the norms of the new society ... Relatedly, in conflicts where one party engages in massive violence against civilians, the other party may practice restraint as a way to demonstrate moral superiority.[77]

As Wood makes clear, however, incentive alone is insufficient, and the group's hierarchy must be sufficiently strong to disseminate and enforce such rules, including a willingness to punish.[78]

I propose that Cuba presents a case in which a repressive government's abuse of civilians, including sexual assault, provided an incentive for the rebels to practice restraint, which leaders had the strength to enforce. My line of analysis builds from Wood's research by inquiring into the rebel construction of the facts surrounding sexual violence. That is, drawing from my analysis of sexual assault in Chapter 6, I explore M-26-7's construction of itself as masculine protector – the force that does not rape but rather sets out to vanquish an army of rapists.

M-26-7's Radio Rebelde broadcasts rallied popular support by referencing women's "sacred condition" and "sullied honor" as well as the "intimate tragedies" the regime inflicted upon women.[79] Rebel testimonies document the particular power of sexualized abuse in turning civilians into rebels. Teté Puebla, for example, described a military offensive, "headed by Sánchez Mosqueda, who was known for his brutality, assassinating, burning houses, raping the daughters of *campesinos*."[80] For her, it was the rape of two women in Yara by government troops that "made us join the struggle."[81] According to Argeo González, a traveling merchant and one of the first regular guerrilla suppliers, early civilian support was earned in large part because, in contrast to the armed forces, the rebels did not mistreat civilians. Batista's Rural Guard would "eat a chick if there was one there, take away a daughter if there was one there – but the rebels were different; they respected everything, and this was the basis of the confidence that they gained."[82] Indeed, González explained, soon rural women were "the first ones to want to join Castro, to help him."[83]

Attention to rural women – actively gaining their trust, sometimes taking them into the guerrilla fold – was an important though largely unappreciated contribution to rebel victory.[84] Addressing sexual violence was one means to this end. As M-26-7 contrasted itself with the abuses committed by the Batista government, it highlighted its own rape-prevention efforts. This both heightened public revulsion toward the regime while also demonstrating the restraint and respect for decency and women's honor that M-26-7 would exercise once in power.[85]

The Rebel Army, as an army of the people, kept tight control over its troops to avoid abuse of the civilian population.[86] This was particularly difficult as armed men roamed the mountains, including army deserters, rebel deserters, and bandits. Civilians were caught between such groups, facing growing anarchy and random violence.[87] Some guerrillas or men claiming to be guerrillas took advantage of the situation to rob, rape, and murder, in the process threatening local support for rebel forces. The recorded rebel response was swift and harsh. The crime of rape, along with desertion, insubordination, defeatism, treason, theft, and lack of discipline, all of which endangered morale or created conflicts between the guerrilla and the local population, was punishable by death.[88]

Evidence is clear that the rebels had the capacity and will to follow through on these punishments. Cuba Archive's Truth and Memory Project documents twenty-two M-26-7 trials ending in execution in the Sierra: three for desertion; eight for collaborating with the Batista military; seven for crimes; and four for assorted other reasons (including two for spying).[89] Out of these executions, four involved crimes with distinct gendered, sexual themes. Ramón Castro, the eldest Castro brother, detailed the strict guerrilla discipline: "Rape, if proven against a guerrilla, allowed for little after-the-fact discussion. Execution was immediate; Raúl Castro personally executed several men for this violation of the guerrillas' code of ethics."[90] M-26-7 documents refer to a member of José Chang's criminal gang as "the rapist"; he was executed by firing squad in October 1957 for raping an adolescent *campesina* while "boasting of his authority as a messenger for the Rebel Army."[91] Che wrote of a rebel named El Maestro (The Teacher) who, posing as Che (and thus a doctor), attempted to rape a young woman who came to him for medical attention.[92] He too was executed for the crime. In another case, Che recorded that during a truce in mid-August 1958: "An army deserter who tried to rape a girl was executed."[93]

In defending women's honor through strict punishments for rape and attempted rape, the rebels modeled honorable, protective masculinity battling against an army of rapists. The guerrillas inserted order and justice in a rural region whose people had been either ignored or abused by the regime. This tactic likely appealed not only to women understood to be vulnerable to rape, but also to the men and women charged with protecting them.

Hailing Honorable Men

However, masculinity is never a given, even for an army of guerrilla men. Rather, it must be earned and defended. Particularly in their first months in the Sierra following the disastrous *Granma* landing, the guerrillas' masculine status was precarious. Indeed, upon arriving in the guerrilla camp in March 1957, the first guerrilla recruits from the *llano* were shocked: Fidel's troops numbered under twenty and "had long hair, beards, ripped uniforms, a sack for a backpack. It was a deplorable situation ... [O]ur hearts sank to our feet."[94] Entries in Che's diary confirm their early rag-tag existence.[95] Such a small and poorly supplied unit could hardly be considered a guerrilla army, much less a viable threat to the Batista government. Their physical appearance also called into question their status as honorable men. They faced, then, significant disadvantages on both the military and symbolic front.

The rebels responded with a two-year gendered offensive that, in redefining masculine honor, targeted government soldiers' will to fight, attracted them to the rebel cause, and promised humane treatment upon surrender.[96] In return, the rebels gained new recruits among defecting soldiers (along with their weapons) and were increasingly effective in combat. The following documents specific ways in which masculinity was deployed in this multi-pronged tactic.

To begin, Castro used Radio Rebelde to disabuse regime soldiers of the idea that they must either win or die trying: "What the dictatorship would like is not for us to cure the wounded soldiers and respect the lives of our prisoners, but for us to murder them without exception, so that every member of the armed forces would feel bound to fight and give his very last drop of blood."[97] From Castro's tactical perspective, then, compassion could be more effective than aggression. Furthermore, in his rendering, the masculine attributes of honor, strength, and courage were confirmed in *not* killing one's enemies. In contrast, Batista's forces, by killing innocents and rebels after capture, proved themselves to be substandard men, even subhuman animals. In an August 1958 radio address, for example, Fidel compared the hundreds of captured soldiers released by the rebels to the civilians killed by the regime: "Killing does not make anybody stronger. Killing has weakened the enemy forces. By not killing we have become strong."[98] He added, "only cowards and hounds murder an adversary who surrenders."[99]

M-26-7 propaganda, however, did not treat Batista's military monolithically. It took advantage of the fractured nature of the military identified by Pérez and exacerbated it, distinguishing between most soldiers – men of honor – and *Batistianos* – thugs, rapists, and assassins.[100] Castro invited "those honorable officers and thousands of soldiers who ... do not want to be traitors to their people" to fight alongside the rebels.[101] Thus, the rebels included as latent allies most of the men with whom they engaged in combat. The real enemies for rebels and honorable soldiers alike, then, were Batista and his henchmen. Fidel made this point repeatedly. For example, he issued a message on July 3, 1958, condemning Batista's reluctance to receive wounded soldiers held by the rebels: "These are ... wounded soldiers of his own army, and only a traitor and a man feeling no gratitude towards the men who serve him would refuse the Red Cross ... permission to give them care they need."[102] The rebel war of ideas also focused upon military corruption among the officer elite. During the summer offensive, for example, rebel planes dropped photos of army officers in brothels and elite Havana nightclubs to soldiers in the field.[103] These formulations gave an air of inevitability to rebel victory. As Castro asserted, "Wars are won, not by those who have the most weapons or soldiers, but rather by those who are in the right ... [*Batistianos*] have waged a war against rightness and they are losing the war."[104] The victory, though, was not foreordained but rather lay in the rebels' ability to construct the popular notion that they were in the right.

Building upon such representations, rebel leadership called upon all good military men to defect. Castro appealed directly to surrounded soldiers, encouraging surrender and promising medical attention for the wounded, prompt release of prisoners, provisions (cigars, food, and "everything they need"), updates to soldiers' families, and protection from interrogation, mistreatment, or humiliation.[105] Such portrayals of rebel humanity were consistently posed against Batista's inhumanity and refusal (or inability) to protect his own men. Importantly, promises of humane treatment also significantly lowered the costs of surrender.

Veteran war correspondent Dickey Chapelle, embedded with the guerrillas, later elaborated on the psychological advantage in releasing Batista soldiers:

When [Castro] was done with them he did not need to feed or bury them. They remained a problem only to Batista; they had been unfitted to fight, certainly to fight against Castro again.[106]

She observed Raúl Castro calling upon captured soldiers to join the rebels:

If you decide to refuse this invitation ... you will be delivered to the custody of the Cuban Red Cross tomorrow. Once you are under Batista's orders again, we hope that you will not take up arms against us. But if you do, remember this – We took you this time. We can take you again. And when we do, we will not frighten or torture or kill you, any more than we are frightening you in this moment. If you are captured a second or even a third time we will again return you exactly as we are doing now.[107]

According to Chapelle, "This expression of utter contempt for the fighting potential of the defeated had an almost physical impact. Some actually flinched as they listened."[108] In its benevolence, Raúl's speech struck at soldiers' masculinity – they had been defeated by men who feared them so little that they set them free.

Fidel was still more pointed in his open letters to soldiers. For example, in October 1958, he clarified he was *not* addressing "those military who have stained the uniform."[109] Rather, he spoke to military men who joined out of legitimate pride in the military as a profession, [who] did not assassinate and have not tortured, have not robbed, have not raped and who still have time to embrace the cause of justice and gain the gratitude, affection, and recognition of the people, instead of engendering death, without glory and without honor, like obscure criminals of an infamous cause.[110]

Other rebel leaders expressed similar themes. Camilo Cienfuegoss responded to a petition of concern for the well-being of a rebel-held officer: "Your petition is unnecessary, because under no condition would we put ourselves at the same moral level as those we are fighting ... [W]e cannot, as men of honor and as dignified Cubans, use the low and undignified procedures that our opponents use against the people and against us."[111]

Rebel broadcasts sometimes referenced soldiers' loved ones to appeal to and shame soldiers. Fidel's October 23, 1958 speech over Radio Rebelde warned of the "infinite shame" that would befall each man in uniform after rebel victory:

Their children and their wives will reproach them each hour, each minute, that they wear that uniform of infamy ... A truly honorable soldier would never fight for a regime that rapes women, tortures citizens, and assassinates even wounded prisoners ... Batista has turned the Army into a national stain, an international shame.[112]

Here, Castro is both forecasting and producing a sense of shame. Such men must side with the rebels or be cast the same as those beyond shame and thus unredeemable.

In a separate example, Fidel noted that on the same day two military commanders threw grenades and sprayed bullets into a vehicle to kill already-wounded rebels, rebel doctors saved the lives of an officer and several soldiers: "If we had deprived of life all the prisoners we have freed and those we hold, more than 700 Cuban mothers would be dressed in mourning and thousands of children would have been needlessly orphaned."[113] This extract also displays Fidel's multi-layered discourse, in which in the process of emphasizing military debasement and rebel honor, he also boasts by alluding to rebels' battle prowess through the many soldiers they have wounded and captured.

Rebel self-abnegation and benevolence was a related theme. On Christmas Eve 1958, the rebel army called a ceasefire, prepared holiday food, and encouraged family visits to Batista soldiers in the field, bringing "a heartfelt kiss ... [and] Christmas Eve treats."[114] Radio Rebelde advertised their largesse: "[r]ebel soldiers, far from our loved ones, do not have Christmas Eve nor the kiss of loved ones, but in our immense love of Cuba we permit the soldiers of the dictator that which we cannot today enjoy."[115] This gesture conveyed at least three points. First, it established that rebels – not the government – controlled much of Oriente. Second, it demonstrated rebel benevolence, in contrast to a cruel regime. Third, it suggested the rebels to be "real" men, tough enough to forgo privileges in order that civilians and Batista soldiers might enjoy them.

Castro's tactics were sometimes lost on his own officers, including Che, who later came around to Castro's way of thinking: "Over time this difference [between the rebel code of conduct and that of the military] had an effect on the enemy and it was a factor in our victory."[116] Such acts aimed at demoralizing Batista soldiers by demonstrating the rebels as magnanimous, humane, principled, disciplined, and tough.[117] *Batistianos* were thus cast as the corresponding contrasts: greedy, inhumane, unprincipled, undisciplined, and soft. Increasingly, then, the spreading revulsion at Batista's rule penetrated into Batista own military, undermining its ability and will to carry out its offensive.[118]

Counter-Hegemonic Masculinity and the Real Man

For the guerrillas, simply surviving and maintaining a presence in the Sierra "assumed a symbolic value out of proportion to [rebel] military capability."[119] Fidel in particular reaped the benefits. As Bonachea and San Martín explain, Castro's civilian supporters assumed his death to be inevitable and the challenge would be to "meet defeat with dignity and honor."[120] His survival rallied many, and Castro profited immensely, "for his decision to remain in Sierra Maestra was for most people an act of incredible courage, one more proof of his *machismo*."[121]

As this suggests, Fidel was a prime marker of rebel masculinity. The dangerous and physically demanding trials of the Sierra Maestra was a common theme.[122] When his guerrilla column was on the move, weighted down with heavy packs, Fidel set off each morning with huge strides "and one had to hurry to avoid being left behind."[123] He was called "El Caballo" (the horse), purportedly because of his strong will and ability to hike faster and farther than others.[124]

Another representation of Fidel's masculine exceptionalism was his refusal to issue battle commands from a safe distance. Batista and his generals, in contrast, issued their orders from afar, a position many condemned as cowardly and thus unmanly.[125] In late March 1958, out of concern to ensure their leader's survival, guerrilla officers opposed Fidel's direct participation in combat, writing to him and even appealing to Celia, "who was always the mother up there," warning that they would refuse to fight if he was in the battle.[126] Fidel seemed to concede at the battle of San Ramón, but once "the action started, there was Fidel in the middle of the shooting."[127]

Che, of course, was also prominent in performing guerrilla masculinity and policing its boundaries.[128] He told a journalist, "I've found that gunpowder is the only thing that really relieves my asthma."[129] Newly arrived rebel men had to earn their place in the masculine hierarchy. After the long trek with a pack into the Sierra, Filiberto Olivera arrived in camp exhausted to the point of vomiting. Che greeted him by asking, doubtfully, "You're a *guerrillero*?" and demanded Olivera's gun. "I got pissed off. I said to [Che], 'What is this? I am a revolutionary. I came to fight.' He just replied: 'Here, you need to earn it.'"[130]

In these cases, the attributes associated with hegemonic masculinity – toughness and courage – were not in dispute so much as the struggle revolved around who truly performed it. But the rebels also succeeded in weaving counter-hegemonic versions of masculinity into the Cuban social fabric. Hegemonic masculinity of the 1950s entailed a clean-cut look, and the rebels' beards called their honor and respectability into question. Indeed, the beards summoned interpretations of the rebels as irresponsible, uncivilized, and dirty.[131] However, as the guerrilla group survived and grew, the beards were increasingly a symbol of rebellion and a counter-hegemonic physical marker of real manhood. The Sierra guerrillas became known as *Los Barbudos* (the Bearded Ones). Those guerrilla men unable to grow respectable beards compensated in other ways. Seventeen-year-old Rogelio Acevedo, a member of Che's Column 8, was scrawny and too young to grow a beard. "To compensate, he let his brown hair lengthen until it touched his shoulders."[132] Notably, Raúl Castro, who also struggled unsuccessfully to grow a full beard, grew his hair long.

In preparation for the April 1958 general strike, Castro considered ordering the men to shave to make a good impression on the civilian population should the rebels move into the *llano*. Indeed, the regime portrayed the guerrillas as "a bedraggled and filthy bunch."[133] The matter was weighty enough to prompt a rebel meeting, at which Spanish journalist Meneses pointed out, "any photographs in existence anywhere in the world at the time would lose their news-value if the rebels were to shave off their beards."[134] There was the additional concern that Batista troops would kill *campesinos* and claim the victims to be rebels. The beards helped distinguish "between rebel combatants and ordinary *campesinos*. The photos of rebels killed by the Army, unless they showed copious beards, deceived nobody in Cuba."[135] After several hours, the decision was made: keep the beards for the duration.

Though the beards first appeared because the *Granma* survivors' lacked razors, then as a means of identification, they came to confer status within the masculine hierarchy. With the rebel victory, this counter-hegemonic masculinity had significantly displaced the previously hegemonic masculinity, and even men who had never set foot in the Sierras were growing beards.[136]

Critiques of the rebels' beards and unkempt appearance was not the *Batistianos'* only gendered weapon. In making their case against M-26-7 to an increasingly cynical US embassy, Batista allies used gender and sexuality in ways that implied rebel leaders were irrational and perverse. In a November 1958 meeting with US Ambassador Smith, President-elect Andrés Rivero Agüero characterized Fidel as a sick man with "a syphilitic inheritance" – an insult to both Fidel and his mother that also called into question Fidel's sanity.[137] Cuban presidential candidate Carlos Márquez Sterling told Smith that both Fidel and Raúl had been his students at the University of Havana, and he considered both men to be "mentally unbalanced."[138] Sterling elaborated, "When Raul was attending Havana University there was talk that he was homosexual."[139]

In contrast, women guerrillas, unable to mark their status through beards, were often described with markers of traditional femininity.[140] Indeed, Celia Sánchez presented an idealized feminine contrast that complemented the counter-hegemonic rebel masculinity. The feminine to Fidel's masculine, Celia is often mentioned as marching with him, hurrying so that "she wouldn't be left behind."[141] Though she was the first woman to carry a gun in the Sierra and fire it at the enemy, media sources labeled Celia as "Castro's own 'Girl Friday'" or "faithful assistant."[142] She served as "the right hand of Fidel in the endless gathering of funds and supplies."[143] Such references detailed her femininity in a way that complemented and confirmed, by way of contrast, Fidel's masculinity. He generated the big ideas and grand schemes, while she attended to the small details. He was an imposing and impressive figure, and she was self-abnegating and humble, working behind the scenes. He grew a beard and smoked cigars; she wore a gold chain on her ankle and a Mariposa flower in her hair. Binary opposites of revolution, they completed each other. But with Celia at his side, it was always clear that Fidel was in charge, the ultimate authority, the commander in chief.

In sum, although the Cuban War Story and much of the literature focus upon the military engagements of the guerrilla war, the improvised bombs, bullets and battle tactics, I argue for not only an increased appreciation for the war of ideas but also a recognition of the ways that it relied upon and revolved around gender, particularly masculinity. The rebels, in a multi-pronged gender offensive, attacked Batista and his military by impugning their masculinity and posing the rebels as real men.

Notes

1. Bonachea and San Martín (1974, 173).
2. Ibid.
3. Dubois (1959, 172).
4. Espín (1975).
5. Ibid.
6. Ibid.
7. Sweig (2002, 49, 54).
8. Letter to Sánchez, August 11, 1957, in Franqui (1980, 220).
9. Dubois (1959, 175). See also Pérez (1976), especially regarding the drafting and deployment of inexperienced men.
10. Bonachea and San Martín (1974, 96).
11. Sweig (2002).
12. Mirta Rodríguez Calderón, "Hilos para halar ..." *Granma* April 21, 1988, 3.
13. Ibid.; Pastorita Núñez, interviewed in Jiménez, *Tribuna de la Habana* July 21, 2007.
14. Meneses (1966, 79).
15. Dubois (1959, 252–3).

16. Ibid., 253–4. Pérez (1976, 144) reports ninety-one rebels killed in Havana following the strike.
17. Sweig (2002, 136).
18. Park F. Wollam, "Letter from the Consul at Santiago de Cuba (Wollam) to the Officer in Charge of Cuban Affairs (Leonhardy)," Foreign Relations of the United States, 1958–1960, June 4, 1958.
19. Sweig (2002, 137).
20. Eugene A. Gilmore, Jr., "Despatch from the Embassy in Cuba to the Department of State," Foreign Relations of the United States, 1958–1960, February 28, 1958.
21. Phillips (1959, 353).
22. Sweig (2002, 137). Vilma had transferred to the Sierra in early 1958 for safety (Espín 1975). In March 1958, Raúl left for the Second Front, and Vilma remained with Fidel.
23. Sweig (2002, 137, 141–2).
24. Ibid., 140–1. There were many complications to René's plan. Raúl, Almeida, and Che also criticized it.
25. Espín (1975).
26. Hart (2004, 327); Sweig (2002, 148).
27. Espín (1975).
28. Sweig (2002, 150).
29. Szulc (1986, 442–3); Bonachea and San Martín (1974, 215–16).
30. Sweig (2002, 153).
31. There is little information in Cuban sources about Melba during this time. A journalist observed her in fall 1958 in Juan Almeida's column in the Sierra (Dubois 1959, 334).
32. Haydée discusses this decision in a 1980 interview (Tad Szulc Collection of Interview Transcripts 1984–1986, University of Miami).
33. With soft power, one coopts and attracts others to want what one wants (Nye 2004, 1).
34. Sweig (2002, 139).
35. Bonachea and San Martín (1974, 216). Carlos Franqui also joined the leadership. René Ramos Latour died in battle on July 30, 1958. David Salvador Manso was arrested in the fall of 1960 for counter revolutionary acts and then went into exile. Carlos Franqui broke with Castro in 1968, going into exile.
36. Vilma and Raúl were engaged by April 1958 (Sweig 2002, 142).
37. Wollam (1958).
38. Arenas (1986 [1994], 42).
39. Ibid.
40. Sweig (2002, 116).
41. Macaulay (1978, 288).
42. Bonachea and San Martín (1974, 182–3).
43. Ibid., 184.
44. Ibid., 186. However, the DR suffered internal divisions.
45. Some DR members left Cuba once Castro was in power, then returned in the Bay of Pigs invasion. Others became government officials.

46. Draper (1962, 13).
47. Pérez (1976). See also García-Pérez (1998).
48. Pérez (1976, 139, 143), citing *El Mundo* September 15, 1957, A-8. Moncada and the *Granma* landing played toward the Batista military's strengths. Rural guerrilla warfare did not produce clear rebel victories so much as it interrupted the military's capacity to do so.
49. Pérez (1976, 141).
50. Ibid., 142.
51. Ibid., 145, 147, 153. In 1961, Arthur Schlesinger Jr. maintained that the rebels succeeded not on guerrilla action alone but also owing to growing civilian opposition, "which undermined the morale of the superior military forces of Batista and caused them to collapse from within" (cited in Kling 1962, 45).
52. Pérez (1976, 153).
53. Ibid., 153. García-Pérez (1998, 10) notes that by 1958 military desertion to the rebels was widespread.
54. Pérez (1976, 157, 161); Smith (1962, 48).
55. Pérez (1976, 156).
56. Ibid., 156.
57. See Castro (2011, 13).
58. Phillips (1959, 362).
59. Bracero Torres (2007).
60. Rodríguez Reyes (2010).
61. Phillips (1959, 362).
62. Ibid., 344.
63. Pérez (1976, 153).
64. Chapelle (1962b, 271–2). See also Guevara (1961) 1985, 62.
65. Pérez (1976, 154).
66. Castro (2011, 306).
67. DuBois (1959, 295–6).
68. Chapelle (1962b, 271–2).
69. Ibid.
70. Pérez (1976, 154); Suárez Pérez and Caner Román (2006, 345).
71. Pérez (1976, 154).
72. See Dietrich Ortega (2012) for varied masculinities experienced and individually expressed by Latin American guerrilla combatants.
73. Sjoberg (2013, 218).
74. Wood (2009); see also Viterna (2013, 112–13). Both authors point to the Salvadoran case as one in which leftist guerrillas did not practice rape while government forces did. Viterna finds the guerrillas encouraged women to join to protect themselves from potential rape by government forces.
75. Wood (2009, 136).
76. Ibid.
77. Ibid., 141.
78. Ibid., 137. To determine hierarchical strength, Wood (2009, 142) uses two indicators that are observable apart from sexual violence: the organization's punishment of combatants who break rules and norms, and its ability to

effectively tax civilians without redirection of funds for personal use. I document the punishment in this chapter; the literature agrees that Cuban rebel leaders followed through with capital punishment for a variety of offenses, amply documented in guerrilla memoirs, including Guevara (1971) and Macaulay (1970).

79. Princeton University Library microfilm, Radio Rebelde abril 8, 1958; Radio Rebelde broadcast reprinted in *Granma* September 18, 1978, 2. See Chapter 6 for discussion.
80. Puebla interview, Lyn Smith Cuba Collection; Puebla interviews in Waters 2003, 28, 45, 52.
81. Ibid., 28.
82. Szulc (1986, 390).
83. Ibid.
84. Stout (2013, 60–1) finds that Celia Sánchez visited women in the Sierra who had been raped by soldiers.
85. Stout (2013, 61).
86. Che discusses the guerrillas' successful practice, particularly in its early months, of using an "iron fist" to "inflict exemplary punishment in order to curb violations of discipline and to liquidate the nuclei of anarchy" (Guevara 1971, 183). See Yuval-Davis's (2004, 177) and Wood's (2009, 133) cautionary notes regarding inferring frequency of sexual violence.
87. Anderson (1997, 282).
88. Bonachea and San Martín (1974, 90). After two weeks with the guerrillas, *The New York Times* journalist Homer Bigart reported to the US embassy that the rebels had drawn up a legal code under which sixty people were tried, with twenty-eight convicted, and eight executed by firing squad. Crimes punishable by death were murder, rape, banditry, and espionage (Gilmore, Jr. 1958). See also Guevara ([1961] 1985, 62–3): "A fundamental part of guerrilla tactics is the treatment accorded the people of the zone... Conduct [should respect] all the rules and traditions of the people of the zone, in order to demonstrate effectively, with deeds, the moral superiority of the guerrilla fighter over the oppressing soldier." The guerrillas also pursued deserters from their own ranks and civilians suspected of collaborating with the military – tracking them down and hanging them. For example, during Macaulay's (1970, 47, 50, 73–5, 79) two months as a guerrilla, he saw six men hanged by his small squad – some of whom he suspected were not spies as charged but simply Batista supporters. In one incident, three policemen and a spy were captured; only the latter was executed while the three police switched to the rebel side (Macaulay 1970, 73–4, 109). The guerrillas often considered deserters and spies to be irredeemable and untrustworthy, whereas police and soldiers were potential converts.
89. Werlau (2011, 25–6).
90. Bonachea and San Martín (1974, 197), citing their interview with Ramón Castro, March 10, 1960.
91. Guevara (1971, 180).
92. Ibid., 182; see also Anderson (1997, 286). The Rebel Army also executed a *campesino* named Dionisio, who in addition to committing murder, stole

llano provisions sent for the guerrillas to support his wife and two mistresses. Che, with gallows humor, wrote: "At that time in the Sierra, a man's wealth was measured essentially by the number of women he had. Dionisio, faithful to custom and taking himself for a pasha, had [stolen enough to support] three households ... In the course of his trial, faced with Fidel's indignant reproaches concerning his abuse of trust, his treason, and his immoral conduct – was he not supporting three women with the people's money? Dionisio maintained, with a good measure of peasant artlessness, that it was not three but two, since one of the three was his legitimate wife (which was true)!" (Guevara 1971, 181–2).

93. Guevara (2013, 250).
94. Eloy Rodríguez, interviewed by Stout (2013, 170).
95. Guevara (2013).
96. This rebel policy varied. For example, on December 30, 1958, Castro threatened the troops stationed at the Maffo outpost that if they didn't surrender, he was going to "fry" them in their warehouses by filling a fire department pump truck with gasoline, spraying the building, and setting it on fire (Dorschner and Fabricio 1980, 334–5).
97. Fidel Castro, radio address August 20–21, 1958, quoted in DuBois (1959, 294–5).
98. Ibid. Castro goes on to emphasize that "the seed of brotherhood must be sown" to avoid vengeance and political crimes in post-Batista society and the importance of setting an example for future generations.
99. Fidel Castro, radio address, August 20–21, 1958, quoted in DuBois (1959, 294–5).
100. Pérez (1976).
101. Suárez Pérez and Caner Román (2006, 341).
102. Perret Françoise (1998).
103. Pérez (1976, 206n7). Pérez cites Marta Rojas, "El Segundo Frente Oriental 'Frank País': El reencuentro de los hermanos heroes," *Bohemia* 51 (August 16, 1959), 104.
104. Fidel Castro, radio address, October 23, 1958; Princeton University Library microfilm, Radio Rebelde collection.
105. Perret (1998).
106. Chapelle (1962b, 272). Batista officers recognized the impact of the rebels' symbolic offensive on troop morale. General Eulogio Cantillo reported to Batista: "One of the main problems affecting morale was the troops' ... awareness that there is no strong penalty against those who surrender or betray their unit, and that falling prisoner to the enemy ends all their problems" (Bonachea and San Martín 1974, 248).
107. Chapelle (1962b, 273). This observation contrasts with Bonachea and San Martín's (1974, 197n73) claim that, in contrast to Fidel, Raúl did not treat prisoners humanely.
108. Chapelle (1962b, 273).
109. Suárez Pérez and Caner Román (2006, 339). Similarly, prior to the Batista coup, Castro pursued corruption cases of exploited soldier labor on the farms of politicians and military officials (Castro 2011, 26–8).

110. Suárez Pérez and Caner Román (2006, 339).
111. Farber (2006, 42–3); translated by Farber from William Gálvez, *Camilo: Señor de la Vanguardia* Havana: Editorial de Ciencias Sociales, 1979, 357–8.
112. Fidel Castro, radio address, October 23, 1958; Princeton University Library microfilm, Radio Rebelde collection.
113. Suárez Pérez and Caner Román (2006, 340).
114. Ibid., 387–8. See also Dorschner and Fabricio (1980, 260–3), describing Camilo's attempt on Christmas Eve 1958 to persuade Batista troops to surrender. Camilo offered them a good dinner, distributed cigars and cigarettes, and repeated the argument that M-26-7 was at war with the regime, not the soldiers themselves – but to no avail. To add insult to injury for the surrounded soldiers, a Batista plane dropped two boxes by parachute for the surrounded troops. Unfortunately, one fell in rebel territory and the other in the neutral zone. Believing them to be ammunition, soldiers recovered one box under rebel fire only to discover it to be filled with food. Finding it not worth their lives, they returned empty-handed and that night suffered through radio broadcasts of rebels loudly smacking their lips as they ate the soldiers' Christmas Eve dinner: "What's this? A leg of lamb?... And here is some rice. And black beans. And roast pork. And look what we have here for dessert."
115. Suárez Pérez and Caner Román (2006, 387–8).
116. Guevara (1971, 59). In another example of differences over tactics, specifically Fidel's concern for the long-run impact and the battle for hearts and minds over Che's orientation toward immediate tactical advantages, in May 1957 Che advocated ambushing a military truck, but Castro insisted on attacking military barracks, as that would have a bigger psychological impact nationwide. "Today ... I must recognize that Fidel's judgment was correct ... In that period, our yearning for combat always led us impatiently to adopt drastic attitudes, without seeing the more distant objectives" (Guevara 1971, 110). See also Guevara (2013, 139); Castañeda (1997, 103).
117. Farber (2006, 41).
118. Draper (1962, 14); Pérez (1976).
119. Pérez (1976, 152).
120. Bonachea and San Martín (1974, 232).
121. Ibid.
122. There are numerous instances of tests Fidel posed to confirm masculinity; see, for example, Bonachea and San Martín (1974, 349n9).
123. Meneses (1966, 55). However, Meneses observed that Fidel and Celia's belongings were carried by a "robust rebel *guajiro*." Thus unburdened, and at 6 feet 3 inches tall, it is less remarkable that Fidel trekked faster than his guerrilla followers.
124. Others suggest the nickname "El Caballo" implies that he is endowed "like a horse" and more generally was a reference to his sexual success with women (a stud). See Montaner (1976, 112).
125. Bonachea and San Martín (1974, 233).
126. Raúl Castro Mercader testimony, "Acontecimientos de Marzo del '58" (n.d.), in *Cubasocialista.com: Revista Teorica y Politica, Comité Central del*

Partido Coumunista de Cuba. Phillips reported a "big argument" prior to the guerrilla attack near Estrada Palma, in which rebel officers told Castro he could no longer lead the attacks, arguing that if he were killed, "the rebellion will split into many groups' and lose" (Phillips 1959, 325–6).

127. Castro Mercader (n.d.).
128. See Rodríguez (1996, 50).
129. Meneses (1966, 67).
130. Olivera interview in Báez (1996, 250–1). See also Bayard de Volo (2012); Rodríguez (1996); Cabezas (1985).
131. See Meneses (1966, 135); Weldes (1999, 98).
132. Dorschner and Fabricio (1980, 183).
133. Teté Puebla, in Waters (2003, 39).
134. Meneses (1966, 56).
135. Ibid.
136. "[S]ome time after the victory, everyone except Fidel Castro and a few others was ordered to shave, because beards were being sported for their own personal advantage by people who had never been near the Sierra Maestra" (Meneses 1966, 57).
137. Earl T. Smith, "Memorandum of a Conversation Between the Ambassador in Cuba (Smith) and President-Elect Rivero Agüero," Foreign Relations of the United States, 1958–1960, Volume VI, Document 154, November 15, 1958.
138. Earl T. Smith, "Telegram from the Embassy in Cuba to the Department of State," Foreign Relations of the United States, 1958–1960, Volume VI, Document 147, October 22, 1958.
139. See also Schoultz (2011, 77); Bardach (2003, 68).
140. See, for example, Bardach (2003, 51).
141. Alberto, *Verde Olivo* January 20, 1980, 4. See also Armando Hart's eulogy in *Verde Olivo* January 20, 1980, 8.
142. No author, "Celia, cabal imagen del pueblo," *Granma* January 11, 1982, 2; Bethel (1969, 113); Meneses (1966, 55). Celia participated in the battle of El Uvero on May 28, 1957.
143. No author (1982, 2).

CHAPTER 9

Women Noncombatants

Multiple Paths and Contributions

Women comprised about 5 percent of the Cuban guerrilla in the Sierra by late 1958, most serving in rearguard positions.[1] Although the women combatants (discussed in the following chapter) have received much of the attention, most women rebels in the Sierra were not combatants and did not carry rifles. Rather, they worked in areas such as couriers, teachers, nurses, and cooks. Che Guevara's globally influential writings on guerrilla warfare, which lauded women's contributions while channeling them into feminized tasks, have served as a primary source for guerrillas and scholars alike. Accordingly, I examine them here as a means of organizing and analyzing the diverse and sometimes contradictory messages about Cuban women's actual and proper participation in guerrilla warfare. I then trace women's paths into the guerrilla forces, finding that they were ideologically drawn to the rebels, pushed by the repression, and called up from the *llano* for their skills.[2] There were also class distinctions in the work assigned to women. Growing numbers of relatively well-educated middle- and upper-class women were forced from the *llano* to the relative safety of the guerrilla camps. Instead of the low-status feminine work of cooking and cleaning, these women helped replace the state in guerrilla-controlled regions, supplying rebel tax collection, education, and healthcare. I argue this to be another aspect of the hearts and minds campaign, providing incentives for civilians to collaborate and increasing their support for the rebels' vision of governance.

189

CHE IN LOVE AND WAR

A primary argument barring women from militaries is that their presence will distract men and lead to sexual tensions. Accordingly, before examining women's noncombatant contributions, I first consider heterosexual relations in the Sierra. Che, as archetype of guerrilla machismo and author of the how-to handbook on guerrilla warfare, was both a model and catalyst for revolutionary movements elsewhere.[3] His own relations with women in the guerrilla as well as his writings on the role of women in the struggle are thus a productive though underexamined starting point.

In his guerrilla diary, in the rare instances Che writes of specific women, he evaluates them on more personal terms than he does men. Of Liliam Mesa, a young and well-off Havana rebel who drove journalist Herbert Matthews to his interview with Fidel in February 1957, Che's diary entry read: "[She is a] great admirer of the Movement who seems to me to want to fuck more than anything else."[4] He elaborates in the same entry: "Of the women, Haydée seems to be the one with the clearest political ideas and Vilma the most interesting one. Celia Sánchez is very energetic."[5]

Che nonetheless reassures readers of his guerrilla handbook that with "adequate indoctrination" in the troops, women do not create sexual conflicts that would hurt morale.[6] Indeed, "Persons who are otherwise free and who love each other should be permitted to marry in the Sierra and live as man and wife."[7] He is, however, much stricter with the urban underground, which he equates with men: "If an individual repeatedly disobeys orders of his superiors and makes contacts with women, ... he should be separated immediately" for the danger posed as well as the lack of discipline.[8] Women, for clandestine rebels, are hazards: "contacts [with women] of any type should be prevented by every means. However positive the role of women in the struggle, it must be emphasized that they can also play a destructive part. The weakness for women that young men have when living apart from their habitual medium of life ... is well known."[9] Thus, women pose a danger to the urban underground owing to men's weakness for them. Che's logic indicates women's participation to be auxiliary and provisional in nature – women are included or excluded depending upon usefulness.

Heterosexual couples did form in the Sierra, and some later married. Guerrilla Isabel Rielo explained, "Wherever there are men and women, feelings of love can develop. This was not prohibited; it was controlled so that discipline did not break down ... But nothing was prohibited to any *compañera* or any *compañero* within the moral parameters and normal relations."[10]

Indeed, Che had at least two sustained relationships with women in his second year in the Sierra. The first, which is not well known, was with Zoila García.[11] As an eighteen-year-old Afro-Cuban single mother (Che turned thirty in 1958), Zoila met Che in spring 1958, when he arrived at her father's blacksmith shop to have his mule Armando shoed. Through her father, Che encouraged Zoila to collaborate with the guerrilla, including a rebel mission to Manzanillo. Che personally debriefed her and soon gave her additional missions. According to Zoila, "One day he decided that I would stay permanently in the Minas del Frío camp, helping in everything, in the kitchen and the hospital, and I worked hard."[12] Soon after, they moved into a hut set off from the rest of camp. Zoila recalled, "I fell deeply and sweetly in love. I was committed to him not only as a fighter, but as a woman."[13] The relationship only lasted several months, and by August, as plans for Che's transfer to the distant Las Villas province were finalized, Che did not allow Zoila to accompany him. Instead, as the column headed out, he tasked Zoila with caring for his mule. Zoila confirmed: "I looked after [that mule] as if he were human."[14]

Evidently, with regard to guerrilla relationships, Che's theory and practice did not always coincide. In his handbook, he indicates that a couple should first marry, then live as husband and wife – a sequence he did not follow. His relationship with Zoila was short-lived, and he was married to someone else. Indeed, his wife Hilda, who had trained with the Cuban exiles in Mexico City, still hoped to join Che in the Sierra now that their daughter was old enough to be cared for by family. He turned Hilda down, explaining that the conflict was too dangerous.[15]

In the final months of the insurrection, in the Escambray Mountains of Las Villas, Che met Aleida March, who would soon become his second wife. Aleida was a blonde, white, twenty-one-year-old, trained as a teacher.[16] She had joined M-26-7 in 1956, around the age of nineteen. Now a trusted rebel with two years' experience, she accompanied the M-26-7 financial officer to deliver a very large sum of money to Che in October 1958.[17] While there, her house was searched, and she was ordered to remain with the guerrillas for safety.[18] In her own words, she was atypical of the Escambray rebels: "I hardly looked like a tough guerrilla fighter. I was quite a pretty young woman, looking anything but a battle-ready combatant."[19]

The transition from the urban underground to the guerrilla was difficult for Aleida, as she thought her prior clandestine work had earned her the right to take up arms. Che, however, disagreed. In the last weeks of the war, she became Che's personal assistant (like an orderly and not, she insists, his secretary).[20] On December 28, a few days before Batista fled, Aleida finally got her gun: "Che gave me an M-1 rifle, saying that I had earned it. This was my first important achievement as a combatant; I was keenly aware of how strict Che was in his criteria for who should receive weapons."[21] Also in late December 1958, Che broached the subject of his wife: "He told me about his marriage to Hilda Gadea ... and his daughter, Hildita ... [F]rom the way that he spoke about her, I sensed he no longer loved her, or at least he wasn't in love with her ... In fact, he was trying to tell me he was no longer married."[22] This is a different characterization of the marriage than that reported by Hilda, who clearly understood her marriage to be intact.[23] Che soon divorced Hilda and married Aleida on June 2, 1959.

In sum, in opening guerrilla ranks to women, Che indicated a traditional and rather formal path by which heterosexual relationships could be formed and recognized. Notably, Che himself did not follow the traditional path that he later advocated, though with no apparent harm to troop morale. Furthermore, although the evidence supports Che's assertion that mixed-gender units did not undermine combat effectiveness, he blocked the combat aspirations of women with whom he was personally involved.

CHE ON WOMEN IN THE GUERRILLA

Beyond personal relationships, how does Che instruct future revolutionaries regarding the place for women in guerrilla warfare? In his handbook, he tells us, "the woman is a companion who brings the qualities appropriate to her sex, but she can work the same as a man and she can fight; she is weaker, but no less resistant than he."[24] Indeed, women are capable of "the most difficult tasks, of fighting beside the men."[25] He further notes the barriers women face: "The part that the woman can play in the development of a revolutionary process is of extraordinary importance. It is well to emphasize this, since in all our countries, with their colonial mentality, there is a certain underestimation of the woman which becomes a real discrimination against her."[26] As these quotes imply, Che affirmed women's abilities and contributions but largely equated guerrillas with men.

Feminist research in international relations finds that military women "are threatening unless controlled and distinguished from male soldiers by an emphasis on their femininity."[27] Indeed, Che repeatedly notes women's femininity and its usefulness in meeting the needs of male combatants. He remarks favorably on women's domestic skills, their "habitual tasks of peacetime" transferred to guerrilla life.[28] Women, for example, are skilled in social work and are naturally suited to be nurses, and "even" doctors, as they are gentler than their "rude companion in arms, a gentleness that is so much appreciated at moments when a man is helpless, without comforts, perhaps suffering severe pain and exposed to the many dangers."[29] More generally, he lauds women who "provide an enormous encouragement by their presence and who will do such auxiliary tasks ... as cooking, taking care of the wounded, giving final comfort to those who are dying, doing laundry, in a word, showing their companions-in-arms that they will never be absent in the difficult moments of the Revolution."[30] All the better since "it is easier to keep her in these domestic tasks; ... all works of a civilian character are scorned by those [men] who perform them; they are constantly trying to get out of these tasks in order to enter into forces that are actively in combat."[31] These qualities – women's willingness to perform low-status, feminized work eschewed by men, their inclination to subordinate their own interests for the good of the whole, not to mention the apparent morale boost to male guerrillas that their presence brings – helps explain guerrilla leaders' openness to women in the guerrilla rearguard.

Many women rebels did not seek out combat and by their own accounts found meaning in traditionally feminine guerrilla work. However, as the next chapter details, some women strained against the limits imposed by this gendered division of labor. Though women's rearguard contributions to the guerrilla camps – such as cooking, cleaning, and first aid – were welcomed, many guerrilla men strongly opposed women's efforts to move into armed combat.[32]

In addition to men's conditional acceptance of women in the camps provided they perform traditionally feminine work, women faced structural barriers. Che identified the best age for a guerrilla to be between twenty-five and thirty-five years, "a stage in which the life of most persons has assumed definite shape. Whoever sets out at that age, abandoning his home, his children, and his entire world, must have thought well of his responsibility and reached a firm decision."[33] This is, however, the age at which Cuban women were most likely to be pregnant or have preadolescent children and were least likely to join the guerrilla camps. In effect, then, because they were mothers, a significant percentage of women in Che's ideal guerrilla age range were seen and saw themselves as disqualified from guerrilla status.[34] According to all evidence, the overwhelming

number of women in the camps were either childless (many young and single) or had older children able to care for themselves. In sum, Che both challenged traditional representations of women's capabilities and worked within them, often representing women and their appropriate role in revolution in ways that mirrored those of bourgeois society at the time – women were men's helpmeets and auxiliaries more than political actors.

BARRIERS AND PASSAGES: MOTHERHOOD, THREAT, AND IDEOLOGY

Comparative research confirms the barriers suggested by analysis of Che's writings. Linda Lobao Reif identifies women's reproductive roles and traditional gendered ideological constraints as significant barriers to women's entry into guerrilla camps.[35] Cuba presented a more urban middle-class rebel base than later Central American guerrilla armies, as well as a significantly lower rate of single female-headed households. The constraints identified by Linda Lobao Reif concerning the traditional gendered division of labor apply to Cuba, and most women in guerrilla camps were either young, single, and childless or women whose children were old enough to live independently, along with middle-aged women without children. Examining the biographies I compiled on women in guerrilla camps, I find many were teenagers or in their early twenties, whereas women in the twenty-five to thirty-five range were relatively scarce, with a higher number of women over thirty-five. Middle-aged women leaders who served in the Sierra, with ages ranging from thirty-five to forty years, included Haydée Santamaría, Melba Hernández, Pastorita Núñez, Celia Sánchez, and María Antonia Figueroa.[36] None of these women had children. Vilma Espín was the rare leader in the twenty-five to thirty-five age range – also without children. As these cases suggest, age and motherhood influenced women's paths into guerrilla camps. Notably, middle-aged women sometimes followed sons into the guerrilla camps and took up rearguard roles, a path that was at least as common as women following husbands into camp.

Mady Segal identifies the level of threat and the availability of alternatives as two factors influencing women's military participation: women are more likely to join armed groups if the threat is high and they lack other options for survival.[37] David Mason makes a similar case for the Central American guerrillas: women activists (like many men) "saw that joining the guerrillas provided them a better chance of survival than did remaining where they were and awaiting the death squads."[38] Guerrilla groups can offer protection for those identified by government forces as suspected rebels or sympathizers. In Cuba, many rebel women were sent into the Sierra because they were *quemada* ("burned," sought by authorities) and *llano* work had become too dangerous. This included rank and file members such as fifteen-year-old Consuelo Elba Álvarez, who was sent to the Sierra after having been twice jailed for rebel activities.[39] However, regime violence in Cuba, though brutal, was less indiscriminate than cases such as the Salvadoran civil war and less likely to target women. Accordingly, unlike the cases of El Salvador and Nicaragua, mothers with young children were less prominent among women guerrillas in Cuba. Most were either single and childless or, less commonly, mothers of adult children. I also found no indication of children under fourteen and only rare cases of fourteen- to sixteen-year-olds (such as Consuelo) in guerrilla camps.

The leftist ideology of rebel armies is another factor influencing women in guerrilla groups – both attracting women (and men) and influencing leaders to open their ranks to women. Some women who ascended the Sierra as volunteers were pulled by ideology without being simultaneously pushed by dangers posed in the *llano*.[40] For their part, Cuban rebel leaders were influenced by the logic Timothy Wickham-Crowley identifies: "Feminism, in a sense, *had* to emerge sooner or later on the radical left, due to the patent cultural contradiction between an ideology of equality ... and the obvious subordination of women."[41] In this sense, women's inclusion in the camps complemented the rebels' leftist ideology.

Fidel might never have uttered the word "feminism," but he grasped the symbolic importance of inclusion of the formerly marginalized, including women. Susan Eckstein, however, has argued convincingly that Castro's policies were ideologically consistent when it suited his pragmatic goals.[42] Thus, we must consider motivations for guerrilla policies beyond ideology and official reasons. As this chapter and the next show, Castro permitted and sometimes encouraged women's participation, a seemingly normative position but one that also complemented his effort to build a movement and later a revolutionary state. Inclusion of women, first and foremost, made pragmatic, tactical sense.[43]

Paths to the Guerrilla

Given the impediments to their participation, what paths did women take into the guerrillas? I identify several, which frequently intersected.

Campesinas in the Sierra were recruited as collaborators, typically to remain at home and aid the guerrillas with supplies, shelter, and information. Virtually all *llano* women were attracted for ideological reasons. However, only a few of these sought out the guerrilla on their own, while most awaited orders from the *llano* leadership, which sent women to the Sierra for their safety or for their skills. Some women fled on their own to the guerrillas to escape dangers. Finally, some were attracted for familial reasons, following husbands or adult children into the camps without first receiving *llano* permission. In what follows, I review these often-intersecting paths in greater detail.

To begin, the guerrillas recruited women living in areas they controlled or traversed as collaborators who could be relied upon to shelter rebels, provide information about Batista's troop movements, or otherwise contribute to guerrilla camps as rearguard support. The rebels enjoyed the collaboration of numerous middle-aged and older *campesinas* in the Sierra, such as Ponciana "Chana" Pérez Rigar. Chana figures in the war story as a much-loved *campesina* who prepared food for passing guerrillas. She tells of meeting Fidel and Celia in May 1957, when Fidel approached her house and greeted her: "*Mi vieja*, ... I am looking for the way to free Cuba."[44] Che writes fondly of the complicity and generous protection of "Old Lady Chana" upon which his guerrillas depended during their "sedentary stage" at El Hombrito.[45]

Information on the *campesina* experience of the conflict is relatively scarce. The observations of journalists and diplomats who ventured into the Sierra and Escambray mountains and guerrilla memoirs provide glimpses. Insights can also be gleaned through the testimonies of women published in Cuban media, such as that of Hilda Labrada Díaz, mother of eleven combatants in the Escambray mountains, who transported messages secured with a safety pin in her undergarments. She also hid rebels in her home and fondly recalled "watching over the combatants as they slept."[46] Lest such rearguard contributions be interpreted as low-risk, in one terrifying instance her home was partially destroyed by a military plane when she was hiding ten rebels within.

By mid-1958, the guerrillas mobilized women in greater numbers and in increasingly diverse ways as they gained trust among *campesinas* and more women rebels were sent from the urban underground. For example, in September 1958, Zaída Romero Sánches, one of two women delegates to the Congress of Armed Campesinos, was recruited into the *Comité Femenino* "Mariana Grajales" in August 1958 to contribute to the guerrillas, tasked with familiar feminine rearguard jobs.[47]

As their forces grew, the guerrillas also set about normalizing their stronghold, imposing law and order and providing public services. This process boosted M-26-7's hearts and minds strategy, as the guerrillas replaced the government by providing services in areas M-26-7 controlled (a point I develop more fully at the end of this chapter). From a makeshift camp of half-starved *Granma* survivors in early 1957, by 1958 the network of guerrilla fronts represented an alternative state with infrastructure that included schools, hospitals, radio stations, a command headquarters, roads, and even airstrips. The physical appearance of the guerrillas also notably improved, as they increasingly sported new uniforms that were freshly laundered and even ironed. This transition called for more diversified work for guerrillas and collaborators, and the *llano* sent skilled women to the Sierra for these tasks.

Familial ties were another factor that attracted women to the guerrilla camps, and women such as Olga Lara García mobilized to be close to her guerrilla husband, as well as to set up a sewing workshop in the Sierra. Clara "Clarita" Lull was a *madre* of Raúl Castro's Second Front "Frank País," which formed in March 1958. These *madres* supplied the Front "so that Raúl didn't lack anything."[48] Clarita's contributions were maternally motivated in two ways and apply to a subset of women within the guerrilla: not only did she "mother" the troops by securing needed supplies, but she felt that through her contributions, she was protecting her guerrilla son. She helped collect and transport weapons and medicines, obtaining medical supplies from a doctor and a pharmaceutical salesman, which she hid in her skirt as she rode to the Second Front in a jeep. Clarita described how they passed safely through the military checkpoints, "looking like tourists on a country excursion."[49] Despite the danger, she recalled, "This was the happiest time of my life. There was a fraternity, we cared so much about each other."[50] Such emotional and maternal ties were often mentioned by middle-aged women as motivating factors.

Women, particularly mothers, also served as informal liaisons between the *llano* and the Sierra. When Aída Bles Montenegro's sons were forced into the Sierra in 1958, she delivered food to them at night. "I had to be strong and not cry in front of people so that they wouldn't know that I knew where [my sons] were and discover them."[51] While mothers such as Clara and Aída concentrated on supplying the guerrillas that now included their children, some mothers made other sacrifices. Enerdina Díaz Bárcenas, mother to fifteen children, described herself as actively encouraging her sons to join the guerrillas: "Up there, one has to *vencer o morir* [win or die]."[52] Taking a page from the Mariana Grajales legend, she added, "I turned to Rafaelito, the youngest, and said to him, 'Listen, son, … to my boys that are up there … Tell them for me that I don't want to find out that anything has happened that is cowardly, because in my house I don't want cowards or deserters.'"[53] Seven of her children joined the Second Front, and another was imprisoned. In June 1958, Enerdina, her husband, and four of their daughters arrived in the territory of guerrilla Column 19 and remained until Batista's overthrow.[54]

Some *llano* women forced into the Sierra were prominent and highly skilled rebels. One such case was Pastorita Núñez, a middle-aged M-26-7 member who had worked with Fidel in the Orthodox Party a decade earlier.[55] A founding member of *Las Martianas*, she later directed the *Comando Femenino* in the April 1958 strike.[56] When the strike failed, she transferred for safety to the guerrilla command headquarters in La Plata. Rebel men with such skills and stature would often become guerrilla leaders in the Sierra. However, Pastorita was first assigned tasks in camp such as cleaning, counting bullets, and sewing uniforms. In late August 1958, Fidel, looking to put her skills to use and under pressure from Pastorita herself, assigned her to collect war taxes from the growers in Oriente and Camagüey: "In one month we'll have all the cash we need to buy arms, feed the troops, and pay for the coffee harvest."[57] This was challenging work, as Pastorita had to threaten to burn sugar mills or fields if growers did not pay. On occasion, she ordered a warehouse or a portion of the crop burned to prod a reluctant owner.[58] Ultimately, she collected nearly 4 million in Cuban pesos, all carefully documented with receipts.[59]

WOMEN COURIERS: LIDIA AND CLODOMIRA

As in the urban underground, the guerrillas deployed tactical femininity in the Sierra, particularly with women couriers. In part because Che later extolled the benefits, this practice is well known and features prominently in the Cuban War Story and even academic accounts.[60] First, "women can transport [supplies and messages] using a thousand tricks," such as hiding bullets and explosives under wide skirts and taping money to their torsos.[61] Second, "it is a fact that however brutal the repression, however thorough the searching, the woman receives a less harsh treatment than the man, … attracting less attention and at the same time inspiring less fear of danger in the enemy soldier."[62] Femininity, in this sense, was a guerrilla tactic to ensure safer passage of guerrilla communications and supplies.

Though Che's observations generally held, the work was nonetheless dangerous. For example, Olga Lara, entrusted for crucial supply missions including transport of large sums of money, was detained by the military and tortured for information about the rebel camps, the beatings so severe as to permanently affect her health.[63]

The deaths of two women couriers, Lidia and Clodomira, prominent in the post-1958 Cuban War Story, are the most well-documented examples of the danger. Outside of Cuba, little has been written about Lidia and Clodomira. Like Urselia Díaz and the Giralt sisters discussed in Chapter 6, they are among the few women martyrs of the insurrection recognized within Cuba. However, unlike those cases, Lidia and Clodomira were from economically marginalized backgrounds, and Clodomira was triply marginalized as a mixed race, poor *campesina*.

Through a fictional account of 1950s Cuba, Graham Greene suggests a distinction between the torturable and nontorturable classes: the former expect (and are expected) to be tortured while the latter "would be outraged by the idea."[64] For Greene, economic class and nationality mark the distinctions; however, with the complexity supplied by an intersectional lens, we can add that in 1950s Cuba, people of color were more torturable than whites. In this formulation, Lidia and especially Clodomira, as a woman of color, fell into the torturable class as distinct from many other women rebels. At the time, they were mourned in their guerrilla units, but in seeming confirmation of Greene's distinction, their deaths were not acknowledged more widely until the post-1958 revolution elevated them as an example of the support and sacrifice of women and the poor.

Lidia Esther Doce Sánchez, born in 1916, was an Oriente mother of three grown children.[65] After divorcing her second husband in 1956, she moved to Havana and struggled to support herself as a domestic worker and through embroidery work.[66] When Lidia received news that her eldest son Efraín had been killed in the guerrilla, she rushed back to Oriente. The news turned out to be false, but she decided to remain near her children. In a house on the banks of the Yao River, Lidia began her guerrilla collaboration, sewing flags and uniforms as well as delivering supplies.[67]

Lidia soon became a trusted messenger. By all reports, she was a brave woman, full of life and contagiously optimistic about rebel victory.[68] She committed herself to Che in particular, and he recalled Lidia with unusual fondness: "When I mention her name, there is something more than an affectionate appreciation ... she had a particular devotion to me and preferred to work under my orders."[69] A Che biographer elaborated: "Lidia was to become one of Che's most revered revolutionary personalities."[70]

Che placed her in charge of an auxiliary camp in "la Cueva," a risky location. "We wanted to remove her from that command because it was too dangerous a spot ... I tried to have Lidia transferred from there once and for all; but I succeeded only when she followed me to the new fighting front."[71] He also recalled that Lidia had led the men in camp "with spirit and a touch of high-handedness, causing a certain resentment among them, since Cubans weren't accustomed to taking orders from a woman."[72] Indeed, according to Che, she was so fearless in her work that male messengers avoided her: "I remember very well the opinion – a mixture of admiration and resentment – of one of them, who told me: 'That woman has bigger [balls] than Maceo but she's going to get us all killed.'"[73]

Lidia was sometimes sent to Santiago and Havana with sensitive documents from Fidel and Che; on the trip back, she would carry medicines, weapons, and other supplies.[74] On those trips, "she liked to dress elegantly," altering her hair color, glasses, and clothing, to evade the authorities.[75] A Cuban magazine article recounted twenty-five years later: "If Batista's soldiers engaged in conversation with her, you could hear her talk and talk for hours without anything happening. The words and laughter of Lidia would only serve to convince them that they are speaking with a *criolla* without a care in the world, totally apart from matters of revolution."[76]

Clodomira Acosta Ferrales was a common companion for Lidia. In her early twenties (and twenty years younger than Lidia), Clodomira was from a very poor family in rural Oriente.[77] Recollections of Clodomira often note her physical appearance – she is described as slight and sickly-looking, with rough skin, frizzy hair, and no front teeth. Lilia Galiano remembered asking Clodomira why she had not had her teeth fixed, and Clodomira replied: "Because I don't have the resources, but when we triumph there will be a new Clodomira."[78] Celia worried that given her appearance, Clodomira would stand out when she went to Havana on rebel business, so she sent her to a friend in Santiago with instructions to get Clodomira's teeth fixed and take her to a beauty salon.[79] Like many poor Afro-Cuban and mixed-race *campesinas* (she is described as *mulata*), she was illiterate. At the age of nine, she left home for domestic work in the city.[80] By the time she was twenty, she had returned to the countryside and begun to collaborate with the rebels when a military offensive developed near her home in June 1957. At first she washed clothes, carried water, and did other feminized tasks of the camp.[81] Her intelligence and commitment caught leaders' attention, and she became a trusted messenger and envoy. She was adept at (memorizing messages,) a skill that made her particularly valuable, and was sent on highly sensitive missions.[82] For example, Fidel sent Clodomira as his envoy in mid-February 1958 to meet with the *Directorio Revolucionario* (DR) rebels on their return from exile in Miami to establish a guerrilla base in the Escambray.[83] According to Celia, Fidel was struggling to determine which DR guerrillas were in Escambray and how they were establishing their base.[84] Clodomira established the connection between the two armed groups.

To evade detection, Clodomira at times traveled with a friend's young daughter who carried a small doll that hid secret documents.[85] During the April 1958 strike, Fidel had an urgent message for the *llano*, but the military blocked the highway. Clodomira managed to get through the roadblock by making a scene, insisting that she had to visit her gravely ill mother.[86] During her missions, Clodomira was twice taken prisoner but managed to escape both times.[87]

Castro planned for Clodomira to lead the Marianas women's platoon in September 1958 once she returned from a mission to Havana.[88] As Mariana member Lilia Riero recalled: "Based upon her merits, her experience, and her trustworthiness, Fidel ... told Clodomira to return quickly to begin organizing the platoon. Clodomira went off this last time to Havana very pleased."[89]

On their last mission, Lidia joined Clodomira in Havana on September 11, 1958 at a safe house.[90] Four young rebel men were in hiding there after having executed a police informer.[91] In the early morning, the police forced their way into the dwelling.[92] The men were killed in the apartment, while the women, badly beaten, were taken alive.[93] Lidia was in a state of semi-consciousness; however, Clodomira reportedly fought back. (It is said that one policeman, at his execution in 1959, still bore Clodomira's bite marks on his shoulder.[94]) Their bodies are thought to have been taken out to sea.[95] Lidia's son learned of the news by chancing upon a front-page headline at guerrilla headquarters.[96] The news hit their guerrilla units hard. One ex-combatant recalled, "[It] moved us deeply ... Camilo [Cienfuegos] called the troops together and spoke of the responsibilities and the role that Lidia and Clodomira played ... We were talking about them for days after."[97]

Lidia and Clodomira are recurring figures in the Cuban War Story, often accompanying the "Even the Women" narrative, echoing Martí, in which women's participation in the struggle demonstrated the justice and invincibility of the rebel cause.[98] As nonelite women, relatively rare in the dominant state narrative on the guerrillas, representations of Lidia and Clodomira powerfully convey for the revolution a broad appeal across class, gender, and racial lines. The established narrative surrounding them has an intersectional advantage, helping secure the claim that all Cubans rose up against Batista, not just those relatively privileged categories represented by the leaders.

SUPPLANTING THE GOVERNMENT: CAPTURING HEARTS AND MINDS THROUGH EDUCATION AND HEALTHCARE

Although the Cuban guerrillas are typically analyzed and idealized in terms of military engagements, I have stressed that much of their success relied upon achievements beyond combat. Such achievements included development of social services, which addressed dire needs in the areas they controlled, highlighted shortcomings of the current government, and promised a better future. This process can be examined through Raúl Castro's establishment of the Second Front in the Sierra Cristal in March 1958. The new front had to respond to the many civilians and *llano* rebels (especially young men) arriving there for safety, as well as capture the support of the largely poor and historically neglected *campesinos/as* in the area. Soon, they also confronted the dictatorship's 1958 Summer Offensive, engaging with the Batista military at least 247 times, inflicting thousands of casualties and capturing airplanes, ships, and trains.[99] In late June 1958, the rebels captured fifty North Americans, billing it an anti-aircraft operation, *Operación Antiaérea*, as the military's intense aerial bombardment reportedly slowed to avoid harming the North American captives.[100] Raúl used the one-month respite to convert the Second Front into its own republic: "we supplanted the old authority of the regime in that territory and made the new authority prevail."[101] The guerrilla-held zones levied taxes on large landowners, resolved workplace disputes, built roads, administered justice, taught literacy, treated illnesses, and even performed marriages.[102] By October, the Second Front had a military and administrative structure and seven departments: War, Justice, Public Health, Propaganda, Education, Finances, and Construction and Communications.[103] In this way, the guerrilla replaced the old, corrupt authority of Batista with a more effective and just revolutionary authority.

Raúl later claimed the creation of an educational system in this zone with high illiteracy to be one of the Front's greatest nonmilitary achievements.[104] He identified health as another: "Right from the start, the medical personnel who took care of our troops in the Second Front also treated the peasant population that, as a rule, lacked any kind of health care and lived in areas where epidemics, malnutrition, and endemic illnesses prevailed," along with high infant mortality.[105] Rebel leadership understood these projects "as an incentive to collaborate with the Rebel Army and greatly contributed to increasing their respect for it ... [They] showed the population in that territory very graphically what the triumph of the revolution would signify."[106] Women were concentrated in this work, which was another vital though barely recognized contribution, overshadowed by the fifty-plus-year spotlight focused on military engagements.

The Rebel Army reopened schools closed by the government during the conflict and set up additional mobile and makeshift schools, calling for teacher volunteers. M-26-7 sent up women to serve as teachers as well as nurses. For example, in early 1958, Che requested a teacher and a nurse for his Column 4, and sisters Lilia and Isabel Rielo joined Che's column in early March 1958.[107] Lilia, who had completed two years of high school, helped create a mobile school, able to evade the military during Batista's military offensive.

In August 1958, Raúl assigned Asela de los Santos, a central member of M-26-7 in Oriente with a doctorate in pedagogy, to be director of the rebel Department of Education.[108] With deputy director Zoila Ibarra, Asela oversaw hundreds of rebel schools and also formed literacy groups for combatants in the camps.[109] According to Asela, Raúl channeled resources as well as men and women newly arrived from the *llano* to work in education. The Department of Education was structured into columns and companies, headed in each case by someone trained as a teacher.[110] Such rebel resources and attention to the rural poor, so long severely neglected and largely illiterate, aimed to broaden rural support. This was also an effective way to put unarmed rebels to work in the Sierra, as volunteers continued to outnumber rifles.

Administering to local health needs was another means, and like education, this effort also relied heavily on women. Emma Carnet, a young woman with only a modest background in health, was summoned to the Sierra in the summer of 1958 to work as a medical assistant.[111] At its peak, the medical department of the Second Front had a staff of 160, including nineteen doctors and five dentists, as well as pharmacists, X-ray and lab technicians, medical students, nurses, and helpers.[112] Reportedly, the field hospitals had operating rooms, radiology, laboratories, blood transfusion centers, and other services.[113]

Built quickly in rebel-held territory and with supplies that had to be smuggled in, the medical field hospitals were rather rudimentary. In December 1958, US journalist Dickey Chapelle was injured and taken to a rebel hospital (a converted coffee-drying shed) staffed by two doctors, "a bearded older man and a sturdy light-haired woman."[114] As she recalled, "Under the sheet-metal roof of the shed hung two flickering kerosene lanterns. Toward one end stood six shabby beds and a canvas cot … In the center of the space stood a dining room table. A white enamel basin and a canvas roll of surgical instruments gleamed on it."[115] Chapelle watched the woman doctor use the last anesthetic on a patient, then "all the casualties from the mortar barrage arrived at almost the same minute. Before the next hour passed, there were a dozen newly wounded in the hospital. Four bodies, candles burning at their feet, lay in a row at the dark end of the shed. The floor was wet with blood."[116]

In addition to providing care for rebel and civilian injuries received in battle and aerial bombardments, basic healthcare for the population was also a means by which the rebels appealed to the surrounding population, demonstrating care in obvious contrast to the often-indiscriminate attacks of Batista forces. Chana Pérez, the elderly *campesina* discussed earlier, remembered Che for his medical attention: "If I sent him a message that I was sick, whatever hour of the night he would arrive at my house and say, 'Here I am *mi vieja* – what do you need.' He would examine me and Che himself would give me the money for the medicine. He loved me a lot."[117]

Thus, through supplanting government services and improving upon them, the guerrilla pursued a hearts and minds campaign in the Sierra that relied heavily on the work of unarmed women rebels. As I have argued, the gendered struggle to win over the support of the Cuban people was at least as important as the casualties the guerrillas inflicted in battle. Indeed, M-26-7's success in winning popular support through education and health services was such that the revolution in power prioritized this strategy over nearly six decades, both domestically and in its international relations.

Notes

1. Chapelle (1962a); Wickham-Crowley (1992, 216–17); Kampwirth (2002, 3); Foran et al. (1997, 32–3).
2. Bayard de Volo (2001, 185–9); Viterna (2006).
- Guevara (1961) 1985.

4. Anderson (1997, 238). Anderson based this account on his access to Che's diary (Guevara 2013, see February 18, 1957 entry, 76).

5. Guevara (2013, 77).

6. Guevara (1961) 1985, 132.

7. Ibid., 133.

8. Ibid., 157.

9. Ibid., 157.

10. Nydia Sarabia, "Mujeres guerrilleras en la batalla de Guisa," in *Bohemia* November 24, 1967, 53–4; Silvia Bota and Adelina Vázquez, "La razón para vivir," *Mujeres* September 1983, 6.

11. See Castañeda (1997, 113, 120). As Taibo (1997, 160) wrote: "Zoila described the meeting years later, breaking the silence that until then had covered that part of Che's life."

12. Zoila Rodríguez García testimony, *El Nuevo Fénix* (originally published in Cupull and González, 1992).

13. Taibo (1997, 161–2) (Taibo's translation).

14. Ibid., 183.

15. Gadea (2008, 218).

16. March (2012, 13–14, 42).

17. Ibid., 37. The peso was pegged to the US dollar; she delivered $50,000 in 1958, worth over $410,000 in 2016 US dollars.

18. Taibo (1997, 213).

19. March (2012, 6).

20. Barrio and Jenkins (2003, 124); March (2012, 43).

21. March (2012, 47).

22. Ibid., 49–50.

23. See, for example, Gadea (2008, 218).

24. Guevara (1961) 1985, 133.

25. Ibid., 132.

26. Ibid., 132.

27. Yuval-Davis (2004, 177); Enloe (2000).

28. Guevara (1961) 1985, 133. He adds that education can be a task "of great importance for women," as they "arouse more enthusiasm among children" (ibid., 133).

29. Ibid., 134.

30. Ibid., 177–8.

31. Ibid., 133.

32. Bota and Vázquez (1983, 6–8).

33. Guevara (1961) 1985, 85. Che is primarily concerned with setting a lower age limit, noting that younger combatants (especially under sixteen) are not effective and even constituted a burden for the guerrillas. He also sets the upper age limit at 40, at least for the stage of guerrilla combat that involves constant movement without a set base camp.

34. Lobao Reif (1990); Kampwirth (2002).

35. Lobao Reif (1990, 183). David Mason (1992) explains later Central American guerrilla groups' higher percentage of women through economic shifts in agriculture, which produced a rise in female-headed households

206 Women and the Cuban Insurrection

and in turn a rise in women's participation in social organizations, challenging traditional roles while also increasing their exposure to regime repression. This combination pushed women, often with children, into guerrilla camps for safety (see also Viterna 2006 and 2013; Kampwirth 2002, 8–9).

36. Ages calculated for December 31, 1957 to capture the last year of the insurrection: Haydée Santamaría (35), Melba Hernández (36), Pastorita Núñez (36), Celia Sánchez (37), María Antonia Figueroa (39), and Lidia Doce (41).

37. Segal (1995, 762).

38. Mason (1992, 83). See also Luciak (2001, 70); Shayne (2004, 3, 115); Viterna (2013).

39. Rose Ana Dueñas, "Heroic Combatants, Anonymous Women," *Granma Internacional* (Havana) April 11, 2006.

40. See Viterna (2006).

41. Wickham-Crowley (1992, 217).

42. Eckstein (2003, 12–13).

43. Scholars have noted that dominant notions of femininity can give an advantage to women rebels and activists. See Byrd and Decker (2008); Shayne (2004, 9, 43–4); Bouvard (1994); Decker (1991); Schirmer (1993); Fisher (1989).

44. Pérez Rigar interview, "Ah caray, este mismo es el hombre," *Verde Olivo* February 18, 1979, 8.

45. Guevara (1971, 184).

46. Juan Carlos Rivera, "Savia joven en las venas," *Verde Olivo* January 8, 1987, 43.

47. Magaly Sánchez Ochoa, "La batalla por la tierra," *Mujeres* May 1979, 4–5.

48. Prada, *Verde Olivo* November 1988, 24. Carmen Matos is a similar case; she mobilized into the Second Front with her daughter Iris (Triay, *Mujeres* September 1983, 15).

49. Prada (1988, 24).

50. Ibid. Her son died in the last months of the conflict.

51. Marilys Suárez, "Con cariño de madres," *Mujeres* April 1978, 4.

52. Alfredo Reyes Trejo, "Una familia de la Revolución," *Verde Olivo* March 13, 1983, 40. Aída Bles also told her sons, "If you die, let it be with weapons in hand" (Suárez 1978, 4).

53. Reyes Trejo (1983, 41).

54. Ibid.

55. Rebel-turned-CIA informer Frank Sturgis, in testimony to the Rockefeller Commission, described Pastorita Núñez as "a Commander and a lesbian" (Mary Ferrell Foundation Archives, Rockefeller Commission Testimony of Frank Sturgis, April 3, 1975). This appears as a criticism of Núñez in other anti-Castro sources.

56. Rodríguez Calderón, *Granma* April 21, 1988, 3.

57. Pastorita Núñez, "Pastorita Núñez, sus recuerdos: Guerrillera en las calles y en la Sierra, constructora de sueños" (excerpts from Pastorita Núñez's unpublished autobiography) *Granma* 10(117), April 27, 2006. The Rebel Army took on the coffee harvest in the area since Batista's military offensive had blocked access into and from the Sierra.

58. Núñez, *La Jiribilla* VII, January 3–9, 2009.
59. Ibid.
60. For Che, women were effective spies: "[especially women] should be in permanent contact with soldiers and gradually discover what there is to be discovered" (Guevara (1961) 1985, 147). However, there is little concrete evidence that women were often utilized for this work in the Sierra.
61. Guevara (1961) 1985, 132–3.
62. Ibid.,133.
63. Sánchez Ochoa, *Mujeres* May 1980, 9.
64. Greene (1958) 2007, 159.
65. Her name is sometimes written as "Lydia."
66. Marilys Suárez, y Clodomira: Las mensajeras de la Sierra," *Mujeres* November 1976, 51; Heidy González Cabrera, "Mujeres increíbles que no flaquearon," *Mujeres* September 1983, 38–41.
67. Suárez (1976, 51); Vilma Espín, "Como dignas continuadoras del Pelotón Mariana Grajales crecen en todas partes las Unidades Femeninas de las Milicias de Tropas Territoriales," September 4, 1983 speech, Granma Province, transcribed in *Granma* September 5, 1983, 2; Guevara (1971, 160). Column Four met Lidia around September 1957, when the rebel army took San Pablo de Yao.
68. Espín (1983, 2).
69. Suárez (1976, 51); González Cabrera (1983, 38–41); Katia Valdes, "Las dos mensajeras," *Verde Olivo* September 8, 1983, 25; Katia Valdes, "Dos caracteres y una misma estirpe," *Verde Olivo* September 10, 1978, 40–3. See also Guevara (1971, 147).
70. Anderson (1997, 321).
71. Guevara (1971, 148).
72. Ibid.
73. Guevara (1971, 147–8). Ellipses in the original; *tener más cojones que* [independence hero Antonio] *Maceo* (to have bigger balls than Maceo) is a common Cuban phrase indicating great bravery.
74. Nidia Díaz, "Lydia y Clodomira," *Granma* September 17, 1983, 2.
75. González Cabrera (1983, 38–41).
76. Valdes (1983, 24–7). *Criolla* indicated a white woman of Spanish descent.
77. Iraida Campo, "XX aniversario: Lydia y Clodomira," *Mujeres* September 1978, 12–13.
78. Ibid., 13. This question, put to someone as poor as Clodomira, suggests the disconnect between the Cuban middle class and the rural poor at the time.
79. Stout (2013, 267).
80. Suárez (1976, 51); Espín (1983, 2).
81. Ibid.
82. Gonzáles Cabrera (1983, 38–41).
83. Testimony of Armando Fleites, in Hernández (2013).
84. EcuRed (n.d.), Síntesis biográfica, Clodomira Acosta. In addition to the DR guerrillas, the Second Front was in the Escambray, an armed group financed by ex-President Prío.
85. Espín (1983, 2).

86. Gonzáles Cabrera (1983, 38–41).
87. Suárez (1976, 51).
88. Valdes (1983, 6–9).
89. *Bohemia* July 28, 1967, 14–17.
90. Valdes (1983, 26). Griselda Sánchez Manduley and Gaspar González-Lanuza Rodríguez were overseeing Lidia's stay. González-Lanuza maintained that Lidia sneaked back to the apartment where Clodomira was staying after he had dropped her off at another safe-house earlier that night (González-Lanuza, "Heroínas de la Sierra y el llano," *Juventud Rebelde* September 13, 2012, 4).
91. Suárez (1976, 51). The four men were Reinaldo Cruz, Alberto Álvarez, Onelio Dampier, and Leonardo Valdés. The informer, "Manolo el relojero," was believed to be spying for the notorious police lieutenant colonel Esteban Ventura.
92. Ibid.
93. One body had fifty-two bullet holes (González-Lanuza 2012, 4).
94. Espín (1983, 2).
95. Valdes (1983, 26). *The New York Times* correspondent Ruby Hart Phillips wrote that in September 1958, "I learned that two girls had been arrested after several boys had been killed in a gun battle with police in a Havana suburb. I called Pizzi [de Porra, Batista's propaganda chief, who had previously successfully intervened in arrests]. He said he would check into the matter. I learned later that the two girls, one of them from the Sierra Maestra Mountain headquarters of Fidel Castro, here on a mission, had been beaten to death by the police. Their bodies were almost unrecognizable when their relatives got them out of the morgue" (Phillips 1959, 365). Given the date and the general description, it is likely these were Lidia and Clodomira. According to Cuban sources, the women's bodies were never recovered.
96. González Cabrera (1983, 41).
97. Dariel Alarcón Ramírez in Suárez (1976, 53).
98. See Chapter 3; Yuval-Davis (2004, 172).
99. Bonachea and San Martín (1974, 191).
100. Park Wollam, the US Consul sent to negotiate the release, witnessed the targeting of civilians by Cuban Air Force planes, which dropped a bomb on a Baptist church and strafed people indiscriminately as Wollam hid nearby (Paterson 1994, 162–3). This occurred after the Cuban military had pledged to stop such air attacks as the United States negotiated for release of the hostages. The US hostages also later noted the danger posed by these indiscriminate air attacks, contrasting them to the relatively humane treatment they received from the rebels. Rebels took the hostages to view the damage created by the airstrikes, and at least several captives informed Wollam they had become rebel sympathizers (Paterson 1994, 164, 166). Wollam reported that rebels "became emotional about the women and children being bombed and strafed in their territory" (Paterson 1994, 196).
101. Raúl Castro Ruz, "How Rebel Army Spread Revolutionary War" (Interview), *Granma International Weekly Review* March 15, 1988.

102. Ibid.; Bonachea and San Martín (1974, 191); *Bohemia* July 28, 1967, 14–17.
103. Castro, *Granma International Weekly Review* March 15, 1988.
104. Ibid.
105. Ibid.
106. Ibid.
107. *Bohemia* July 28, 1967, 14–17.
108. Luis Hernández Serrano, "El magisterio de Fidel se multiplica en pueblos y generaciones," *Juventud Rebelde* December 21, 2009.
109. Stoner and Serrano Pérez (2000, 113); Marilys Suárez Moreno, "Asela," *Mujeres* (4) 1990, 7–8. With the overthrow of Batista, she became Provincial Superintendent of Education in Oriente, and in 1960 she worked with Vilma in the creation of the Federation of Cuban Women.
110. Hernández Serrano (2009).
111. Isolina Triay, "Emma Carnet: La voluntad de vencer," *Mujeres* June 1986, 14–15.
112. Castro (1988).
113. Ibid.
114. Chapelle (1962b, 266).
115. Ibid.
116. Ibid., 267.
117. Rigar (1979, 8); see also Guevara (1971, 184).

CHAPTER 10

Las Marianas

Even the Women in Arms

9/4/58 = Las Marianas

On September 4, 1958, Fidel christened the all-women's platoon "Mariana Grajales" in honor of the Afro-Cuban woman heroine of the independence wars and mother of the heroic Maceo brothers.[1] The Mariana Grajales Platoon (*Las Marianas*) is well known, having received coverage both domestically and internationally. But the Marianas numbered at most fourteen, engaged in only a limited number of battles in the last months of the insurrection, and did not make a discernible difference to the outcome of a battle. Gender research on war tells us that all-women's units such as Las Marianas are extremely rare cases in the history of warfare, which tend to form in response to extreme military personnel shortages or as the nation faces an existential threat.[2] However, the formation of Las Marianas was not a decision made by a desperate military suffering severe attrition but rather an increasingly successful one with more volunteer combatants than it could put to use.[3] Furthermore, Cuban guerrilla men's initial opposition to arming women is well documented. Why, then, did the guerrilla leadership make this unusual, initially unpopular, and militarily unnecessary decision to arm women?

Though the Marianas proved effective combatants, I propose that the platoon's formation is not sufficiently explained by its potential contribution to guerrilla battlefield effectiveness. The Marianas represented a small fraction of the guerrillas' already small fighting force, a detail easily lost given the considerable attention they receive in the Cuban War Story.[4] Nearly all instances of guerrilla women in combat occurred in the last six months of the insurrection, by which time the tide had turned in the rebels' favor. By July 1958 the US embassy and state department, for example, considered M-26-7 victory a real possibility.[5] Guerrilla confidence, too, was higher following the military's failed 1958 Summer Offensive, and Fidel was contemplating the postwar period. Accordingly, rather than contributions to fighting effectiveness, the Marianas formation is best explained by the convergence of four factors: the symbolic power of such a platoon, M-26-7's official ideological commitment to ending discrimination, pressure from women who sought combat, and an increase in available rifles.[6] Of these, the driving cause was the symbolic effect of armed women. Certainly women's willingness to go to battle, the availability of combat weapons, and ideological resonance were important, but they are conditions that made possible a gender tactic aimed at popular support – one with immediate benefits but that also looked beyond the guerrilla war to postwar revolutionary governance.

This gender tactic was multivalent. First, Las Marianas conveyed the Even the Women narrative, affirming that armed resistance expressed the will of the people and thus was both righteous and invincible.[7] The gendered logic is somewhat complex, as women are supposed to be peaceful and apolitical, not violent.[8] When a woman commits an act of violence, hegemonic discourse often downplays her political agency through alternative explanations: deviance, mental illness, irrationality, or pressure from a male companion.[9] Yet when multiple women unite with men in taking up arms, they are often endowed with an air of righteousness. As Jocelyn Viterna explains: "Precisely because women are considered peacemakers, and precisely because they are considered the subordinated sector of society, their widespread participation in violent groups often adds an aura of legitimacy to the politics of the armed organization."[10] Indeed, armed groups amplify the images and rhetoric of the women in their ranks "to portray their cause as so just that *even women* are willing to risk their lives, and the lives of their children, to support it."[11] There are additional facets to the "even the women" gendered logic here. The presence of women within guerrilla units can help garner civilian sympathy and trust.[12] Furthermore, as with the Cuban Mambí army over half a century prior, the high moral caliber of the guerrilla men was demonstrated by the fact that women were willing to fight alongside them.[13]

Second, armed women shamed guerrilla men into bravery and undermined the morale of the enemy. The literature cites a number of cases in which militaries have mobilized women to shame men into joining the military or advancing forward on the battlefield.[14] A tactic practiced by the Mambisas in Cuba's wars of independence, the M-26-7 guerrillas made use of it as well.[15] However, the Cuban case presents an additional gendered shaming tactic aimed at demoralizing the enemy. In Cuba, armed guerrilla women not only demonstrated the rightness and popularity of the cause but also called into question the masculinity of government soldiers. The gendered logic was that each battlefield loss inflicted deeper psychological wounds when the victorious troops included women.

Third, the Marianas confirmed women's capability and right to participate fully in the revolutionary process. Indeed, after 1958, the Cuban state media celebrated the Marianas and periodically featured interviews with members. Decades later, state media used representations of Las Marianas to mobilize women into militias during Cuba's 1980s defense buildup.[16]

Scholarly literature tends to focus on Che's writings to illustrate the lack of women in combat and sexism in guerrilla armies.[17] However, Fidel's statements and Cuban media representations present intriguing and meaningful contrasts. Fidel emerges as the ultimate hero of the Marianas legend because, as the Cuban War Story goes, owing to his faith in women and commitment to equality, he defended the women against the strenuous objections of male guerrillas, personally trained them, then placed them as his advance guard and deployed them in combat.[18] The main elements of the narrative can be found in this 1976 article:

Fidel, demonstrating his celebrated vision, saw women's liberation in the context of the struggle of society as a whole for liberation from exploitation and imperialist domination and for elimination of all forms of injustice, discrimination, and inequality ... This idea was put into practice through women's presence in the most important revolutionary actions ... The maximum leader of the Revolution always supported and promoted this participation, confronting the prevailing prejudices ... [Women] had earned the right to carry a gun and to demand their place in society ... Upon arriving in Santiago de Cuba in early January 1959, the commander in chief reiterated: ... "When in a nation, the men fight and the women can fight, this people is invincible."[19]

The above is but one example of the long life of this gendered tactic in the war for hearts and minds. Beginning in 1958 and extending for decades, the arming of the Marianas signaled the revolution's commitment to equality, celebrated the maximum leader's faith in women, mobilized women into militias and mass organizations, and rallied a nation to support Cuba's foreign wars and national defense.

WOMEN BARRED FROM COMBAT

Regarding Latin American guerrilla armies, Wickham-Crowley asks whether women were in noncombatant roles out of personal preference or because they were barred from combat.[20] A key question, it must be approached by differentiating between women. The Cuban case provides numerous examples, discussed in previous chapters, of women who embraced traditional gender roles within the guerrilla camps. This chapter covers the smaller number of women who sought combat assignments and were initially barred. Given that the first impulse within the guerrilla army was to bar women from combat, what broke down this resistance? In this section, I explore three women's efforts to enter combat and Che's resistance to those efforts. As is evidenced in this section and the guerrilla case more generally, discrimination against rebel women took the forms identified in Chapter 5: redirecting women from participation; undercutting their authority or capability; and undermining their ability (often in the guise of protection).

Part of the problem was the scarcity of rifles and bullets. As Fidel later explained, "We used to gauge the success of the military operations by the number of weapons seized."[21] Indeed, guerrilla correspondence is filled with details on captured weapons. Men and women alike who arrived at the guerrilla camps unarmed were typically turned away, being told to return once they had captured a rifle from a *guardia* (government soldier). In this context, women were marginalized with an argument in which gender bias was disguised as common sense: if so many men were unarmed, how could women be given rifles?

Aleida March's experience is instructive. She explains that although she was an experienced and trusted *llano* rebel:

[I]n the mountains I was just another insignificant person expected to follow orders ... My new challenge was to become a soldier ... I met with [Che] one evening and we talked about this. He proposed that I stay on in the camp as a nurse ... I responded bluntly, explaining that I thought my two years of clandestine work gave me the right to be incorporated into the guerrilla unit. He didn't agree.[22]

Instead, she became Che's assistant and was not issued a rifle until the final days of the insurrection.

More generally, despite mounting counter-evidence, guerrilla leaders such as Che saw women as less physically resilient and in need of protection. Oniria Gutiérrez was only seventeen years old when she arrived in Che's camp on August 3, 1957. Though she had wandered around the countryside a month before finding them, Che initially refused to let her stay: "He told me that it was totally impossible, that it would be very hard for a woman in my physical condition, that I would be more useful in the cities, and I don't know what else."[23] She argued "for a good long time," pointing out that Celia Sánchez's presence in the Sierra Maestra "demonstrated that women too could fight."[24] Oniria proposed a trial period, "I begged him: 'Come on, commander, please, don't be bad,' over and over again" until he agreed.[25] Soon after, as the men prepared for a battle, she tried to accompany them. Again, Che at first refused, then relented: "he put me 'in charge' of watching his field glasses and his coat while they fought, and gave me a small revolver for my personal defense."[26] However, during the battle of Mar Verde, a more dangerous situation with enemy troops nearby, Che ordered all women and wounded men to evacuate to safety and was furious when Oniria sneaked back to camp. He also refused her when he left for the Escambray: "He ... told me that it was impossible, that I wouldn't be able to withstand that campaign. I protested that Joel Iglesias, who also was very young and had been injured a short time before, was going. But he did not want me to go with them."[27]

Several other rank and file women sought combat outside of the Marianas.[28] Among these, Mimí's story stands out for her determination to not simply follow her husband into war but fight alongside him. It also alerts us to the tensions women in the guerrilla faced, ranging from cussing and other masculinized behavior deemed offensive to women, to privacy while going to the bathroom, to questioning and even threats to women's honor through sexual advances.

Zobeida "Mimí" Rodríguez and husband Israel Chávez, both *llano* rebels, joined the famous Column 8 Ciro Redondo in the Escambray Mountains in 1958, leaving their two children in the care of others.[29] Chávez left first, and Mimí followed after a police officer warned that his lieutenant was coming for her.[30] The movement originally told her to leave for the United States because "in the Escambray [guerrillas] there are no women."[31] She refused exile, so they sent her to a nearby city to hide in a hotel. Mimí, a white woman, recounted how the police sergeant, "a big black man," reviewed the hotel's guest list and thought she was a prostitute. He sent word that he would be back to see her with a case of beer and, she implies, an expectation of sexual services.[32] She fled again and eventually arrived in camp: "My arrival in the mountains was not rosy. Not even Chávez himself was happy to see me. I had to explain in great detail that I had no other choice, so that he would understand."[33]

Chávez was apprehensive about her living with a group of men: "Within a few hours of her arrival, the insinuations began on the part of some misunderstandings, which like weeds, crop up everywhere. I didn't feel comfortable in the first days with her there among the men ... who were always ready to mortify and with vulgar language."[34] A guerrilla captain reassured Chávez not to fear for Mimí's safety and met with the troop to declare: "[Mimí] was the only woman and the wife of a combatant in the group, and it was necessary to respect [her]."[35] Notably, the concern was for what the men in the guerrilla might do, not the danger posed by guerrilla warfare. In response to this threat, Mimí re-oriented the gender dynamics, telling the men: "From now on you are all my sons, and you will occupy the space of my two children that I had to leave behind."[36] Although the guerrilla men were roughly her own age if not older, her maternal conversion "neutralized them from whatever possible presumptions they had."[37] *Meter?*

Mimí's experience reveals the very constricted range of identities that women in this context could fill: sexualized object or mother. Despite the fact that she was married to one of their own, both Mimí and her husband worried that she was viewed as sexually available by their predatory fellow guerrillas. Her declaration as the men's mother-figure "neutralized" this tension. However, part of this maternal performance entailed a desexualized "purity," and she refrained from sleeping near her husband "to avoid any temptation."[38]

When Che arrived in the Escambray, he addressed their troop without realizing that Mimí was a woman. According to Mimí, because she was thin and wore her hair back in a ponytail, like some rebel men, newcomers assumed she was a man.[39] She volunteered and headed out under Che's leadership along with several hundred others, pleased because now that Che had arrived, she expected she would receive a rifle.[40] Mimí walked ahead of the rest: "if I had to urinate, that gave me some time before the rest caught up."[41] But Che soon heard that one of the officers had a woman in the troops. According to Chávez, Che thought that she was a woman Chávez had there on the side and that he was abusing his authority.[42] Che was surprised to learn they were married. Nonetheless, he insisted that she had to leave.[43] Hearing that Mimí had been with the troop for four months after fleeing the *llano* and leaving her two children behind, his attitude softened.[44] Che allowed, "For the time being she will continue on as a nurse, an aide, because as it is, this is very bad, and when things normalize, we will see."[45] Mimí, who "had never cured a sick person," learned some nursing skills and in several battles administered first aid.[46]

Yet Mimí was intent on combat and decided to earn her gun like the men. As the guerrillas prepared for the battle at Fomento, she was left behind with six men to guard packs and supplies. But once the fighting began, she convinced those six to leave the packs and accompany her to the battle: "It's the only way to capture a gun. If they kill us, that's our bad luck.'"[47] She was among the first to enter the captured barracks and found an abandoned rifle. Che saw this and grabbed her by the ponytail, demanding, "What are you doing here?" She responded: "You said that we had to earn our weapon, and I came to earn me one, and I did."[48] His response was severe, threatening to discipline her:

He ordered me, forcefully: "Give me that rifle." Big tears started to roll down my face, I started to cry and to say that after such a good job that I had done, how could this happen to me, that I could even be sanctioned. Then the *compañeros* said to Che [sympathetically]: "Comandante, look at how Mimí is crying." He came and grabbed me by my ponytail and said to me: "You are undisciplined, but really ballsy. The gun is yours, you earned it."[49]

After that, Mimí passed into the combat troops as a member of her husband's platoon, accompanying him into battle. In the final offensive, Che issued Chávez a recently captured 30 mm machine gun—the biggest the troop had—and assigned Mimí as his assistant. Chávez reflected, "It was a way of following through on his word, of recognizing our union in the guerrilla."[50] In one battle, as Chávez tells it, he was wounded in the head, with blood pouring out; Mimí, looking him over, said "Stop fucking around, you're fine," then took over the gun and started firing.[51]

These three cases illustrate some women's determination to take up arms on par with men. All three occurred in the same period that the Marianas formed, though Che initially barred each from combat even as Fidel armed and trained the Marianas. Che was unconvinced that women could perform as well as male combatants and, as Mimí's case reveals, was also concerned with morale problems or sexual tensions in introducing armed women into the elite mobile units that he led in the Escambray. I propose that the difference between Che and Fidel in this regard had less to do with differing commitments to equality and more to do with the driving impetus for arming women. That is, in arming women, Fidel aimed at the level of ideas, thinking of symbolic efficacy more so than battlefield efficacy. But guerrilla men still needed to be convinced that in battle women, at the least, could be trusted not to abandon their precious weapons to flee.

TETÉ AND THE TRUCE

Delsa Esther "Teté" Puebla's role in a temporary truce helped chip away doubts about women's courage and trustworthiness in dangerous situations. It thus served as a step toward arming the Marianas. Teté, one of nine children, was born into a poor, rural family in 1940.[52] She was studying to become a teacher, but when the *Granma* landed, she joined an underground cell. Many cell members were her relatives, and her home was the M-26-7 headquarters in town.[53] She soon questioned, "If I can do all the work – transporting arms and *compañeros* into the Sierra, selling rebel war bonds – why not leave to join the war?"[54] By July 1957, "We finally reached a point when it was no longer safe to go into town anymore because of the repression. We had to go up to the Sierra."[55] M-26-7 refused her permission to join the guerrilla, but she left anyway with two other women, Gena Verdecía and Ileana Rodés, and some sixty men.[56] According to Teté, when they arrived in camp, someone asked, "What is this *mocosa* [snot-nose kid] doing here?" – a nickname she bore for the duration.[57] But Fidel embraced her, held her up, and exclaimed, "Now we will win the war!"[58] Only 16, she claimed to be a year older, and Fidel allowed her to stay.[59]

Teté performed typical feminized tasks and served as Celia Sánchez's assistant. But she wanted to fight and begged to go into battle: "I had to shoot and receive my baptism of fire."[60] She accompanied Raúl Castro into the battle of Oro de Guisa in early 1958.[61] Fidel tried to bar her from combat, so she had to sneak into her next battle at Madre Vieja.[62] Conflicts intensified during the 1958 Summer Offensive, and women were called upon to deliver food to the male combatants who were in position.[63] Teté drove a team of mules to bring food to combatants in remote areas. This work exposed the women to gunfire as well as strafing and bombing from planes.

By July 1958, the rebels held hundreds of captured soldiers, some seriously wounded. The government military refused a truce that would allow the International Red Cross to receive prisoners of war.[64] To get around this impasse, Che proposed sending a woman to negotiate. As Teté explained, "if a man were sent, he would have been killed," but "[o]ur estimation was that because of my age, and the fact that I was not an ugly young woman at the time," the army might not shoot.[65] Once she accepted the risks, Che told her: "wash your uniform, iron it well, you have to go there very pretty with your 26 of July armband."[66] Teté set off with a white flag on mule-back into the tense situation. As military planes strafed and bombed, the mule threw her and ran off.[67] She continued on foot to the Las Vegas de Jibacoa military post. The arrival of a woman guerrilla was reportedly "cause for great excitement among the guards."[68] She remained there three days, during which time they treated her "with every courtesy," even wooing her with chocolates and perfume.[69] Teté was free to move about the base, and the captain gave over his sleeping quarters to her – all in all, a more positive reception than a man would likely have received.

The commander was, according to Teté, concerned that his troops would be demoralized to receive their own defeated comrades.[70] Nonetheless, he composed a message for her to deliver. Teté's comrades triumphantly carried her on their shoulders upon her return, relieved she had not been killed.[71] She returned to the military base that evening with Fidel's response, and eventually the truce was secured. Red Cross delegates described the transfer of prisoners: "a woman bearing a white flag approached on horseback. The woman told them that 50 wounded prisoners were nearby. She was then joined by Che Guevara, who told the delegates that 200 more prisoners were a bit further away."[72] The Cuban army accepted all 253 prisoners, the most seriously wounded carried in by their comrades.[73]

As a gendered tactic, rebel leaders deployed a woman to get through enemy defenses, assuming correctly that soldiers would not react aggressively to a woman emissary. Use of this tactic, in turn, helped pave the way for women in combat. As Teté put it, after that, "how could they refuse to give us, women who have had direct participation in all aspects of the Revolution, our gun?"[74] On her last trip to Santiago as a courier, she heard talk of a women's platoon.[75]

LAS MARIANAS: THE WOMEN'S PLATOON

Cuban sources list fourteen women as Marianas: Isabel Rielo, Lilia Rielo, Teté Puebla, Orosia Soto, Edemis Tamayo, Olga Guevara, Ada Bella Acosta, Juana Peña, Angelina Antolín, Rita García, Eva Palma, Norma Ferrer, Lola Feria, and Flor Pérez Chávez.[76] Teté recalled, "We were 16, 17, 18 years old."[77] Some, nonetheless, were mothers who had left their children with relatives.[78] Angelina, a mother of three, lost her means of financial support when her husband joined the rebels: "My economic situation became difficult ... [and] I was denounced for hiding messengers from the Sierra. One day the Batista army placed a machinegun on my patio to watch me."[79] She escaped to a coffee farm but was captured and imprisoned. She told her interrogators she was searching for condensed milk for her children, but "In those days, to talk of condensed milk was a crime, so immediately they had me figured as one of the 'mau-maus' [rebels]."[80] The farm owner intervened to free her, alleging that Angelina's husband had mistreated and abandoned her. With few options, she left her children with her sister and set out for the Sierra.[81] Several other young mothers were also in the guerrilla camps because they had little choice, including Rita (at twenty-six, the oldest Mariana and a widow) and Mimí Rodríguez.[82]

Isabel explained that those selected as Marianas had already completed "heroic missions," like Teté's role in the truce.[83] Some, such as Rita and Eva, had survived direct military attacks unarmed.[84] More generally, the women had proven themselves disciplined, trustworthy, and brave under fire, all characteristics highly valued by the guerrillas. In guerrilla communications and memoirs, leaders frequently comment on problems of discipline and lack of preparation among newly arrived combatants (overwhelmingly men).[85] In the Escambray, for example, Che instructed an advance team to break any bottles of rum in the shops, "so that if some rebel wanted to get drunk, he wouldn't be able to find any alcohol."[86] There were also problems of carelessness, desertion, cowardice, demoralization, and treachery. So, guerrilla women who had already proven themselves along these lines would bring valuable qualities to combat troops.[87]

The Marianas had also already shown they could withstand the privations of guerrilla life and work alongside men. Teté recalled the rough conditions in 1957, almost daily on the move, with the army close behind: "We had a plastic sheet, and we used it between three or four *compañeros*, because if not, when it rained, the water fell on us and then dried on our bodies, because we had only one change of clothing. For us this was difficult, above all on those days that we women have every month."[88] She went on, "War is very hard, but we united with the men. We came to blend in so much that at times they didn't notice we were women. We lived together like brothers and sisters."[89] Women had thus proven themselves as sufficiently tough and disciplined in working side by side with men. They were relatively seasoned guerrillas before they were armed, more mentally disciplined, physically fit, and familiar with guerrilla warfare than many new male volunteers from the cities.[90] The nomadic guerrilla life typical of 1957 transitioned to more fixed camps in 1958, and new men arrived from the *llano*. With these changes came some women's realization: "we cared for wounded, we cooked, we withstood the bombings. We did it all. Then why wouldn't they give us a gun?"[91]

Given that all-female military units are extremely rare cases, how and why did the women's platoon form?[92] The Cuban War Story gives Fidel nearly all the credit.[93] Supplementing that explanation with a broad array of additional sources, in the following section I explore factors that converged to produce this radical departure from conventional warfare: pressure from trusted and tested women, an increase in available weapons, M-26-7's official opposition to discrimination, and most importantly, the symbolic value of armed women. The debates leading up to the formation of the Marianas, charted through retrospective accounts and archival sources, provide rich detail as to the resistance to arming women as well as openings that made it possible and the benefits that made it desirable.

The Marianas' First Battle – Against Machismo

Mariana member Rita García recalled how guerrilla men's support for women in the camps turned to opposition with the question of combat:

I think the *compañeros* felt very good when we joined the guerrilla. They thought we wouldn't do anything but help, cure the wounded plus wash some things, and they felt fine about that ... But the opposition came when Fidel called the roundtable to establish the Mariana Grajales Platoon. They didn't realize that we would also fight; rather, they thought we would do the so-called women's work.[94]

Reportedly, tears were shed on both sides, such was the opposition to arming women. In the midst of the Marianas' first struggle – the struggle over their right to bear arms – Fidel declared, "Compañeras, if you can win this fight, you're going to win them all."[95] This section details this opposition and the main arguments lodged on both sides, which mirrored the classic equality-versus-difference debate: were women to be treated as individuals with an equal right to prove themselves or were women fundamentally different from men such that all women should be barred (or protected) from combat?

In essence, the women who approached Fidel for permission to fight wished to be judged on their individual abilities and were convinced they had earned the right to be armed.[96] The men who opposed them drew from traditional gender characteristics ascribed to all women to argue that women were unfit for combat, or at the least, less deserving of a gun than any man. Working through this discursive struggle, questions of men's duty to protect, women's courage, strength, and resistance, weapon scarcity, and the basis of merit (who deserved a rifle) were central and often interwoven. What emerged was a dominant narrative in which Fidel (modeling the role later taken up by the revolutionary state) protected women from discrimination and in which women confirmed their right to full participation in the revolutionary society through having taken up arms in the insurrection alongside men. As I have argued in prior chapters, women's participation in armed conflict lent a sense of righteousness and thus legitimacy to it through the "even the women" logic.

To begin, men objected to women in combat on the basis of the danger it posed, which was informed by the traditional gender notion of men's duty to protect women, who were naturally timid and tender-hearted. Some men maintained, "women, by their own nature, were sentimental and if they saw someone fall, even the enemy, they would leave their combat post to come to their aid."[97] Teté recalled someone arguing that all the military would need to do is throw a lizard at the women, and they would "drop their guns and run away."[98] Accordingly, "giving a rifle to a woman would be the same as throwing it away."[99] In response, the women pointed out that guerrilla life was dangerous whether armed or not, and they had proven themselves capable of confronting the dangers. For example, on July 11, 1958, a shell landed on the hut where eight rebels were sheltered, including Eva and Rita, who were not yet armed combatants but rather caring for men lying wounded or sick.[100] Three of the men died, and Eva was wounded. Normita argued: "[W]hen we were cooking, we did it under gunfire; we went to the trenches to deliver food, and we had to return to camp ... under fire and bombardments. So then we were not going to accept that the men tell us, 'No, the danger!'"[101]

There were also arguments as to women's and men's natural abilities. Some, including the doctors, objected that if women were mobilized to fight, "there wouldn't be anyone to care for the wounded or sew the uniforms for the troops" – the assumption being that men could not fulfill such roles (or, more realistically, would refuse).[102] Through similar logic, men questioned women's strength and resistance to withstand guerrilla warfare. The doctors insisted that women did not have the same resistance as the men.[103] The women countered this by pointing out that unarmed guerrilla women were hardly spared heavy labor and furthermore had proven themselves capable of the long marches and nomadic lifestyle of the guerrilla in its first year of existence. Lilia recalled that in August 1958, Fidel saw Lilia and her sister Isabel returning from a supply run "with our enormous packs on our backs under a torrential rainfall" and declared, "Women, if you are capable of handling the weight of these enormous packs, you can carry a gun."[104]

Weapons were scarce, and most aspiring guerrillas who arrived without a rifle were turned away. This scarcity led to rationing and rationalizations: "naturally" men deserved rifles over women. I suggest that

Collny Pılo
question
course
of men

not only rifles were at stake but also the gendered meanings associated with combat. If women deserved a rifle and saw combat, then perhaps men's heroism was not so special, their own masculinity not secured. Nonetheless, the women saw opportunity when new rifles arrived. According to Isabel, "[Once] a large number of guns were seized, each one of the women demanded a gun."[105] Edemis summarized:

> [T]hey didn't allow us in combat. The scarcity of weapons influenced this at first. It was said that as long as there was even one man without a gun, how could they be distributed to women, when it was likely that the women would just abandon the guns somewhere. Then we asked the Commander in Chief, if we participated in everything, why were we still discriminated against?[106]

Fidel's recollection concurs: "I had to fight hard against machismo up there, because we had a group of the lightest weapons reserved for the women, and some men said, 'How can we give a woman an M-1? ... I'd say, '... because they're better soldiers than you are.'"[107] In fighting machismo, Fidel thus shamed men, applying pressure to improve their own combat performance.

The more abstract arguments in defense of women's capabilities and rights as well as the tactical advantages of a women's platoon were primarily expressed by or attributed to revolutionary leaders, particularly Fidel. Indeed, the women's platoon served as a confirmation of women's equality. According to Edemis, Fidel was convinced "the women were going to prove they could do battle the same as men."[108] Lilia noted that Fidel wanted women in combat because "women weren't only for washing, cooking, attending the wounded, getting water, but also it was important to claim their social position."[109] She described the mobilization as producing the necessary proof for the postinsurrection revolutionary society: "Fidel felt that the war was almost over. He decided that women should take up the gun because their selfless service to the troops earned them the right to confront the enemy. And there was no better way than creating a platoon in which women could demonstrate their capabilities as combatants."[110]

Why did Fidel buck the gender norms so radically to create an all-women's combat unit? While women's willingness, M-26-7's ideological commitment to equality, and the growing availability of weapons are important factors, the key, as I have suggested, lies in their symbolic value more so than any military advantage in fighting effectiveness.[111] In the short run, women guerrillas undermined the enemy's morale. Lilia explained: "as another means of demoralizing the military, women were going to take up the gun to throw them out."[112] According to Isabel, arming women "had great political significance, as much to demonstrate to the enemy that women were capable of defending, with consciousness, the Revolution, as to also impart the lesson to our own *compañeros*."[113] In the long run, the post-1958 Revolution held up Las Marianas as a symbol of women's equality, which in turn called upon Cuban women to participate in national defense.[114] Furthermore, any celebration of the Marianas was an opportunity to celebrate Fidel: "Fidel was the principal defender of the legitimate right of the Marianas to engage in combat. In the face of the opinions 'of the men,' the Commander in Chief showed unlimited confidence in those women."[115]

This latter message is conveyed primarily through the story of the guerrilla roundtable that deliberated on arming women, which Fidel called on September 10, 1958.[116] A few men defended the women, including Orlando Lara, who had a broken leg. Isabel recalled "[We] were rushing around, trying to borrow a horse from a *campesino* to bring him [to the meeting], because we knew that he would defend us."[117] But most opposed arming women, some to the point of tears as they rehearsed the objections detailed above.[118]

Writing immediately following Batista's overthrow, Ruby Hart Phillips, a *New York Times* correspondent, had not received the Fidel-centric version of the Marianas. The narrative she recites inflates the platoon's size and frames the women as avenging the deaths of loved ones: "Fifty women under command of Doctora Isabel Rojas [Rielo] had a skirmish with soldiers near Holguin and killed several. The women had named their group *Mariana Grajales* … Reportedly every one of the women had lost some member of her family in the struggle against the Batista regime."[119]

Fidel, of course, emerged quickly as the protagonist in the official story. In the face of stiff and emotional opposition, Fidel reportedly argued for six hours in defense of the women, drawing from the nineteenth-century struggles for independence and maintaining that since the women have withstood the military bombardments, they "deserved a gun as much as the best soldier."[120] He also pointed to the symbolic value of arming women.[121] As Lilia explained, Fidel was looking ahead: "he wanted women to test ourselves in battle, as a precedent to women's function, their mission, during the revolutionary process following the war."[122] At last a vote was taken and the platoon approved, with Fidel responsible for their training.[123] He cautioned, "*Muchachitas*, you have seen how I had to argue for you so that you could fight. Don't make me look bad."[124]

Guarding Fidel

With the matter decided, Fidel hiked to Radio Rebelde with some of the Marianas to broadcast the news. He oversaw their training, with long marches and target practice, "but always," claimed Edemis, "with the attitude that [the women] were like any other soldier."[125] He had originally planned for Clodomira to head the platoon, and upon her death in Havana just days after the roundtable, Fidel held a shooting contest to select the leader. Isabel won, with Teté second in command, and both with the grade of lieutenants. To demonstrate his confidence in the Marianas, Fidel employed them as his advance guard and bodyguard. People began to recognize them: "From that day ... the people would say, 'Here comes the Marianas, the *Comandante* [Fidel] is coming.'"[126] Normita explained, "We kept watch while he slept ... We took great zeal in looking after Fidel ... If even a mouse moved, it wouldn't move again!"[127]

The Marianas' first battle was at Cerro Pelado on September 27, 1958, which, according to Edemis, was both a "baptism by fire" and a vindication: "we didn't betray the confidence Fidel had in us, and we returned with our weapons."[128] Radio Rebelde transmitted the news: "[T]he enemy suffered 67 casualties, both dead and wounded ... The platoon of women rebels 'Mariana Grajales,' entered into action for the first time in this battle, firmly withstanding, without moving from their positions, the shelling from the Sherman tanks."[129] The platoon participated in other battles and skirmishes: La Presa de Holguín, Los Güiros, Velasco, La Cadena, Gibara, Las Uñas, Puerto Padre, Delicia, Guisa, and Maffo.[130]

The Education of Eddy Suñol

Eddy Suñol had been among the most vocally opposed to arming women. Perhaps not unrelatedly, he was married to Mariana member Lola Feria (a point rarely mentioned in the literature).[131] Both Suñol and Lola were *llano* rebels, and when Suñol transferred to the Sierra, Lola soon followed. Suñol recalled, "Fidel asked me if, despite my having been opposed to arming women, I was ready to lead a squad of women who were armed with 10 M-1s and had already been tested at Cerro Pelado."[132] Suñol refused until Fidel informed him that if he didn't take *las muchachitas*, he would not be going to battle at all.[133]

Thus, when Suñol led his 3rd Platoon of Column 14 "Juan Manuel Márquez" down from the Sierra, on October 9, 1958, he also led five women: his wife Lola, Teté, Isabel, Lilia, and Edemis.[134] The remaining Marianas were in Column 1 with Fidel. Suñol's platoon, with sixty-four combatants but only sixty-one weapons, arrived in Holguín on October 20 and saw combat the next morning. Suñol wrote to Fidel of the battle to capture the lightly guarded dam: "Here the women fought, and I tell you they all fought like heroines."[135] Roughly forty soldiers had arrived unexpectedly, and eighteen rebels, including four women, were surrounded by several military vehicles with limited options for retreat.[136] As the story goes, Suñol asked, "*Muchachitas, what do we do?*" and the women responded, "Die fighting!"[137] The rebels opened fire and drove the soldiers off, with only two rebel men wounded. As was common, Suñol's battle report listed the results in terms of dead (three soldiers), wounded (two rebels), and weapons captured (thirteen guns, hundreds of bullets).[138] The women's conduct in battle was praised on Radio Rebelde, and, according to Teté, "After this combat, all the guerrilla columns wanted women combatants."[139]

Twelve days later, on November 2 at Los Güiros, Suñol's troops, including Isabel, Lilia, and Teté, killed twenty soldiers, wounded three, and captured two along with all the weapons.[140] A contrite Suñol, himself wounded, reported to Fidel on November 4:

[A]fter having been one of the main opponents of women's integration, I'm now completely satisfied. I congratulate you once again because you are never wrong ... I wish you could see – even if just on film, so you could smile with joy – the actions of Teté in particular, as well as the other *compañeras*. When the order was given to advance, some of the men stayed behind, but the women advanced in the vanguard. Their courage and calmness merits the respect and admiration of all.[141]

Radio Rebelde announced the victory at Los Güiros (also known as the battle of Cerro de Uñas): "New and crushing rebel victory in the zone of Holguín ... Rebel troops for Company 3 of Column 14 and forces of the women's platoon Mariana Grajales staged ... one of the most devastating battle victories of the rebel forces."[142]

The broadcast's special mention of the women's platoon was, I propose, not incidental but rather a maneuver in the war of ideas. The symbolic effects of women in combat were multiple. Lilia explained that Suñol became "our number one defender" because "as long as we fought, he didn't have a single coward among the [male] soldiers."[143] Thus, in fighting the Marianas also performed a more tactical function through a mix of inspiring and shaming their male comrades. When women held firm under fire, how could men retreat?

Sensing that victory was near, Fidel instructed Suñol to send the women back to his column. But Suñol asked to extend their stay, and the

Marianas participated in the battle for the city of Holguín and were in the first rebel car that entered the city.[144] Isabel, Lilia, and Teté continued on together until the end of the war.[145] After several additional military engagements, they entered Puerto Padre on December 24 and Gibara five days later.[146] Fidel wrote again for the women to return, this time with "no excuses."[147] They rejoined Fidel and the rest of the Marianas in Santiago in time to catch the Victory Caravan as it made its way across the island to Havana.[148]

The Battle of Guisa

Other Marianas also saw combat. As Gonzalo Camejo prepared to lead his troops into the *llano* in September, his cousin Angelina asked him to talk with Fidel and Braulio Coroneaux, Camejo's immediate superior, so that the remaining Marianas could accompany them.[149] Not only were Angelina and Camejo cousins, but Eva and Camejo were a couple, two guerrilla "lovebirds" (as Isabel put it) who later married.[150] Thus Eva, Flor, Bella, Rita, and Angelina joined Coroneaux's troops. Camejo had strict orders from Fidel: "Do not give them any [rifles], they themselves are going to capture them."[151] Camejo later explained, "We took them unarmed from the Sierra so that they could seize a gun like any other combatant: in combat. Fidel told them: 'There you are going to demonstrate that you are brave, as brave as the bravest here.'"[152]

These five Marianas were part of the 220-strong guerrilla force at the battle of Guisa that lasted from November 20 to November 30, 1958, an important battle for its duration and the number of weapons captured. Eight rebels died, and seven were wounded. As per instructions, the women went into the battle unarmed (though Bella had a handgun).[153] According to Angelina, they used men's rifles while the latter prepared mortars. Camejo told of when Bella accompanied rebel men to approach a group of surrendering soldiers:

[They found] a *guardia* behind a rock, and Bella with her revolver said: "Give yourself up, *casquito* [little helmet-head]." He surrendered his rifle to Bella and then said, "If I had known that you were a woman, I wouldn't have surrendered." And I said, "Bella, give him back his rifle, and you two can shoot it out," and he said, "No, no, I surrender anyway." Bella herself marched the *casquito* to Fidel, as he was about three or four kilometers away. Bella on her own delivered the *casquito* to Fidel![154]

After the first day of battle, as rebels had gathered arms abandoned by soldiers, Fidel asked Coroneaux how the *compañeras* had performed in the battle. Angelina recalled, "Coroneaux told him that we had behaved very calmly and bravely in spite of being unarmed, that we deserved a gun."[155] Fidel, pleased, ordered Coroneaux to distribute rifles to the Marianas.[156]

For Angelina, once armed "We felt great esteem and with more courage than ever, proud to have a rifle. We returned again to our positions, but now it was different, because we were armed, and these arms had to be put to use."[157] More military arrived, and in the second battle, rebel mines failed to stop an approaching tank. Its mortars destroyed Angelina and Eva's trench, half burying them, also killing Coroneaux.[158] Stunned, temporarily deaf, and badly bruised, the women had to be dug out. A rebel came with orders "that the women should go to the rear to rest, because we had spent many days in combat ... But none of us women abandoned the frontline."[159]

As with the Marianas in Holguín, the battle of Guisa became a means by which to document women's military competency and later mobilize them to defense. In the rebel newspaper *Sierra Maestra* and over Radio Rebelde, Fidel reported that "A squad of the women's 'Mariana Grajales' platoon also fought bravely during the ten days, ... withstanding the bombardment of the planes and the artillery attacks of the enemy."[160] Their battle exploits continued to pay off for the revolution decades later. In 1981, introducing the Territorial Militia Troops in Cuba's buildup for national defense that would rely heavily on women, Fidel spoke (with exaggeration) of the "large number of women" in this battle: "Their leader was seriously wounded. As a general rule, a patrol or a platoon had the habit of withdrawing when its leader was wounded ... [T]he platoon of women was not discouraged in spite of the fact that its leader was seriously wounded. It continued the fight. It destroyed the truck and seized all the weapons. It was truly exceptional conduct."[161]

In sum, while the Marianas were a test case for women's bravery under fire, the reality of their small number and formation at a time of guerrilla success rather than existential threat leads me to emphasize the symbolic nature of their contribution to the insurrection. They were a powerful example of what I have termed the Even the Women narrative, in which women's presence in the struggle lent it legitimacy, demonstrating the justness of the cause and the moral caliber of the men.

Another finding has to do with issues of propriety and women's honor. Leaders were uncomfortable with having just one woman in an otherwise all-men's unit, concerned about appearance and respectability or, more specifically, concerned for the woman's honor amid a group of crude, sexually aroused men. The literature has emphasized female combat units as forming under conditions of extreme threat, an act of desperation, though one in which women proved themselves competent fighters.[162] However, the Cuban case suggests that leaders formed all-women's units for propaganda purposes and as a means to protect women and their reputation. They colocated small groups of women combatants with a larger all-male unit headed by a boyfriend, cousin, or husband of one of the women – possibly so that women could watch out for each other under the command of a man who presumably shared their concerns for protection and propriety. I found no record of sexual assault of women combatants, though sexual attraction was another matter, and several Marianas met and later married guerrilla men.

Notes

1. Puebla interview in Báez (1996, 415); Isabel Rielo interview in Bota and Vázquez, *Mujeres* September 1983, 8.
2. Segal (1995, 760); Goldstein (2001, 77).
3. Goldstein (2001, 64–5, 70, 72).
4. The M-26-7 guerrilla was relatively small until the insurrection's final months, with estimates ranging from totals of 1,000 (Draper 1962, 13) to 7,250 (Macaulay 1978, 285–6, 291) by January 1, 1959.
5. C. Allan Stewart, "Memorandum from the Deputy Director of the Office of Middle American Affairs (Stewart) to the Deputy Assistant Secretary of State for Inter-American Affairs (Snow)," Foreign Relations of the United States, 1958–1960, July 24, 1958; No author, "Draft Memorandum Prepared in the Office of Middle American Affairs," Foreign Relations of the United States, 1958–1960, July 25, 1958.
6. Castro's August 1955 "Manifesto No. 1 to the People of Cuba" outlined a sociopolitical program of change, including "adequate measures in education and legislation to put an end to every vestige of discrimination for reasons of race or sex" (Smith and Padula 1996, 25).
7. See Chapters 3 and 9 for additional instances of this narrative.
8. Sjoberg and Gentry (2007, 2).
9. Alison (2009); Sjoberg and Gentry (2007).
10. Viterna (2013, 208).
11. Ibid., 208–9; see also Bayard de Volo (2001); Sharoni (1995, 44–5); Goldstein (2001, 80). In World War II, the USSR's mobilization of women into combat was spurred by the existential threat posed by Nazi Germany; Goldstein (2001, 65) notes that this "helped the formidable Soviet propaganda machine to raise morale in a dispirited population, and spur greater sacrifices by the male soldiers." The Salvadoran guerrillas highlighted the military exploits of its all-women Silvia Battalion while sending them into few battles (Viterna 2013, 208–9). Wickham-Crowley (1992, 216) suggests

Latin American guerrillas inflated the percentage of women in their ranks "for western intellectual consumption."

12. In El Salvador, Viterna finds guerrilla leaders used young women as expansion agents because their femininity helped gain civilian sympathy (Viterna 2013, 208).

13. Prados-Torreira (2005, 61).

14. Goldstein (2001, 72–6); see also Power (2002). In El Salvador, the guerrilla used women as recruiters to subtly shame young civilian men (Viterna 2013, 208–9).

15. Prados-Torreira (2005, 5).

16. Bayard de Volo (2012). "Castro ... mentioned the heroism of the Mariana Grajales Platoon ... which is considered a precursor to the current mass incorporation of women in defense work ... The new *Marianas* also know how to protect the future to the ultimate consequences" (Vilma Espín, "Como dignas continuadoras del Pelotón Mariana Grajales crecen en todas partes las Unidades Femeninas de las Milicias de Tropas Territoriales," September 4, 1983 speech, Granma Province, transcribed in *Granma* September 5, 1983, 2).

17. See, for example, Lobao Reif (1986, 153); Mason (1992, 64); Kampwirth (2002, 128); Shayne (2004, 45); Luciak (2001, 2). Referring to Che, Mason maintains that women have been ignored in theories of revolution because they are understood as inessential and relegated to noncombat tasks (Mason 1992, 64).

18. See Saldaña-Portillo (2003, 74–5). In 1988, Vilma Espín, as head of the Cuban Women's Federation, referenced Las Marianas to illustrate the "beautiful link between Fidel and Cuban women": "[Fidel] understood the basic principle of justice [in arming women rebels]. He had always thought of women's right to equality ... as one of the greatest goals to which society should aspire" (in Espín 1990, 30–1).

19. No author, "La Revolución cuenta con la mujer," *Mujeres* November 1976, 11. Fidel paraphrases Martí in the last line.

20. Wickham-Crowley (1992, 22).

21. Fidel Castro speech, January 20, 1981 "Castro Marks Territorial Militia Units' Formation" (Guisa, Granma Province), LANIC Castro Speech Database.

22. March (2012, 38).

23. In the camp, Oniria helped the rebel soldiers by mending and washing their clothes. But Che ordered her to stop. "Before you came," he said, "everyone took care of their own problems here" (Oniria Gutiérrez, "'I Argued That Women Too Could Fight': Interview with the first woman to join Che Guevara's column of Rebel Army," *The Militant* 60(7), February 19, 1996).

24. Ibid.

25. Ibid.

26. Ibid.

27. Ibid.

28. Lupiáñez Reinlein (1985, 104, 115). Dueñas (*Granma Internacional* April 11, 2006) has several examples. Nancy Ojeda, at 17 took part in the August 1958 rebel assault on a train to free Carlos "Nicaragua" Iglesias, an action

in which several rebels died. Previous to that, Ojeda had been captured and tortured by regime officers. Also, rebel messenger Herenia Vázquez asked Che to transfer to the Sierra as a guerrilla combatant.

29. Fulgueiras (2004, 107). She left her infant daughter with her mother and her young son with a Santería priest.
30. Fulgueiras (2004, 112).
31. Ibid.
32. Ibid., 112–13. I suggest Mimí mentions his race to heighten the sense of sexual threat he posed.
33. Ibid., 113. Commander Bordón had known Mimí for years, as they both attended Chávez's fights when he was the boxer Kid Relámpago (Kid Lightning) (Fulgueiras 2002, 12). He explained his unusual decision to allow her to remain in the troops: "I knew the odyssey she had faced below, and I was impacted by her attitude of leaving her children to join the struggle. I immediately knew that she was a brave compañera. Also, there were no women in the camp and to me this was something that the guerrilla lacked" (ibid., 76).
34. Fulgueiras (2002, 76). See Viterna (2013, 152–8) for an analysis of the successful management of (hetero)sexual tensions within the Salvadoran guerrilla.
35. Fulgueiras (2002, 77–8); Fulgueiras (2004, 113).
36. Fulgueiras (2002, 77; 2004, 113).
37. Fulgueiras (2004, 113).
38. Ibid.
39. Ibid., 114.
40. Fulgueiras (2002, 102–3).
41. Fulgueiras (2004, 113).
42. Fulgueiras (2002, 110). See also Fulgueiras (2004, 106–7).
43. Fulgueiras (2004, 114).
44. Israel Chávez's testimony in ibid., 106–7.
45. Ibid., 107.
46. Ibid., 116.
47. Dueñas (2006).
48. Fulgueiras (2004, 117).
49. Zobeida Rodríguez testimony, *El Nuevo Fénix* (originally published in Cupull and González 1992); see also Fulgueiras (2004, 117).
50. Chávez's testimony in Fulgueiras (2004, 107). This size machine gun required at least two people to operate and carry it.
51. Dueñas (2006). Mimí fought in the battles of Guayos, Placetas, Santo Domingo, Mordazo, Manacas, and the Río Sagua Bridge.
52. Puebla interview in Báez (1996, 412).
53. Bota and Vázquez (1983, 5); see also *Bohemia* July 28, 1967, 14–17.
54. Bota and Vázquez (1983, 5).
55. Waters (2003, 31).
56. Bota and Vázquez (1983, 5); Waters (2003, 32).
57. Puebla interview in (no author) "Lo que demostraron aquellos fusiles," *Mujeres* November 1976, 55.

58. Puebla in *Mujeres* November 1976, 55; Puebla interview in Báez (1996, 412).
59. Some sources put Teté as seventeen years old when she arrived in the Sierra (for example, no author 1976, 55).
60. *Bohemia* July 28, 1967, 14–17.
61. Ibid.; Puebla interview in Báez (1996, 413).
62. No author (1976, 54–5); Puebla interview in Báez (1996, 413).
63. Báez (1996, 43).
64. *Bohemia* July 28, 1967, 14–17; Bota and Vázquez (1983, 7); Puebla interview in Báez (1996, 414).
65. Bota and Vázquez (1983, 7); Waters (2003, 37).
66. Delsa "Teté" Puebla Viltres testimony, *El Nuevo Fénix* (originally published in Cupull and González, 1992); Puebla interview, Lyn Smith Cuba Collection.
67. Puebla interview in Báez (1996, 413).
68. Castro (2011, 298).
69. *Bohemia* July 28, 1967, 14–17; Puebla interview, Lyn Smith Cuba Collection.
70. Puebla interview in Báez (1996, 414).
71. Ibid.
72. Entry for 16 July 1958, in Perret (1998).
73. Ibid.
74. Bota and Vázquez (1983, 7).
75. Valdes, *Verde Olivo* March 3, 1983, 6–9.
76. Ferrer Gómez et al. (2014).
77. Bota and Vázquez (1983, 6); Puebla in *Mujeres* November 1976, 54.
78. "Mimí" Rodríguez also left children in the *llano*.
79. *Bohemia* November 24, 1967, 55.
80. Ibid.
81. Antolín in *Mujeres* November 1976, 55; *Bohemia* November 24, 1967, 55.
82. Bota and Vázquez (1983, 6); *Bohemia* November 24, 1967, 54. Rita lived near a guerrilla camp and was recruited for her skills in shoe repair.
83. Bota and Vázquez (1983, 5).
84. Castro (2011, 226).
85. See, for example, Macaulay (1970); Guevara (2013).
86. Zobeida Rodríguez testimony, *El Nuevo Fénix* (originally published in Cupull and González 1992).
87. See Viterna (2013, 66) on trustworthiness as a key characteristic sought by Salvadoran guerrilla recruiters.
88. Bota and Vázquez (1983, 5).
89. Ibid., 6.
90. In the Salvadoran case, Viterna (2013, 66–7, 91) finds that trustworthiness – which meant the ability to keep a secret, intelligence, integrity, cleverness, and bravery in the face of violence – was a highly valued trait in the guerrilla.
91. Bota and Vázquez (1983, 6).
92. Goldstein (2001, 77).
93. For example, "The vision of Fidel prevailed" (Valdes 1983, 6). Celia Sánchez was also a principal promoter of the platoon, and set a precedent as "the

first woman who took up arms in the Sierra" at the battle of Uvero (Puebla interview in Báez 1996, 415); Espín, *Granma* September 5, 1983, 2.

94. Bota and Vázquez (1983, 7).
95. Ibid., 8.
96. *Bohemia* November 24, 1967, 55; Bota and Vázquez (1983, 7); Stoner (2003, 86).
97. Nidia Díaz, "Gardenias que un día se hicieron leonas ..." *Granma* September 3, 1983, 4. Lilia: "For us, a guardia was the hated enemy ... That was how it was in combat, but after, it made us sad to see them abandoned by their troops and dying alone. I remember that after the battle of Presa de Holguín, one was mortally wounded, and one of us *compañeras* approached him, moved, and asked if he had children, if he wanted to send a message, what was his name, where was he from ..." (Rielo in *Mujeres* November 1976, 57).
98. Suárez and Caner (2006, 296–7). See also Puebla (1990, 46–7, 49).
99. Puebla in *Mujeres* November 1976, 56.
100. Rita García's testimony, *Bohemia* November 24, 1967, 54. One man died in this bombing (Castro 2011, 226).
101. Normita in Bota and Vázquez (1983, 7). Notably, the Marianas escaped serious injury in combat. Flor Pérez is described as the only Mariana wounded in combat at the battle of Maffo (Díaz, *Granma* September 3, 1983, 4; Waters 2003, 29).
102. Antolín in *Mujeres* November 1976, 56–7. Orosia and Juana had been aids to the camp doctors (Castro 2011, 226). Rita and Angelina were at the time cooks at the rebel hospital (Lilia Rielo in *Bohemia* July 28, 1967, 14–17). See also Viterna (2013).
103. Lilia Rielo, *Bohemia* July 28, 1967, 14–17; Antolín in *Mujeres* November 1976, 56–7; Bota and Vázquez (1983, 8).
104. *Bohemia* July 28, 1967, 14–17; Diaz, *Granma* September 3, 1983, 4. Che wrote, "[T]he basic tactic of the guerrilla army is the march, and neither slow men nor tired men can be tolerated. Adequate training therefore includes exhausting hikes day and night ... Resistance and speed will be fundamental qualities of the first guerrilla nucleus" (Guevara [1961] 1985, 131).
105. Bota and Vázquez (1983, 7).
106. Edemis Tamayo Nuñiz, in María Elena Pérez, "Reencuentro con las historia," *Verde Olivo* February 11, 1979, 4.
107. Castro and Ramonet (2008, 235). See also Espín, *Granma* September 5, 1983, 2.
108. Tamayo Nuñiz in Pérez, *Verde Olivo* February 11, 1979, 4.
109. *Bohemia* July 28, 1967, 14–17.
110. Rielo in *Mujeres*, November 1976, 56. See also *Bohemia* July 28, 1967, 14–17; Castro (2008, 235).
111. See, for example, Bota and Vázquez (1983, 8).
112. Rielo in *Mujeres* November 1976, 56. See also *Bohemia* July 28, 1967, 14–17.
113. Bota and Vázquez (1983, 8).
114. Fidel remained surprisingly invested in this narrative for over five decades. In his autobiography, he recalled the women's platoon was not conceived of until after the military's summer offensive, at which point "it was organized through my initiative" (Castro 2011, 225).

115. Bota and Vázquez (1983, 8).
116. Tamayo Nuñiz in Pérez, *Verde Olivo* February 11, 1979, 4. It was held at the *Estado Mayor* of Column 1 at the field hospital. Between Lilia and Angelina's recollections, the following were present: Padre Guillermo Sardiñas (a priest), Dr. Ordaz, Faustino Pérez, Eddy Suñol, Carlos Franqui, Quevedo, Paco Cabrera, Orlando Lara, Julio Camacho, Celia, Isabel, Rita, Olga, Normita, Angelina, and Lilia. Lilia Rielo, *Bohemia* July 28, 1967, 14–17; Antolín in *Mujeres* November 1976, 56–7.
117. Bota and Vázquez (1983, 8).
118. Isabel Rielo, *Mujeres* September 1983, 8.
119. Phillips (1959, 376).
120. Díaz, *Granma* September 3, 1983, 4; Antolín in *Mujeres* November 1976, 56–7.
121. Isabel Rielo in Bota and Vázquez (1983, 8).
122. *Bohemia* July 28, 1967, 14–17.
123. Tamayo Nuñiz in Pérez, *Verde Olivo* February 11, 1979, 4.
124. Díaz, *Granma* September 3, 1983, 4.
125. Tamayo Nuñiz in Pérez, *Verde Olivo* February 11, 1979, 4. See also *Bohemia* July 28, 1967, 14–17; Puebla interview in Báez (1996, 415).
126. Suárez and Caner (2006, 296–7). See also Marianas en Combate 46–7 and 49.
127. Bota and Vázquez (1983, 9).
128. Tamayo Nuñiz in Pérez, *Verde Olivo* February 11, 1979, 5.
129. Radio Rebelde transcript, August 27, 1958 (from Princeton University Library microfilm collection). Note, the transcript date should read September 27, 1958, given the date of the Cerro Pelado battle.
130. Díaz, *Granma* September 3, 1983, 4.
131. No author (1976, 56); Abreu Cardet (2009), "Guajiros clandestinos: Familia campesina y líderes de barrio en el clandestinaje (1956–1958). Eddy and Lola married in 1956 and divorced in 1961" (EcuRed [n.d.], Síntesis biográfica, Eddy Suñol).
132. Suñol interview, published in Suárez and Caner Román (2006, 317).
133. Puebla interview in Báez (1996, 416).
134. Ferrer Gómez et al. (2014). See also Antolín in *Mujeres* November 1976, 56–7. Teté later married an officer in this platoon, Raúl Castro Mercader.
135. October 23, 1958 letter; *Bohemia* July 28, 1967, 14–17; Abreu Cardet, "Los ataques a guarniciones enemigas en el Cuarto Frente Simón Bolívar," (2009).
136. Ferrer Gómez et al. (2014).
137. Ibid. See also Puebla interview in Báez (1996, 416–17).
138. Abreu Cardet 18 de Agosto de (2009).
139. Puebla interview, Lyn Smith Cuba Collection. See also Antolín in *Mujeres* November 1976, 57.
140. *Bohemia* July 28, 1967, 14–17.
141. Espín, *Granma* September 5, 1983, 2, quoting Suñol, November 4, 1958 in a letter to Fidel. See also Puebla (1990, 55). During this 25-minute battle, the three Marianas, who were with Suñol when he was wounded, transported him to a safer location (EcuRed [n.d.], "Combate del cerro de Uñas").

142. Radio Rebelde transcript, estimated November 5, 1958, Princeton University Broadcast Transcripts. Date not specified, but the same radio announcement detailed the battle of Alto Songo, which had just ended.

143. No author (1976, 57).

144. Ibid.

145. *Bohemia* July 28, 1967, 14–17.

146. Ibid.

147. No author, *Mujeres* November 1976, 57.

148. Ferrer Gómez et al. (2014); Puebla interview in Báez (1996, 417).

149. Bota and Vázquez (1983, 7). See also Angelina Antolín's account in Alfredo Reyes Trejo, "Una escuadra de mujeres," *Verde Olivo* December 1, 1983, 27.

150. Bota and Vázquez (1983, 6). See also *Bohemia* November 24, 1967, 53–4; Reyes Trejo, *Verde Olivo* December 1, 1983, 27.

151. Bota and Vázquez (1983, 7).

152. Ibid.

153. Viterna notes similar expectations for guerrilla men and women in the early years of that conflict: "they'd put it to you really simply, they told you there weren't any arms and that you had to go get your gun from the army. And with your hands" (2013, 91).

154. Bota and Vázquez (1983, 7). See also Antolín's account in Reyes Trejo, *Verde Olivo* December 1, 1983, 27.

155. Antolín, in Reyes Trejo, *Verde Olivo* December 1, 1983, 27

156. Angelina, in *Bohemia* November 24, 1967, 55.

157. Antolín, in Reyes Trejo, *Verde Olivo* December 1, 1983, 27.

158. Angelina, in *Bohemia* November 24, 1967, 55.

159. Ibid.; Antolín in Reyes Trejo, *Verde Olivo* December 1, 1983, 28.

160. Sarabia, *Bohemia* November 24, 1967, 50–5. Radio Rebelde, December 4, 1958, Princeton University Library microfilm collection, Radio Rebelde transcripts; see also Carlos Del Toro, "El Pelotón de Mujeres Mariana Grajales," *Granma* September 3, 1988, 2, which records the date as in November and the speaker as Fidel.

161. Castro, "Castro Marks Territorial Militia Units' Formation," January 20, 1981, LANIC Castro Speech database; Castro, "Guisa: discurso pronunciado por Fidel Castro Ruz," January 20, 1981, in Cuban State database *Discursos e intervenciones del Comandante en Jefe Fidel Castro Ruz*. On this day of Ronald Reagan's 1981 presidential inauguration, Castro announced plans to increase the size of the military by mobilizing women, using women's participation in the battle of Guisa as the prime example of their capacity to serve: "[Women's military mobilization] is not a case of a political question or simply a struggle for equality ... It is a necessity and it is an extraordinary potential force that we have in women as combatants for defense of the country" (ibid.). See also Stone (1981, 8).

162. Goldstein (2001, 64, 70, 72).

CHAPTER II

Past Is Prologue

Victory and Consolidation

THE THEATER OF WAR

Though war stories are largely written by the victors, the past remains a site of struggle. One lesson that emerges from this research is that it is not enough to have won the war, it also matters how the war was won. Writer Reinaldo Arenas, a Castro critic in exile, tells us of his time as a guerrilla, "I never even witnessed a battle; those battles were more myth than reality."[1] Dismissing the insurrection as "a war of words," Arenas dismisses Castro as having "won a war that had never been fought."[2] Echoes of Arenas reverberate elsewhere in the anti-Castro literature: Castro is a blustering leader who gained power through an inflated war record.[3] Meanwhile, from the pro-Castro perspective, despite the considerable rebel effort to capture the hearts and minds of domestic and international audiences, the post-1958 official story marginalizes this theater of war by its celebration of heroics on the physical battlefield. The academic literature has often followed suit, if not celebrating guerrilla war at least prioritizing it as a subject of study.

This book has not set out to determine which theater of war – the war of flesh and blood or the war for hearts and minds – is more real or worthy of victory. Rather, it is a call for balance – for greater recognition and thus analysis of the more mundane and incremental process of building legitimacy and popular support for armed conflict. The kinetic nature of the Cuban insurrection is undeniable, as bullets and bombs killed thousands. But as this book insists, militaries also fight their battles with carefully deployed language and actions aimed at gaining symbolic terrain across hearts and minds. And this battle is a gendered one. Gender both produces and is produced by war.[4] As a central organizing principle of society, gender structures how actors understand violence, enmity, and heroism, making certain forms of violence thinkable and thus possible, and exposing certain military weaknesses while shoring up others. To the extent that scholarship on the Cuban insurrection and war more generally ignores this gendered theater of war, it fails to fully grasp how such struggles are waged and won. Thus, a key question has been, how was this war gendered – both in terms of gendered individuals as actors and victims, and in terms of the means by which gender structured the understandings of this insurrection.

Because of this coconstitutional relationship between war and gender, war also has an impact on gender that informs the postwar society. Yet the armed insurrection did not produce a revolution in gender relations so much as replace one version of hegemonic masculinity with another.[5] In what follows, I maintain that M-26-7 pursued armed insurrection in a way that both integrated women and even exaggerated their contributions while leaving the gender binary and thus gender power differentials intact.

In post-1958 revolutionary Cuba, the state controlled the traditional agents of hegemony – notably the media, politicians, teachers, artists, and academics – weaving through the social fabric a revolutionary worldview built upon a foundational narrative, the Cuban War Story.[6] This included a hegemonic masculinity, largely adopted and accepted as normal and against which, for men, nonconformity was evaluated and punished.[7] Femininity served as a binary complement to masculinity, necessary as a means to measure and celebrate masculinity by way of contrast. In this most fundamental of ways, the New Woman existed in the shadow of the New Man, struggling to measure up to a masculine standard while embracing femininity.

Gender Tactics and Masculine Terrain

Rebels have long recognized femininity as a tactic of war and thus exploited traditional femininity as a diversion in order to smuggle weapons, provide safe houses, and hide rebel men. In Cuba, women deployed this tactic in the independence wars of the late nineteenth century and again in the Cuban insurrection of the 1950s. I have also identified masculinity as a rebel tactic. Less recognized as such in the literature, it operates through a different gendered logic. Whereas rebel women often performed femininity as a cover or diversion to perform war work that was gender-nonconforming, rebel men's masculine performance was itself a propaganda piece. That is, they performed masculinity not to distract attention from their rebel work but rather to attract attention to it, and with it, fear or admiration. The rebels' gain was Batista's loss — with each rebel act of courage, toughness, and audacity, Batista and his military appeared less manly, less honorable, less fit to rule. That is to say, Batista's forces were increasingly the feminine to the rebels' masculine. As the rebels' masculinity outperformed the government's, the binary opposition masculinity/femininity remained intact, with femininity the devalued term. This masculinity-as-message influenced popular conceptions of the rebels and revolution more powerfully than the femininity-as-diversion approach.

Thus, while both femininity and masculinity were deployed tactically, the latter prevailed as the revolution was imprinted with a pronounced masculine character. As Carlos Alberto Montaner tells us, "The Cuban Revolution is the business of machos."[8] To the extent that the insurrection succeeded through its war of ideas, masculinity was one of its foremost weapons. Or rather, the war itself was fought over masculine terrain, which the rebels ultimately dominated. Through the Cuban War Story, the gender binary held firm and indeed was foundational in reproducing gendered oppositions that continued to mark hierarchy.[9] Although officially committed to the liberation of women and invested in celebrating women's contributions to the insurrection, the devaluation of the feminine undergirds gender inequality. In this way, the manner in which gender differences structure actors' understanding of themselves and the world around them remained largely undisturbed by the insurrection, despite women's contributions and the prominence of women heroines. In what follows, a brief overview explores the overthrow of Batista and the subsequent revolutionary era, with particular attention to women and militarization.

A Militarized Path to Women's Liberation

The provincial capital of Santa Clara fell to the rebels on December 30, 1958, as most of Batista's army "simply melted away."[10] As Batista fled on New Year's morning, M-26-7 rebels scrambled to secure control across the island. Fidel directed Che Guevara and Camilo Cienfuegos to Havana while he headed to Santiago. In his first public address to a post-Batista

Cuba, Castro marked the path for women's emancipation that revolutionary Cuba would follow for the next three decades:

> [W]hen our people are threatened, it will be ... 300,000 or 400,000 or 500,000 Cubans who will fight, men and women who can take up guns. There will be enough weapons to arm all who want to go to battle, when the time comes to defend our freedoms, because it has been shown that not only the men fight, but also in Cuba the women fight, and the best proof of this is the Mariana Grajales platoon ... I wanted to show that women could be good soldiers, and that there were many prejudices against women, and that women are a sector of this country that also needs to be redeemed, because they are victims of discrimination ... When in a nation the men fight and the women can fight, this nation is invincible. We will organize and train women's militias or reserves on a voluntary basis. And these young women whom I see here dressed in the black and red of the 26th of July, I hope that you too learn to handle weapons.[11]

As if to highlight and underline the militarized path to women's liberation, the Marianas featured prominently in the rebel victory caravan as it made its way west from Santiago to Havana. Fidel had earlier insisted that the Holguín faction of the women's platoon rejoin the rest, and along the way, the caravan picked up more women rebels, inducting them into the Marianas.[12] The women rode atop captured tanks as the caravan entered the capital: "In the front line, as if escorting Fidel's tank, there they were, the 'Marianas' in whom [Fidel] always believed, [and] who didn't let him down."[13] The Marianas were reportedly hailed by the crowds: "men yelled up to them, 'Look! Here are the most beautiful women in Cuba!'"[14] Mariana member Rita García recalled, "The women asked, 'You fought? You shot a gun?' And when we said, 'yes,' many of them embraced us, crying."[15]

Despite the Marianas' high profile in the victory caravan and Fidel's glowing praise of women's contributions in his first 1959 speech, Michelle Chase points out that he called for no specific policies that would address discrimination.[16] However, in hindsight gained through the Cuban War Story, we see that Castro revealed his blueprint for women's emancipation by emphasizing women's participation in Cuba's national defense. Indeed, the War Story marks Fidel's January 1959 speech in Santiago as a watershed moment for women's liberation. A 1967 magazine article explained: "With that [speech], Cuban women won one more battle for their social, economic, and political emancipation. With these words, a series of bourgeois prejudices were swept away."[17]

Not only was armed defense of the revolution crucial to women's liberation, but women were also represented as crucial to the revolution's defense. Revolutionary Cuba experienced a series of Cold War security events that sustained a high level of military mobilization: the Bay of Pigs invasion and Cuban Missile Crisis in the 1960s; the African engagements including the Angolan War (1975–91); and the massive domestic defense buildup (referred to as the War of All the People) in the 1980s. Cuba thus operated as a militarized society under varying degrees of heightened alert until the early 1990s post-Soviet economic crisis. This militarization informed women's place in society and the state-led steps toward gender equality. As Stoner explained, "By militarizing many aspects of life, Castro has made heroines out of all women and consecrated the Revolution by making the least militaristic members of society the greatest revolutionaries. Thus, he has succeeded in framing Cuba as a nation in constant struggle … [and] rebellion."[18] Because of the purported symbiotic relationship between women's liberation and the revolution's survival, revolutionary Cuba did not follow the course of many postwar societies in downplaying women's contributions once the insurrection was won; rather, in this state of constant struggle, women's contributions continued to be touted and even exaggerated.[19]

In 1960, Vilma Espín issued a call for women to join the National Revolutionary Militias (MNR), declaring: "Women also have a place in this struggle."[20] As a counter revolutionary invasion seemed increasingly likely, Fidel explained on December 31, 1960, that Cuba must convince the United States of the fierce resistance invading forces would encounter:

In no way could they destroy [our resistance] in a matter of hours, nor destroy it ever, for as long as a man or a woman with honor remains in this country, there will be resistance; [we aim] to convince [the US] that with thousands of paratroopers and some ships they are not going to take [Cuba] … [I]t would take more … than what it cost them to land at Normandy.[21]

By this logic, militarily mobilizing women increased the resistance an invading army would face, thus working to dissuade invaders. The "Even the Women" logic also contributed to Cuban morale in these tense times. Both factors comprised key though underappreciated facets of Cuba's post-1958 security policy.

In a televised four-hour speech on April 20, 1961, Fidel explained Cuba's victory against the Bay of Pigs (Playa Girón) invasion: "Imperialism examines geography, analyzes the number of cannons, of planes, of tanks, the positions. The revolutionary examines the social composition of the population. The imperialists don't give a damn about how the population there thinks or feels."[22] Always the underdog, the David to a Goliath – first Batista, now the United States – this attention to hearts and minds continued to be a relatively unacknowledged factor in Castro's post-1958 military strategy, and as he notes, his enemies have ignored it at their peril. Rather than writing off women in the insurrection and national defense, Castro actively courted them as potential combatants and as symbols to rally a nation.

Though only rarely acknowledged publicly, militarily mobilized women met resistance in Cuba. In the early 1960s, some Cubans outspokenly questioned the morals of the militia women who dressed like men and carried guns.[23] Such "counterrevolutionary elements" reportedly threw rocks at the women when they went out to drill.[24] Geoffrey Fox found a major reason working-class men left Cuba in the 1960s had to do with changing gender roles – women took on roles previously gendered exclusively masculine, which many perceived as a challenge to men's status.[25] The "participation of women in the regular and irregular armed forces" was one of the gender-based changes that most disturbed this group of men.[26]

In the face of such opposition, glowing profiles of the Marianas through various state outlets including speeches, the media, and school materials lent legitimacy to armed women.[27] Teté Puebla explained: "Fidel likes to say that the Mariana Grajales Platoon was a forerunner, setting the example of women defending our homeland."[28] From the revolution's first days, as the Marianas entered Havana on top of tanks, armed women occupied prominent symbolic real estate. For example, in 1981 during the first oaths of the newly formed Territorial Troops Militia (MTT), which relied heavily on women, the ceremony included the handing over of two rifles used in the insurrection, one of which had belonged to Mariana leader Isabel Rielo.[29] As women's participation in armed national defense was a means to achieve women's liberation, Marianas were represented as the origin of this struggle. A 1983 article in the daily *Granma* described Mariana member Angelina Antolín as understanding her right "to go into combat, to face the enemy and fight with a rifle the same as her *compañeros* [male comrades]. It would be as if she herself, without anyone's help, broke the chains that society of that era imposed upon her."[30] Although the claim was that the Marianas fought like men, Cubans were reassured that "none of this made them less delicate and feminine."[31] As Stoner argues, Castro also used the Marianas to shore up support for the revolution: Castro "glorified [women combatants'] importance to the Revolution and used the new icon to keep Cubans on perpetual military alert and politically loyal ... Since 1959, the Pelotón Mariana Grajales has led military parades and been the first squadron to present arms to their *comandante en jefe*."[32] Such ceremony and proclamations linking them to the heroic Marianas helped secure women soldiers "as a beloved symbol of loyalty, militancy, and sacrifice to a male leader and a nation."[33]

In sum, the revolutionary state claimed a symbiotic relationship in which women's liberation and national defense mutually benefitted each other. However, this in effect meant that women's liberation must always be in sync with the demands and aims of the revolutionary state and could not proceed as a goal in and of itself.[34] The limits of this approach are particularly clear in instances in which women's loyal but autonomous organizations were forced to disband and also through the limited goals of state feminism, which did not disturb the gender binary.[35] While arming women did not make them men, it also did not secure them the status that attaches to masculinity. As the revolution hailed the New Man for the New Society, courage, toughness, boldness, certainty, decisiveness, confidence, and leadership remained coded as masculine, legitimating and protecting power enjoyed by "real men" to the disadvantage of those many not included in that category.[36]

WAR – A GENDER OPPORTUNITY?

Las Martianas dissolved on January 28, 1959, less than a month after the revolution came to power. All the civic groups of Santiago, the schools, and the revolutionary organizations marched to Martí's tomb in the Santa Ifigenia cemetery, where Aida Pelayo spoke the final words of the *Frente Cívico de Mujeres Martianas*.[37] At this point, the new revolutionary state deemed such organizations no longer relevant, and members were instructed to dissolve them to focus energies on the new task of consolidating the revolution.[38] In her rich and detailed account, Michelle Chase makes the case that activist women pushed for inclusion in a grassroots manner in this early period of revolutionary consolidation when the revolution was at its most open and fluid.[39] The revolution, however, responded with a top-down, centralized approach that incorporated women as a mass, state-sanctioned organization with Vilma Espín at the helm.[40] This led to a less radical version of women's emancipation than that envisioned by women's more autonomous early organizations.[41] Such visions and such women must be viewed as on the losing side of this insurrectionary war, which produced a centralized, socialist, mobilizing regime.

In this system, women's gains, which included their participation in armed defense, were argued to be thanks to the revolution. Bernal, writing on women combatants in the Eritrean national liberation struggle, captures the logic and its downside: "Women's involvement in the nationalist struggle is treated as [a guerrilla] achievement – another testimony to the goodness and justice" of the cause.[42] Bernal echoes other feminist research in critiquing the feminism articulated by revolutionary socialist regimes, which failed to achieve gender equality in part because such efforts were "top-down and male-led, rather than rooted in the empowerment of women themselves, and because [they] relied heavily upon enforced compliance rather than voluntary change."[43]

Gladys Marel García-Pérez, a Cuban feminist historian, notes that despite the greater gender parity among rebels during the insurrection, women rebels "were not conscious of their role as the vanguard for women and did not include their [gender-based] demands" among the goals of the revolution.[44] Women's liberation, then, was state-led and served as testimony to Fidel's benevolent generosity as well as his commitment to equality.

But as women were argued to benefit from the revolution, the success of revolution was purported to depend upon women's participation. In this regard, revolutionary Cuba also bore similarities to earlier socialist revolutions. Four decades prior, Lenin proclaimed in a speech to the First All-Russia Congress of Working Women: "The experience of all liberation movements has shown that the success of a revolution depends on how much the women take part in it. The Soviet government is doing everything in its power to enable women to carry on independent proletarian socialist work."[45] However, the impact of mobilizing women is limited when women's rights and participation are not the goal but rather the means to a larger national goal.[46]

One related question that arises in research on gender and war is whether war challenges traditional gender relations or reinforces them. Feminist studies have produced seemingly contradictory findings, arguing both that war and militarism shore up patriarchy, and that they engender women's political and economic empowerment.[47] Indeed, both processes might well be at work. Often, women's active contributions, including as fighters, are framed as achievements of the guerrilla organization and evidence of the goodness and justice of the new government. Insurrectionary wars and revolutions are implicitly masculine projects, with women as one of the beneficiaries. Such top-down, male-led efforts at gender equality in the postwar period, often labeled "state feminism," have produced disappointing records for gender equality.[48] In particular, policies aimed at women's emancipation that arise from state feminism are likely to fall far short if the primary aim is not actually women's rights but rather the use of women's rights toward a larger national goal.

There are additional contributing factors arising from the research presented in this book that help explain Cuba's limited progress on gender equality. Once the armed insurrection ended and rebel men were no longer a persecuted group, women lost much of the gendered advantage that they lent to the cause. That is, they were no longer needed to deliver messages or deflect suspicion from men under the guise of feminine innocence. Marriage and pregnancy also aligned with the broader social expectations, supported by the rhetoric drawing on Martí and the Even the Women discourse in which women engage in politics under extraordinary circumstances. Prominent women rebels to varying degrees retreated toward more traditional relationships.[49] Once the end of the war appeared imminent, Vilma and Raúl delayed their 1958 Christmas Eve wedding so that "she could have a real wedding in Santiago itself."[50] Their early 1959 wedding featured markers of traditional femininity such as an elegant white wedding dress and bridal bouquet, which were dramatically juxtaposed with the new masculinity represented by the bearded rebels in attendance, wearing berets and battle fatigues. The wedding, featured as photo spreads in the Cuban papers and *Life* magazine, visually indicated a return to traditional emphasized femininity alongside a newly ascendant hegemonic masculinity.[51] *Life* magazine's photo spread was entitled "Raul Castro Is Captured," implying that Vilma had ensnared in her matrimonial trap the rebel man who so successfully evaded Batista's forces. Such representations eclipsed an alternative interpretation of the dynamics, in which it was rebel heroines such as Vilma who were ensnared and tamed to traditional feminine subordination in the revolutionary New Society. For many, including Vilma, Haydée Santamaría, and Che's new wife Aleida March, babies soon followed. The sources available do not indicate that these women were overtly pressured into domesticity and decreased authority. Rather, traditional emphasized femininity was central not only to how male revolutionaries understood women but also to how many women rebels understood themselves, and many returned to a more traditional gender path with the end of the conflict.

In contrast, the 1950s machismo discussed in Chapter 5 was in some ways amplified by the revolution. Given that the Cuban revolution is "a matter of machos," Carlos Alberto Montaner asks[52]:

How are they going to comfortably integrate women in this process that is so markedly masculine? The very revolutionary mechanism, unconsciously, rejects them ... The truth is that, to make space for women, in addition to creating child care centers ... you have to de-masculinize the nation. Loosen the straitjacket of sexual roles ... so that sex ceases to be a determining factor in the location of people within society ... Women are not integrated because they almost have to stop being women to integrate ... [T]o take the right path [revolutionaries] would have to write another mythology, adopt other gestures, castrate the revolution ... If revolutionizing is tearing down structures and replacing them with others more just, the revolutionary act would be to take away the masculine accent, the macho style that governs Cuban public life, but that would be like asking for a different revolution than the one we have.[53]

An intersectional approach lends depth and nuance to the analysis, for this macho revolution was also informed by race and sexuality. The proportion of Afro-descendants in revolutionary Cuba grew, as emigrants were largely white. In contrast to Castro's explicit recognition of discrimination against women, the revolution pursued a "raceless" society through prohibiting race-based discrimination while declaring racism solved.[54] By virtue of their disproportionate representation among the poor in prerevolutionary Cuba, Afro-Cubans were advantaged by revolutionary policies focused on income redistribution, education, and healthcare. However, in more recent decades Afro-Cubans have been disproportionately disadvantaged by the post-Soviet economic shifts, as they are significantly less likely to receive remittances from relatives abroad and are less likely to work in the relatively lucrative tourism sector.[55] The structural pressures introduced via international investment and tourism are argued to leave Afro-Cuban women particularly disadvantaged, a point difficult for the state to address given its reluctance to acknowledge the significant vestiges of racism.

Homosexuals, most notably gay men, were disadvantaged by the gender logic of the Cuban revolution and were persecuted in revolutionary Cuba. Most infamously, from 1965 to 1968, the revolutionary state sent suspected homosexuals to forced labor camps. Treatment was harsh, with guards especially targeting the more feminine gay men and transwomen for abuse.[56] The late 1960s and 1970s also saw a rise in purges of homosexuals from jobs and universities, and the Ministry of Culture ordered that all homosexual artists be fired. In roundups, police went about harassing and arresting those they suspected of being gay on the streets and in bars. Such arrests and purges combined with an ailing economy to culminate in the Mariel boatlift, in which members of the LGBT community were prominent.

Like women, gay men functioned as a binary opposite to the revolutionary New Man and were represented in terms of a failed, effeminate masculinity: the man who was afraid, soft, and morally or physically weak.[57] Thus, this has much to do with gender binaries and the forms of rebel hegemonic masculinity discussed previously. The Cuban armed insurrection, though officially committed to equality, was hierarchical, and gender continued to mark hierarchy.[58] Though the Cuban revolution, too, was officially committed to the liberation of women, the devaluation and rejection of the feminine worked to maintain gender hierarchy, which in turn was further demarcated by race and sexuality.

In sum, the post-1959 militarized revolutionary state, battle born through a strict chain of command, was tactically reliant upon a pronounced masculinity in its struggle for hearts and minds, which also entailed exaggerating the two-year guerrilla war at the expense of the longer urban struggle. Women were enjoined to participate in the new revolutionary society, even taking up arms to defend the nation, but all the while reassuring that their traditionally understood femininity was intact. To achieve gender equality would require a revolution in the gender binary, or more specifically, its undoing. And that would entail a very different revolution than the one to which Cubans awoke on January 1, 1959.

Notes

1. Arenas (1986 [1994], 43).
2. Ibid., 43–4.
3. See, for example, de la Cova (2007).
4. Goldstein (2001).
5. Bayard de Volo (2012).
6. Eagleton (1991, 116). The War Story also drew upon Cuba's Independence Wars of the late nineteenth century. See Olcott (2005) for a key comparative case of women and citizenship in post-revolutionary Mexico.
7. Connell and Messerschmidt (2005).
8. Montaner (1981, 87).
9. See Bayard de Volo (2012).
10. McCormick et al. (2007, 345).
11. Castro (2012, 613–14).
12. López Larosa interview, Lyn Smith Cuba Collection.
13. Nidia Díaz, "Gardenias que un día se hicieron leonas," *Granma* September 3, 1983, 4.
14. Espinosa Hechevarría, *Mujeres* May 1975, 73.
15. Ibid.
16. Chase (2015, 115).
17. Sarabia, *Bohemia* November 24, 1967, 50–5.
18. Stoner (2003, 88).
19. Segal (1995, 761); Cooke (1993, 178).
20. Espín (1990, 8, 10).
21. Castro, "Discurso pronunciado por el Comandante Fidel Castro Ruz, Primer Ministro del Gobierno Revolucionario, en Ciudad Libertad," December 31, 1960, in Cuban State database Discursos e intervenciones del Comandante en Jefe Fidel Castro Ruz.
22. Wyden (1979, 295).

23. Stone (1981, 9).
24. Ibid.
25. Fox (1973).
26. Ibid., 287.
27. Stone (1981, 8); Stoner (2003, 87).
28. Teté Puebla in Waters (2003, 54). See also, for example, Jorge Luis Blanco, "Las flores se visten de verde olivo," *Verde Olivo* March 15, 1984, 4–5.
29. José Gabriel Guma, "Prestaron juramento las primeras unidades de las Milicias de Tropas Territoriales en Plaza de la Revolución," *Granma* March 9, 1981, 3.
30. Díaz (1983, 4).
31. Valdes, *Verde Olivo* March 3, 1983, 6–9.
32. Stoner (2003, 87).
33. Ibid.
34. Molyneux (1985); Bayard de Volo (2012).
35. Fernandes (2005, 434, 440); Luciak (2007, 27).
36. Hawkesworth (2005, 149–50); Fowler (1998, 30, 86).
37. Izquierdo, *Tribuna de la Habana* (n.d.).
38. Salas Servando, *Radio Metropolitana* March 6, 2008.
39. Chase (2015, 106–7).
40. Ibid., 107.
41. Ibid.
42. Bernal (2000, 64).
43. Ibid., 72; see also Chase (2015).
44. García-Pérez (1999, 73).
45. Lenin, "Speech at the First All-Russia Congress of Working Women," November 19, 1918.
46. Bernal (2000, 72).
47. Ibid. See Luciak (2001); Enloe (1990); Badran (1996); Tetreault (1994).
48. Bernal (2000). See Bengelsdorf (1988).
49. For an excellent analysis of the revolutionary state's Operation Family promotion of heterosexual marriage in its first decade, see Hynson (2014, 63–100). For policies and practices of heterosexuality in contemporary Cuba, see Lundgren (2011).
50. Dorschner and Fabricio (1980, 267).
51. *Bohemia* 51:5, February 1, 1959, 98–100; "Raul Castro Is Captured" (no author), *Life* 46:6, February 9, 1959, 37. Connell (1987, 187–8).
52. Montaner (1976, 110).
53. Ibid., 112–13.
54. "Raceless" refers to the post-1958 Cuban state's efforts to achieve a color-blind society involving the combined effect of Latin American exceptionalism, which denied that racism existed in the region, and a Marxist approach, in which a classless society would resolve other forms of oppression (Sawyer 2006, xviii).
55. Roland (2011).
56. Lumsden (1996, 69).
57. Bayard de Volo (2012); Rodríguez (1996).
58. Bayard de Volo (2012, 414); White (2007).

Bibliography

Alison, Miranda. 2009. *Women and Political Violence: Female Combatants in Ethno-National Conflict*. New York: Routledge.

Álvarez, Santiago. 1980. *La guerra necesaria*. Havana: El Instituto Cubano del Arte e Industria Cinematográficos.

Álvarez, José. 2009. *Frank País: Architect of Cuba's Betrayed Revolution*. Boca Raton, FL: Universal Publishers.

Anderson, Jon Lee. 1997. *Che Guevara: A Revolutionary Life*. New York: Grove Press.

Andux González, Teresa, Haydée Laborí Ripoll, and José M. Leyva Mestre. 1990. *La Capital en el Moncada*. Havana: Editorial de ciencias sociales.

Arenas, Reinaldo. 1986. *Necesidad de libertad*. Mexico City: Editorial Kosmos.
1994. *Before Night Falls*. Translated by Dolores M. Koch. New York: Penguin Books.

Báez, Luis. 1996. *Secretos de Generals*. Havana: Editorial Si-Mar S.A.

Badran, Margot. 1996. *Feminists, Islam, and Nation*. Princeton, NJ: Princeton University Press.

Bardach, Ann Louise. 2003. *Cuba Confidential: Love and Vengeance in Miami and Havana*. New York: Vintage.
2007. "Introduction." In *The Prison Letters of Fidel Castro*, edited by Ann Louise Bardach and Luis Conte Agüero, vii–xv. New York: Nation Books.
2009. *Without Fidel: A Death Foretold in Miami, Havana, and Washington*. New York: Simon & Schuster, Inc.

Bardach, Ann Louise and Luis Conte Agüero, eds. 2007. *The Prison Letters of Fidel Castro*. New York: Nation Books.

Barrio, Hilda and Gareth Jenkins. 2003. *The Che Handbook*. New York: St. Martin's Press.

Bayard de Volo, Lorraine. 2001. *Mothers of Heroes and Martyrs: Gender Identity Politics in Nicaragua, 1979–1999*. Baltimore, MD: Johns Hopkins University Press.

2012. "Revolution in the Binary? Gender and the Oxymoron of Revolutionary War in Nicaragua and Cuba." *Signs: Journal of Women in Culture and Society* 37(2):413–39.

Bayard de Volo, Lorraine and Lynn K. Hall. 2015. "'I Wish All the Ladies Were Holes in the Road': The U.S. Air Force Academy and the Gendered Continuum of Violence." *Signs: Journal of Women in Culture and Society* 40(4 Summer):865–89.

Bengelsdorf, Carollee. 1988. "On the Problem of Studying Women in Cuba." In *Cuban Political Economy: Controversies in Cubanology*, edited by Andrew Zimbalist, 119–36. Boulder, CO: Westview Press.

Bernal, Victoria. 2000. "Equality to Die For? Women Guerrilla Fighters and Eritrea's Cultural Revolution." *PoLAR* 23(2):61–76.

Bethel, Paul D. 1969. *The Losers: The Definitive Report, by an Eyewitness, of the Communist Conquest of Cuba and the Soviet Penetration in Latin America.* New Rochelle, NY: Arlington House.

Biddle, Stephen. 2008. "The New U.S. Army/Marine Corps Counterinsurgency Field Manual as Political Science and Political Praxis." *Perspectives on Politics* 6(2):347–50.

Bockman, Larry James. 1984. "The Spirit of Moncada: Fidel Castro's Rise to Power, 1953–1959." Marine Corps Command and Staff College, accessed January 11, 2017. www.globalsecurity.org/military/library/report/1984/BLJ .htm.

Bonachea, Ramón L. and Marta San Martín. 1974. *The Cuban Insurrection 1952–1959.* New Brunswick, NJ: Transaction Books.

Bonsal, Phillip. 1971. *Cuba, Castro and the United States.* Pittsburgh, PA: University of Pittsburgh Press.

Bouvard, Marguerite Guzman. 1994. *Revolutionizing Motherhood: The Mothers of the Plaza de Mayo.* Lanham, MD: SR Books.

Bunck, Julie Marie. 1994. *Fidel Castro and the Quest for a Revolutionary Culture in Cuba.* University Park, PA: Penn State University Press.

Byrd, Miemie Winn and Gretchen Decker. 2008. "Why the U.S. Should GENDER Its Counterterrorism Strategy." *Military Review* 88(4):96–101.

Cabezas, Omar. 1985. *Fire from the Mountain: The Making of a Sandinista.* Translated by Kathleen Weaver. New York: Crown Publishers.

Cámara Betancourt, Madeline. 2000. "Between Myth and Stereotype: The Image of the Mulatta in Cuban Culture in the Nineteenth Century, a Truncated Symbol of Nationality." In *Cuba, the Elusive Nation: Interpretations of a National Identity*, edited by Damián J. Fernández and Madeline Cámara Betancourt, 100–15. Gainesville, FL: University of Florida Press.

Campanaro, Jocelyn. 2001. "Women, War, and International Law: The Historical Treatment of Gender-Based War Crimes." *Georgetown Law Journal* 89(8):2557–92.

Casal, Lourdes and Virginia R. Domínguez. 1987. "Images of Women in Pre- and Postrevolutionary Cuban Novels." *Cuban Studies* 17:25–50.

Casals, Elena. 1989. "Un ayer de barbarie." In *Semillas de fuego: Compilación sobre la lucha clandestina en la capital* 2, edited by Partido Comunista de Cuba Sección de Historia en Ciudad de La Habana, 161–5. Havana: Editorial de ciencias sociales.

Castañeda, Jorge. 1997. *Compañero: The Life and Death of Che Guevara*. New York: Knopf.

Castro Porta, Carmen. 1990. *La lección del maestro*. Havana: Editorial de Ciencias Sociales.

Castro, Fidel. 1976. *La historia me absolverá*. Madrid: Biblioteca Júcar.

Castro, Fidel, Deborah Shnookal, and Pedro Álvarez Tabío. 2005. *Fidel: My Early Years*. Melbourne: Ocean Press.

Castro, Fidel and Katiuska Blanco Castiñeira. 2011. *Guerrillero del tiempo: Conversaciones con el líder histórico de la Revolución Cubana*. Havana: Casa Editora Abril.

Castro, Fidel. 2011. *La victoria estratégica: Por todos los caminos de la Sierra: La contraofensiva estratégica*. Mexico City: Ocean Sur.

2012. *La victoria estratégica: La contraofensiva estratégica*. Madrid: Ediciones Akal.

Castro, Fidel with Ignacio Ramonet. 2008. *MyLife: A Spoken Autobiography*. Translated by Andrew Hurley. New York: Scribner.

Casuso, Teresa. 1961. *Cuba and Castro*. Translated by Elmer Grossberg. New York: Random House.

Chapelle, Dickey. 1962a. "How Castro Won." In *Modern Guerrilla Warfare: Fighting Communist Guerrilla Movements, 1941–1961*, edited by Franklin Mark Osanka, 325–35. New York: Free Press of Glencoe.

1962b. *What's A Woman Doing Here? A Reporter's Report on Herself*. New York: William Morrow and Company.

Chase, Michelle. 2010. "Women's Organisations and the Politics of Gender in Cuba's Urban Insurrection (1952–1958)." *Bulletin of Latin American Research* 29(4):440–58.

2015. *Revolution within the Revolution: Women and Gender Politics in Cuba, 1952–1962*. Chapel Hill, NC: University of North Carolina Press.

Childs, Matt D. 1995. "An Historical Critique of the Emergence and Evolution of Ernesto Che Guevara's 'Foco' Theory." *Journal of Latin American Studies* 27(3):593–624.

Clausewitz, Carl von. 1832 [1976]. *On War*. Edited and translated by Peter Paet and Michael Howard. Oxford: Oxford University Press.

Coltman, Leycester. 2003. *The Real Fidel Castro*. New Haven, CT: Yale University Press.

Connell, R.W. 1987. *Gender and Power: Society, the Person and Sexual Politics*. Palo Alto, CA: Stanford University Press.

Connell, R.W. and James W. Messerschmidt. 2005. "Hegemonic Masculinity: Rethinking the Concept." *Gender & Society* 19(6):829–59.

Cooke, Miriam. 1993. "[WO]-man, Retelling the War Myth." In *Gendering War Talk*, edited by Miriam Cooke and Angela Woollacott, 177–204. Princeton, NJ: Princeton University Press.

1996. *Women and the War Story*. Berkeley, CA: University of California Press.

Cuadriello, Juan Domingo. 2009. *El exilio republicano español en Cuba*. Madrid: Siglo XXI de España Editores.

Cupples, Julie. 2006. "Between Maternalism and Feminism: Women in Nicaragua's Counter-Revolutionary Forces." *Bulletin of Latin American Research* 25(1):83–103.

Custodio, Isabel. 2005. *El amor me absolverá: La pasión secreta de Fidel Castro en México*. Mexico City: Plaza y Janés.

Daynes, Gary. 1996. "Finding Meaning in Moncada: Historical Memory in Revolutionary Cuba." *Caribbean Quarterly* 42(1):1–13.

De la Cova, Antonio Rafael. 2007. *The Moncada Attack: Birth of the Cuban Revolution*. Columbia, SC: University of South Carolina Press.

De la Fuente, Alejandro. 1998. "Race, National Discourse, and Politics in Cuba." *Latin American Perspectives* 25(3):43–69.

——— 2001. *A Nation for All: Race, Inequality, and Politics in Twentieth-century Cuba*. Chapel Hill, NC: University of North Carolina Press.

Debray, Regis. 1967. *Revolution in the Revolution? Armed Struggle and Political Struggle in Latin America*. New York: Monthly Review Press.

Decker, Jeffrey Louis. 1991. "Terrorism (Un)Veiled: Frantz Fanon and the Women of Algiers." *Cultural Critique* 17:177–95.

DePalma, Anthony. 2006. *The Man Who Invented Fidel: Castro, Cuba, and Herbert L. Matthews of the New York Times*. New York: Public Affairs.

Díaz Vallina, Elvira. 2001. "The Invisibility and the Visibility of Women in the History of Cuba." In *Cuban Women: History, Contradictions and Contemporary Challenges*, edited by Colleen Lundy and Norma Vasallo Barrueta, 1–21. Ottawa: Carleton University Graphic Services.

Díaz Vallina, Elvira, Olga Dotre Romay, and Caridad Dacosta Pérez. 1994. "La mujer revolucionaria en Cuba durante el periodo insurreccional, 1952–1958." *Revista de Ciencias Sociales de la Universidad de Puerto Rico* 3:24–32.

Dietrich Ortega, Luisa Maria. 2012. "Looking Beyond Violent Militarized Masculinities." *International Feminist Journal of Politics* 14(4):489–507.

Domínguez, Jorge I. 1975. "Book review of Ramón Bonachea and Marta San Martín's The Cuban Insurrection, 1952–1959." *Worldview* 18(5):56–8.

——— 1976. "Racial and Ethnic Relations in the Cuban Armed Forces: A Non-Topic." *Armed Forces & Society* 2(2):273–90.

——— 1978. *Cuba: Order and Revolution*. Cambridge, MA: Belknap Press of Harvard University Press.

——— 1989. *To Make a World Safe for Revolution: Cuba's Foreign Policy*. Cambridge, MA: Harvard University Press.

Dore, Elizabeth. 2012. "Foreword: Cuban Voices." In *Sexual Revolutions in Cuba: Passions, Politics, and Memory*, by Carrie Hamilton, vii–xi. Chapel Hill, NC: University of North Carolina Press.

Dorschner, John and Roberto Fabricio. 1980. *The Winds of December*. New York: Coward, McCann & Geoghegan.

Dosal, Paul J. 2004. *Comandante Che*. University Park, PA: Penn State University Press.

Draper, Theodore. 1962. *Castro's Revolution: Myths and Realities*. New York: Frederick A. Praeger.

Dubois, Jules. 1959. *Fidel Castro: Rebel, Liberator, or Dictator?* Indianapolis, IN: Bobbs-Merrill.

Eagleton, Terry. 1991. *Ideology: An Introduction*. London: Verso.

Eckstein, Susan Eva. 2003. *Back from the Future: Cuba under Castro*. 2nd ed. New York: Routledge.

Editora, Girón. 1961. "Ramón Calviño Inzua pertenecía a los Servicios Represivos de la tiranía de Fulgencio Batista." Filmed September 8, 1961. Posted December 27, 2010. www.youtube.com/watch?v=t7XYpHGT74k.

Elshtain, Jean Bethke. 1987. *Women and War*. New York: Basic Books.

English, T.J. 2007. *Havana Nocturne: How the Mob Owned Cuba ... and Then Lost It to the Revolution*. New York: Harper Collins.

Enloe, Cynthia. 1990. *Bananas, Beaches and Bases: Making Feminist Sense of International Politics*. Berkeley, CA: University of California Press.

1993. *The Morning After: Sexual Politics at the End of the Cold War*. Berkeley, CA: University of California Press.

2000. *Maneuvers: The Militarization of Women's Lives*. Berkeley, CA: University of California Press.

2014. *Bananas, Beaches and Bases: Making Feminist Sense of International Politics*. 2nd ed. Berkeley, CA: University of California Press.

Espín, Vilma. 1975 [2006]. "Entrevista" [Spanish for interview]. Santiago 18–19 (June–September). Reprinted in Vilma Espín Guillois. 2006. *Inolvidable Frank*, 11–48. Havana: Editorial de la Mujer.

Espín, Vilma. 1990. *La mujer en Cuba*. Havana: Editora Política.

Espín, Vilma and Deborah Shnookal. 1990. *Three Decades after the Revolution: Cuban Women Confront the Future*. Melbourne: Ocean Press.

Estefanía, Carlos Manuel. 2006. "Cuba: tierra de mujeres guerreras," *Cuba Nuestra*, February 23, 2006. www.cubanuestra.nu/web/article.asp?artID=3426.

Falk, Pamela. 1988. "Washington and Havana." *The Wilson Quarterly* 12(5):64–74.

Farber, Samuel. 1976. *Revolution and Reaction in Cuba, 1933–1960: A Political Sociology from Machado to Castro*. Middletown, CT: Wesleyan University Press.

2006. *The Origins of the Cuban Revolution Reconsidered*. Chapel Hill, NC: University of North Carolina Press.

Fernandes, Sujatha. 2005. "Transnationalism and Feminist Activism in Cuba: The Case of Magín." *Politics & Gender* 1(3):431–52.

2006. *Cuba Represent! Cuban Arts, State Power and the Making of New Revolutionary Cultures*. Durham, NC: Duke University Press.

Ferrer Gómez, Yusbel, Mayelín Diéguez Torres, Madelaine Almaguer Sosa, and Yadira Cruz Hernández. 2014. "52 Aniversario del Pelotón Femenino 'Mariana Grajales,'" *Revista de historia* 2. www.baibrama.cult.cu/instituciones/patrimonio/revista/r_artic.php?idarticulo=29.

Fisher, Jo. 1989. *Mothers of the Disappeared*. Boston, MA: South End Press.

Fontova, Humberto. 2008. *Exposing the Real Che Guevara: And the Useful Idiots Who Idolize Him*. New York: Sentinel.

Foran, John, Linda Klouzal, and Jean-Pierre Rivera. 1997. "Who Makes Revolutions? Class, Gender, and Race in the Mexican, Cuban, and Nicaraguan Revolutions." *Research in Social Movements, Conflict, and Change* 20:1–60.

Fowler, Víctor. 1998. *La maldición: una historia del placer como conquista*. Havana: Editorial Letras Cubanas.

Fox, Geoffrey. 1973. "Honor, Shame, and Women's Liberation in Cuba: Views of Working-Class Émigré Men." In *Female and Male in Latin America: Essays*, edited by Ann Pescatello, 273–90. Pittsburgh, PA: University of Pittsburgh Press.

Franqui, Carlos. 1980. *Diary of the Cuban Revolution.* New York: The Viking Press.

Friedman, Edward. 1970. "Neither Mao, Nor Che: The Practical Evolution of Revolutionary Theory. A Comment on J. Moreno's 'Che Guevara on Guerrilla Warfare.'" *Comparative Studies in Society and History* 12(2):134–9.

Fulgueiras, José Antonio. 2002. *Víctor Bordón: El nombre de mis ideas.* Havana: Editorial deportes.

———. 2004. *Cerca del Che.* Havana: Editora Política.

Gadea, Hilda. 2008. *My Life with Che.* New York: Palgrave Macmillan.

García-Pérez, Gladys Marel. 1998. *Insurrection and Revolution: Armed Struggle in Cuba, 1952–1959.* Boulder, CO: Lynne Rienner.

———. 1999. "Algunos apuntes sobre estudios de casos y familias a partir de la perspectiva de la nación y la emigración." *Santiago* 86(8):114–34.

———. 2009. "Mujer y Revolución: Una perspectiva desde la insurgencia Cubana (1952–1959)." *Ruth* 3:51–76.

Geyer, Georgie Anne. 1991. *Guerrilla Prince.* Boston, MA: Little, Brown and Company.

Goldstein, Joshua. 2001. *War and Gender.* Cambridge: Cambridge University Press.

Greene, Graham. 1958 [2007]. *Our Man in Havana.* New York: Penguin Books.

Guerra, Lillian. 2012. *Visions of Power in Cuba: Revolution, Redemption, and Resistance, 1959–1971.* Chapel Hill, NC: University of North Carolina Press.

Guevara, Ernesto Che. 1961 [1985]. *Guerrilla Warfare.* Lincoln, NE: University of Nebraska Press.

———. 1965 [1969]. "Socialism and Man in Cuba." In *Che: Selected Works of Ernesto Guevara,* edited by Rolando E. Bonachea and Nelson P. Valdes, 155–69. Cambridge, MA: MIT Press.

Guevara, Ernesto Che. 1971. *Reminiscences of the Cuban Revolutionary War.* Translated by Victoria Ortiz. New York: Monthly Review Press.

———. 2013. *Diary of a Combatant: The Diary of the Revolution that Made Che Guevara a Legend.* Melbourne: Ocean Press.

Halperin, Maurice. 1993. "Return to Havana: Portrait of a Loyalist." *Cuban Studies* 23:187–93.

Hamilton, Carrie. 2012. *Sexual Revolutions in Cuba: Passions, Politics, and Memory.* Chapel Hill, NC: University of North Carolina.

Hampsey, Russell J. 2002. "Voices from the Sierra Maestra: Fidel Castro's Revolutionary Propaganda." *Military Review* 82(6):93–8.

Harding, Sandra. 1986. *The Science Question in Feminism.* Ithaca, NY: Cornell University Press.

Hart, Armando. 2004. *Aldabonazo: Inside the Cuban Revolutionary Underground 1952–1958.* New York: Pathfinder Press.

Hawkesworth, Mary. 2005. "Engendering Political Science: An Immodest Proposal." *Politics and Gender* 1(1):141–56.

Hegel, Georg Wilhelm Friedrich. 1977. *Phenomenology of Spirit.* Translated by Arnold V. Miller. Oxford: Clarendon Press.

Hernández, Félix José. 2013. "Mi participación en la Expedición de Nuevitas (Armando Fleites testimony)," *Cuba Nuestra*, February 9, 2013. https://cubabuestra7eu.wordpress.com/2013/02/09/mi-participacion-en-la-expedicion-de-nuevitas/.

Holgado Fernández, Isabel. 2000. *¡No es fácil! Mujeres cubanas y la crisis revolucionaria*. Barcelona: Icadia Editorial.

Hunt, Krista and Kim Rygiel. 2006. "(En)Gendered War Stories and Camouflaged Politics." In *(En)Gendering the War on Terror: War Stories and Camouflaged Politics*, edited by Krista Hunt and Kim Rygiel, 1–24. Burlington, VT: Ashgate.

Huston, Nancy. 1983. "Tales of War and Tears of Women." In *Women and Men's Wars*, edited by Judith Hicks Stiehm, 271–82. Oxford: Pergamon Press.

Hynson, Rachel M. 2014. "Sex and State Making in Revolutionary Cuba, 1959–1968." Ph.D. Dissertation, Department of History, University of North Carolina.

Jaquette, Jane S. 1973. "Women in Revolutionary Movements in Latin America." *Journal of Marriage and Family* 35(2):344–54.

Judson, C. Fred. 1984. *Cuba and the Revolutionary Myth: The Political Education of the Cuban Rebel Army, 1953–1963*. Boulder, CO: Westview Press.

Kalyvas, Stathis. 2005. "Warfare in Civil Wars." In *Rethinking the Nature of War*, edited by Isabelle Duyvesteyn and Jan Angstrom, 88–108. Abingdon: Frank Cass.

Kampwirth, Karen. 2002. *Women and Guerrilla Movements: Nicaragua, El Salvador, Chiapas, Cuba. Pennsylvania*. University Park, PA: Penn State University Press.

Kaplan, Fred. 2013. *The Insurgents: David Petraeus and the Plot to Change the American Way of War*. New York: Simon & Schuster.

Kling, Merle. 1962. "Cuba: A Case Study of a Successful Attempt to Seize Political Power by the Application of Unconventional Warfare." *Annals of the American Academy of Political and Social Science* 341(1):42–52.

Klouzal, Linda A. 2008. *Women and Rebel Communities in the Cuban Insurgent Movement, 1952–1959*. New York: Cambria Press.

Kutzinski, Vera M. 1993. *Sugar's Secrets: Race and the Erotics of Cuban Nationalism*. Charlottesville, VA: University Press of Virginia.

Lancaster, Roger N. 1992. *Life Is Hard: Machismo, Danger, and the Intimacy of Power in Nicaragua*. Berkeley, CA: University of California Press.

Laqueur, Walter. 1998. *Guerrilla Warfare: A Historical and Critical Study*. New Brunswick, NJ: Transaction.

Lewis, Oscar, Ruth M. Lewis, and Susan Rigdon. 1977. *Four Women: Living the Revolution, an Oral History of Contemporary Cuba*. Urbana, IL: University of Illinois Press.

Llerena, Mario. 1978. *The Unsuspected Revolution: The Birth and Rise of Castroism*. Ithaca, NY: Cornell University Press.

Llovio-Menéndez, José Luis. 1988. *Insider: My Hidden Life as a Revolutionary in Cuba*. Translated by Edith Grossman. New York: Bantam Books.

Lobao Reif, Linda. 1986. "Women in Latin American Guerrilla Movements: A Comparative Perspective." *Comparative Politics* 18(2):147–69.

1990. "Women in Revolutionary Movements: Changing Patterns of Latin American Guerrilla Struggle." In *Women and Social Protest*, edited by Guida West and Rhoda Lois Blumberg, 180–204. New York: Oxford University Press.

Luciak, Ilja. 1998. "Gender Equality and Electoral Politics on the Left: A Comparison of El Salvador and Nicaragua." *Journal of Interamerican Studies and World Affairs* 40(1):39–66.

2001. *After Revolution: Gender and Democracy in El Salvador, Nicaragua, and Guatemala.* Baltimore, MD: Johns Hopkins University Press.

2007. *Gender and Democracy in Cuba.* Gainesville, FL: University Press of Florida.

Luke, Anne. 2012. "Creating the Quiet Majority? Youth and Young People in the Political Culture of the Cuban Revolution." *Bulletin of Latin American Research* 31(1):127–43.

Lumsden, Ian. 1996. *Machos, Maricones, and Gays: Cuba and Homosexuality.* Philadelphia, PA: Temple University Press.

Lundgren, Silje. 2011. *Heterosexual Havana: Ideals and Hierarchies of Gender and Sexuality in Contemporary Cuba.* Dissertation, Sweden: Department of Anthropology and Ethnology, Uppsala University.

Lupiáñez Reinlein, José. 1985. *El movimiento estudiantil enSantiago de Cuba 1952–1953.* La Havana: Editorial de Ciencias Sociales.

Macaulay, Neill. 1970. *A Rebel in Cuba: An American's Memoir.* Chicago, IL: Quadrangle Books.

1978. "The Cuban Rebel Army: A Numerical Survey." *Hispanic American Historical Review* 58(2):284–95.

Machover Ajzenfich, Jacobo. 2001. *La memoria frente al poder: Escritores cubanos del exilio: Guillermo Cabrera Infante, Severo Sarduy, Reinaldo Arenas.* Valéncia: Universitat de Valéncia.

Mack, Andrew. 1975. "Sharpening the Contradictions: Guerrilla Strategy in Imperialist Wars." *Race & Class* 17(2):161–78.

Maclean, Betsy. 2003. "Introduction." In *Haydée Santamaría: Rebel Lives*, edited by Betsy MacLean, 1–10. Melbourne: Ocean Press.

Maloof, Judy. 1999. *Voices of Resistance: Testimonies of Cuban and Chilean.* Lexington, KY: University Press of Kentucky.

March, Aleida. 2012. *Remembering Che: My Life with Che Guevara.* Melbourne: Ocean Press.

Martínez Triay, Alina. 2006. "Bay of Pigs: Who were the 'Liberators'? Torturers 'Made in USA.'" *PA: Political Affairs*, April 4, 2006, www.politicalaffairs .net/bay-of-pigs-who-were-the-liberators-torturers-made-in-usa/.

Mason, David T. 1992. "Women's Participation in Central American Revolutions: A Theoretical Perspective." *Comparative Political Studies* 25(1):63–89.

Matthews, Herbert. 1961. *The Cuban Story.* New York: George Braziller.

McCormick, Gordon H, Steven B. Horton, and Lauren A. Harrison. 2007. "Things Fall Apart: The Endgame Dynamics of Internal Wars." *Third World Quarterly* 28(2):321–67.

Meneses, Enrique. 1966. *Fidel Castro.* Translated by J. Halcro Ferguson. New York: Taplinger Publishing Company.

Miller, Francesca. 1991. *Latin American Women and the Search for Social Justice.* Hanover, NH: University Press of New England.

Miller, Nicola. 2003. "The Absolution of History: Uses of the Past in Castro's Cuba." *Journal of Contemporary History* 38(1):147–62.

Minority Rights Group International. 2015. "Afro-Cubans." June 19, 2015. http:// minorityrights.org/minorities/afro-cubans/, accessed February 19, 2016.

Molyneux, Maxine. 1985. "Mobilization without Emancipation? Women's Interests, the State, and Revolution in Nicaragua." *Feminist Studies* 11(2):227–54.

Montaner, Carlos Alberto. 1976. *Informe secreto sobre la revolución cubana.* Madrid, Spain: Ediciones Sedmay.

——— 1981. *Secret Report on the Cuban Revolution.* London: Transaction Books.

Moore, Carlos. 2008. *Pichón: Race and Revolution in Castro's Cuba: A Memoir.* Chicago, IL: Chicago Review Press.

Moreno, José A. 1970. "Che Guevara on Guerrilla Warfare: Doctrine, Practice and Evaluation." *Comparative Studies in Society and History* 12(2):114–33.

Navarro, Marysa. 1989. "The Personal Is Political: Las Madres de Plaza de Mayo." In *Power and Popular Protest: Latin American Social Movements*, edited by Susan Eckstein, 241–58. Berkeley, CA: University of California Press.

Noonan, Rita. 1995. "Women against the State: Political Opportunities and Collective Action Frames in Chile's Transition to Democracy." *Sociological Forum* 10(1):81–111.

Nye, Joseph S. 2004. *Soft Power: The Means to Success in World Politics.* New York: Public Affairs.

Olcott, Jocelyn. 2005. *Revolutionary Women in Postrevolutionary Mexico.* Durham, NC: Duke University Press.

Oltuski, Enrique. 2002. *Vida Clandestina: My Life in the Cuban Revolution.* Translated by Thomas and Carol Christensen. New York: Wiley.

Paterson, Thomas G. 1994. *Contesting Castro: The United States and the Triumph of the Cuban Revolution.* Oxford: Oxford University Press.

Pedraza, Silvia. 2007. *Political Disaffection in Cuba's Revolution and Exodus.* Cambridge: Cambridge University Press.

Pérez Jr., Louis A. 1976. *Army Politics in Cuba 1898–1958.* Pittsburgh, PA: University of Pittsburgh Press.

——— 1980. "In the Service of the Revolution: Two Decades of Cuban Historiography, 1959–1979." *Hispanic American Historical Review* 60(1):79–89.

——— 1990. *Cuba and the United States: Ties of Singular Intimacy.* Athens, GA: University of Georgia Press.

——— 1998. "Foreword." In *Insurrection and Revolution: Armed Struggle in Cuba, 1952–1959*, edited by Gladys Marel García-Pérez, ix–x. Boulder, CO: Lynne Rienner.

——— 2013. *The Structure of Cuban History: Meanings and Purpose of the Past.* Chapel Hill, NC: University of North Carolina Press.

——— 2015. *Cuba: Between Reform and Revolution.* 5th ed. New York: Oxford University Press.

Pérez Cabrera Arístides, Ramón. 2006. *De Palacio hasta Las Villas: En la senda del triunfo.* Havana: Nuestra America.

Pérez-Stable, Marifeli. 1987. "Cuban Women and the Struggle for 'Conciencia.'" *Cuban Studies* 17:51–72.

Perret, Françoise. 1998. "Activities of the International Committee of the Red Cross in Cuba 1958–1962" *International Review of the Red Cross* 325, December 31, 1998, www.icrc.org/eng/resources/documents/article/other/57jpjk.htm, accessed September 9, 2016.

Peterson, V. Spike. 2010. "Informalization, Inequalities and Global Insecurities." *International Studies Review* 12:244–70.

Peterson, V. Spike and Anne Sisson Runyan. 1999. *Global Gender Issues*. 2nd ed. Boulder, CO: Westview Press.

Phillips, R. Hart. 1959. *Cuba: Island of Paradox*. New York: McDowell, Obolensky.

Power, Margaret. 2002. *Right-Wing Women in Chile: Feminine Power and the Struggle against Allende, 1964–1973*. University Park, PA: Penn State University Press.

Prados-Torreira, Teresa. 2005. *Mambisas: Rebel Women in Nineteenth-Century Cuba*. Gainesville, FL: University Press of Florida.

Puebla, Teté. 1990. *Marianas in Combat: Tete Puebla and the Mariana Grajales Women's Platoon in Cuba's Revolutionary War 1956–58*. New York: Pathfinder Press.

Randall, Margaret. 2015. *Haydée Santamaría, Cuban Revolutionary: She Led by Transgression*. Durham, NC: Duke University Press.

Ricks, Thomas E. 2006. *Fiasco: The American Military Adventure in Iraq*. New York: Penguin.

Rodríguez, Ileana. 1996. *Women, Guerrillas, and Love*. Minneapolis, MN: University of Minnesota Press.

Rodríguez Calderón, Mirta. 1990. "¡Torturados!" In *Semillas de fuego: Compilación sobre la lucha clandestina en la capital 2*, edited by Partido Comunista de Cuba Sección de Historia en Ciudad de La Habana, 62–70. Havana: Editorial de ciencias sociales.

Rojas, Marta. 1979. *La Generación del Centenario, 3a edición*. Havana: Editorial de ciencias sociales.

———. 1988. *El juicio del Moncada*. Havana: Editorial de ciencies sociales.

Roland, L. Kaifa. 2006. "Tourism and the Negrificación of Cuban Identity." *Transforming Anthropology* 14(2):151–62.

———. 2011. *Cuban Color in Tourism and La Lucha*. Oxford: Oxford University Press.

Rosendahl, Mona. 1998. *Inside the Revolution: Everyday Life in Socialist Cuba*. Ithaca, NY: Cornell University Press.

Rosete, Hilario. 2002. "Con Natalia Bolívar." *AfroCubaWeb*, www.afrocubaweb.com/bolivar.htm, accessed July 14, 2009.

Ruddick, Sara. 1989. *Maternal Thinking: Towards a Politics of Peace*. Boston, MA: Beacon Press.

Saldaña-Portillo, María Josefina. 2003. *The Revolutionary Imagination in the Americas and the Age of Development*. Durham, NC: Duke University Press.

Santamaría, Haydée. 1967. *Haydée habla del Moncada, Ediciones El orientador revolucionario 21 (pamphlet series)*. Havana: La Comisión de Orientación Revolucionaria del Comité Central del Partido Comunista de Cuba.

2003a. "A Personal Account of the Moncada." In *Haydée Santamaría: Rebel Lives*, edited by Betsy MacLean, 13–17. Melbourne: Ocean Press.

2003b. "All of Us Are Part of the Same Whole." In *Haydée Santamaría: Rebel Lives*, edited by Betsy MacLean, 20–59. Melbourne: Ocean Press.

Sarabia, Nydia. 1980. *Tras la huella de los héroes*. Havana: Gente Nueva.

1983. *Moncada: Biografía de un cartel*. Havana: Editorial de Ciencias Sociales.

Sawyer, Mark. 2000. "Unlocking the Official Story: Comparing the Cuban Revolution's Approach to Race and Gender." *UCLA Journal of International Law and Foreign Affairs* 5:403–17.

2006. *Racial Politics in Post-Revolutionary Cuba*. Cambridge: Cambridge University Press.

Schirmer, Jennifer. 1993. "Those Who Die for Life Cannot Be Called Dead." In *Surviving Beyond Fear: Women, Children and Human Rights in Latin America*, edited by Marjorie Agosín, 31–57. Fredonia, NY: White Pine Press.

Schlesinger, Arthur M., Jr. 1965. *A Thousand Days: John F. Kennedy in the White House*. Boston, MA: Houghton Mifflin.

Schoultz, Lars. 2011. *That Infernal Little Cuban Republic: The United States and the Cuban Revolution*. Chapel Hill, NC: University of North Carolina Press.

Scott, Joan Wallach. 1988. "Deconstructing Equality-versus-Difference: Or, the Uses of Poststructuralist Theory for Feminism." *Feminist Studies* 14(1):33–50.

1999. *Gender and the Politics of History*. New York: Columbia University Press.

Segal, Mady W. 1995. "Women's Military Roles Cross-Nationally: Past, Present, and Future." *Gender & Society* 9(6):757–75.

Sepp, Kalev I. 2005. "Best Practices in Counterinsurgency." *Military Review* 85(3):8–12.

Sharoni, Simona. 1995. *Gender and the Israeli-Palestinian Conflict: The Politics of Women's Resistance*. Syracuse, NY: Syracuse University Press.

Shayne, Julie D. 2004. *The Revolution Question: Feminisms in El Salvador, Chile, and Cuba*. Piscataway, NJ: Rutgers University Press.

Sjoberg, Laura. 2013. *Gendering Global Conflict: Toward a Feminist Theory of War*. New York: Columbia University Press.

Sjoberg, Laura and Caron E. Gentry. 2007. *Mothers, Monsters, Whores: Women's Violence in Global Politics*. New York: Zed Books.

Skierka, Volker. 2004. *Fidel Castro: A Biography*. Translated by Patrick Camiller. Cambridge: Polity.

Smith, Earl E.T. 1962. *The Fourth Floor: An Account of the Castro Communist Revolution*. New York: Random House.

Smith, Lois M. and Alfred Padula. 1996. *Sex and Revolution: Women in Socialist Cuba*. Oxford: Oxford University Press.

Stephen, Lynn. 1995. "Women's Rights Are Human Rights: The Merging of Feminine and Feminist Interests among El Salvador's Mothers of the Disappeared (CO-MADRES)." *American Ethnologist* 22(4):807–27.

1997. *Women and Social Movements in Latin America: Power from Below*. Austin, TX: University of Texas.

Stiehm, Judith Hicks. 1982. "The Protected, the Protector, and the Defender." *Women's Studies International Forum* 5(3):367–76.

Stone, Elizabeth. 1981. *Women and the Cuban Revolution*, Ed. Vol. New York: Pathfinder Press.

Stoner, K. Lynn. 1991. *From the House to the Streets: The Cuban Woman's Movement for Legal Reform, 1898–1940*. Durham, NC: Duke University Press.

———. 1997. "Ofelia Domínguez Navarro: The Making of a Cuban Socialist Feminist." In *The Human Tradition in Modern Latin America*, edited by William H. Beezley and Judith Ewell, 181–203. Wilmington, DE: SR Books.

———. 2003. "Militant Heroines and the Consecration of the Patriarchal State: The Glorification of Loyalty, Combat, and National Suicide in the Making of Cuban National Identity." *Cuban Studies* 34:71–96.

Stoner, K. Lynn and Luís Hipólito Serrano Pérez. 2000. *Cuban and Cuban America Women: An Annotated Bibliography*. Wilmington, DE: Scholarly Resources.

Stout, Nancy. 2013. *One Day in December: Celia Sánchez and the Cuban Revolution*. New York: Monthly Review Press.

Suárez Pérez, Eugenio and Acela A. Caner Román. 2006. *Fidel: De Cinco Palmas hasta Santiago*. Havana: Casa Editorial Verde Olivo.

Suárez Suárez, Reinaldo and Oscar Puig Corral. 2010. *La complejidad de la Rebeldía*. Havana: Ediciones La Memoria.

Sweig, Julia E. 2002. *Inside the Cuban Revolution: Fidel Castro and the Urban Underground*. Cambridge, MA: Harvard University Press.

Szulc, Tad. 1986. *Fidel: A Critical Portrait*. New York: William Morrow and Co., Inc.

Taber, Robert. 1961. *M-26: Biography of a Revolution*. New York: Lyle Stuart.

Taibo, Paco Ignacio. 1997. In *Guevara, Also Known as Che*, edited by Martin Michael Roberts. New York: St. Martin's Press.

Taylor, Diana. 1997. *Disappearing Acts: Spectacles of Gender and Nationalism in Argentina's "Dirty War"*. Durham, NC: Duke University Press.

Taylor, Verta. 1989. "Social Movement Continuity: The Women's Movement in Abeyance." *American Sociological Review* 54(5):761–75.

Tetreault, Mary Ann, ed. 1994. *Women and Revolution in Africa, Asia, and the New World*. Columbia, SC: University of South Carolina Press.

Theidon, Kimberly. 2012. *Intimate Enemies: Violence and Reconciliation in Peru*. Philadelphia, PA: University of Pennsylvania Press.

Thobani, Sunera. 2002. "War Frenzy." *Meridians* 2(2):289–97.

Thomas, Hugh. 1998. *Cuba, or, the Pursuit of Freedom*. New York: Da Capo Press.

Thomas-Woodard, Tiffany A. 2003. "'Towards the Gates of Eternity': Celia Sánchez Manduley and the Creation of Cuba's New Woman." *Cuban Studies* 34:154–80.

Tickner, J. Ann. 2001. *Gendering World Politics: Issues and Approaches in the Post-Cold War Era*. New York: Columbia University Press.

United Nations Department of Economic and Social Affairs. 2015. World Population Prospects. http://esa.un.org/unpd/wpp/DataQuery/.

United States Senate, Sub-Committee on Internal Security Hearings, "Communist Threat to the United States Through The Caribbean: Hearings Before the

Subcommittee to Investigate the Administration of the Internal Security Act and Other Internal Security Laws of the Committee on the Judiciary," *United States Senate, Eighty-Sixth Congress, Second Session, Part 9*, August 27, 30, 1960.

Ustariz Arze, Reginaldo. 2008. *Che Guevara: Vida, muerte y resurrección de un mito*. Madrid: Ediciones Nowtilus, S.L.

Vellinga, M. L. 1976. "The Military and the Dynamics of the Cuban Revolutionary Process." *Comparative Politics* 8(2):245–71.

Vilas, Carlos. 1986. *The Sandinista Revolution: National Liberation and Social Transformation in Central America*. New York: Monthly Review Press.

Viñelas, Estrella Marina. 1969. *Cuban Madam: The Shocking Autobiography of the Woman who Ruled Castro's White Slave Ring*. New York: Paperback Library.

Viterna, Jocelyn. 2006. "Pulled, Pushed, and Persuaded: Explaining Women's Mobilization into the Salvadoran Guerrilla Army." *American Journal of Sociology*. 112(1):1–45.

   2013. *Women in War: The Micro-Processes of Mobilization in El Salvador*. Oxford: Oxford University Press.

Waters, Mary-Alice, ed. 2003. *Marianas in Combat: Teté Puebla and the Mariana Grajales Women's Platoon in Cuba's Revolutionary War, 1956–68*. New York: Pathfinder Press.

Waters, Anita and Luci Fernandes. 2012. "Representing the Revolution: Public History and the Moncada Barracks in Santiago de Cuba." *Canadian Journal of Latin American and Carribean Studies* 37(73):125–54.

Weldes, Jutta. 1999. *Constructing National Interests: The US and the Cuban Missile Crisis*. Minneapolis, MN: University of Minnesota Press.

Werlau, María C. 2011. *Ché Guevara Forgotten Victims*. Washington, DC: Cuba Archive of Free Society Project Inc. http://cubaarchive.org/home/images/stories/che-guevara_interior-pages_en_final.pdf.

White, Aaronette M. 2007. "All the Men Are Fighting for Freedom, All the Women Are Mourning Their Men, but Some of Us Carried Guns: A Raced-Gendered Analysis of Fanon's Psychological Perspectives on War." *Signs: Journal of Women in Culture and Society* 32(4):857–84.

Wickham-Crowley, Timothy P. 1992. *Guerrillas and Revolution in Latin America: A Comparative Study of Insurgents and Regimes since 1956*. Princeton, NJ: Princeton University Press.

Wood, Elisabeth Jean. 2009. "Armed Groups and Sexual Violence: When Is Wartime Rape Rare?" *Politics & Society* 37(1):131–62.

Wyden, Peter. 1979. *Bay of Pigs: The Untold Story*. New York: Touchstone.

Yaffe, Helen. 2014. *Ernesto "Che" Guevara: Socialist Political Economy and Economic Management in Cuba, 1959–1966*. Dissertation, London: London School of Economics and Politics.

Young, Iris Marion. 2003. "The Logic of Masculinist Protection." *Signs: Journal of Women in Culture and Society* 29(1):1–25.

Yuval-Davis, Nira. 2004. "Gender, the Nationalist Imagination, and Peace." In *Sites of Violence: Gender and Conflict Zones*, edited by Wenona Giles and Jennifer Hyndman, 170–89. Berkeley, CA: University of California Press.

Žarkov, Dubravka. 2007. *The Body of War: Media, Ethnicity, and Gender in the Break-up of Yugoslavia*. Durham, NC: Duke University Press.

MEDIA ARTICLES AND INTERVIEWS

Abreu Cardet, José. 2009. "Guajiros clandestinos: Familia campesina y líderes de barrio en el clandestinaje (1956–1958)," *RadioAngulo*, October 19, 2009.

Abreu Cardet, José. "Los ataques a guarniciones enemigas en el Cuarto Frente Simón Bolívar," *RadioAngulo*, 18 de Agosto de 2009.

Álvarez Tabío, Pedro. "Celia Sánchez: A Maker of Cuban History," *Bohemia*, May 4, 1990. Translated and reprinted in *The Militant*, 60(8), February 26, 1996, www.themilitant.com/1996/608/608_23.html, accessed June 8, 2008.

Amador Morales, Dora. 1991. "La larga noche: mujeres en el presidio político cubano," originally published in *El Nuevo Herald*, March 10, 1991; reprinted www.palabracubana.org/Articulos-Blog/1991-03-10.htm, accessed July 15, 2009.

Amat, Carlos. *Santiago* June–Sept 1975. Excerpts of Amat interview, translated and reprinted in "How swift action saved life of Cuban revolutionary leader Armando Hart," *The Militant* 68:1, January 12, 2004; www.themilitant.com/2004/6801/680156.html, accessed August 30, 2012.

Archilla, Daniel. "Isabel Custodio, la novia de Castro antes de la Revolución" (interview), *Ya era hora*, December 19, 2008, http://yaerahoraenlaradio.blogspot.com/2008/12/isabel-custodio-la-novia-de-castro.html, accessed November 18, 2016.

Barreado, Arianna, Paula Companioni, Rosario Alfonso, and Alejandro Ruiz. "La luz que desafio a la dictadura batistiana," *Juventud Rebelde*, January 26, 2008, www.juventudrebelde.cu/cuba/2008-01-26/la-luz-que-desafio-a-la-dictadura-batistiana/, accessed June 16, 2009.

Bello Expósito, Elizabeth. "Una marcha de luz," *Alma Mater*, January 28, 2010, www.almamater.cu/sitio%20nuevo/paginas/universidad/2010/marcha%202.htm, accessed February 2, 2010).

Bosch, Adriana. 2005. "Huber Matos: A Moderate in the Cuban Revolution" (interview), PBS *The American Experience*, www.pbs.org/wgbh/amex/castro/peopleevents/e_moderates.html, accessed May 12, 2016.

Bracero Torres, Josefa. "Ricardo Martínez Víctores y su legado a la radiodifusión cubana," *Radio Cubana*, September 3, 2007. www.radiocubana.cu/glosario-de-terminos-radiofonicos/32-historia-de-la-radio-cubana/memoria-radial-cubana/878-ricardo-martinez-victores-y-su-legado-a-la-radiodifusion-cubana, accessed September 18, 2016.

Carriera Martínez, Alina. "El precio de retar al tirano," *Cuba Ahora*, November 7, 2007. www.cubahora.cu/index.php?tpl=buscar/ver-not_buscar.tpl.html&newsid_obj_id=1022413, accessed July 27, 2010.

Casán, Rosita. *Santiago* June–Sept 1975, excerpts of the Casán interview, translated and reprinted in "How swift action saved life of Cuban revolutionary leader Armando Hart," *The Militant* 68:1, January 12, 2004. www.themilitant.com/2004/6801/680156.html, accessed August 30, 2012.

Castro Mercader, Raúl. "Acontecimientos de Marzo del '58" (testimony) in *Cubasocialista.com: Revista Teorica y Politica, Comité Central del Partido Coumunista de Cuba*, n.d. www.cubasocialista.cu/texto/acontmarzo.htm, accessed August 3, 2010.

Castro Ruz, Raúl. "How Rebel Army Spread Revolutionary War" (interview), *Granma International Weekly Review*, March 15, 1988.

Davison, Phil. "Vilma Espin Guillois: Hero of the Cuban Revolution Who Became a Powerful 'First Lady' and Advocate for Women's Rights," *The Independent* (UK), June 20, 2007. www.independent.co.uk/news/obituaries/vilma-espin-guillois-453833.html, accessed May 19, 2010.

Díaz Acosta, Rebeca. 2010. "Aleida Fernández, la joven que desafió al tirano," *Radio Güines, 11 de Febrero de 2010*. www.radioguines.icrt.cu/index.php/memo/4401-aleida-fernandez-la-joven-que-desafio-al-tirano, accessed July 27, 2010.

Dueñas, Rose Ana. "Heroic Combatants, Anonymous Women," *Granma Internacional*, April 11, 2006, www.granma.cu/ingles/2006/abril/mar11/15mujeres-i.html, accessed March 13, 2008.

Gálvez, William. "Crónicas de la lucha revolucionaria preparando la guerra VIII a X partes," *Publicación Semanal* 3(156), December 29, 2006, http://librinsula.bnjm.cu/1-205/2006/diciembre/156/documentos/documento461.htm, accessed July 14, 2011.

González–Lanuza, Gaspar. "Heroínas de la Sierra y el llano," *Juventud Rebelde*, September 13, 2012, 4.

Gutiérrez, Oniria. Reprinted "'I Argued that Women Too Could Fight': Interview with the First Woman to Join Che Guevara's Column of Rebel Army," *The Militant* 60:7, February 19, 1996, translated and reprinted from *Bohemia* October 20, 1967. www.themilitant.com/1996/607/607_30.html, accessed June 3, 2013.

Gutiérrez Bourricaudy, Jorge Eduardo. "Tortura y represión hacia la mujer durante el Batistato," *Caliban: Revista Cubana de Pensamiento e Historia*, Octubre-diciembre, 2011. www.revistacaliban.cu/articulo.php?numero=11&article_id=124, accessed May 12, 2014.

Hernández Serrano, Luis. "El magisterio de Fidel se multiplica en pueblos y generaciones," *Juventud Rebelde*, December 21, 2009. www.juventudrebelde.cu/cuba/2009-12-21/el-magisterio-de-fidel-se-multiplica-en-pueblos-y-generaciones/, accessed September 29, 2010.

Infante, Enzo. "Santiago Uprising: A Harbinger of Victory." *Verde Olivo*, November 27, 1966. Translated and reprinted in *The Militant* 60(9), March 4, 1996. www.themilitant.com/1996/609/609_23.html, accessed September 3, 2016.

Izquierdo, Irene. "La 'maldita' Aida Pelayo," *Tribuna de la Habana*, n.d. www.tribuna.co.cu/mujere/historia/maldita1.htm, accessed June 16, 2009.

Jiménez, Argentina. "Rescate de los restos de los mártires del Moncada," *Tribuna de la Habana*, July 21, 2007. www.tribuna.co.cu/etiquetas/26-julio/rescate-%20restos-de-los-martires-moncada.html, accessed May 21, 2012.

No Author, "Cuban Army Style Note: No More Sack Dresses," *Chicago Daily Tribune*, July 6, 1958, 3.

Núñez, Pastorita. "Tengo la Revolución en la sangre" (interview), *La Jiribilla* VII, January 3–9, 2009. www.lajiribilla.cu/2009/n400_01/400_09.html, accessed June 17, 2016.

Padura Fuentes, Leonardo. "Recuerdan aniversario 50 del asesinato de Josué País, Floro Vistel y Salvador Pascual," *Diario de la juventud cubana*, June 30, 2007. www.juventudrebelde.cu/cuba/2007-06-30/recuerdan-aniversario-50-del-ase-sinato-de-josue-pais-floro-vistel-y-salvador-pascual-/, accessed June 15, 2016.

Reyes, Mariusa. "Castro y el amor en México," *BBC Mundo*, December 19, 2005. http://news.bbc.co.uk/hi/spanish/misc/newsid_4536000/4536852.stm, accessed March 12, 2017.

Rodríguez, G., Rosa. "Mujer pueblo, mujer nación," *Tribuna*, n.d. www.tribuna.co.cu/mujeres/historia/frente%20civico.htm, accessed June 19, 2009.

Rodríguez Reyes, Juan Fidel. "Violeta Casal en la memoria." *La Jiribilla*, IX, August 7–13, 2010. www.lajiribilla.co.cu/2010/n483_08/483_13.html, last accessed September 17, 2016.

Salas Servando, Matilde. "Aida Pelayo: cubana símbolo de valor y dignidad," *Radio Metropolitana*, March 6, 2008. www.radiometropolitana.cu/2008/secciones/historia/marz/aida%206.htm, accessed June 16, 2009.

Sartre, Jean-Paul. "In a Cuban Prison" (Letter to the Editor), *New York Review of Books*, 25(19), December 7, 1978.

Silva León, Arnaldo. "Moncada: A Vision from Afar," *Cuba Socialista: Revista Teórica y Política*, November 2003, www.cubasocialista.cu/texto/csi0013.htm, accessed June 24, 2009.

Stein, Jean. 2011. "All Havana Broke Loose: An Oral History of Tropicana," *Vanity Fair*, September 2011, www.vanityfair.com/culture/features/2011/09/tropicana-201109, accessed June 8, 2014.

Suárez Ramos, Felipa. "15 de mayo de 1955: la profecía de Fidel," *Trabajadores*, December 22, 2006. www.trabajadores.cu/materiales_especiales/suple-mentos/memoria-historica/guerra-de-liberacion-1/15-de-mayo-de-1955-la-profecia-de-fidel/?searchterm=su%C3%A1rez, accessed August 10, 2009.

Valenzuela García, Teresa. "Cuando se conquistó el cielo," *Pionero*, March 3, 2010, www.pionero.cu/2010/secciones/nuestra%20historia/marzo/cuando.htm, accessed June 3, 2013.

www.radioangulo.cu/columnistas/memoria-Holguínera/6713-Los%20ataques%20a%20guarniciones%20enemigas%20en%20el%20Cuarto%20Frente%20Sim%C3%B3n%20Bol%C3%ADvar%20.html, accessed December 16, 2009.

www.radioangulo.cu/columnistas/memoria-Holguínera/7802-Guajiros%20clandestinos-%20Familia%20campesina%20y%20l%C3%ADderes%20de%20barrio%20en%20el%20clandestinaje%20%281956-1958%-29%20.html, accessed December 16, 2009.

ARCHIVAL SOURCES

Newspapers

Cuban:

- *Bohemia* (weekly magazine)
- *Diario de la Marina* (national daily)
- *Granma* (national daily)

- *Mujeres* (monthly women's magazine)
- *Verde Olivo* (weekly military magazine)

United States:

- *The New York Times*

ONLINE ARCHIVES AND DATABASES

Discursos e intervenciones del Comandante en Jefe Fidel Castro Ruz, Presidente del Consejo de Estado de la República de Cuba, Versiones Taquigraficas – Consejo De Estado (Cuban State online archive of Fidel Castro's speeches, 1959–2008). www.cuba.cu/gobierno/discursos/.
EcuRed, www.ecured.cu/

- Acosta, Clodomira
- Araujo Pérez, Leocadia
- Combate del cerro de Uñas
- Ros Reyes, Amalia
- Suñol, Eddy
- Véliz Hernández, Pedro

El Nuevo Fénix, www.fenix.co.cu/che/hastalavictoria.htm, accessed July 5, 2016. Testimonies originally published in Adys Cupull and Froilán González, *Che entre nosotros* (Havana: Ediciones Abril, 1992):

- Puebla Viltres, Delsa (Teté), "Teté, no traiciones."
- Rodríguez Ferreiro, Zobeida (Mimí), "Che: Como caído del cielo."
- Rodríguez García, Zoila, "Ernesto Che Guevara: un hombre extraordinario."

LANIC Castro Speech Database 1959–1996, Latin American Network Information Center, The University of Texas at Austin, http://lanic.utexas.edu/la/cb/cuba/castro.html.
Antonio de la Cova Latinamericanstudies.org Archive

- Ochoa, Emilio. April 9, 1990. "Entrevista de Antonio Rafael de la Cova con Emilio Ochoa Ochoa," Miami, Florida. www.latinamericanstudies.org/moncada/Ochoa.pdf.
- Suardíaz Fernández, Manuel. April 29, 1990. "Entrevista de Antonio Rafael de la Cova con Manuel Suardíaz Fernández." Queens, New York. www.latinamericanstudies.org/moncada/Suardiaz.pdf.
- Smith, Earl T., August 7, 1957. "Foreign Service Despatch, from the Embassay in Cuba to the Department of State" 737.00/8-757(w), 1–6. Havana. www.latinamericanstudies.org/embassy/R7-107-8-7-1957.pdf.
- United States Senate, Sub-Committee on Internal Security Hearings, "Communist Threat to the United States Through The Caribbean: Hearings Before the Subcommittee to Investigate the Administration of the Internal Security Act and Other Internal Security Laws of the Committee on the Judiciary," United States Senate, Eighty-Sixth Congress, Second Session, Part 9, August 27, 30, 1960, www.latinamericanstudies.org/us-cuba/gardner-smith.htm.

Mary Ferrell Foundation Archives. www.maryferrell.org.

- Rockefeller Commission Testimony of Frank Sturgis, 04/03/1975, Agency: SSCIA; Record Number 157-10005 10125, p. 56; Originally classified as Top Secret.

Tad Szulc Collection of Interview Transcripts 1984–1986, University of Miami Libraries digital collections, http://merrick.library.miami.edu/cubanHeritage/chco189/.

Department of State, Office of the Historian, 1955–1957, Volume VI https://history.state.gov/historicaldocuments/frus1955-57v06/d276.

- Gardner, Arthur. October 16, 1956. "Telegram From the Ambassador in Cuba (Gardner) to the Secretary of State," Document 286, Havana.
- Hoyt, Henry A. July 1, 1955. "Memorandum of a Conversation, Department of State," Document 276, Washington.
- Smith, Earl T. September 16, 1957. "Despatch From the Ambassador in Cuba (Smith) to the Department of State," Document 295, Havana.

US Department of State, Office of the Historian, 1958–1960, Volume VI http://history.state.gov/historicaldocuments/frus1958-60v06/.

- Braddock, Daniel M. February 18, 1958, *Counselor of Embassy*, "Despatch From the Embassy in Cuba to the Department of State," Document 14. Havana, Cuba.
- Gilmore, Jr., Eugene A. February 28, 1958. "Despatch From the Embassy in Cuba to the Department of State," Document 21, Havana.
- Guerra, Oscar H. February 21, 1958. "Despatch From the Consulate at Santiago de Cuba to the Department of State," Document 18, Santiago de Cuba.
- No author. July 25, 1958. "Draft Memorandum Prepared in the Office of Middle American Affairs," Document 112, Washington.
- Smith, Earl T. October 22, 1958 "Telegram From the Embassy in Cuba to the Department of State," Document 147, Havana.
- Smith, Earl T. November 15, 1958. "Memorandum of a Conversation Between the Ambassador in Cuba (Smith) and President-Elect Rivero Agüero," Document 154, Havana.
- Stewart, C. Allan. July 24, 1958. "Memorandum From the Deputy Director of the Office of Middle American Affairs (Stewart) to the Deputy Assistant Secretary of State for Inter-American Affairs (Snow)," Document 111, Washington.
- Wollam, Park F. June 4, 1958. "Letter From the Consul at Santiago de Cuba (Wollam) to the Officer in Charge of Cuban Affairs (Leonhardy)," Document 62, Santiago de Cuba.

OTHER

26th of July Movement. 1958. Shadow of Cuba: Story of a Dictator, Facts and Articles Published, Compiled and Translated by the "26th of July Movement" for the History of Cuba. Parts 1 & 2 (no page numbers). June 1958. Miami, FL: Counselor VEDC.

Federación de Mujeres Cubanas (FMC) Archives, Havana, Cuba.

Lyn Smith Cuba Collection: oral histories of women collected 1988 and 1990. US Library of Congress (audio transcribed by author). English and Spanish Sound Recording.

- Melba Hernández
- Marta Fuego Rodríguez
- María López Larosa
- Esther Lina Milanés
- Teté Puebla

Princeton University Latin American Documents of the Movimiento 26 de Julio, May 1957–December 1958 (correspondence); Princeton University Latin American pamphlet collection. Politics in Cuba; P0901, Pt. 1, Reel 2–3.

Princeton University Broadcast Transcripts of Radio Rebelde, May 1957–December 1958 (Princeton University Latin American pamphlet collection. Politics in Cuba; P0901, Pt. 1, Reel 1).

Index